M<small>ARGARET</small> S<small>ULLAVAN</small>

MARGARET SULLAVAN

The Life and Career
of a Reluctant Star

MICHAEL D. RINELLA

McFarland & Company, Inc., Publishers
Jefferson, North Carolina

LIBRARY OF CONGRESS CATALOGUING-IN-PUBLICATION DATA

Names: Rinella, Michael D., 1962– author.
Title: Margaret Sullavan : the life and career of a reluctant star /
Michael D. Rinella.
Description: Jefferson, North Carolina : McFarland & Company, Inc.,
publishers, 2019 | Includes bibliographical references and index.
Identifiers: LCCN 2019027226 | ISBN 9781476675237 (paperback : acid free paper) ∞
ISBN 9781476636054 (ebook)
Subjects: LCSH: Sullavan, Margaret, 1909–1960. | Motion picture actors and
actresses—United States—Biography.
Classification: LCC PN2287.S85 R56 2019 | DDC 791.4302/8092 [B]—dc23
LC record available at https://lccn.loc.gov/2019027226

BRITISH LIBRARY CATALOGUING DATA ARE AVAILABLE

ISBN (print) 978-1-4766-7523-7
ISBN (ebook) 978-1-4766-3605-4

Front cover: Publicity photograph of Margaret Sullavan
(courtesy of Peter Doyle)

Printed in the United States of America

McFarland & Company, Inc., Publishers
Box 611, Jefferson, North Carolina 28640
www.mcfarlandpub.com

To the memory of my mother
Carole Louise Rinella
(1936–2017)
who shared her love of classic movies with me at an early
age, thus forming a bond between us that endured long
after the onset of Alzheimer's robbed her of the ability to
place a name to a well-beloved face on the screen

Acknowledgments

First, I would like to thank my wife Julie and our children Paul, Martha and Faith for their support and encouragement; I am particularly grateful to Martha for assisting me with ordering DVDs and photographs online and for taking me to libraries for last-minute research. I am grateful to Tracy Whitney and the staff at Marion Public Library for their invaluable assistance, and am deeply grateful to Cheryl Blue for cheerfully fulfilling my neverending requests for books through the interlibrary loan system. Without Cheryl's assistance, this book would be not as complete as I had envisioned. I am deeply indebted to Christopher Frank and James Hallahan of the Association for the Blind and Visually Impaired (ABVI) of Rochester for their assistance with adaptive technology; I am grateful to the two authors who "beat me to the punch" with the Kay Francis project, Scott O'Brien and Lynn Kear, for their words of encouragement. Lynn was particularly helpful in guiding the development of this book. I would like to thank G.D. Hamann for compiling articles into *Margaret Sullavan of the 30s*; Troy Valos of Slover Library of the Norfolk Public Library system for his invaluable assistance in locating hard-to-find information regarding Margaret Sullavan's early life; William Black of Chatham Hall for information regarding Chatham Episcopal Institute; Diane Buckley and Dorothy Williams of Meyera E. Oberndorf Central Library in Virginia Beach for information regarding Ms. Sullavan's little-known appearance with the Little Theater of Norfolk and the obituary notice for Garland Council Sullavan, respectively; Jeff Korman of the Baltimore Public Library for assistance with the University Players repertory season of 1931–32; and Kim Stucko of the Field (Peekskill NY) Library for providing invaluable access to New York newspapers. I would also like to thank the staff of the New York Public Library (Billy Rose Theater Division) as well as the following public libraries: Indianapolis (Mike Perkins); Cambridge (MA) Public Library (Anne Crockett); White Plains, NY (Miriam Berg Varian); Poughkeepsie, NY (Kira Thompson); Nyack, NY (Kathleen Sullivan); Falmouth, MA; Pittsburgh, PA; Mt. Kisco, NY; Rochester, NY; Brighton, NY; East Rochester, NY; Fairport, NY; Greene, NY; Macedon, NY; Newark, NY, and Pittsford, NY, as well as the following universities: SUNY Brockport, SUNY Cortland, SUNY Geneseo, Cornell University, Syracuse University and the University of Rochester.

I am also grateful to the following for their assistance in obtaining photographs for this book: my family, with Martha again playing a critical role in this area; William Black of Chatham Hall; Troy Valos of Slover Library; Tom Lisanti of the New York Public Library; Brooke Hayward Duchin for her permission; Gary Combs and Peter Doyle.

Finally, I am grateful to God, in whom all things are made possible.

Table of Contents

Introduction
Clarity of Vision

"I have never been what you would call a 'dedicated actress'."[1]

On the set of *Three Comrades* (1938), Gladys Hall of *Motion Picture* magazine asked Margaret Sullavan, "What do you consider the outstanding quality you bring to the screen?"

Sullavan was characteristically unaffected and to the point: "Blest if I know," she replied. "I'm not pretty, not glamorous. Better on the stage, the footlights help me to create an illusion."[2]

Despite her tremendous overnight success in motion pictures back in 1933 and the box office and critical success of the recent Broadway play *Stage Door* (1936), Margaret Sullavan was still unsure of her value as an actress. She continued to have such doubts until her death 21½ years later. Her lack of an actor's ego significantly limited her output as an actress. Considering other popular film stars of the 1930s, Sullavan's body of work (16 films in all) is rather small. Only one film, *The Shop Around the Corner* (1940), has been rightfully recognized as an enduring classic; all of her other films are mostly forgotten or underappreciated today. As a consequence, her star shines far less brightly today than stars of similar appeal like Jean Arthur.

Other popular female stars, such as Bette Davis, Joan Crawford and Katharine Hepburn, combined an identifiable cinema personality with acting talent and, consequently, achieved legendary status that lasts to this day. Sullavan was first and foremost an actress, who so completely submerged her personality in each of her roles that she never became an easily identifiable "film type." Most comedians can do recognizable imitations of Davis and Hepburn. Could there ever be a "Sullavan" type to imitate? She was simply too individual for that. As a researcher once aptly remarked, "Defining the qualities that made Sullavan special is like trying to capture air."[3] Most modern movie fans know of her performance in *The Shop Around the Corner*, but may be hard-pressed to come up with another film role. After all, there are still those who refer to her as Jane from the Tarzan movies (Maureen O'Sullivan, if you please).

It could be argued that her lack of an actor's ego and "type" became her greatest asset. She was an exceptionally instinctive actress who found success in several media: film, theater, radio and television. At her peak, she was considered by many notable critics to be the best actress in the entertainment field. Throughout her career, she received nominations and awards for performances on the screen, stage and television. Sullavan had the uncanny ability to inject just enough of her personality to enhance any role without overpowering it as Davis or Hepburn so often did. Whatever the role—the idealistic young wife of *Little Man, What Now?* (1934); the guileless young orphan of *The Good Fairy* (1935); the tubercular fraulein of *Three Comrades*; the long-suffering mistress of *Back Street* (1941); the terminally ill housewife of *No Sad Songs for Me* (1950)—Sullavan was able to create individual screen characters who were essentially soul sisters, yet varied and quite different from each other.

What was it about Sullavan that made her so hauntingly memorable on the screen? Many critics and film historians refer to her charmingly husky voice, her luminous presence, her expressive, melancholy eyes. I believe that her enduring appeal goes deeper than that. In watching her best work on film, I have noticed a common thread among them which elevates her performances into something special and exquisite. I vividly recall encountering this for the first time when I watched *Back Street* as a young teenager. This was my initial exposure to Sullavan and, after more than 40 years, the impression still haunts me. I call this characteristic "clarity of vision." Simply put, it is that rare ability to clearly communicate to the audience the purpose of his or her very existence. It is the inherent ability of knowing who they are and remaining steadfastly true in that conviction no matter what life may throw in their paths. Ironically, this marvelous quality eluded her in real life and she was left to cope with crippling insecurity and nagging self-doubts.

Through Sullavan's words, actions and, in particular, expressive eyes on the screen, the audience feels an intense emotional connection to a woman who seems so *real* and *life-like.* Although I realize that I am perhaps inviting some unwanted controversy, I contend that few actresses of the 1930s and 1940s share this trait, this "clarity of vision." One can admire Joan Crawford's performances in *The Women* and *Mildred Pierce*, but these characterizations bear no resemblance to real life. The same can be said for Bette Davis. While always watchable, she was not exactly lifelike because she was most often much larger than life.

On the other hand, the great Greta Garbo most certainly had this quality in such films as *Queen Christina* and *Camille*. While something of a goddess at times, she was also incredibly human. Ann Sheridan was another star who had this instinctive quality. *Kings Row* and *City for Conquest* confirm this beyond a doubt. Another sublime example is my favorite "personality star," Kay Francis. Films such as *One Way Passage, Cynara* and even *In Name Only* emphasize her own unique clarity of vision. In those films, she was immensely real and moving. When cast in films such as *First Lady* and *Comet Over Broadway,* which went against this quality, she was startlingly artificial and unconvincing.

Sullavan, supreme actress that she was, was convincingly real and intensely personal in her connection to the audience. They not only believed in the character she was playing, they believed in *her.* Even today, her performances have such a natural quality that she is still contemporary to modern audiences. One is rarely aware of the impression that she is acting. There may have been the rare occasion in which her character lacked this clarity of vision—the Virginia military ball scenes in *Only Yesterday* (1933) and the latter sections of *Back Street*—and, not surprisingly, she seems to be a different, distant person altogether. Fortunately, these instances only amounted to fleeting moments on the screen.

A conversation with a family friend, Lauren, was the impetus for this book. Although she has more than a passing knowledge of classic movies, Lauren was still at a loss to place a face to the name Margaret Sullavan. "What has she done?" was her inevitable question. Picking the most obvious and accessible choice, I replied, "*The Shop Around the Corner* with Jimmy Stewart and Frank Morgan." "Oh, *everybody* knows Jimmy! And Frank Morgan, wasn't he the Wizard from *Wizard of Oz*?" she asked. "But I don't recall having ever seen Margaret Sullavan." Lauren had never seen the movie but promised to see it soon.

So, given that all-too-familiar scenario, I became more resolved to shed light on Sulla-van's life and career for all of those who still have trouble putting a face to the name. It is time that she received renewed attention on her amazingly diverse and rewarding film work. It is my deepest wish to restore the luster of her once-brilliant light in that constellation of stars in a heaven called Hollywood.

1

Untamed Spirit

There was so much prissy propriety and sexual prudity and emotional repression among the people who inhabited my early life, that I suppose I went to the other extreme.[1]

In a three-part series of articles called "Beloved Brat" for *Photoplay* magazine in 1938, which covered Sullavan's early life, Howard Sharpe made this claim: "If she'd been born 50 years earlier she would have been Scarlett O'Hara, with all of Scarlett's charm and her fury and all her vital disregard of custom and, in addition, intelligence that Scarlett never had. She would have been Jezebel, what's more, and have loved it."[2] As one becomes more familiar with Sullavan's life, this remark is not that far-fetched.

Margaret Sullavan was born into a prominent Virginian family with a rich ancestral history and deeply rooted Southern values. Her father Cornelius Hancock Sullavan was born on September 3, 1877, in Lancaster County, Virginia, to John L. and Mary Chowning Sullavan. He came from a wealthy family, whose background consisted of Irish-American stock dating back to the pre–American Revolutionary days. The spelling of Sullavan with an "a" instead of an "i" reflects the family's ties to Ireland's northern regions. Once in America, the family maintained this spelling rather than adopting the more commonly used Sullivan.

Margaret's mother, Garland Council, was born into an affluent family in Aberdeen, Virginia, on April 13, 1876. She was the fourth child of James Calvin Council (born 1825) and Mary Smith (born 1834). Her family tree was as notable as Cornelius' as it consisted of prominent Virginians such as State Senator James Smith and Confederate General Robert E. Lee. Sometime between 1901 and 1902, Garland married Lewis Gregory Winston. He died of typhoid fever after three months of marriage and left behind a grieving, pregnant widow.

According to Sullavan's biographer Lawrence J. Quirk, Garland mourned the loss to an obsessive degree. She carried a picture of Lewis in her locket (behind her second husband's picture) for many years. In 1902, their daughter Lewise was born in Richmond.

A few years later, Cornelius, then an affluent produce and farm supplies broker (not a stockbroker as recorded), met Garland. According to census records from that time, they were married either in 1906 or 1907. It has been insinuated that this marriage was one of convenience rather than that of passion or even love. Sullavan always felt that her mother never really stopped loving her first husband.

The family relocated to Norfolk, Virginia, in early 1909 and settled into a spacious three-story red brick house on Westover Street. It was there that the couple's first child was born on May 16, 1909 (not 1911, as many publications have printed). Cornelius and Garland's daughter was christened Margaret Brooke Sullavan; the name Brooke was from a maternal great-grandmother, Priscilla Brooke Lee Smith. The infant was given the nickname Peggy, which Sullavan later said she hated. In accordance with family tradition, the nickname persisted until her twenty-first birthday at which time she chose a new nickname, Maggie. Only those closest to her were allowed to call her Peggy. A second child, Cornelius Hancock Sullavan Jr., was born in 1914. His nickname was Sonny. Their older half-sister's nickname was Weedie.

According to Sullavan's daughter Brooke Hayward, her mother's childhood memories were conflicted: There was "deep pride about her Southern ancestry and customs, offset by a rebelliousness against that pride."[3] Throughout her life, Sullavan detested the smug, pompous attitude in those who valued social status.

Early on, Sullavan was afflicted with a painful condition that caused muscular weakness in both legs. As she recalled, "I was sick.... I was all arms and legs and weakness."[4] Due to this condition, she did not walk on her own until the age of five or six. This prevented her from playing with other children and she spent many lonely days within the confines of her home. Her parents lavished their attention on her to the extent of being overbearing and protective. Actor Kent Smith, her lifelong friend, recalled that, despite their warm and kind demeanor, her parents were reserved physically as well as emotionally. As a result, Sullavan vowed to be more emotionally involved in her children's lives.

Hayward's earliest recollections of her grandparents were much more charitable than her mother's. She recalled that Cornelius was "spry and gay" and Garland "plump and charming." She recalled that both were short, which seemed "to be the only respect in which Mother [at 5'2"] took after either of them."[5] Sullavan claimed she was tiny during her growing years. "I didn't grow until I was 19. When I was 19, I sprouted."[6] She was often being referred to as a "mere slip of a girl" all her life, but the headstrong Sullavan personality proved much more formidable.

Peggy's rebellious nature surfaced early. By her own admission, she was a "nasty little girl."[7] To another interviewer, she explained, "I was a temperamental youngster and I grew up with the notion that I could do ... whatever pleased me at the moment."[8] A childhood friend later recalled, "The parents doted on her—but I think she always wanted more."[9]

By the time she was six, Sullavan had the full use of her legs. "It wasn't until I heard someone say I'd never live to see my sixteenth birthday that I really set my mind on getting well," Sullavan reminisced. "I had to show 'em. That's part of the Sullavan in me."[10] She quickly embraced the life of a rambunctious tomboy. For her class-conscious parents, this new behavior brought new concerns. To make matters worse, the child preferred the company of children from the "other side of town." Unlike most girls of her social status, Sullavan enjoyed the company of both boys and girls. With the boys, she engaged in roughhousing and highly physical activities. At the same time, her years of isolation enabled her to be deeply sympathetic to girls and their difficulties.

In desperation, her parents exposed her to other interests. "Because I drew a good pig at three years of age, my family wanted me to be an artist," Sullavan recalled. However, her interest in art did not satisfy her restless nature for long. Sullavan also loved participating in Sunday School at St. Andrew's Episcopal Church where Cornelius served as a vestryman. It was there that Sullavan first experienced the excitement of performing as a dancer in front of an audience. From this point on, she focused on dance classes with aspirations of becoming a dancer. Her parents encouraged her interests in art and dance because, according to Margaret, "those were nice ladylike accomplishments."[11]

But not all of her interests were acceptably feminine. Sullavan inherited an appreciation for hunting from her father, who enjoyed the reputation as one of the best shots in the state. Her father's Parker 28 gauge shotgun was passed down to her. With its handle engraved with game birds and animals, this gun was cherished greatly. Her family took her all over Virginia and North Carolina on fishing and hunting trips to build up her physical strength. "All it did was to give me a taste for the simple life," Sullavan reflected. "Ever since, I've doted on living outdoors."[12] Like Carole Lombard, she was an anomaly among the stars for her love of hunting and camping in the rugged outdoors.

Weedie's friend Louisa Venable Kyle recalled that Sullavan "often proved the pest that any younger sister can prove." Even then, there was something that set Peggy apart from other girls her age:

> I remember that even as a wisp of a child, she had the temperament of the artist. She was all grace and possessed a pixie quality. Her golden head, well set on her shoulders, was carried with a certain air. She was winsome and affectionate and impish and she formed many friendships among the young people in Norfolk.[13]

When she was eight, Sullavan was enrolled at the Walter Taylor Grammar School, located on 1410 Clairmont Avenue in Norfolk. The school was named after Lt. Col. Taylor, an aide to General Lee. The building, listed on the National Register of Historic Places listings in Norfolk, was demolished in 1999.

By adolescence, Sullavan developed an interest in boys and took more than the casual interest in what made them tick. She later regaled her daughters with stories of spending countless hours entertaining smitten young boys, much to the irritation of her brother Sonny. In an attempt to tame her rebellious nature, her parents enrolled her in a series of boarding schools for girls. Although her father's produce business suffered a bit during the slow post–World War I recovery period, Sullavan attended prestigious private schools such as St. George's Private School in Norfolk and Miss Turnbull's Norfolk Tutoring School for Girls before settling in at Chatham Episcopal Institute in Chatham, Virginia, in the fall of 1925. Sullavan later admitted that this period was filled with loneliness as she detested being away from home. As a result, the teenaged girl worked hard to be a problem child. As she recalled, "I learned the surface manners and niceties that went with being a well-brought-up young lady of good stock, but inwardly I was an anarchist of the deepest dye."[14] She had a "partner-in-crime" in her roommate, Martha "Cree" Justice Pender, who became a lifelong friend. "We sure had some wild times there," Pender recalled. "We were really terrible." She recalled that, at the beginning of their time at Chatham, a new principal arrived. A free-thinking, progressive woman, the principal decided that rules were not needed as girls with social status were expected to act like young

Sullavan's senior high school picture (1927). She had already demonstrated her many talents as well as her rebellious nature (courtesy Chatham Hall).

ladies. Sullavan and Cree were placed on probation the next night for having slept outside on the porch.

During the summers, Sullavan attended summer camps to build her physical strength and stamina. It was another attempt by her parents to keep their daughter preoccupied. Hayward recalled her mother boasting of her being named the best all-round athlete one summer.

During her senior year at Chatham, Sullavan was involved in multiple clubs and activities. She participated in the French Club, Varsity Basketball, and Dramatic and Art Clubs, among others. It is no wonder she was voted "Most Talented" of her class. As Cree recalled, "Peggy was one of the most remarkable talents I ever knew. Not only in her acting ability, but in art, dancing and writing as well."[15] For the May Day celebration, Sullavan appeared as Puck in the senior class production *The Queen of Youth*. Hayward claimed that her mother, as president of the student body, delivered the salutary oration at the 1927 graduation ceremony. Chatham Episcopal Institute was renamed Chatham Hall the following year and continues to operate as an exclusive all-girl boarding school. Other notable graduates include artist Georgia O'Keeffe (class of 1905) and Pulitzer Prize–winning poet Claudia Emerson (1975).

It was expected that Sullavan would attend Hollins College in Roanoke County. To no one's surprise, she chose to enroll in Sullins College in Bristol, Virginia, instead. Founded in 1868, Sullins was once both a high school and a junior college for girls operated by the Methodist Church. After a fire destroyed the building in 1915, Sullins became an exclusive women junior college that appealed to a clientele of rich families throughout the southeastern region. Sullins remained in operation as a girls' college until it closed in 1976.

Margaret's parents needed very little persuasion to let her attend this prestigious college. She entered Sullins in the fall of 1927 and quickly embraced every activity she undertook and was voted most popular girl of her class. Away from her parents' watchful eyes, she enjoyed unbridled sexual freedom. It was the Roaring Twenties and women enjoyed a looser standard of sexual conduct. Years later, *Photoplay* editor Ruth Waterbury shared one of Sullavan's college friend's memories of the star's views on love and sex: "I fall in love too often and too head-over-heels. So then I shift from the romantic to the sexual just to get my balance back, so I can be more detached, so I can be and feel less vulnerable to hurt."[16]

Burgess Meredith, whom Sullavan befriended in the early 1930s, recalled, "She didn't really pay any attention to men unless she was interested in them sexually. You *knew* when Sullavan was interested in you, and there weren't many men who could resist her because she was so predatory about seduction."[17] One of Sullavan's closest friends, Millicent Osborn, offered her perception that Sullavan was raised in a culture "with the understanding … that she had to charm every man that she came across." Summing up the enigma of Margaret Sullavan, Osborn reflected, "She was like a Fitzgerald creature, the Southern belle. But there was nothing substantial about her flirtatiousness."[18] Sullavan's views of love and sex were very masculine in nature, but there was also an element of insecurity and fragileness that permeated her thinking. These opposing feelings never were resolved and she was haunted by her inability to find true and lasting love with any man.

Sullavan's first love was Hunter Hogan of Norfolk. According to Hogan, they met at a dance when she was 16 and he was only 15. "She was captivating," Hogan remembered. "Peggy had to be one of the most attractive women I have ever met.." He reminisced about the time she attended a winter dance with him at the University of Virginia. "She just walked in and took the place over. Peggy was a sensational dancer."[19] They broke up around the time Sullavan began pursuing a serious stage career, but remained close friends all her life.

Sullavan claimed that it was at Sullins that she began to entertain the notion of being an actress. As she explained, she was overwriting every essay in the hope of striking the main idea at some point. The English Literature professor tried to discourage this practice and requested that she stop acting on the margins of a paper. "It made me think," Sullavan related. "Maybe I could act."[20] Later that year, she appeared in *The Girl with the Green Eyes*. At the end of the play, Sullavan's character commits suicide by sticking her head in the oven. According to Cree (who was Sullavan's roommate again), there wasn't a dry eye in the house: "Anyone would have known then that she was going places."[21]

After her freshman year, Sullavan returned to Norfolk. She quickly became restless and desired something more than what the inevitable, respectable future held in store. The previous summer, she had met a family from Boston at camp. Through a casual conversation, she learned about the Denishawn School of Dance in Boston. The family encouraged her to pursue dancing at that notable school. Emboldened by her year at college, Sullavan was determined to leave home. Breaking this news to her parents required different tactics. Although the following excerpt sounds suspiciously like fabricated publicity, it is nonetheless an interesting read: Sullavan told her parents: "I've always done as you asked. I've always obeyed the essentials. But you must understand; I can't be a polite sub-deb who paints wishy sunsets in water color and keeps her eye peeled for a husband. And I'm sorry, but I'm going to Boston."

"Fantastic," said Cornelius. "I forbid it."[22]

Sullavan was not dissuaded and her parents reluctantly agreed that she could move to Boston and live with Lewise. She told them she would attend secretarial school, but instead she secretly enrolled at Denishawn.

The Denishawn School of Dancing and Related Arts opened in Los Angeles in 1915. It was founded by Ruth St. Denis and Ted Shawn, who raised some eyebrows by living together before marriage. One of its most famous pupils was legendary silent film star Louise Brooks.

Once at Denishawn, Sullavan did not last more than a few weeks. Perhaps she found the methods of dance instruction too restricting. Sullavan then decided to pursue a new interest: acting on the stage. She had gone to see *The Connecticut Yankee* presented by the E.E. Clive Copley Dramatic Players. As she watched the performance of the company's ingénue, she thought that she could do better. At that moment, a determined young lady knew what she had to do next.

2

Frolicking with the Players

I more or less wandered into the theater. It was really part of the business of youthful rebellion.[1]

When her parents learned from Lewise that Peggy had dropped out of secretarial school, they were furious. As Sullavan recalled, "My family shuddered with horror when they first discovered I wanted to be an actress."[2] To make matters worse, Lewise had written that Peggy was "absolutely man-mad! And I for one just hope that our Peggy doesn't get into trouble" with all of those infatuated Harvard boys.[3]

Despite her family's concerns, Sullavan would not budge. As she explained, "I wanted to break away from home.... The theater seemed like an easy and interesting and glamorous way to do it."[4]

Cornelius cut her allowance, hoping to deter her from her unsanctioned activities. That only strengthened her resolve. Sullavan secured an $18-per-week clerk job at the Harvard Cooperative Bookstore to pay for her studies at Clive's. Sullavan claimed, "I was a marvelous saleswoman. I used to make more sales than anyone else because I'd tell the boys I had cheaper copies than they were looking at."[5] She didn't keep that job for long.

Sullavan always referred to 1928 as the year her life began. Not only had she found the long-desired freedom from her oppressive upbringing, but she also had a purpose in her life that provided a suitable outlet for her restless spirit. "The need to act had become an urge so strong that nothing could stop me. It had to do with a need to express certain feelings inside me."[6]

Clive, a Welsh-born stage actor, operated an all–British repertory company and dramatic school during the 1920s and early 1930s. One of his most famous students was Rosalind Russell, who appeared in several productions in 1929. A small, mild-mannered man in person, Clive was a taskmaster with his students. He taught it was the blending of personal experience with the truth of the character that was an essential element to a performance. While Sullavan never appeared in any Copley Players productions, she made an impression. In 1934, Clive shared his memories of Sullavan for *Photoplay*: "She had an instinctive grace, a voice that promised depths, yet to be explored, and an earnestness rather surprising to find in a little Southern girl whom the Harvard boys were only too eager to make a belle of the ball."[7]

Along with her studies, Sullavan was busy with her personal life as she was receiving plenty of attention from college boys. The most persistent admirer from Harvard was a wealthy young man, Charles Crane Leatherbee (class of 1929). Leatherbee, despite his poise and sophistication, was hopelessly smitten with Sullavan. Certainly, her parents would have approved. His grandfather, Charles Richard Crane, was an American diplomat and founder of the Crane Plumbing Company. Leatherbee's stepfather Jan Masaryk was the Czechoslovakian Minister to the Court of St. James. Unfortunately for her parents, Leatherbee's influence on their daughter would be professional rather than personal.

In May, the Harvard Dramatic Society production was a musical comedy entitled *Close Up*, written by senior Bernard Hanighen, who later gained recognition as a Broadway and Hollywood composer. Having served as the head of the Dramatic Society in 1928, Leatherbee got Sullavan assigned to the chorus. When a part in a comedy sketch became available, she secured that part as well. Appearing in the sketch was a young actor who played a significant role in her life. His name was Henry Fonda.

Despite a vastly different background, they shared many similarities, including the same birthday. He was born in 1905 in Grand Island, Nebraska. His father, William Brace Fonda, was in the advertising and printing business. His mother was Elma Herberta Jaynes. His paternal ancestors emigrated from the Netherlands to the Dutch colony of New Netherland in 1642. His ancestors, among the first Dutch settlers in what became upstate New York, founded the town of Fonda. By the late 1800s, many of their descendants relocated to Nebraska. Fonda spent most of his childhood and early adulthood in Omaha. His family was close, religious and supportive. As a young man, Fonda was a bashful, athletic person who avoided girls. He studied journalism at the University of Minnesota for two years before flunking out. By 21, he gravitated toward working full-time with the Omaha Community Playhouse over his father's objections. Initially, he was only interested in the behind-the-scenes aspects of stage production. However, after performing the lead in *Merton of the Movies*, Fonda recalled, "That was the first time I realized what acting meant. It also dawned on me that for a self-doubting man, this was the answer."[8] With his father's approval, Fonda pursued a new career.

While working with a Washington, D.C. stock company, Fonda received word from Hanighen, a friend from Omaha, about a comedy sketch in *Close Up*. Fonda recalled, "This was a typical burlesque type of comedy and one of the pieces of business was [Sullavan] crosses the stage while I'm going in the other direction. I do a big take, make some gesture or comment, she turns and slaps me and just keeps walking."[9] What should have been a standard routine became more complicated than Fonda anticipated. "We rehearsed that bit for a week or ten days and every time she slapped me, she rocked me. Every time she hit me, I saw a flash. It seemed to say, 'You'd better, by God, notice me.' And I did. I fell in love with her, too."[10]

Sullavan managed to be featured in a *Boston Post* photograph. Under the caption of "High Steppers," she is identified as Peggy Sullavan of Norfolk, Virginia. She made her stage debut on May 8 when *Close Up* premiered at Brattle Hall. The college newspaper, the *Harvard Crimson,* called it "a gay and tuneful frolic obviously hugely enjoyable to its participants and contagious in its entertainment value. Audiences will please not look for professional smoothness in the dancing sequences, but they should be charmed by the players' spirit of genuine enjoyment."[11]

Sullavan claimed to recall very little about the play except "it gave her delight to save all her strength and deliver a resounding smack across [Fonda's] cheek. Otherwise, she insists that she didn't notice him."[12] Despite that assertion, sparks of mutual attraction ignited and Sullavan was intrigued by the lanky young actor. Josh Logan recalled the 24-year-old Fonda. In addition to "that beautiful male face, when Fonda smiled, you were uplifted."[13] The budding romance between Fonda and Sullavan might have gone nowhere had Leatherbee not invited her to join the University Players for the summer season in Falmouth, Massachusetts.

The University Players Guild was the brainchild of Leatherbee, who already had a small amateur stock troupe, the Juniper Point Players, in the Cape Cod area. With Bretaigne Windust, they established the University Players Guild, which was based in Elizabeth during the summer of 1928. The four founding members included Erik Bannouw and Windust of Princeton and Kingsley Perry and Leatherbee of Harvard. Each contributed $100 toward the start-up funds. Other members of this group included undergraduates from the prestigious universities Harvard, Princeton, Vassar and Radcliffe.

What is remarkable about this group is the level of success many of its prominent members achieved. In his book *But Not Forgotten*, Norris Houghton reflected, "The University Players remains an unfulfilled dream—that did not fail to touch every single Player. The failure of the whole has in some measure have been vindicated by the accomplishments of the individuals."[14] Windust became a prominent film, stage and television director and producer. Myron McCormick had a productive career as a film, stage and radio actor who won a Tony for his supporting role in *South Pacific* (1949). Logan achieved distinction as a stage and film director and writer. Among his notable directorial credits were the play, *Mister Roberts* (1948, with Henry Fonda) and his Oscar-nominated direction of *Picnic* (1955) and *Sayonara* (1957). Johnny Swope became a noted Hollywood photographer for *Life* magazine and an airplane pilot. With Leland Hayward and John H. Connelly, Swope co-founded Southwest Airways (no relation to Southwest Airlines). While not as commercially successful as his colleagues, Norris Houghton has been recognized as the premier American expert of 20th-century Russian theater as well as a major force in developing the Off-Broadway movement during the 1950s. In addition to this distinguished lineup, several other members who had their first professional acting experience included James Stewart, Barbara O'Neil and Kent Smith. As for Leatherbee, his contribution to the theatrical world was cut short when he died of pneumonia in January 1935 at the age of 27.

The University Players' guiding philosophy was simple: "The idea of theater artists working together over a long period of time subordinating themselves to the whole and finding therein a satisfaction beyond that accruing from individual glory."[15] The finished product (the performance) was the ultimate goal rather than any individual contribution. All members were involved in every aspect from building sets, designing costumes and serving in the tea room. For the troupe, it was an exhilarating experience. Logan wrote,

> Inside each member burned hot love not only for the theater but for their company—yes, and for each other. We actually believed we were better than anyone. We would have challenged any company in the country. It was only this blind, idiot confidence that could make us accept minor parts, odd jobs with the crew, our meager salary of five dollars a week less laundry, our frayed clothing and our repetitious skimpy sets.[16]

With the summer season a few months away, the Players needed an ingénue after Eleanor Phelps joined a national touring production. Sullavan readily accepted Leatherbee's invitation. However, she would need the others' approval. Houghton recalled, "She was not exactly beautiful. She was a little shy. She had a husky voice with a strong Southern accent. She was about 18, slight with sandy-blonde hair. But Windy knew at once that Charlie had made a real discovery. There was electricity there, a wonderful arresting magnetism."

Enchanted, the men didn't ask her to read. They didn't even ask her what she had done. They just asked her if she would join them. Remembering the stipulation that they only hired undergraduates from distinguished universities, Windust asked her where she attended college. "I went to Sullins College," she informed a dubious Windust.

"Sullins?"

The University Players in Baltimore. Left to right: Henry Fonda, Joshua Logan, Sullavan, Myron McCormick and Barbara O'Neil in *Holiday*. Sullavan often regarded her association with the University Players as among the happiest in her career.

"For a whole year."

"Sullins?"

"It's one of the finest colleges in Virginia," she said firmly.[17]

With an offer of $10 a week and board, the company had their newest ingénue. Then Leatherbee made a strange request. He advised Sullavan not to cut her hair in the fashionable bob of the 1920s, because he knew that it would not be appropriate for some of her roles. Besides, he disliked the style intensely.

Sullavan's arrival in late June was an indication of the excitement she would bring in successive months for she had cut her hair in that bob so detested by Leatherbee. Furious, he threatened to fire her. Sullavan, instead of being apologetic, was indignant that a big fuss was made over such a small matter. Cooler heads prevailed and Sullavan remained. She had won her first—but certainly not the last—professional skirmish.

Among the prominent members that summer were Elizabeth Fenner, Aleta Freel, Kent Smith—and Henry Fonda. For the first production, Windust and Leatherbee chose *The Devil in the Cheese*, a complicated and difficult show as it required multiple props.

The start of the season found the Players in total disarray. No longer operating in Elizabeth, the company moved to Old Silver Beach in West Falmouth. They had decided to build their own theater with a $20,000 loan from Leatherbee's grandfather. With the season's opening performance scheduled for July 2, construction of the theater began in early June. The new theater included a stage, a tea room and dance hall. Sporadic rehearsals took place amongst the busy carpenters and other contractors. Prior to the opening, Windust suspended rehearsals so the company could finish the construction. By opening night, frantic last-minute preparations took place as an exhausted company nervously prepared to perform. Finally, after a lengthy delay, the curtains rose at 9:30 p.m. What transpired after would be a disaster on every imaginable level.

According to various recollections, the comedy was a doomed enterprise from the beginning. Fonda recalled, "Sullavan and I were supposed to be the leads, but a vicious sea robin who tried to claw me to death and a crazy tortoise who wandered on and off stage at will stole the damn show."[18] Props were misplaced, cues were missed, special effects involving water ruined the fresh paint, expensive apparatus malfunctioned, and a monkey urinated on Sullavan's shoulder.

Despite her inexperience, Sullavan made a great impression. Her first line ("Now, don't worry, Mother, everything's all right") was delivered "with such calm authority" in all the chaos that Logan shook Leatherbee's hand. "What a wonderful actress we have," he whispered.[19] The curtains came down around one a.m. to lay this disaster to rest. The audience burst into loud applause. Houghton remembered, "Instead of being resentful at the inadequacies of the evening, they seemed to appreciate the dogged determination with which this band of youngsters had carried through…. The audience then and there became our fast friends."[20] The next day, the *Falmouth Enterprise* wrote,

> Rising superbly over a multitude of vicissitudes, the University Guild Players in their first production, Monday night, in their new theater, carried their audience with them by sheer contagious youthful enthusiasm and excellent acting…. They went bravely on the stage and played as though everything in the world were breaking right for them. The play was incredibly smooth, forgotten lines were covered up and passed over, and the players remained cool and confident.

The critic also opined, "Miss Sullavan is extremely pretty and her first-night nervousness will doubtless disappear with more experience." Logan was enthusiastic: "The only bright, competent figure—the only ray of hope in all that despair was radiant little Margaret Sullavan."[21]

Sullavan reveled in her newfound freedom. Sharpe theorized,

> The turbulent spirit of Margaret Sullavan found exceptional happiness…. She walked along the beach in the early twilight, reminding herself that this was the liberty she had always wanted; this the escape from the sharply raised eyebrows of a family and friends whose opinions were rooted in the Old South and whose rules for living were deadlocked with those of Maggie Sullavan, the rebel.[22]

From the beginning, Fonda was uncomfortable with Sullavan's presence. Logan recalled, "She could be a real bitch. But she was also a great deal of fun and very passionate."[23] Fonda was confused by her capricious nature. So far, his experience with her "added up to a kind of nightmare," Fonda admitted.[24] That she was Leatherbee's girlfriend did not help matters. Fonda warned Leatherbee that she was trouble, but he only replied, "You'll fall for her yourself, Hank—everyone does, in time."[25]

Logan was one of the many enchanted by Sullavan:

> [She] had a pulsing and husky voice, which could suddenly switch in emotional moments to a high, choir-boy soprano. Her beauty was not obvious or even standard. It showed as she tilted her head, as she walked, as she laughed, and she was breathtakingly beautiful as she ran. One of my girlfriends complained that I talked too much about Sullavan, and she was right. We were all in love with her.[26]

Fonda succumbed once again. Slowly, throughout the summer, it became romantic. "She was fun-loving, fun on the beach playing games. If she found a water pistol, she was the one who squirted water on everybody."[27] For the dour, brooding Fonda, her free-spirited nature was irresistible. Their burgeoning romance set the background of an interesting quadrangle between Leatherbee, Fonda, Sullavan *and*, according to Devin McKinney, Logan, who harbored "sexually or at least sensually ambivalent" feelings for *Fonda*.[28]

Windust, Leatherbee and Logan knew that they had an exceptional actress in their midst. As Logan explained to Hayward, "She had, from the beginning, that magic, that indescribable quality that is extremely rare."[29] But the University Players believed that all actors had the same opportunities to play leading roles. Therefore, Sullavan only appeared in two more leading roles and a smaller part in an unidentified play. The other time was mostly spent behind the scenes. In 1950, Houghton mused, "Imagine the summer theater manager today who had the privilege of Miss Sullavan's services for ten weeks and employed her as a waitress for more than half the season."[30]

Sullavan played the ingénue role in *Crime*, presented in early August. She and Fonda were cast as the two innocent victims implicated in a criminal act. This was the first play in which the couple had a love scene to play. As the week progressed, the company noticed the increasing ardor the scene took on. "Although they pretended to despise each other offstage," Logan recalled, "they caught fire when the curtains went up."[31] All of this must have been a painful development to Leatherbee, who was cast in the role of the criminal mastermind.

Crime was well received by the *Falmouth Enterprise*: "It is a good show, with plenty of actions and thrills, and well cast." As Annabelle, "petite Peggy Sullavan wins all hearts," while Fonda was judged as "handsome, but more or less dumb." The critic also noted, "Each week the theater of the University Guild plays to larger houses; Monday's opening this week was exceptionally crowded, and the Guild seems established as a permanent asset to the Falmouth summers." This was good news as the company's dream was now a profitable reality.

Sullavan had finally fallen completely in love with Fonda and, despite Leatherbee's presence, they were open about their feelings. A cast member recollected, "She was going to marry Hank and together they would soar to stardom."[32] The couple spent a lot of time together lying on the beach, swimming and rehearsing their lines.

There were constant requests for Fonda and Sullavan to appear together. "I kept after Charlie to do something truly romantic with them," Logan recalled. "They were both 'naturals'—consummate actors but with an animal attraction that was quite apparent."[33] In September, Sullavan and Fonda were teamed in the final production, *The Constant Nymph*. The highly romantic story involved a teenage girl who falls in love with a family friend. Her love for him remains unrequited as he marries her cousin. Under Leatherbee's direction, the play was an ambitious undertaking with its complicated sets and large cast. This production was considered to be among the company's best efforts and the experience was magical. Logan recalled a particularly memorable moment: "[Fonda and Sullavan] had to sing a Lewis Dodd composition, 'Ah, Say Not So, Another Love Will Find Thee.' Even though Hank was able to sing on key, his voice was described as an on-key whine. Sullavan was so insecure musically that she never settled on any key. It didn't seem to matter. Everyone melted the moment they appeared."[34]

The other unforgettable moment was the final scene where Sullavan laid dying in Fonda's arms. After watching Sullavan's performance, Houghton asserted, "it was clear to everyone that in this little hoyden who refused to wear shoes and stockings except on stage it had one of the best, if not the best, talent in the company."[35]

The *Enterprise* called the play a bit of an anticlimax "after the gorgeous costumes, colorful setting and satiric drama of *The Czarina* played last week. The modern costumes and mise en scène suffered by contrast with last week's splendor inevitably." Fonda was praised for being "well-cast" and Sullavan was "adorable." In recognition of the Players' efforts, the *Enterprise* wrote, "The Guild have been a hardworking, enthusiastic, likable crew. Falmouth is pleased with their presence and proud of their success…. Next year is pleasantly anticipated."[36]

In recalling her experience with the University Players, Sullavan said, "It was grand fun."[37] With memories of carefree days, it is little wonder that another noted, "When she speaks of those days, she glows with pleasure."[38]

3

"Local Girl Makes Good"

Margaret was a career girl, and nothing meant more to her than that.[1]
—*Joshua Logan*

At the end of summer, Sullavan received a wire from her father. The message was brief: "We expect you at once."[2] Cornelius enclosed money to cover the train fare.

She knew that her formal debut into Norfolk's society was dear to her parents' hearts. But it would be difficult to go back to the life that she detested. At some point, she must have decided to obey her parents as it was announced in the *Falmouth Enterprise* that "[p]retty Peggy Sullavan is to be a debutante in Norfolk, Virginia."

After the summer, however, Sullavan impulsively decided to join Fonda in seeking acting jobs in New York. She used Cornelius' money to pay for her tickets. Leatherbee was already working as an assistant stage manager for the Theatre Guild and got a bit part for Fonda in a Guild play, *The Game of Life and Death*. With Leatherbee's connections, Sullavan was offered an off-stage voice part in the Guild's production of *Karl and Anna*. She was also offered the lead in a touring production. Sullavan accepted the Guild's offer, reasoning that the association with the famed Theatre Guild would be good for her career. It looked as if both Sullavan and Fonda were off to a good start. Fonda took her to a theatrical agent he had heard of, in hopes that he would sign both of them. The agent, Leland Hayward, was not interested.

Before rehearsals began, Cornelius arrived in New York City to bring his wayward daughter back home. According to Sharpe's account, Cornelius spoke quietly, but firmly, about fulfilling her obligation according to family values. "We ask a year of your time to finish what we've started," he requested. "If you won't give us that … you're running out on an obligation."[3]

Knowing that he was right, Sullavan left with her father that night. She made her social debut in mid–November at the German Club Debutante Ball. As Sullavan reflected, "I had a dreadful year … living the sort of life they wanted me to live. I was utterly miserable."[4]

She couldn't have been too miserable, for Sullavan appeared with the Little Theater stock company in Norfolk. She had small roles in two productions, *Dear Brutus* (presented February 4–6) and *Lady Windermere's Fan* (May 13–15). Rose Johnson Willis, the company's director, recalled, "She was beautiful to look at and to listen to."[5] Sullavan also performed dramatic readings for the Women's Club of Queen Anne County on March 11. The *Virginian Pilot and the Norfolk Landmark* interestingly noted that she was "a student of dramatics at Harvard." As for Fonda, his association with the Theatre Guild was short-lived due to the Stock Market Crash in October 1929. A few acting jobs here and there did not last long and a depressed Fonda went back to Omaha.

By mid–July 1930, Sullavan was back with the University Players to resume her acting career—and her romance with Fonda.

The University Players Guild had been in operation since late June thanks to Leatherbee's grandfather, who helped fund the season. They used Sullavan in three supporting roles. Her only lead, in her fourth play, was given to her by default.

Sullavan first appeared in the obscure Czechoslovakian fantasy drama *The Makropolous Secret*. Houghton felt the play was too extreme for the summer theatergoers, but the *Falmouth Enterprise* called it as "outstanding." The critic noted that one of the minor roles was capably played by Sullavan. Two weeks later, she appeared opposite Fonda in minor juvenile roles in *The Firebrand*. The play was well received by the *Enterprise*, who declared, "Gorgeous settings and costumes of great charm ... give color to the Guild's play." Sullavan and Fonda's roles were so trivial that they did not rate any mention.

Two weeks later, Sullavan and Fonda appeared opposite each other in *The Mar-*

Margaret Sullavan

Disregard the Universal Studios logo in the lower left corner; this photograph was most likely taken in 1929 when Sullavan was in New York, hoping to conquer Broadway.

quise, one of Noël Coward's lesser-known plays. A romantic comedy set in an eighteenth century French chateau, it was one of the Players' finest productions. The *Enterprise* offered its commendation to "Charles Leatherbee, Henry Fonda and Margaret Sullavan [who] play a youthful triangle with ingenious appeal."

It is ironic that the casting of Leatherbee, Fonda and Sullavan in a romantic triangle on-stage was a situation that continued off-stage. Houghton noted, "Hank was much in love with Peggy, and Peggy thought she might be in love with Hank. But there was also Charlie and he, too, was devoted to her, which pleased and somewhat flattered her."[6] Fonda, however, was someone with whom she could have more fun than with anyone else, including Leatherbee. The problem was that Fonda and Sullavan were just not a good match. As Houghton reminisced, "They seemed to prove the truth of the adage: She couldn't stand to be with him, she couldn't stand to be without him." Leatherbee was not totally out of the picture. "Peggy knew he would be there in case of need. And the need would come whenever Hank fell into one of his dark, brooding moods—usually brought on by Peggy herself. It was not a bad arrangement, although a little rough on Charlie."[7]

The last play of the summer, J.M. Barrie's *A Kiss For Cinderella*, was a gentle fantasy that required perceptive handling. Fonda had already appeared in the production in Washington, D.C., and Omaha (where a 13-year-old actress named Dorothy McGuire appeared opposite him). Given his familiarity with the play, it was decided that Fonda would direct, design the sets and perform the leading male role. The leading lady, Susan Gill, had been abroad all summer and arrived ill-prepared. After two days of rehearsals, Fonda convinced her to withdraw. Sullavan was assigned the part and began rehearsals four days prior to opening night. Given the nature of their romantic relationship, things did not go smoothly. Fonda recalled, "Sullavan took directions well on stage, but off-stage she was a true Southern rebel. Peggy was Scarlett O'Hara before Margaret Mitchell even dreamed of her."[8]

None of this acrimony reflected in the performance. Sullavan mesmerized the audience with her simple, yet touching, portrayal. Logan told Hayward, "She, more than anyone else, put us all on the map. The audiences in Falmouth fell madly in love with her."[9]

The *Enterprise* critic enthused, "To little Margaret Sullavan … and to Henry Fonda go the honors this week for their performances."

The third summer season came to a close and everybody either returned to college or sought theatrical employment. Sullavan went straight to New York City to try her luck again. Sullavan accepted Brock Pemberton's offer to understudy Elizabeth Love in the southern tour of *Strictly Dishonorable* at a weekly salary of $75. The hit play had opened in September 1929 and was still playing on Broadway when a few touring productions were sent out on the road.

Strictly Dishonorable arrived in Norfolk on October 6 for a four-night run. Taking advantage of the hometown connection, it was announced, "Local Girl Makes Stage Debut Here" for the Wednesday matinee performance. A capacity audience was in attendance to see her. Also in the audience were Cornelius and Garland, who had only found out that morning from the newspaper. Given the risqué nature of the play (a womanizing singer falls in love with an old-fashioned Southern belle, who already has a fiancé), her parents squirmed in their seats. Sullavan recalled, "Remember in the second act when I disrobe on the stage? I wish you could have seen Mother's mortified expression—and was Daddy's face red!"[10] Sullavan made a hit with the Norfolk community. The *Virginian-Pilot and Chronicle* critic pronounced that she "justified fully the high hopes the home folks had of her" and performed like "a genuine artist." From this point on, her parents ceased trying to talk her out of an acting career.

As the tour progressed, newspaper accounts reported that Sullavan began playing the leading role for a week's run, while Love played a smaller part. The two actresses alternated the lead role until disaster struck. Love was stricken with appendicitis prior to Memphis and Sullavan took over the role opposite Cesar Romero. In Atlanta, the *Constitution* critic judged the play the "cleverest, wittiest, and most delicious thing of a half-dozen seasons…. [Sullavan] makes of Isabelle a character so lovable and delightful that no man or woman could fail to adore her. She plays an intensely hard role with perfect tact."

Sullavan continued playing the lead until Love recovered to re-assume the role in Indianapolis in late December.

While appearing in Philadelphia, Sullavan attracted the attentions of a scout. She was summoned to New York to meet producer Lee Shubert. There are varying accounts of how Sullavan came to star on Broadway. The most widely believed account first appeared in print in *Collier's* magazine in 1934 and has been reprinted in several books, including *Haywire*. In this version, Sullavan, supposedly ill with a bad cold, was ushered into Shubert's office, where he asked:

> "Who are you and what sorts of parts do you want, and all that sort of thing?" She told him. "You're hired," said the great Mr. Shubert, getting up and reaching for his derby. "What do you mean— hired? You haven't even heard me read a part." "You have a voice like Helen Morgan, a voice like Ethel Barrymore," said the great Mr. Shubert. "What I have is a bad case of laryngitis." "Laryngitis or no laryngitis," replied the great Mr. Shubert, "you have a voice like Ethel Barrymore and you're hired. Report on Wednesday to Elmer Harris."[11]

Great story, but it sounds like Hollywood fabrication. Given her ambition to act on Broadway, it is unlikely that she would be so blasé in the presence of someone who could propel her to stardom. Other stories place Sullavan in Princeton while she appeared in a different play with Shubert himself in the audience. That account seems the least likely as it is doubtful that a famous producer would be in attendance of a minor college play. Sullavan would offer her own explanation, which will be forthcoming shortly.

What is known is that Sullavan was offered an exclusive two-year contract with the Shubert Brothers. Afterwards, she returned to Philadelphia and soon withdrew from *Strictly Dishonorable* early in February 1931. Back in New York, Sullavan received an urgent message from Antoinette Perry, who had co-directed *Strictly Dishonorable* with Pemberton on Broadway. Perry's daughter Margaret was unable to fulfill her commitment in a Princeton University play. Little did Sullavan know at the time that this minor engagement would introduce her to two important individuals at a crucial point of her early career.

The first person was the student stage manager, a junior classman who became a lifelong friend. For him, Margaret Sullavan would embody the ultimate unrequited love of his life. His name: James Stewart.

Years later, Stewart recalled meeting Sullavan to biographer Michael Munn. "I thought she was a really nice girl, and we had a friendship that lasted till she…." According to Munn, Stewart paused mid-sentence as his eyes began to brim with tears. "Till she passed away." Despite his shyness, Stewart mustered up the courage to ask her to be his escort to a reception hosted by the Charter Club. Sullavan told Logan, "It was the longest, slowest, shyest but most sincere invitation she'd ever received from a man, and she fell for him too. There was love between them from the very start." Logan claimed, "When they first met, they did have an affair. And it was a passionate one. But their love affair was short-lived because a Broadway producer came to see the show at Princeton, and a few weeks later, Margaret was making her debut on Broadway."[12] However, there were many who doubted such an affair ever occurred. Myrna Dell, who dated Stewart in the mid–1940s, remarked, "Everyone in Hollywood knew the stories about Jimmy and Margaret Sullavan. I'm about as certain as a third party can be that they didn't go to bed together."[13] Regardless of the exact nature of their relationship, Sullavan enjoyed a special friendship with Stewart unlike any other relationships she had.

Now we can examine Sullavan's version of how she was seen by Elmer Harris, the other significant person, who was responsible for her Broadway debut. *Three Artists and a Lady* was an offering of Princeton's Theatre Intime, instead of a touring production as claimed by many (including Hayward, Stewart and Logan). The play was written by two Princeton undergraduates and was directed by senior Myron McCormick (who had spent the previous summer with the University Players). It concerned the satirical attempts of three young artists to mold a young, innocent maiden (Sullavan) into a great poetess. The play wasn't much, but the *Drama Magazine* praised its "amusing situations" and called the dialogue "sophisticated." The college newspaper noted that Sullavan "showed herself so absolutely natural and entertaining without the slightest exaggeration."[14]

Sitting in the audience was Harris, a prolific playwright who specialized in racy, cheap sex comedies. His most recent production, *Young Sinners* (1929), was a huge financial success. It has been reported in various accounts that Harris was sent to Princeton by the Shuberts to see if Sullavan might be appropriate for the lead in a play he's just written, *A Modern Virgin*. As Sullavan recalled, "We were having a lot of fun the closing night, practically kicking each other around the stage." During intermission, word was sent back that Harris was in the audience.

Suddenly feeling terrified, "we did our very best in the last act," she recalled.[15] A week later, Sullavan received a telegram from director Stanley Logan requesting a meeting at the Shuberts' office. In the margin, Sullavan wrote "Finally!."[16] As Sullavan recounted the story,

I was to have an interview with [Harris], which I realized might result in a part in the show.... Well, on the morning of the great day, when I woke up I couldn't utter a sound. My voice, without any warning whatsoever, had just disappeared. In desperation I decided to save whatever scrap of it I had left, by not talking until the appointment late that afternoon and chancing Mr. Harris' wrath. The hour arrived and I walked into his office, my hands shaking. Fortunately he did most of the taking, but my replies were so low they frightened me, yet, if I raised my voice, even faintly, I knew I would sound like a foghorn. Imagine, then, my surprise when at the end of the interview he said: "I'll give you the part. What impresses me most about you is your voice. It is exactly the type I had in mind for the heroine."

Sullavan walked out of Harris' office elated, but then remembered that it was not her normal voice Harris had admired. She decided that she would keep her husky voice from returning to its normal tones. She threw her coat open and exposed her ailing throat to the cold. She continued this practice, along with sitting in drafts and getting her feet wet. "It worked, though," she confided, "for to this day my voice haven't gone back to normal."[17]

There were those who disputed such stories. Rose Willis told a reporter in 1934, "All this talk from the critics about Margaret's charming voice being the result of laryngitis is so much foolishness. That girl always had a lovely voice—and it's just as natural as can be."[18] However, it turns out that there may be some truth to the stories. After Sullavan's death, her otologist, Dr. Julius Lempert, reported she had "deliberately developed for her work what I should call a cello voice, which was not her natural voice."[19]

Sullavan found it amusing that she debuted on Broadway in the role of a Southern girl. She recalled that E.E. Clive once told her, "My child, you'll never get anywhere with that Southern accent," and then her first line on Broadway was "What you all doing out theah?"[20] This was her big break. Sullavan recalled, "You can imagine how thrilled I was with the opportunity."[21] In her usual perfectionist manner, she learned her entire part before rehearsals began.

Prior to the start of rehearsals, Sullavan became very ill. "By morning," Sullavan recalled, "I reaped that it was something more than excitement that I had felt and continued to feel with increasing discomfort. Twelve hours later I was operated upon for appendicitis."[22] Deeply disappointed with this turn of events, she sent word to the Shuberts that she was recuperating and would be unable to appear in the play in time. To her deep relief, they wired back that they would wait for her.

It was also a smart move on their part. The producers must have known that, without Sullavan in the stellar role, there really wasn't much to the play, particularly its plot. It concerned a wealthy, rebellious young girl named Teddy (Sullavan), who desires a "liberal education" in matters of the opposite sex. She is surrounded by older men who are not above manipulating her into marrying a middle-aged "man about town," whom she dislikes. It all works out in the end, however, with Teddy being persuaded to marry her fiancé in order to escape her guardian aunt.

With a cast of seasoned actors such as Herbert Rawlinson, Nicholas Joy and Roger Pryor, the play began its three-week try-out tour on April 27 in Atlantic City, New Jersey. During the tour, it received decent reviews, but nothing to suggest anything out of the ordinary.

When *A Modern Virgin* premiered at Broadway's Booth Theatre on May 20, no one was prepared for the attention Sullavan received as she was hailed an overnight sensation.

Even though the slightly objectionable play was considered third-rate, Sullavan was an unqualified success—almost. The *Billboard* drama critic was disgusted: "It's one of those cheap and frowsy little pieces." As for Sullavan's performance, he dug further into his contempt: "She is too all-fired cute to be true, and, tho the audience seemed to like her, she left this reporter something more than cold."[23]

Fortunately, the general consensus among the other critics was highly favorable. *The New York Post* enthusiastically judged, "Miss Sullavan is in reality what the old phrase calls a 'find.' She has youth, beauty, charm, vivacity, and intelligence.... Last night the evening was hers, as many other evenings should be in the future."[24] Columnist Mark Harron wrote, "A Bright Star": "*A Modern Virgin* is distinguished by the electrifying performance of Margaret Sullavan (spelled with an 'a' or she'll knock your block off). The enthusiastic, bronze-haired actress has a deep, husky voice that reminds one now of Ethel Barrymore and then of Jeanne Eagels."[25] A reporter from Norfolk's *Tidewater Trail*,

Despite her overnight success in *A Modern Virgin* (1931), Sullavan was unable to land a successful play until she replaced another actress in *Dinner at Eight* in 1933.

making the trip to New York, found their hometown girl's performance "impressive" and noted that she had "scored an enviable triumph" in her Broadway debut.

Little Peggy Sullavan had become a star beyond anyone's wildest imagination.

4

The Volstead Ingénue
Steps Out

When I first went on the stage, I made up my mind that I would be myself at all times.[1]

Despite expectations that *A Modern Virgin* would last the summer, the play closed on July 5 after 53 performances. Once the novelty of an overnight star wore off, theatergoers were left with a bad play. Despite this, the producers made plans to reopen the play on August 3.

Despite the short run, Sullavan made a big impression in the theatrical world. She rated a mention in Gilbert Swain's nationally syndicated article "Volstead Ingénue is Standard Role." What exactly is a Volstead Ingénue? "The new type is, almost invariably, a sweet young thing from the South with a fresh, soft accent," Swain offered. "She fairly exudes naïve, inexperienced; she is innocent but in search of 'flaming youth.' She becomes just about the naughtiest gal to be found in the Broadway belt."[2] Other purveyors of the new type included Mary Howard, Muriel Kirkland and Dorothy Appleby. This characterization fitted her to a t and Sullavan was typecast during her early years on Broadway with little success.

Sullavan also acquired the services of the agent she and Fonda had visited back in 1929, Leland Hayward. He advised her to turn down offers of five-year film contracts from Paramount and Columbia Studios. She wasn't leaving Broadway any time soon.

In one article, "Margaret Sullavan Star in Spite of Family's 'No!,'" a brief rundown of her road to fame was given. The rest of the article provides a fascinating insight into her talent at this early juncture:

> Not every professional life snaps into it so quickly nor in such a brilliant manner. Miss Sullavan is unique in that she manages to bring her own girlish naturalness into prominence on the stage. She has an inborn method of imparting her feelings to her audiences so that they live the part through with her.[3]

With the prospect of having the summer off, Sullavan took the opportunity to rejoin University Players (Guild had been dropped from its name) after it had started its third season. When she resumed her turbulent relationship with Fonda, Leatherbee wised up to the fact that he would forever play second fiddle. Little did he or anyone else in the troupe know that the couple had applied for a marriage license with the New York State Department of Health back on June 2, but did not follow through with a ceremony. Sullavan kept this license among her personal possessions.

Sullavan's return brought a lot of excitement to the group. As Houghton remembered,

"Peggy was the first University Player to make it big and the company was very proud of her."[4] The publicity surrounding her return was substantial as a legitimate Broadway star was in their midst.

There was also the long-awaited reunion between Sullavan and Fonda. At the time, Fonda was sporting an odd-looking moustache. He was self-conscious about it and the brutally honest reception by Sullavan, so he hid among the rafters under the pretense of fixing a pulley. After Sullavan had crossed the stage, Fonda called down to her. Looking up, Sullavan remarked, "Fonda, shave off the damned fool moustache," and walked on.[5]

Sullavan arrived in time for *Mr. Pim Passes By*. However, she accidentally tumbled on the beach and sprained her back two days prior to opening night. Katherine Hastings replaced her. Sullavan recovered and played the role of Norma Bresant in *Coquette* the following week. *Coquette* was a huge Broadway and London success for its star, Helen Hayes, and its producer, Jed Harris. Given its distinctive pedigree, there was considerable surprise when the relatively inexperienced Logan was assigned as director. He later recalled that during rehearsals, the cast was "suspicious, then astonished at my newfound intensity. To my surprise, for the first time ever, they welcomed my help. And I thoroughly enjoyed my role as director." The part of a flirtatious Southern belle, who faces tragedy when her father kills her lover, was Sullavan's most ambitious part to date and gave her something substantial to work with. Also in the cast were Fonda, who played the lover, and Kent Smith as Dr. Bresant. The performances in the play exceeded expectations. According to Logan, "Sullavan was at her best" and Fonda "projected intensity and masculinity that galvanized their romance."[6] The *Falmouth Enterprise* enthusiastically endorsed the production:

> No wonder the weather has been humid and wet all week; the University Players and Director Joshua Logan are to blame for the production of *Coquette* which reduced so many of the audience to tears of sympathy for charming Peggy Sullavan's dramatic sufferings…. Coquette [is] played with a marvelous range of emotion and charm by Miss Sullavan.

Sullavan was set for the leading role in the following week's production *Her Cardboard Lover*; however, she received word from New York that *A Modern Virgin* was being sent on a tour and she needed to report back immediately. (Katherine Hastings replaced her in *Her Cardboard Lover*.) A new actress, Merna Pace, was brought into the company to take over Sullavan's spot for the remainder of the summer. She also took over Sullavan's spot in Fonda's disillusioned heart.

With most of its Broadway cast intact, *A Modern Virgin* began its tour on August 3 at the Brighton Beach in New York before heading out to Chicago. Chicago critics were not impressed, but Sullavan received favorable notice. "A promising young actress named Margaret Sullavan plays this rampant girl with high animation and decided charm. She is the most striking reason for attendance," according to the *Chicago Tribune*.

After five weeks of mediocre business, the play descended upon Detroit for a four-week engagement. Critical reactions were not that much different. According to *The Detroit News*, "The leading roles are so nicely performed that the beholder is almost convinced—occasionally—that he is watching a good play." Once again, Sullavan won effusive notices:

> Miss Sullavan is a newcomer and quite a lot might be written about her. In the first place, in the matter of her face, she looks like a youthful edition of Ethel Barrymore. There is really a striking resemblance. Whether a throaty, English-hora sort of voice is just another coincidence, one couldn't say, but that's the kind of voice she displays…. She is a wholesome, cheery young person, utterly at ease in her stage behavior and with an undoubted charm that is basic and personal…. She is a very promising young woman.

Lackluster business caused the producers to shut the play down after only one week in Detroit and cancel the rest of the tour. Sullavan returned to New York and was loaned out to appear in what would be the first of several flops in a row, *If Love Were All*. The comedy, by Cutler Hatch, originally debuted as *The Other Fellow* during its summer stock engagement at Mt. Kisco in mid–July. It was presented at the Booth Theatre on November 13, 1931, and closed after 11 performances. The stars were Walter Kingsford and Aline MacMahon as an older married couple whose daughter Janet (Sullavan) discovers that her mother is having an affair. With the aid of the other man's son, Janet attempts to rectify the situation before the unsuspecting spouses find out. The "surprise" ending reveals that, not only did all of the adults know, but they were okay with the arrangement.

Critical reviews were mixed. The *Billboard* critic found it to be "an amusing, charming and—at least to one spectator—a thoroly delightful play." But the same critic had a few sharp words for Sullavan: "Margaret Sullavan returned to New York with a bit more weight and a bit more acting ability than when she made her debut in *A Modern Virgin* last spring. But she still has her annoying Southern accent, and she still spends almost all of her time being cute—far too cute for the taste of this department." The magazine *The Commonweal* lambasted the play for being "as strange a concoction of dramatic mistakes as we have seen for a long time. *If Love Were All* … is styled on the program as a 'gentle comedy.' It is certainly gentle enough—in the wrong way. But whatever else it may be, it is certainly not comedy." As for the actors: "It is rather sad that such capable actors as Walter Kingsford, Aline MacMahon, and Hugh Buckler, not to mention that delightful young person, Margaret Sullavan, should have to sustain the burden of so much concentrated rubbish. Through sheer personal excellence, they almost make you believe for brief moments in the author's absurd creations." *Variety* observed, "Miss Sullavan needs some toning down, being a bit flouncy and jumpy. That showed when she played in *Modern Virgin*, since which time she has improved." The critic predicted that Sullavan "will probably reach Hollywood sooner or later. She is under contract to Shuberts and reputedly was unable to take advantage of film offers because of that fact."

With the closing of the play, the Shuberts once again had nothing for Sullavan. Winter season on Broadway was typically slow after the onslaught of new plays in the fall and Sullavan would not have anything until early spring. Once again, she contacted the University Players, now based in Baltimore for its first winter season. With permission from the Shuberts, Sullavan let the Players management know that she was available. As usual, this announcement induced a great deal of drama among the group members, but not for the reasons one would have expected.

Since the group's inception, it had been Leatherbee and Windust's dream that the University Players would develop into a year-round venue. Back in mid–August, the directors (Leatherbee, Windust, and Logan) were contacted in Falmouth by the manager of the Maryland Theater in Baltimore. He offered the troupe the opportunity to rent the Maryland for a season of repertory theater. For Leatherbee and Logan, this was their moment to shine; Windust, on the other hand, was not sure that the troupe was ready for such a big challenge. The decision was made in favor of Baltimore and a jubilant troupe spent two months in preparation for their Baltimore debut. The concept of Repertory Theatre (to present a different play each night of the week) was an ambitious undertaking, but they enthusiastically tackled all of the details. Plays and casts were carefully chosen and rehearsed.

When the Players arrived in Baltimore in late October, they were prepared to take the city by storm. Houghton gave an example of how this looked at the time: *Hell Bent for Heaven* was presented on Tuesday evening; *Mr. Pim Passes By* on Thursday and Saturday nights; the week's opening play, *The Silent House*, was presented on Monday, Wednesday and Friday nights as well as the two weekend matinees. An ambitious undertaking to be sure and one that failed during the initial weeks of the season. Most theatergoers were confused that a different play was presented every night. As a result, the paying customers stayed away in droves despite the good reviews. Under great pressure, the Players' Directors reluctantly abandoned the Repertory Theatre concept and began to operate as a winter stock company with the presentation of *The Constant Nymph* scheduled for mid–November.

The main issue regarding Sullavan's return was that many felt that the company had been operating as a close-knit group for a few months and Sullavan's re-entry would upset the balance. Roles that had been selected for the actresses would have to be reassigned to accommodate Sullavan's return and many believed that it would not be fair. Even Fonda was opposed to Sullavan's return, particularly since he had become well-acquainted with Merna Pace since the summer. Pace, who was hired to handle the "Sullavan-type" parts, stood to lose the most, and sympathy for her ran high. Finally, there was the feeling that Sullavan would expect star treatment, which went against the dictate that no one individual's contribution would outweigh that of the group's.

The Maryland Theater managers, however, were much more financially motivated. They reasoned that Sullavan's presence would bring a touch of "Broadway Glamour" to Baltimore and boost the sluggish box office. In the end, the Players' Directors discarded their democratic ideals for practicality. After all, they knew that, unless they started to earn a profit, the University Players would not be operating in Baltimore much longer. After much debate, a compromise was reached. Sullavan would be allowed to rejoin the group with the understanding that she would not receive any special treatment. She would be given the leading role in *The Constant Nymph*, but after that, she would have to share the starring roles with Pace for the season. The company's third ingénue, Cynthia Rogers, was dismissed as there was no need for four leading ladies. The *Constant Nymph* opening was delayed a week to give Sullavan sufficient time to arrive in Baltimore for rehearsals. *The Silent House* was presented in its place.

Sullavan's return would provide financial impetus to the struggling enterprise, thus ensuring the future viability of an organization in the short term. For Fonda, her arrival would culminate in the bleakest period of his personal and professional life.

5

The Winter of Their Discontent

It was a strange winter ... isolated from the world.[1]*—Norris Houghton*

Fonda still had strong feelings for Sullavan. Of her arrival, he remembered: "The expression they used in those days was 'She looked like a million,' and she sure did. When she smiled at me, I thought, 'I ain't ever gonna let this girl get away from me again!'"[2] And with that, the embattled lovers resumed their romance.

With Sullavan and Fonda reprising their original roles, *The Constant Nymph* was presented with much hope. Reviews were respectful but not what the Directors hoped. The *Baltimore News* observed, "The play is not a particularly brilliant one, but it serves to pass an interesting evening." Sullavan was praised for being "especially satisfying as Teresa, and her coming should be a big help to the University Theatre." Opening night business was good, but the rest of the week slowed. The Directors took drastic measures and reduced ticket prices.

Desperate to keep from folding, the company decided to present *Death Takes a Holiday*. The play had never been performed in Baltimore. The story of Death assuming a mortal form for three days had a strong romantic appeal and promised to bring paying customers back. During the week prior to opening night, there was a general sentiment among the company that Kent Smith and Sullavan, playing the leads, bore the primary responsibility for saving the season. A feeling of anxiety pervaded during the final rehearsals.

The reviews dispelled all fears. According to the *Baltimore News*, *Death Takes a Holiday* "should do much to establish the University group here as an acting company. The players move with greater authority than at any times since their arrival and their manner is more professional." Sullavan was also embraced: "Margaret Sullavan, with her charm and throaty voice, proves in the role of Grazia that she is an actress who should climb rapidly." Smith was commended for his "understanding portrayal of Death, very satisfactory." The *Sun* was equally jubilant: "Last night's performance, in point of acting, direction and staging, may rank with the best repertory production ever to appear in this city.... Margaret Sullavan, as Grazia, confirmed the extremely favorable impression she made last week.... She has intelligence and charm and already has an enthusiastic following among Baltimore theatergoers." The play was the critical and financial success needed to ensure their survival in Baltimore.

The following week, Donald Kirkley of the *Sun* reflected, "If the University Players continue on the same high plane reached with last week's production of *Death Takes a Holiday*, their chances of attaining their objective in the city will be very good indeed. For the first time since their arrival they found a happy combination of play, cast and production."[3]

The financial success of *Death Takes a Holiday* did much to energize the University

27

Players, especially since their future had begun to look as bleak as the winter sky over the city. Members of the troupe were homesick for the carefree summer days back in Falmouth. As Houghton observed, "The shadow of America's depression was deepening, but being already as depressed—economically—as we could be, we avoided reading the newspapers and functioned oblivious to the forces around us.... Although close to penniless, we were cheerful and full of hope."[4]

The Players next presented a farce, *It's a Wise Child*. The comedy highlighted the company's versatility and the critics were impressed. The *News* endorsed the offering: "[I]t's a pleasure to record that this company of young 'uns, like good wine, is improving with the passage of time, and it now looks as if its ambition is to be realized—to winter in Baltimore and summer in Cape Cod." Sullavan was deemed "a simon-pure delight as Joyce. 'Twas a ten-strike when she returned to the University fold." Unfortunately, business was not as strong as Christmas was about ten days away; this period is usually regarded as a slow time for theatrical productions. With that in mind, the Players decided to put on an old standby, *The Ghost Train*. Sullavan took that week off and Pace assumed the feminine lead opposite Fonda.

With their recent successes, Smith, Fonda and Sullavan "became Baltimore stars. Crowds waited in the alleyways for autographs, newspapers carried features about their romantic lives."[5] As a result, Sullavan assumed more leads over the next few months. This was good for business but bad for Merna Pace.

Fonda and Sullavan were again embroiled in their usual merry-go-round of intense fighting and reunions. With his insecurities momentarily in check, Fonda was more forceful and combative. He was hoping his assertiveness would finally tame Sullavan's volatile temper. It only fueled her angry outbursts. Fonda's description of her as "cream and sugar on a dish of hot ashes" was spot on as their fighting continued to be as open as their romance. McKinney quoted one unidentified witness: "They fought so terribly, that you had to get out of the room."[6] Despite this, however, Fonda was desperate and continued his seemingly futile quest to marry Sullavan. Logan failed to understand why Fonda acted this way: "She was the most difficult woman I've ever met in my life. She was so attractive, and so beautiful, and she had so many little Southern tricks ... to win you, but she was willful as all get out."[7]

On December 23, the couple applied for their second marriage license. The next day, a *Post* reporter discovered this and investigated further. The reporter came to the Kernan Hotel's dining room during breakfast and asked Sullavan and Fonda for more details. "What! Marry Fonda? Look at him! Who'd ever want to marry him?" Sullavan responded.[8] With that, she left the dining room with Fonda close behind. Not put off so easily, the reporter then spoke to Windust. Oblivious, Windust responded he knew nothing. He did concede that it would not surprise him if they had applied for one in New York. He even joked that the couple was collecting marriage licenses.

When Windust's comments reached Sullavan, she was offended. At that moment, the mercurial Sullavan decided she would marry Fonda once and for all. On Christmas morning, word was passed around for the company to assemble in the dining room at noon. The dining room was soon packed, but there was a delay to the wedding ceremony as there was a newspaper photographer in the lobby and Sullavan refused to leave her room until he left. The ceremony began at 12:15. Kent Smith served as best man and Julia Dorr was the maid of honor. Dr. Horace W.B. Donegan of Christ's Episcopal Church in Baltimore presided over the ceremony.

During the ceremony, Windust played the love song from *The Constant Nymph*. Houghton was struck by the irony of the words: "Ah, say not so! Another love will cheer thee," which was "peculiarly inappropriate and frighteningly prophetic."[9] Logan remembered, at that moment, "We all choked up. We had to. We were their family."[10]

That afternoon, Fonda appeared as a bridegroom in the matinee performance. News of the impromptu wedding had spread throughout the theater during the performance. When Fonda accidentally scattered rice when he pulled a handkerchief from his pocket (part of his character's stage business), the audience applauded wildly. "We thought we'd kept it all a secret," Fonda recalled. "Well, shit! It was on the news before the audience came in for the matinee. They went crazy because they knew about it and found it a lot of fun."[11]

News of the marriage reached New York City in many gossip columns, including this unintentionally funny report by Walter Winchell: "Margaret Sullavan (a's not i's Mr. Printer), whose performance here left the reviewers in a pashy mood, was wedded on Xmas day to Henry *Fonder* [author's emphasis] of the University Players, Baltimore."[12]

Of the next production, *The Royal Family*, the *Sun* observed, "That the University Players got through it as well as they did last night is a tribute to their ability, but it must be admitted that nearly everyone suffered from first night jitters." Sullavan was among those judged "competent." Business continued its post-holiday slump.

The Directors decided to improve things by offering Philip Barry's sophisticated comedy *Holiday*. The story was not particularly challenging but, if done well, could be a sparkling hit. To further enhance the odds, the newlyweds were cast in the leading roles. They were partially successful. The *Post* critic offered faint praise: "It seemed again to be the sort of show an audience wants.... Margaret Sullavan and her becoming garments are bestowed generously on the role of Linda Seton. Her acting gives the piece credibility." Fonda did not fare as well: "Henry Fonda is at ease, or perhaps too much so."

By the new year, the Players were in a rut again as they faced stiff competition from other touring productions in the city. Most troubling was the Group Theatre, which was presenting *The House of Connelly*. The Group Theatre was an adversary unlike anything they had known in Falmouth. It was time to present their trump card: Margaret Sullavan in *Coquette*.

With *Coquette*, Sullavan conquered Baltimore and brought in the needed financial revenues. The press was enthralled. The *Sun* reported, "It is very probable that both in selection and treatment, this is the high water mark of the University Players' Baltimore season to date." Sullavan won the lion's share of the accolades. The *Sun* wrote, "Miss Sullavan struck some new, deep chords of emotion and shone with a new luster." Not to be outdone, the *News* critic proclaimed,

> I have written before that the organization at the Maryland Theatre has a very promising young actress in Margaret Sullavan. After seeing her portray Norma Bresant, I arise again to make the same remark, but this time louder and more positively. This charming slip of a girl has the heart and the brain of a true actress and the ripening hand of experience should make of her a star one of these days.

Houghton credited Sullavan's success with revitalizing the economic future of the University Players in Baltimore.

The following week, the Directors struck gold again with *Lysistrata*, in which neither Sullavan nor Fonda were involved. The play was so successful, it was held over for an additional week. During the second week, the newlyweds left for their honeymoon trip to Norfolk. Fonda acquired $75 and bought a 1921 Stutz Bearcat for the trip. Unfortunately, the car broke down outside of Washington, D.C., and the couple took a bus back to Baltimore in time to begin rehearsals for the next play, *Mary Rose*.

Mary Rose was a gentle fantasy whose delicate theme required expert guidance. Logan was selected as the director. For unknown reasons, Sullavan became difficult due to her displeasure over the sets during dress rehearsals. Logan recalled that Leatherbee and Fonda warned him about her temperament. Without realizing it, Logan found himself saying, "If you don't like the set, why don't you go home? Just pack your bags and leave Baltimore. We can't change the set, but we can change you. Merna can learn your part overnight." To his surprise, "Just as abruptly as the tantrum began, it ended. I will never know why. She turned away and continued the scene as if there had never been a break."

According to Logan, *Mary Rose* was "a real achievement. I have seldom seen anything better. Peggy and Hank were unsurpassable and again there were standees the entire week. Baltimore loved us more than ever."[13] The critics were equally impressed. The *Sun* observed, "[T]he players should be commended for their choice of *Mary Rose* as well as for their generally understanding and excellent interpretation." The Players' performance was deemed "a distinguished one, and certainly the acting of Margaret Sullavan in the title role deserves that very word." The *Post* stated that, with Sullavan and Fonda's acting, "the roles scarcely could be handled better."

The following week's play, *The Second Man*, met with favorable reaction. The *Sun* noted, "This comedy was a happy choice.... [T]he manner of telling, subtle and urbane, appeals to the few. As presented at the Maryland Theater by Margaret Sullavan, Kent Smith, Henry Fonda and Elizabeth Fenner, under the direction of Joshua Logan, *The Second Man* offers a rich, beguiling and profitable evening to all." Fonda received the best notices of the night: "Mr. Fonda, submerging his personality completely in that of Austin, gave his finest portrayal to date," while "Miss Sullavan, Miss Fenner and Mr. Smith did ample justice to the other three principal roles."

Two weeks later, Sullavan and Fonda appeared in Rachel Crothers' society comedy *Let Us Be Gay*. As performed, the play proved to have a profitable run. The *Sun* observed,

> Miss Crothers' gift for making her characters distinctive and interesting people, and her flair for producing conversation which not only advances the story, but also is charming in itself are well illustrated in this play.... Margaret Sullavan was charming and expert, as usual ... if one can accept the fact she does not seem quite mature enough for this role. About the same comment will do, too, for Henry Fonda.

The following week brought Philip Barry's *Paris Bound*, a comedy of a married couple who believe in freedom to pursue other romances. Sullavan was cast opposite Peter Wayne instead of Fonda. The *Sun* reviewer wrote that the Players "seems to gain from week to week in smoothness and sureness." Sullavan was judged as "accomplished in the part of Mary and is equal to the scenes that call for the restrained emotion."

Before the next production, *The Trial of Mary Dugan*, began rehearsal, Sullavan received word from New York that she was needed for a new play. With this, she assumed a non-speaking walk-on part so she could focus on learning her lines for the new play. Barbara O'Neil assumed the role of Mary. A young actress named Mildred Natwick, whom Fonda and Smith had worked with in children's theater, made her first appearance with the Players. In the opinions of the *News*, "Bayard Veiller's realistic melodrama, *The Trial of Mary Dugan* ... thrills in the hands of the University Players at the Maryland."

With the final performance on March 12, Sullavan left the University Players for good. In 1950, there was a reunion of its members. Of Sullavan, Houghton wrote, "The years had softened the edge of her unruly gamine girlishness, and given her poise and authority, but her voice retained its provocative huskiness and she was as alluring when she tossed her head as she had been at 19."[14]

Fonda followed Sullavan to New York. Logan recollected, "With a declaration of discontent at the way the University Players was being run, he left the company to find his way alone. He was a tremendous loss. He was the heart of the company."[15] When the next play, *The Ghost Train*, finished its run, the University Players' stay in Baltimore ended. Critically, the season was a success as the critics were supportive. However, the company came close to bankruptcy due to the lack of steady attendance. The winter season proved to be the low point of the Depression, which hit the Baltimore residents hard. The Players went to New Jersey that spring and back to Falmouth for the summer. They directed an original play called *Carry Nation*, which was eventually performed on Broadway for a disappointing run of 30 performances. By late November 1932, the University Players finally fell victim to the harsh conditions of the Depression and folded. Before his death, Leatherbee was determined to resurrect the company once more, but his dream was never realized. Despite this failure, Houghton recalled, "We had the memory of a dream that was not yet really proved vain. It had been a glorious prelude to a life in the theater."[16]

Meanwhile, the newlyweds shared a Greenwich Village flat. Sullavan was brought in as a replacement for Joyce Arling in *Happy Landing* (originally called *Zoom* in Philadelphia), but Fonda struggled to find anything. There were moments when things were good. In a 1934 magazine article, an unidentified person recalled, "I used to see them walking around New York, hatless, hand in hand, courting like two kids in their teens, fresh and unspoiled."[17] These moments, however, were few and far in between. Later, many stories painted a vague picture of the events that transpired during their marriage. According to *Photoplay*, while Sullavan was climbing the ladder of success, Fonda met with continued failure in landing any acting jobs. As this continued, the two drifted apart.

The truth was much more complicated. According to Fonda, "It got to the point where we didn't live on love. We were at each other constantly, screaming, arguing, fighting." Friends were sympathetic to Fonda. In Kent Smith's opinion, "She was too fiery to handle," but Fonda was not going to back down in an argument either. Still, he was no match for her cruelty. "Time after time that slender girl's words stung me like a wasp," Fonda remembered.[18] A rational person would have walked away, but not Fonda, who alternately worshipped and loathed her. It was a hopeless situation. At one point, Fonda explained his point of view on success in acting, "Luck has a lot to do with it." Her response illustrated the key difference in their personal outlooks: "Don't give me that—we make our own luck."[19]

According to Quirk, the other source of friction between the two was their love life. It seemed that Fonda was not experienced enough to know how to satisfy Sullavan sexually and she grew frustrated. She enjoyed sex and was not going to waste any more of her time with Fonda. The fighting between the two continued to escalate until it all came to a head one night. "It's all a blur now," Fonda later recalled. "I don't remember if I stamped out in a rage or whether Sullavan threw me out."[20] After three months, their stormy marriage was over.

6

In Search of a Good Play

*Note to the folks in Norfolk, Va.—Your hometown girl, Margaret Sullavan,
is on her way to be quite an actress hereabouts. Just wait until she gets a
good part![1]—Gilbert Swain*

With Fonda gone, Sullavan wasted no time pursuing and seducing a variety of men, before setting her sights on Jed Harris, then one of the most successful producers on Broadway.

Harris reached prominence when, at 28, he produced four consecutive Broadway hits in 18 months: *Broadway*, *Coquette*, *The Royal Family* and *The Front Page*. With this success, he was featured on the cover of *Time* magazine, an accomplishment for a non-political figure. In later years, screenwriter Frederic Raphael wrote, "Jed Harris invented Broadway.... He also brought to it an extraordinary sense of theater. He had a touch of genius."[2]

At the same time, Harris was greatly despised by many of his peers. A self-absorbed, brooding egomaniac, he enjoyed manipulating people as puppets. *Front Page* writer George S. Kaufman once expressed his fervent wish that, when he died, his body would be cremated so his ashes would be thrown in Harris' face.

A controversial, exciting figure like Harris was very attractive to Sullavan, who would benefit from their romantic relationship. Sullavan finally met a man who satisfied her sexual desires and provided excitement in her life. Harris, however, was a chronic womanizer who lived with actress Ruth Gordon during his affair with Sullavan. The birth of Gordon's son Jones in 1929 brought about Harris' divorce from his first wife. When Gordon learned of the Harris-Sullavan liaison, she left Harris for good.

Sullavan was not bothered by Harris' infidelity as she continued playing the field. She arranged for trysts with other men on different nights. Sullavan's promiscuity and relationship with Harris did not endear her to those in the theater as it was generally accepted she was using him to get ahead in her career. Kent Smith had a charitable view as he later felt her open sex life would have been no big deal in the free-wheeling '60s. In the early 1930s, such conduct was only scandalous for a woman.

Meanwhile, *Happy Landing*, as written by John B. Hymer and William E. Barry, was in trouble. After its Philadelphia opening, *Variety* noted, "The show … has plenty of material that should make for popular appeal. It needs sharpening and tightening and some rewriting." The producers failed to heed this advice. After six weeks of poor grosses and reviews during its try-out tour, the Shuberts casted Sullavan in the lead in hopes of remedying a bad situation.

Happy Landing opened at the Chanin's Forty-Sixth Street Theatre on March 26 to terrible reviews. Sullavan played Phyllis, telephone operator in a small Maine town and sweetheart of a garage mechanic, Blin (Russell Hardie). A novice flier, Blin decides to make a solo, non-stop flight from there to Japan. After a successful flight, he returns to New York a hero. However, he has a hard time adjusting to his sudden fame and falls prey to unscrupulous promoters. Blim finally wises up, denounces his newfound fame and rejoins Phyllis back home.

While the *World-Telegram* reviewer complained that the comedy "lumbers naively along," he also wrote that it was "helped out immeasurably by an excellent cast. Mr. Hardie and Miss Sullavan are, in spite of it all, altogether effective." The other critics were hostile. The *Evening Post* griped, "An unusually inept and clumsy drama ... went its tasteless way.... [Sullavan] is badly miscast as the little girl from Maine. Not only does her voice sound from time to time like a poor imitation of Ethel Barrymore, but she cavorts around the stage in a most disconcerting way." Also in a foul mood was the *Times*: "Everything about *Happy Landing* ... stamps it unmistakably as chow." The *Times* called the writing, acting and direction "unpardonably cheap." There was praise for Sullavan, who "has such a winning personal manner and plays so earnestly that you hope someday she receives the sort of understanding direction she deserves. She has fine possibilities as an actress." With mostly negative reviews, the play folded after only 25 performances on April 16.

With her second flop and no play in the near future, Sullavan's situation was not lost on the casual observer. An article speculated, "Six actresses in search of an author—an author who can fashion worthwhile plays for their talents—have been fairly consistently the fate of a half dozen of Broadway's outstanding feminine players."[3] Among the other actresses mentioned were Alice Brady and Ethel Barrymore.

By this time, Fonda was living in a desolate hotel room located below 42nd Street living a miserable existence. Fonda recounted when he became aware of Sullavan's affair. He was sitting in an agent's office when he overheard gossip. He made a hasty exit.

> I was drawn back to that Greenwich Village area. I'd wait until night and then I'd go by the main house.... I'd stare up at our apartment with the lighted windows on the second floor. I knew Jed Harris was inside with her and I'd wait for him to leave. But instead the lights would go out.... I'd go back to that flea-bitten hotel room and I'd sit in the dark. I couldn't believe my wife and that son of a bitch were in bed together.... That just destroyed me, completely destroyed me. Never in my life have I felt so betrayed, so rejected, so alone.[4]

Devin McKinney analyzed this situation: "Sullavan cursed and gifted Fonda with decades of experience in a few short years. Without her, a man like him might never have known what it meant, in the rawest terms of his own soul, to crash, or to fly."[5]

The other man lamenting Sullavan's absence in his life was graduating from Princeton. One year after their meeting, James Stewart still harbored an intense infatuation for Sullavan. As he once stated, "She makes life extremely vivid for anyone around her.... It's because she's more alive than anyone else."[6] Logan used Stewart's torment to his advantage. Stewart initially declined Logan's offer to join the University Players, declaring he wasn't an actor. "Then I dropped my bombshell," recalled Logan. "I said, 'Margaret Sullavan is one of our company.' That did it."[7] Instead of graduate school, Stewart headed for Falmouth to join the legendary ranks of the University Players and begin an impressive career as an actor. What he did not realize was that Logan had lied. Sullavan was busy elsewhere.

Information on Sullavan's 1932 summer stock appearances may be incomplete as this period has not been covered in other publications. Five plays have been identified; most likely, she performed in more.

Prior to the summer season, Sullavan was announced for two Broadway productions: a last-minute substitute for *Heigh-Ho, Everybody* and the leading role in *The Boy Friend*.

When these plays opened on Broadway in late May and early June respectively, Sullavan's name was not in the cast listings.

During the week of July 4, Sullavan appeared with Geoffrey Kerr in *There's Always Juliet* in Nyack, New York. The *Rockland County Evening Journal* raved that she "charmed everyone in the theater…. She has the spark of true genius that will make her one of the greats some day. Check up in four or five years to see if we're not right." Next, Sullavan reprised her role opposite Tullio Carminati in *Strictly Dishonorable* at the Croton River Playhouse in Harmon-on-Hudson, New York, from July 18 to 23. The *Peekskill Evening Star* noted, "Margaret Sullavan … carried off honors."

For the next three plays, Sullavan joined a troupe that performed in Poughkeepsie one week and repeated the play in Mt. Kisco the following week. On July 25, she appeared in *Paris Bound*. The *Poughkeepsie Daily Eagle* wrote, "[She] is all the things critics say she is. [Her performance] electrified the house in the most satisfying production of the summer."

She next appeared in the premiere performance of a new play, *Men Must Fight*, during the week of August 8. Included in the cast were Alma Kruger, Day Tuttle (who founded the Westchester Playhouse with Richard Skinner) and Kent Smith. The anti-war drama told the tale of a pacifist mother who tries to dissuade her son from enlisting when war is declared in 1940. *The Daily Eagle* called it "the only play of any consequence brought out this season by the summer theaters" and praised it for its "subtlety, humor and great understanding." As for the "star-studded cast [which] provides enough excitement," Sullavan was singled out as she "sweeps the audience with the pathos of the young girl."

The summer stock performance of *Men Must Fight* showed enough promise that it was presented on Broadway in mid–October, 1932. Among the actors were Janet Beecher, Douglass Montgomery and Kent Smith (in his Broadway debut). *Men Must Fight* folded after 35 performances, but reached the screen as an MGM film in early February 1933.

Sullavan completed her commitment to this stock company when she performed in *There's Always Juliet* opposite Geoffrey Kerr beginning August 22. The *Peekskill Evening Star* observed, "Miss Sullavan makes the most of a role that gives her a nice opportunity to display her ability." The critic also noted that Sullavan had "become one of the most popular players of the summer theaters in this season."

Meanwhile, her family was affected by the Depression. Her brother Sonny recalled that, by the time he was ready to attend college, the family could not afford it. Sullavan had saved enough money to finance her brother's education at the University of Virginia. "She made it possible for me to go," he gratefully acknowledged.[8]

Soon after the summer stock season, Sullavan was offered parts in two promising Broadway productions. The first was the role of Paula Jordan in *Dinner at Eight*. Written by George S. Kaufman and Edna Ferber, the play boasted a cast of prominent players such as Conway Tearle, Constance Collier and Cesar Romero. At last, Sullavan had a play worthy of her talents. However, she was tired of playing society girls in comedies, so she instead accepted the gangster's moll part in *Chrysalis*. Big mistake. *Dinner at Eight* was a smash hit and became a glittering film classic, required viewing for anyone wishing to see one of Hollywood's finest examples of filmmaking.

Chrysalis showed great promise during its summer stock premiere in Westport, Connecticut, with its positive reviews and brisk business. In its Broadway cast were prominent actors Osgood Perkins (father of Anthony Perkins), Elisha Cook Jr. and Humphrey Bogart. As fate would have it, the producers re-assigned Sullavan to the society girl part prior to rehearsals. The play was sent to Newark, New Jersey, for one week of try-outs on November

7 before its opening at the Martin Beck Theatre on November 15. This was a bad sign as most plays enjoyed three or four weeks of try-outs in major cities. After opening night on Broadway, the play was regarded as a major disappointment.

Written by Rose Albert Porter, the overwrought drama dealt with Lyda (Sullavan), a strong-willed socialite who, out of boredom, becomes involved with Don (Bogart), an undergraduate expelled from Princeton. He is an unsavory type who seduces Lyda after getting her drunk. And that's just the beginning of her troubles. Lyda and Don are implicated in a robbery committed by a gangster and his moll. There's a whole lot of melodramatic contrivances before the play ends with the deaths of the criminals and a chastened Lyda now seeing life in a different light.

Chrysalis was widely panned. The *Daily Mirror* observed that the play "obviously suffered from sour production and awkward direction [and] is best listed as a show that might have been better." There was some praise: "Miss Sullavan again offers a delightful account of herself." Other critics did not disguise their contempt. The *Evening Post* sniped, "Not only is its writing woefully exaggerated, but it is the sort of pretentious melodrama which makes you feel sorry for everyone concerned." The critic was sympathetic to the performers: "It makes you feel sorry for Margaret Sullavan, who is forced to waste her beauty and her charm, not to mention her mannerisms upon a part which is so wildly overwritten and incredible that ten Bernhardts at their best could not make it believable." A rare complaint regarding Sullavan's performance came from the *Herald-Tribune*: "Miss Sullavan plays the azure nincompoop eagerly in the early Ethel Barrymore manner, desperate, frenetic and confused." This fiasco lasted 23 performances.

Chrysalis was adapted for the screen in 1934 by Sidney Buchman and esteemed stage and film character actor Thomas Mitchell by Paramount. Retitled *All of Me*, it featured some excellent actors like Fredric March (as an ethical Princeton professor rather than the expelled undergraduate), Miriam Hopkins, George Raft and Helen Mack. The film also flopped.

Thirty years later, Bogart called Sullavan "an uninhibited actress. She could play a scene any place, standing on her head or behind a couch. Most actresses aren't that relaxed."[9] There have been unsubstantiated rumors over the years that Sullavan had an affair with the married Bogart during the play's run. This is entirely possible since Bogart was a womanizer who enjoyed strong, feisty women.

By this time, Fonda had three roommates, Joshua Logan, Myron McCormick—and James Stewart. It was an interesting twist of fate that brought Sullavan's bitter ex-husband and her unabashed admirer together under the same roof. Fonda recalled,

> I just liked him. There was nothing not to like about him. He had this wonderful but quiet sense of humor that appealed to me…. You can never quite put your finger on what makes two people click like that. But we clicked—and kept on clicking all these years…. He's just there for me when I need him. What more can you want from a friend?[10]

Still, it was not an easy situation as Fonda complained about his ex-wife all the time. Valuing his friendship, Stewart kept his thoughts to himself.

Despite their financial difficulties, the roommates rented a speakeasy on West 40th Street every Thursday night. They invited their friends to join a group they dubbed the Thursday Night Beer Club. For two dollars, one could buy beer and a steak. One of the regulars was a struggling musician and actor, Burgess Meredith, who reminisced, "We had some great nights. It kind of became the place to be. There were top musicians there like Benny Goodman and actresses like Ruth Gordon, Helen Hayes and Margaret Sullavan."

With Sullavan back in their lives, this must have made for some interesting dynamics within their social circles. "Sullavan loved Jim and Jim loved Sullavan," Meredith recalled. "It should have been as simple as that. But they never did anything about it. Part of the reason, I would say, was because Jim didn't want to upset Fonda. But it was obvious to everyone that Sullavan thought the world of Jim." Meredith continued:

> With Jim, she was simply affectionate without being predatory. She seemed to want to protect him, to nurture him, to help him become all he could be. I think Jim had made it clear to her at some point that while he may have loved her—and you knew that he was in love with her—they were never going to be lovers…. She never stopped being anything but loving and—well—almost maternal towards him.

Despite steady employment in small stage roles, Stewart doubted his ability to find success. During one of the "Beer Club" evenings, Sullavan announced that Stewart would one day be a major movie star. Logan was convinced that this comment was made as a way to get at Fonda, whose fragile ego she still enjoyed tormenting. But Meredith stated, "[She] never once said anything derogatory about Stewart and she never stopped saying that he would become a star in Hollywood—and when he became a star, she always said, 'I told you so.'" As for Fonda, Meredith conceded, "God knows, she could have said a hundred things just to stick in Fonda's throat—and she *did* say hundreds of things—but she never used Jimmy to do that."[11]

Sullavan's career was stuck in a rut. Her next play, *Bad Manners*, proved an even bigger disaster than her other plays. Written by Dana Burnet and William B. Jutte, it was a throwback to the cheap sex comedies like *A Modern Virgin*. Sullavan is Lois, who is engaged to Jerry. However, she tells the best man, Craig (Bert Lytell), she can't go through with the wedding. Craig, who has a roving eye, invites her to stay in his apartment as his secretary. The two begin a sexual relationship. She rejects his proposal of marriage, but stays on—until she becomes dissatisfied. And so it went, until she and Craig ironed out their issues.

The critics hated this one. While she did receive some good notices, there were a few critics who disliked both the play and her performance. According to *Billboard*, the play was "amusing in spots, but it never manages to become more than one of the minor laugh engagements." Not a Sullavan fan, the reviewer noted that she "still needs a good stiff course in acting." The *Herald-Tribune* complained that *Bad Manners* was "the sort of comedy that induced a mood of mild deprecation, being not good enough to serenade nor bad enough to castigate…. Miss Sullavan exercised all her exuberant talents last night [but] her undisciplined impersonation caused several critics to wonder what she might accomplished if ever she got into a good role in a good play under a good director." The *Evening Post* expressed concern for Sullavan's future:

> It is a pity that Margaret Sullavan has such bad luck in her choice of plays. She is a personable young actress with a real flair for comedy. She is pleasantly vivacious, has a charming smile, and does what she is given to do intelligently and well. But among the talents she has so far exhibited must be listed a gift for bobbing up in scripts which seems calculated not to widen her circle of admirers…. Something ought to be done about Miss Sullavan. Before it is too late.

The play collapsed after eight performances. Sullavan must have felt like kicking herself for turning down *Dinner at Eight*, which was still going strong. As luck would have it, Marguerite Churchill, who was playing Paula Jordan, accepted a film offer in England and was leaving in late March. Sullavan stepped into the role on March 24, 1933. In the play, Sullavan, as the young daughter of a prominent New York family, carries on a secret affair with fading movie actor, Larry Renault (Tearle). The play's plot concerns the various lives of many people who have been invited to a lavish dinner party at the Jordan residence.

Despite her late entry, it must have been gratifying to Sullavan to finally appear in a successful play for which she earned some fine notices. The *Evening Post* found Sullavan "happily poised, intelligent, and right in the emotional attack."[12] The *Journal* opined, "Playing more sincerely and far more ingratiatingly than her predecessor did, she employs her acting assets—her shining youth, her looks, her poise, her healthy eagerness, and her sure sensing of comic and tragic values—that one is almost ready to forgive the foolish way in which these gifts of hers have been squandered on texts that have done them a mean injustice."[13]

Jed Harris was in the process of acquiring the American rights to an English play, *The Lake*, which had its London premiere on March 15. Harris believed this would be *the* play that would bring Sullavan her "big break" on Broadway. Instead, her long-awaited big break came in the most unexpected way.

7

"Discovered" by Stahl

I wanted an unknown actress for that role.[1]—*John M. Stahl*

On January 10, 1933, Elizabeth Yeaman reported in the *Hollywood Citizen News*:

John M. Stahl is searching hopefully for an actress to play the feminine lead in *Only Yesterday*....
He has made screen tests of a score of stars eligible for the role, but he has not found the type he is
seeking. He has agreed to interview any Hollywood actress of experience and personality who
applies to him. He does not care whether the girl comes from the ranks of extras, from independent
productions, from stock companies or from the chorus of a theatrical school.... He wants an intelligent actress with a girlish beauty and a good figure, who can look 18 in the early sequence and 35 in
the final scenes.... A southern accent might help but is not essential.[2]

Thus began one director's quest for his ideal leading lady, similar to David O. Selznick's
search for Scarlett O'Hara a few years later. Like the infamous hoax of Vivien Leigh's "discovery" on the burning Atlanta set, much of the story surrounding Sullavan's discovery
was fabricated as well.

When Universal Studios purchased Frederick Lewis Allen's best-selling book *Only
Yesterday: An Informal History of the 1920s* in 1932, the film was intended to be a special
production like the Academy Award–winning *All Quiet on the Western Front* (1930); in
other words, a critically acclaimed and financially successful film to boost the studio's
dismal profits.

At that time, Universal was in the hands of Carl Laemmle, Jr., son of one of the studio's
founders, Carl Laemmle, Sr. Nepotism was the prevailing modus operandi at the studio
and Carl Jr. (known derisively as "Junior") was given the job of operating the studio for his
21st birthday in 1928. Despite his notable achievement with *Dracula* (1931), *Frankenstein*
(1931) and *All Quiet on the Western Front*, the short-statured executive was considered a
joke within the industry. Notwithstanding the financial success of some movies, he had the
reputation for spending extravagantly on pictures that did not regain their costs at the box
office. By the end of 1935, the studio faced bankruptcy. It's little wonder that contract player
Gloria Stuart stated, "Junior really wasn't qualified to produce pictures." Rose Hobart, so
delicate as Fredric March's fiancée in *Dr. Jekyll and Mr. Hyde* (1931), revealed her sharp
tongue with this blunt statement: "Junior didn't know his ass from a shotgun."[3]

Before the release of one of the studio's biggest successes of 1932, *Back Street* (with
Irene Dunne and John Boles), its director, Stahl, was chosen to direct *Only Yesterday*. Stahl,
a veteran movie director and producer since the late 1910s, was later referred to as "the man
who understood women."[4] He achieved remarkable success as the director of highly profitable "women's pictures," such as the Oscar-nominated *Imitation of Life* (1934), *Magnificent*

Obsession (1935) and *Leave Her to Heaven* (1945). However, he apparently did not have the "Midas touch" with all of his films as evidenced by the dreadfully dull, infamous Clark Gable flop *Parnell* (1937).

With the critical success of Fox's *Cavalcade* in 1933, it was suggested that *Only Yesterday* become an Americanized version of that film. Stahl was against the idea. As he explained,

> [*Cavalcade's*] prevailing theme is loyalty to the crown, loyalty through all manner of trouble and sorrow. For instance, the death of Queen Victoria and its emotional reaction upon the people. I recall only one moment in our history during my lifetime, when the American people reacted similarly to the passing of a leader. That was the death of Theodore Roosevelt. Ordinarily, we live at too fast a pace, are too busy, to be concerned deeply.[5]

Allen's book was an entertaining study of American events and important personalities during the Roaring Twenties. Although it provided a colorful background, Stahl wanted to make a film that had more emotional appeal similar to *Back Street*. Over many months, he commissioned several writers to develop a suitable screenplay. The finished screenplay retained the title of Allen's book but bore little resemblance to that piece of work. Instead, Stefan Zweig's 1922 novella, *Letter from an Unknown Woman*, though not credited, provided the basis for the film. Zweig's work has already been filmed in Germany in 1929. While the setting was transferred from the early twentieth century Vienna to post–World War I America, the essential plot elements were intact and the similarities between the film and Zweig's novella are unmistakable. With the production ready to begin with John Boles in the male lead, there remained one more problem: Who would play the heroine?

Stahl offered the role to prominent stars like Claudette Colbert of Paramount and Irene Dunne of RKO, but they turned it down. Likewise, RKO's Ann Harding declined Stahl's offer of a weekly salary of $7300. Helen Hayes was another possibility, but the studio could not afford to borrow her from Metro-Goldwyn-Mayer. Gloria Stuart, a young starlet who was being heavily promoted by Universal, was also under consideration. All of this is in contrast to Stahl's later assertion that he would only consider an unknown actress. The "search" was just a publicity stunt, dreamed up by either Stahl or Universal in order to promote interest in the film. Consider the following news item by Wood Soanes in February 1933:

> Junior Laemmle is given to making announcements, but occasionally utters something of significance.... The studios, he said, waste about a half million dollars a year trying to discover new talent from among college stars, former silent picture players and athletic celebrities. Universal alone has spent $300,000 during the last year seeking actors whose ability would equal their publicity build-up. He has been forced to postpone production for nearly two months on *Only Yesterday* because he has been unable to find a girl equal to opportunities similar to those given Irene Dunne in *Back Street* and Ann Harding in *Holiday*.[6]

Another month passed and there was still no leading lady. Dissatisfied with the choices at hand, Stahl widened his search. Many in Hollywood wondered what all the fuss was about. After the film's release, Stahl addressed the naysayers:

> To begin with, the part was so well written as to be almost foolproof. Any actress of ability could have given a creditable performance. But I wanted an unknown actress for a different reason. In the story, the star is forgotten by the man who she loves and by whom she bears a child. But if that star had been Irene Dunne or some other well-known star, audiences could not have believed that the soldier lover could forget her.... I wanted the audience to start off on the same footing as that man, so they could understand why he forgot her. If the audience did not understand that one point, the whole drama would have fallen to pieces.[7]

The studio finally announced in mid–April that Irene Dunne was the likely candidate to appear opposite Boles. There was little doubt the financial success of *Back Street* would be replicated with the reunion of these two popular stars. Production was slated to begin on May 1. With that casting issue resolved, Stahl decided to take a quick trip to New York City. There he encountered Margaret Sullavan appearing in *Dinner at Eight*. During the performance, Stahl came to the unmistakable conclusion that he had finally found the actress who would play his heroine. The rest, they say, is history.

Great story. The only problem is it isn't true.

One of the challenges in telling the story of a deceased person's life is separating the facts from fiction. The Hollywood publicity department in Hollywood's "Golden Age" often published stories which bore little relationship to the truth. For this book, I have made every effort to substantiate information by using multiple sources or personal testimony.

This widely accepted account of Sullavan's discovery first surfaced in a June 16 article in the studio's trade paper. This account was repeated a few months later in the *Photoplay* article "She Abhors Being Beautified." The initial indication that this might be fabrication is that the details of her discovery are told in the third-person point of view. There are no direct quotes from either Sullavan or Stahl to confirm the story. Furthermore, since Stahl is often credited with discovering Sullavan for the screen, it is odd that I have yet to come across evidence that corroborates this claim. Adding to the confusion a few years later, there was columnist George Ross' claim that a movie scout was in attendance at the play; Stahl's name does not appear anywhere in the article. Sullavan herself did little to clear up the confusion as she said she was "playing on the New York stage in *Dinner at Eight* when I was shown the movie script of *Only Yesterday* and was offered the leading part."[8] The only piece of information that disputes Stahl's involvement comes from a 1934 Stahl interview in which he stated, "I had seen Margaret in the New York production of *Chrysalis*." The next statement from Stahl offers the most conclusive rebuttal: "Later, I saw a test of her out here [in California]."[9]

So, if Stahl didn't discover Margaret Sullavan, who did?

The answer comes from a January 1934 *Modern Screen* article entitled "How a Star Was Created." The by-line of the article makes it clear that Charles Beahan is solely responsible for Sullavan's discovery. As Beahan, a story editor assigned to Universal's New York office, recalled, he had asked her to come to his office "for I felt that she was the most promising young actress on the New York stage and potentially a great screen bet. It was my job to find personalities who would click at the box office."[10]

It was not an easy task to convince Sullavan as she wasn't interested in making films. As Sullavan informed *Photoplay*, "I loved the theater and I wanted to stay here.... I didn't think I'd like Hollywood, didn't think I'd like pictures."[11] Her response to Beahan's inquiries did not surprise him. As Beaham recalled, Sullavan snapped back, "Listen, Charlie Beahan, why do you want to bother with me? I'll never make the grade in pictures. I'm not pretty enough."

Beahan conceded that, while she lacked the typical Hollywood glamour, she possessed the kind of qualities as an actress that were more lasting. Sullavan responded, "Perhaps someday I will be a fine actress if I work hard enough, but my chance will come on the stage, not in the pictures."[12] Undeterred, Beahan tried a different approach. He brought out the script of *Only Yesterday* and began reading it aloud to her. After a while, she was hooked. As Sullavan recalled, "I loved the story of *Only Yesterday* and I wanted to do it."[13]

Beahan knew a screen test was necessary to convince the executives in Hollywood. Despite her misgivings, Sullavan agreed to make the test in New York. According to Beahan, the screen test "was truly magnificent, because Margaret had put her heart and soul into it."[14] Excited, he wired Junior and had the test reel shipped to Hollywood. Junior was impressed enough to ask Beahan to start negotiating a contract deal. With her agent Leland Hayward, Sullavan secured a lucrative salary of $1200 per week for the duration of the filming. The contract was set up to include six pictures (two pictures per year). There was also the usual six-months stipulation that her services would end if she failed to make an impression with movie audiences.

The pragmatic Sullavan had to admit that she was not progressing far with her stage career. After all, she was only making $300 per week as a replacement in *Dinner at Eight*. Her experience with the theater had been a disappointment. "I wasn't getting anywhere in the theater," she later told an interviewer. "I was in one lousy flop after another." There was another incentive in tackling a new medium: "I went out to Hollywood because I needed the money and because I knew that security would give me independence—the independence to turn down rotten scripts."[15] Furthermore, the notion of *starring* in her first motion picture must have intrigued her. After all, only a handful of Broadway performers like Jeanette MacDonald, Helen Hayes and Katharine Hepburn have found success in their debut films, but none of them had the starring role.

Before signing the contract, Sullavan had more requests, including the condition that she could leave after ten days if she did not like Hollywood or filmmaking. Sullavan also had a stipulation put in that, should Universal decide that she would not make it, the contract would be torn up and she would be paid $2500 for her troubles. Finally, Sullavan demanded that she would not have to be subjected to the standard Hollywood beauty treatment. The executives agreed to her terms. On April 19, Yeaman announced in the *Hollywood Citizen News* that Sullavan had signed the Universal contract.

Ironically, Stahl himself was the last obstacle to overcome. According to Beahan, Stahl would not agree to her as the final selection for the role until she came to the West Coast for additional tests under his direction. Surprisingly, Sullavan agreed to Stahl's terms. If she had any inkling of what lay ahead, she might never have left New York.

In a letter to her brother Sonny, Sullavan wrote that she was really going to Hollywood: "It means discarding what might be termed youthful ideas about Art."[16] Within a few weeks, Sullavan completed the Broadway run of *Dinner at Eight* and Jane Wyatt played the part in the touring production. Sullavan left her car for her brother and her marriage to Fonda behind in New York and boarded an airplane for California. On the way, she stopped in Chicago and began divorce proceedings. Fonda was notified of her intent when he received the letter on May 16, their joint birthday. The irony of the situation was not lost on him. Despite the brevity of the marriage, the impact of its breakup had a lasting effect on Fonda. As his son Peter stated, "His first marriage broke his heart so badly that he never recovered."[17]

8

Creating a Movie Star

When I was in Hollywood five months, I realized one of us must be crazy.[1]

Sullavan arrived in Hollywood on May 16, her 24th birthday. According to *The Hollywood Reporter,* Universal, currently shut down due to financial troubles, would reopen with the filming of *Only Yesterday.* During that time of inactivity, executives made the decision to cut the wages of studio personnel. As a consequence, there was a lot of hope riding on the financial success of this film and a relatively unknown stage actress.

Sullavan later joked, "The renovation of Margaret Sullavan began even before I left New York." A telegram arrived from Hollywood with this message: "Have that wart taken off!"[2] Initially, she vehemently refused to comply with the request. However, it wasn't long before the problematic mole was removed. "They called it a *wart,*" Sullavan explained. "They did! I couldn't possibly keep it after that, could I?"[3] Once in Hollywood, she reported to Universal for additional testing under Stahl's supervision. The makeup department descended upon the newcomer and did what they could to make her more attractive for the camera. She suffered further indignities at their hands:

> Her medium-brown hair was dyed blonde; a shield was put over a front tooth that was short; the top lipstick line on her upper lip was raised to reduce the distance between her nose and mouth; made because the right side of her jaw was lower than the left and her mouth drooped to the right, the corners of her mouth were heightened with lipstick and her right eyebrow line was raised.[4]

The ordeal was far from over. After many sessions in which her looks were closely scrutinized by every makeup artist, hairdresser and cameramen on the lot, a testy Sullavan wondered, "Why on Earth they had employed me…. Why didn't they go out and pick up a $10-a-day extra girl and save money?"[5]

Finally Sullavan was ready for the cameras. Stahl made several tests as a horde of cameramen continued their quest to make her look beautiful. The tests came out worse than anyone had expected until, all of a sudden, there was a lovely girl on the screen. Excitedly, Stahl proclaimed they had finally achieved the desired effect. The problem was, no one could remember how they lit the shot. It was back to the drawing board for several days to recapture that shot. Eight cameramen tried without success. It was the ninth cameraman who solved the problem. Sullavan remembered, "It seems that the trouble was my shallow chin. It wasn't long enough, and threw my face out of balance." That cameraman set the lights over her head and put other lights directed down at her chin. "And there I was, at last, a beautiful girl with a nice, long chin."

Production finally began. Her supporting cast consisted of veteran stage and screen actors: John Boles, experiencing a career boost as a dramatic actor after a brief but highly successful career as a singer in the early talkies; Billie Burke, a renowned stage actress who re-entered films in 1932 with *A Bill of Divorcement* (Katharine Hepburn's debut film) after the death of her husband Florenz Ziegfeld; and Reginald Denny, an English actor with 18 years of experience in films. Sullavan recalled that Stahl and many members of the cast were "marvelous to me, though I must have irritated them frequently. I was jumpy and … had no confidence in my ability to do a good job."[6] With her co-stars' familiarity with film techniques (Boles was particularly helpful), and Stahl's careful guidance, she learned the fundamentals of film acting and scaled back her stage mannerisms. As Boles related to an interviewer, "I should like to be able to say later on, when she is a star, that I helped her in her first film—but the truth is that she needed so little help that I had to put all I knew into my scenes to avoid being overshadowed by her!"[7]

Viewing the early rushes, Sullavan was horrified by her appearance and performance. "I look just like a Pekingese," she complained.[8] She offered to buy out her contract for $2500, but the executives instead renewed her options and presented her with a revised contract: a non-exclusive contract, with script approval and an option for extended leave to appear in plays.

It was still a bold move, since America was in the depths of the Depression. Universal was not in the same league as Metro-Goldwyn-Mayer, Warner Brothers or Paramount and was struggling to stay financially solvent. Earlier that year, the studio had released three of their stars, Lew Ayres, Tala Birell and Boris Karloff. Based on Stahl's reports, Sullavan showed promise in becoming a big moneymaker for the studio. By mid–June, she was heavily promoted as a future box office star in the studio's trade paper, *Universal Weekly*. She joined a group of less expensive players including Paul Lukas, Andy Devine, Tom Brown, Gloria Stuart, Slim Summerville, Zasu Pitts and Ken Maynard.

Sullavan stood in the forefront of Universal's leading actresses since Junior's own discovery, Sidney Fox, had departed the previous year amidst sordid rumors. Not only was Fox romantically linked to Junior, she was also suspected of being intimate with his father. Such unsavory gossip destroyed a once promising career. Coincidentally, Fox married Sullavan's discoverer, Charles Beahan, after leaving Hollywood in 1932. In a sad parallel to Sullavan's life, Fox died of an overdose of sleeping pills in 1942 at the age of 30.

With infinite patience, Stahl worked with Sullavan to boost her confidence. Eventually he was sufficiently satisfied with her progress to proclaim that she'd be a star after the film is released. Stahl told Quirk, "Maggie made the transition from the theater to the screen more easily and readily than most actresses because the essence of her projection was always naturalness."[9]

Despite Stahl's faith, she still found film acting frustrating. Early on, she had to change the way she prepared for a role: "I carefully rehearsed all my lines, from beginning to end, as I would for a play, and then I learned that this diligent effort had done me no good."[10] She found Stahl's painstaking style of direction tedious. The endless retakes of one scene (reportedly as many as 58) drove her insane. The days on the set were long and tiring. The daily grind of makeup, hair and costume preparation wore on her nerves. As a result, tensions festered on the set. One day, she got into a huge argument with Stahl over how to play a scene. Overwhelmed, Sullavan stormed off the set intent on leaving Hollywood that very moment. She made airline reservations for New York. She even intended to repay Universal $2500. After talking to her agent, she settled down and apologized to Stahl by phone. He told her to take the rest of the day off.

To relieve the monotony of filming, Sullavan occupied her spare time learning about moviemaking from behind the camera. She spent considerable amount of time with the carpenters, electricians and camera grips in the interest of learning their crafts. Jerry Lane of *Hollywood* magazine reported an encounter he had with a male extra. The extra asked, "Who is that little scamp climbing up the scaffold? She's been here every day watching things from up on the rafters or on top of the sound booth. Not the script girl, is she?" When Lane told him that that little scamp was the leading lady, the man was taken aback. "*That* little brat in the dirty pants?"[11] Sullavan reportedly shrieked with laughter when told of this exchange.

Sullavan developed a special friendship with young Jimmy Butler, a 12-year-old actor making his debut as her son. She found him to be mature and intelligent for his age and enjoyed his company. Boles joked that those two become so chummy that he felt left out. As for Butler's performance, Sullavan enthusiastically told a *Los Angeles Times* reporter, "The boy is wonderful. As far as I am concerned, he is the best thing in [the film]."[12]

Sullavan film-debuted in *Only Yesterday* (1933) and was hailed an overnight sensation. She portrays an innocent girl who gives birth out of wedlock in this pre–Code woman's picture.

Despite these diversions, filming dragged on. To one reporter, she griped, "I hate Hollywood! I hate the movies! I hate it all! I wish I hadn't stayed!" A moment later, she added wistfully, "Perhaps if I could have just three days' rest I'd probably love it all!"[13]

Filming wrapped in late August and Stahl enthusiastically told Lane, "It is her sincerity and sweetness that stand out. The same qualities that made Janet Gaynor one of the top-notchers. It will be very interesting to see what happens next."[14] Sullavan was not as easily convinced. "You'll see that I'm terrible," she remarked. She was not pleased with her appearance either. "Look at this face," she groused. "Even my best friends can't say it was meant to be in front of a camera," she matter-of-factly told Helen Krumph. With great insight, Klumph managed to capture the essence of Sullavan's appeal by noting that her face may not be conventionally beautiful, "but it's piquant and individual. [It's] a marvelous mirror of moods."[15]

The publicity department started promoting Sullavan as an unconventional girl who shunned glamor in the Hollywood tradition. Universal was capitalizing on Katharine Hepburn's rise to fame as Hollywood's premier nonconformist. An interesting news article appeared in early October. Under a picture of Sullavan was this caption: "Margaret Sullavan, the unknown actress who got a star part while thousands of veterans wanted for jobs." In a diatribe against what was perceived as an unfair practice, the writer proclaimed:

There seems to be more of a chance for an absolute newcomer in Hollywood than for trained screen actors. Not many weeks ago, Margaret Sullavan arrived in the film capital. Not once had she been in front of a motion picture camera. Yet she was brought to the movie capital from New York for the express purpose of playing the leading feminine role in *Only Yesterday*, one of the prize part of the year.... Occasionally a Margaret Sullavan comes along and grabs a role which might have gone to one of their number. That's heartbreaking.

The solution? "If plans now underway materialize, the Will Hays Office is opening an Artists' Service Bureau to be conducted solely for the benefits of the actors and actresses; all freelance players will be engaged through the bureau which will attempt to spread work over a large a field as possible."[16] This accounts for the large number of lesser-known players, such as Bramwell Fletcher, June Clyde and Onslow Stevens, who are given opening credits billing despite their relatively small parts in *Only Yesterday*.

Only Yesterday had its Hollywood premiere on October 27. *Motion Picture Daily* praised Sullavan's performance: "Nobody in the picture approximates Miss Sullavan's performance for understanding and emotional depth. She looks like a real bet.... Histrionically, she has the goods—lots of it." By the time the film was released nationwide on November 7, a new star was born, just as Stahl predicted.

The film opens in New York on October 29, 1929, when the stock market crashed. Stahl inserts effective scenes depicting the rising panic among wealthy businessmen and stockbrokers. After a suicide, the mood changes as a gay couple (one of them played by Franklin Pangborn) discuss plans to attend a cocktail party at the Emersons' apartment. (This scene, along with one featuring a lesbian couple, would not make it past the censors the following year after Breen's Code of Decency took effect.) The party is already underway at Jim Emerson's. The alcohol flows freely, the mood is festive, and sexual tension is pervasive. Featured in this scene is Edna May Oliver, who, despite her screen time of less than three minutes, is accorded third billing in the credits!

Rumors of the crash enter conversations and dampen the mood. Jim (Boles) arrives and confirms the news to his hysterical mistress. Jim locks himself in his study with the intentions of killing himself when he spots a letter on his desk. As he reads it, the viewer is transported back to a military ball in Virginia in 1917.

In a long tracking shot from behind, we are introduced to Margaret Sullavan in her film debut as Mary Lane. "Lt. James Stanton Emerson?" is her first line on the screen. However, something is odd with her performance. Her trademark husky voice registers at a higher pitch than normal. Her acting is also off-kilter. Fortunately, as the film progresses, Sullavan settles into the role with more ease and the familiar and beguiling Sullavan personality emerges.

Mary is smitten and it is not long before Jim's smooth talk sends her into rapturous ecstasy and she gives herself to him in an off-screen scene in the woods. It is her first sexual experience and Sullavan underplays the aftermath beautifully.

It's wartime (war footage courtesy of *All Quiet on the Western Front*) and Jim is soon shipped off to France, leaving a pregnant Mary behind. Mary decides to live in New York with her progressive Aunt Julia (Burke), who has a modern view of such matters as unwed teenage girls and pregnancy. She reassures Mary, "This sort of thing is no longer a tragedy. It isn't even good melodrama. It's just something that happens." Lines like this caused the Breen Office to deny Universal's request to re-issue this film in 1936.

After the Armistice is signed, Mary gives birth to a son named Jimmy. A few months later, returning soldiers parade in the crowded city streets. Mary rushes to one parade in hopes of seeing Jim, so they can be the family she has dreamed of. She spots him quickly in a crowd of thousands. It is not long before Mary realizes that Jim does not remember her. Sullavan's reaction (shown in a tight close-up) is heartbreaking and a testament to her instinctive talents. We can literally see her world shattering through her haunted eyes.

Although Jim's forgetfulness is never clearly explained, the viewer can surmise that he has had so many meaningless sexual encounters that he just plain forgot about Mary. Boles plays this aspect of his character in such a contemporary manner and is so appealing in his sexuality that he is still a likable character. After the Breen Code, such a character would be portrayed in an evil and predatory manner, most notably Basil Rathbone in the underappreciated Kay Francis film *Confession* (1937).

After Jim goes on his honeymoon with his wife Phyllis, Mary resolves to move on with her life, but we all know that's not going to be easy. Fast-forward to New Year's Eve, 1928. Mary is now a successful businesswoman and Jimmy (Butler) is a fine young lad home on holiday break from military school. Jim Sr. has also done well for himself. He is older, still handsome and still married, even though he continues to engage in affairs. He has received another mysterious New Year's Eve letter from "One who does not forget." Apparently, Mary has not let go.

While at a crowded New Year's Eve party, there is a chance encounter between Jim and Mary. This scene is made haunting by the expression of longing and loneliness in Mary's eyes. As the two leave the party, he playfully asks her, "Have we met before?" However, that is part of his seductive tease rather than a legitimate question and she decides to play along in his little game. Mary finally concedes to the fact that Jim is a man who has no qualms about his rampant promiscuity. Despite this, Mary spends a second night with him. This time, it's on her terms and she is clearly the seducer in this tryst.

The film lurches ahead to October and Mary is gravely ill with heart trouble. Despite her weakened condition, she insists on writing a long letter to Jim. When the letter is finished, Mary takes a turn for the worse. In a dreadful scene, Mary is near death and waiting for Jimmy to arrive home from school. This scene is too obvious in its all-out attempt to reduce the feminine audience to tears and Sullavan herself is surprisingly awful.

The film returns to Jim's study and he now has a new lease on life. He bids his wife goodbye and visits the grieving young boy at his mother's apartment. Jim finally tells Jimmy that he is his father. "My father?" the incredulous boy asks and the film comes to a quick conclusion.

Since so much has been written about Sullavan's debut film (little seen since its release), it is unfortunate that one is disappointed by both the film and, to a certain extent, by her performance. *Only Yesterday* suffers from a feeling of *déjà vu* because the screenplay contained so many elements of other films as *The Big Parade* (1925), *Madame X* (1929) and *The Sin of Madeline Claudet* (1931). Furthermore, the viewer is subjected to too many devices designed to wring every tear from even the most reluctant duct. I am not afraid to admit that I can be moved to tears, but I do resent having it poked and prodded out of me. Throughout, the pacing is inconsistent; some scenes end abruptly while others seem to last too long.

In its favor, there are interesting story elements, and Stahl's direction shows flashes of originality. Some of the frank sexual moments are somewhat surprising in that they come from an "old, black-and-white" film. The performances are worthwhile and help to maintain interest. With some minor reservations, Burke and Denny are humorous in their portrayals. Young Butler is affecting and displays nice subtlety in his scenes. Boles is unexpectedly effective. Despite the general ambiguity of his character's motivations, he exudes likable sexuality as the young soldier and older businessman. Sexy is hardly the word that would have been attributed to Boles in later films such as *A Message to Garcia* (1936) and *Stella Dallas* (1937).

This is not one of Sullavan's better performances. Familiarity with her later and more mature work overshadows her portrayal here. Throughout her career, she demonstrated that she was an actress at her best when she was able to display the character's "clarity of vision." She is simply not believable as a naïve young woman who is buffeted about at the hands of cruel fate. Nor is she convincing when she, against her better judgment, willingly submits to a meaningless encounter with Jim. It is this same setup that affected her later scenes in *Back Street*. However, as the young mother, she emerges as the personable and luminous actress we have come to expect. Her scenes with Butler have maternal warmth and believable chemistry between the actors. Likewise, her scenes with Boles in the second half are much more palatable.

In late summer of 1945, producer Felix Jackson, who was responsible for *Back Street* and *Appointment for Love*, contacted the Breen Office about remaking *Only Yesterday*. Breen's response was not surprising. Since the basic story was that of "illicit sex and adultery, without sufficient compensating moral values," the proposed remake would need to be considerably revised in order to satisfy the requirements set by the Breen Office.[17] Not wanting the hassle of reworking the entire film, Jackson abandoned the project. *Only Yesterday* eventually was remade for TV's *Lux Video Theatre* in 1956 with Joan Caulfield and Don Taylor. Zweig's novella, however, served as the basis for several more adaptations including a 1952 *Studio One* TV presentation starring Jean-Pierre Aumont, Viveca Lindfors and Melvyn Douglas; a Russian mono-opera, and a few foreign-language feature films. The most remembered film version is *Letter from an Unknown Woman*, released by Universal in 1948 with Joan Fontaine and Louis Jourdan. This sumptuously produced, leisurely directed "woman's picture" is truer to the flavor of Zweig's work. Fontaine is delicately moving as a young, lovesick girl; however, as the older woman, she comes across foolishly in her undying affection for the unworthy man. The film's biggest flaw is that Max Ophuls' direction is so painstakingly slow in its set-up that the film becomes dull. The end result is a film that, with all of its advantages of filmmaking expertise, is unable to overcome the essential weaknesses of the novella's plot.

Only Yesterday was well received by some and lightly condemned by others. The *Rob Wagner's Script* critic hailed it as "one of the best pictures of the year," but dissenters, like Amy Croughton, film critic for the *Rochester* (NY) *Times-Union,* wrote, "[T]he whole thing is so untrue to human emotion and instinct that one sits wondering where the scenarist's flight of fancy will take him next…. Margaret Sullavan does little to make the character of Mary believable." This critic remained one of the few who was immune to Sullavan's charms throughout her film career. Otherwise, Sullavan's performance was widely heralded as a revelation and Sullavan as a radiant new star. The *Los Angeles Times* astutely noted, "She has an emotional quality which may be very stringently developed. It is immature in this picture, but shows unusual promise, and there was much charm in a majority of her scenes." From the *Oakland Tribune* came this enthusiastic report:

> Miss Sullavan … gives one of the year's best performances in a picture of great box-office proportions…. The success of the project is due, however, not so much to the authors, but to the director and the star and her supporting cast. Without Miss Sullavan or someone of equal talent, *Only Yesterday* would be a rather cheap story.

What did Sullavan think of all the hoopla and fuss back in 1933? No one was able to find out, for she had done the unthinkable. Immediately after completing the film, she had disappeared.

9

A Reluctant Star Takes Flight

I'll probably have to escape rather frequently to keep my perspective in this place.[1]

After the completion of the *Only Yesterday* shoot, Sullavan had so completely pulled off her vanishing act that Hollywood was left scratching its head. Universal was in a panic. Where had she gone? Perhaps if they bothered to read some of Sullavan's recent interviews, they would have realized that she meant what she had been saying all along: She went back to New York.

Sullavan was looking for a play. In mid–September, Elizabeth Yeaman reported that producer Guthrie McClintic was interested in signing Sullavan to replace an ailing Talullah Bankhead in *Jezebel*. Yeaman finished the news item with: "Now if Universal will spare Margaret Sullavan, she will take over the Bankhead role."[2] Miriam Hopkins, herself on hiatus from Hollywood, opened in *Jezebel* in December for a short run. A young director at Universal later suggested that a film version of the play would make a good showcase for Sullavan. His suggestion went nowhere. In 1938, that director, William Wyler (Sullavan's second husband), directed the film with the queen of Warner Brothers' Burbank lot, Bette Davis. Davis' leading man was none other than Henry Fonda.

Sullavan was also sought by Jed Harris for *The Lake*. Believing that she would be perfect for the leading role of the grieving young widow, Harris desperately wanted Sullavan for the production. Again, Sullavan was unavailable and a woefully miscast Katharine Hepburn floundered painfully when it opened in December 1933.

Although the reasons were never given for Sullavan's non-appearance in both plays, one suspects that Universal may have interfered through possible threats of legal action. The following statement, made by Sullavan to an interviewer in 1938 regarding this issue, may shed some light: "For the first time I was in the position to choose a play ... for no other reason than that I wanted to be in it. That was when I began hating the movies." Sullavan was more ambivalent: "I felt that [the movies] were a person ... and I hated that person for keeping me from doing what I wanted to do."[3] Despite the clause in her contract which allowed for an extended vacation time, Universal most likely did not want her to be away from Hollywood for too long a period. If I am correct in the assumption that studio executives prevented her from returning to Broadway, that would certainly explain her animosity toward Universal and her total disregard for her contractual obligations that eventually ended up in court.

Now that Sullavan had been located in New York, Universal tried in vain to get in touch with her. Reportedly, she refused to divulge any clues of her whereabouts. She may have been found, but she was not going to make things easy for them. The studio tried to entice her back to Hollywood with a promising movie project. According to the *Syracuse Herald* in late September, "As a reward for her splendid work in her first picture for Universal.., Margaret Sullavan learned yesterday that she will play the leading feminine role in *Little Man, What Now?*, a screen adaptation of the Hans Fallada best seller."[4] That project piqued her interest and she agreed to return to Hollywood when the script was ready.

By the time *Only Yesterday* played in New York in November, Sullavan was heralded as a new screen sensation. The advertisement pronounced, "Margaret Sullavan will take her place with Garbo, Dietrich, Gaynor, Hepburn and the great stars of all time!"[5] Sullavan's performance was called triumphant and the film was a smash hit all over the country.

The Universal publicity department continued promoting Sullavan as being uniquely different. Yeaman reported, "Mae West, Katharine Hepburn and Margaret Sullavan have proved that the world likes variety. Not one of those three actresses conforms to Hollywood standards of glamor. And, without wishing to detract from their acting ability, I'm convinced that they became popular overnight because they are different."[6] Among Sullavan's most distinctive attributes was her charmingly husky voice. Radie Harris wrote that her voice "is like no one else's you have ever heard." Harris described "its vibrant huskiness [as] a catch between a laugh and a tear."[7] In 1947, Parker Tyler offered this analysis in his book *Magic and Myth of the Movies:* "The opposite of a sissy feminine voice is Margaret Sullavan's, so husky with 'human sympathy,' as I believe it is called, that I have sometimes imagined its quality the result of a sort of fatigue, as though the lady has been carrying around a man-sized load of sentiment for too long a time."[8] In later years, Louise Brooks expressed her admiration when she wrote, "That wonderful voice of hers—strange, fey, mysterious— like a voice singing in the snow."[9]

Her appeal, however, was more than just her haunting voice. In its review of *Only Yesterday*, *Variety* pinpointed the reason for Sullavan's sudden success: "[A]n analysis of why she seems so promising would probably revert to the old truism that the best actors work with their brains and Miss Sullavan seems to possess mentality. Her beauty is not as stunning or vivid as others on the screen but it may be more enduring for it is founded on character and personality." A perceptive *Boston Globe* critic asserted, "Miss Sullavan has not the exotic personality of a Hepburn or a Garbo, but she has something far more enduring—the ability to make people believe in her." Noted film historian David Shipman made this insightful observation on Sullavan's screen performances:

> It was and is a delicate balance, poised between elements of personality, technical knowledge, exhibitionism and a gift for acting—which is perhaps why Miss Sullavan, then in her early twenties, demonstrates it so well. Some performers upset the balance as they age, if their technical mastery increases or their personality strengthens with success—and then they need a strong director. Bette Davis is one such example, with her tendency to demonstrate that she is definitely not coasting through her role. Another is Katharine Hepburn, anxious always to flaunt the admired Hepburn personality. The balance may have been achieved instinctively or with the help of directors, Miss Sullavan did not lose her understanding of it as she aged.[10]

Such is the beguiling magic of Margaret Sullavan, which still resonates more than 85 years after her screen debut.

Despite the widespread critical praise of her performance, Sullavan still resisted seeing the film. According to *Time* magazine, she instead sent her maid Lisbeth. When Lisbeth returned home, she reported that the "picture was wonderful and had made her cry." Sullavan reportedly stated, "Now I know it must be terrible."[11] But her curiosity got the better of her and she eventually saw herself on the screen. "I can't tell you how dreadful I was," she told one reporter. "That's the lucky break about the stage—you can never see yourself."[12]

For the remainder of her film career, Sullavan steadfastly refused to watch many of her rushes or completed films.

With Sullavan's overnight stardom came all of the proposed film projects. No longer under consideration were featured roles in *The Good Red Bricks* for Universal and *A Girl of the Limberlost* on loan-out to Monogram. A far more interesting project was producer Sidney Franklin's live action version of *Bambi*. Franklin had gone as far as recording Sullavan and Victor Jory's voices, but ended up shelving the project., Frank Capra sent a script of a new comedy, *Night Bus*, while Sullavan was still in New York. Like Myrna Loy before her, Sullavan turned it down. Claudette Colbert won her only Academy Award for her performance in the comedy classic, retitled *It Happened One Night*, opposite Clark Gable. One can only imagine the direction Sullavan's film career may have taken had she accepted the part. The notion of a Sullavan-Gable teaming intrigues the imagination as one can only envision the tiny, slightly built leading lady putting the rugged, virile "King" in his place!

Universal Studios worked overtime to promote their radiant new star as a rival to Katharine Hepburn (courtesy Peter Doyle).

Along with these news items came stories of her few months in Hollywood. Many of these stories painted a picture of this new star as a difficult, temperamental non-conformist who despised being in Hollywood. After all, this tactic was working well for Hepburn and Mae West, both of whom were enjoying tremendous popularity. Some of these stories were true; others were taken out of context. As Sullavan recalled, "I was 'hard to handle' because I refused interviews. I didn't care about my career because I went to sleep on the set. I came to the studio with woolen riding gloves, so I was doing it for a gag. I wore pants, so I was going Garbo, Dietrich and Hepburn. Everything I did was wrong."[13]

Consider the following example of the kind of story she was generating: "Every time they need her for a scene, they had to look for her. Once, while working in a beautiful evening gown, she got tired and, not finding a comfortable place to rest, just laid down on the floor for a nap. She's a tomboy too, and the net result of her sleeping and athletic proclivities make her the despair of the wardrobe department."[14] Such stories illustrated how *different* she was in comparison to the "normal" glamor star and Sullavan resented the attention.

While in Hollywood, she eschewed living the high-glamor life of a movie star. Instead of living in a mansion, she rented an apartment. She avoided social gatherings because she detested the night spots. Her disdain for the "star treatment" extended itself to the times at the studio as well. One of the most widely publicized stories illustrates her non-conformist nature. At the studio, it was standard procedure that all of the stars and executives eat in the lavish dining room, "Indian Room." Sullavan preferred to eat at the luncheon counter and refused to comply with their "suggestions." As she explained years later, "I enjoy sitting at a counter, wolfing down a hamburger."[15] She was bound and determined to remain true to herself. If the studio didn't like it, well, they could fire her!

Due to the intense scrutiny of the press and fan magazines, Sullavan began to detest being interviewed. She especially resented being treated as if she were an "insufferable insect," because she refused to answer questions involving private matters.[16] One such private matter involved the issue of her marriage to Fonda. When the news first hit the gossip column, Sullavan categorically denied having ever been married. Eventually, some enterprising reporter dug up the marriage certificate marriage.

If Sullavan's relationship with Fonda had been marked with ups and downs, Sullavan's relationship with Jed Harris was even more intense and mentally exhausting. It was not, in any sense of the word, a healthy relationship, but Sullavan was either unwilling or unable to get out of it. According to biographer Martin Gottfried, Harris is said to have written to his sister Mildred that Sullavan was suicidal. He reportedly told Mildred that Sullavan "asked me why we don't make a suicide pact. She said, 'I'm ready to kill myself out of love for you." If they both killed themselves, "it would prove how much we love each other."[17] According to Quirk, it was Harris who often professed suicidal tendencies when he was needy for attention.

In early December, Louella Parsons reported that Sullavan was due back in Hollywood prior to Christmas to begin work on *Little Man, What Now?* "I crawled on my trip west," Sullavan revealed later. "I wanted to commit suicide because I was going back to a place where I had been unhappy and isolated."[18] Apparently, Sullavan was not adverse to using the word "suicide" to make a dramatic point, either.

When she reported to Universal, she found that the film was not ready to begin. Douglass Montgomery (known as Kent Douglass when he was an MGM contract player in the early 1930s) was borrowed as a replacement for Lew Ayres as the male lead. Director Frank Borzage needed to complete another film commitment before beginning *Little Man, What Now?* Universal hastily announced a new, even more prestigious vehicle, *Elizabeth and Mary*, based on the lives of Queen Elizabeth and Mary of Scots. Actor-turned-Director Lowell Sherman was chosen to direct the project. Sherman has had tremendous success with Mae West in *She Done Him Wrong* and Katharine Hepburn in *Morning Glory* (which earned Hepburn the first of her four Academy Awards).

Sullavan was very enthusiastic about this film. Unfortunately, this project was abandoned after a major dispute arose over the casting of Queen Elizabeth as Sherman unsuccessfully fought for the distinguished English actress, Mrs. Patrick Campbell.

When the *Oakland Tribune* revealed this interesting tidbit, Universal executives must have done a double-take: "Jed Harris managed to place Margaret Sullavan under contract while she was on vacation in New York. Now all he needs is to find a play for her and get her away from Universal long enough to appear in it."[19] Luckily for the studio, that was a legal matter which could be easily resolved. Then came this news item: "Margaret Sullavan is the most recent film actress to take up flying and just has made her first solo fight."[20] She would indulge in her new hobby whenever she felt the need to get away from Hollywood—and, over the years, she would, much to the studio's irritation.

Once again, with no immediate film projects, Sullavan wasted no time leaving for New York without Universal's knowledge. Harrison Carroll reported, "Universal wishes that Margaret Sullavan would let the studio know her new address and telephone number."[21]

Sullavan once again resumed her tumultuous relationship with Harris. It was not long before rumors began to circulate that the two had eloped. In the nation's newspapers, there was a big picture of Sullavan with a small inset of Harris with the caption "Another Runaway Romance?" According to the report, "Hollywood is all agog at persistent reports that Margaret Sullavan, film star, and Jed Harris, New York theatrical producer, have become Mr. and Mrs. by the elopement route. Miss Sullavan's absence from Hollywood and Harris' mysterious departure from Broadway started rumors."[22] Despite the couple's insistent denials, the rumors continued for a long time.

Sullavan was proving to be a thorn in Universal's side. Yeaman reported, "Margaret Sullavan, in her sudden flights to New York, has Universal executives worked up to a high pitch of exasperation. She will not see interviewers nor anyone else and blithely hops a plane every time anyone asked her to do anything."[23]

The script of *Little Man, What Now?* was finally ready and filming was about to commence. When Sullavan returned to Hollywood, little did she realize that she would meet the man who was ultimately responsible for nurturing her enduring screen persona. Stahl may have introduced the actress to moviegoers, but director Frank Borzage was the one who brought her distinctive talent and radiant personality to full, vibrant life.

10

Encountering Hollywood's Great Romanticist

Real acting is to keep your personality entirely out of the picture—to be somebody else—to submerge your individuality in the character you are playing.[1]

What is ironic about this statement is that, under his astute handling, Frank Borzage managed to successfully merge aspects of Sullavan's personality into the character to the extent that the character became uniquely identified with the Sullavan screen persona. Of all of her directors, Borzage understood her the best and elicited some of her most soul-searching performances.

One of Hollywood's most successful directors, Borzage enjoyed phenomenal success with the silent films *Humoresque* (1920), *Seventh Heaven* (1927) and *Street Angel* (1928); for the last two films, he won an Oscar, the first Academy Award for Best Direction. In the early years of the Academy Awards it was common for a single Oscar to represent more than one film. Borzage specialized in lushly photographed films that emphasized deeply sentimental themes, typically that of young lovers battling and ultimately triumphing over life's adversities. He continued to direct notable films in the early 1930s, including *Bad Girl* (1931, which earned him his second Oscar), *A Farewell to Arms* (1932) and *Man's Castle* (1933). However, Borzage had not consistently merged the delicate balance of tender pathos with the gritty reality of the Great Depression as seen in other early sound films. What was lacking was his "inspiration." In the '20s, he utilized the perfect couple to personify his romantic vision in Janet Gaynor and Charles Farrell in a series of highly profitable films. Gaynor has been referred to as his Muse of Silent Films or, as Andrew Sarris dubbed her, his "Madonna of the Streets."[2] In the early 1930s, Borzage explored different types of romantic films, achieving varying degrees of success. Helen Hayes was theatrical in *A Farewell to Arms*, Mary Pickford was too coy for her age in *Secrets* (1933), and Marian Nixon was a cloying, simpering child in *After Tomorrow* (1932). A breathtakingly beautiful Loretta Young came the closest in *Man's Castle*, despite the fact she doesn't quite seem real.

Then Borzage connected with Margaret Sullavan and, with his new "Muse for the Talkies," continued to perfect his craft as Hollywood's greatest romanticist. Sullavan benefited greatly as he elevated her screen appearances to heights not achieved by any other directors. Sullavan's performances in her four films with Borzage revealed her gifts at their most lyrical. Her first Borzage film, *Little Man, What Now?*, inarguably changed the course of her career.

Back in Hollywood, it was obvious that Sullavan had not softened her opinion of the industry. Helen Klumph noted, "Producers think Miss Sullavan is the perfect actress, but they would like to muzzle her because she isn't tactful—her opinions are as honest as her acting."[3] Once again, her words became fodder for public consumption. "I still hate making pictures!" she sniped. After a few more terse comments, she wistfully added, "If only Hollywood will only let me alone to find my way about … I probably will change my feelings about it." Then, her anger quickly flared up as she concluded, "It seems utterly, horribly and completely consuming and interfering. That's my grief against the place. And that's why I am always restless to get out of it the very moment I am able."[4]

Despite her outspokenness, Sullavan continued to attract the attention of members of the film colony. In one widely publicized story, she was approached by actress Lilyan Tashman after the Hollywood premiere of *Only Yesterday*. Tashman gushed over Sullavan: "My dear, you were wonderful in that picture. We're proud of you—really!"[5] Embarrassed, Sullavan responded with a terse "thank you" before walking away. Taking offense, Tashman fumed, "Somebody ought teach that child some manners."[6] When word reached Sullavan, she explained, "I didn't mean to be insulting at all. But what could I say? She told me she liked me in my picture and I thanked her. Should I have said, 'I think I was great, too?'"[7] Sullavan eventually became friendly with some of filmland's prominent players, including Ginger Rogers. As Rogers recalled, "One of the myths about actresses is that we're too self-centered to be friends with other actresses. Well, Maggie Sullavan and I certainly disproved that theory…. I always welcomed Maggie's company and her conversation."[8]

In a thinly veiled swipe at John Stahl, Sullavan stated, "It will be so nice to work for a director whose judgment I respect."[9] She was also enthusiastic about *Little Man, What Now?*'s story and later regarded this film as one of the very few worthwhile things she did on the screen.

Little Man, What Now? Was based on the international bestseller *Kleiner Mann—Was Nun?*, written by Rudolf Ditzen under the pseudonym of Hans Fallada. The novel was a trenchant observation of the social and materialistic atmosphere characteristic of the New Objectivity in post–World War I Germany. While Ditzen aimed some subtle criticism at the Nazi party's ideological views, those in power never caught on as Ditzen successfully diffused the ambiguous criticism by the apolitical attitudes of his main characters. The novel, however, was more than a cautionary tale of an uncertain time. As Ditzen wrote in a letter, "Perhaps I did once … want to write a novel about unemployment, but gradually and imperceptibly, this book became a tribute to a woman." By the time he finished, the book became "a mark of gratitude to a woman, a small part of a large feeling of gratitude."[10] First published in Germany in 1932, the novel emerged as the international best-selling fiction work of 1933.

Ditzen was caught off guard by its phenomenal success as he despised his male protagonist, Johannes Pinneberg, whom he referred to as "that wimp Pinneberg who would be nothing without his wife."[11] The first movie adaptation was made in Germany in 1933. Ditzman was originally involved, but withdrew when he became unhappy with the director's misguided interpretation. The resulting film was terrible and flopped. Due to this, Ditzen later declined Universal's offer to come to Hollywood.

The novel was brought to Junior Laemmle's attention by an European émigré, Edgar G. Ulmer, a set designer. Despite the novel's success in its U.S. edition, Laemmle doubted that filmgoers would pay to see a depressing movie that mirrored their own troubles. Still, he could not deny the novel's success and changed his mind. "There have been lots of Depression stories, but none has done well," Junior told an interviewer. Ever the showman, he painted a different picture. "I think that it will be a big hit," he asserted. "It'll be like *All*

Quiet [on the Western Front], the one war picture of the year that was a tremendous hit."[12] As befitting a "super production," Junior spent a considerable sum. Old sets from *All Quiet on the Western Front* and *Frankenstein* were utilized in recreating authentic-looking German towns.

Some sources claimed that Sullavan insisted on Borzage as director over James Whale due to her admiration for his film *No Greater Glory*. This is not likely since *No Greater Glory* was not even in post-production when he was assigned to direct in October 1933. Douglass Montgomery was cast as Hans, the male protagonist, while Alan Hale, Catherine Doucet, Alan Mowbray and DeWitt Jennings played major supporting roles.

In revising Ditzen's novel, the screenwriters ended the film with the birth of the baby (born in the middle of the novel), rearranged some key incidents, and cut some of the harsher elements, such as the rise of the Third Reich, in order to conform more closely with Borzage's romantic vision of the effects of severe economic and spiritual depression on a young lower-class couple. Filming began on March 9, 1934. In an interview, Borzage remarked, "Once [the actors] have thoroughly absorbed the mood and feeling of a scene, the rest is easy.... I love to get into the hearts and souls of my players and make them live the characters which they portray."[13] Borzage worked hard to avoid obvious displays of pathos and constantly strove for naturalness and spontaneity. "I've finally learned that the first rehearsal—always the first take—is the best," he revealed. "You get a crisp, vital quality in the acting on that first take." As for his leading lady, "She is not camera-proof as stars are. Many of the most famous stars are never photographed from certain angles. Margaret Sullavan doesn't mind. There are many scenes in *Little Man, What Now?* which failed to show her features at her best. To have done so would have spoiled the naturalness of the sequences."[14]

The shoot was not always free of stress as Borzage did not direct his actors as Stahl did. Sullavan, used to Stahl's careful direction and constant coddling, had a hard time adjusting to Borzage's *laissez-faire* style. As Patricia Keats of *Silver Screen* observed, Borzage "kneels down by Margaret Sullavan and goes over her lines with her. He doesn't tell her how to read them, he doesn't tell her how to 'act' them. One, two, perhaps three takes is all he ever needs."[15]

As Sarris later wrote, "Borzage's distinctive temperament on the set is exemplified by his extraordinary treatment of Janet Gaynor and Margaret Sullavan, actresses with screen personalities exalted by him."[16] However, Borzage's directorial habits got the better of the insecure actress and, one day, she blew up on the set. "You never told me I'm rotten," Sullavan screamed. "I can't stand any more silence!" Borzage assured her that, if she was bad, he would have spoken up. "You're doing it perfectly," he added.[17] In time, Sullavan settled down. "I do adore this picture," she told a reporter. "The association of Mr. Borzage and all the lovely cast has really been fun."[18]

Whenever Sullavan was not needed, she seized the opportunity to take a nap—lying face down. This practice often ruined her makeup, and extra time was spent reapplying it. More challenging was that she had taken a strong dislike to Montgomery. Favoring a more virile actor, Sullavan found the high-strung, sensitive actor irritatingly passive. Montgomery was Borzage's personal choice and the director became paternal and protective of the young actor. Montgomery later referred to both Sullavan and Hepburn as "tiger cats."[19]

Dealing with his leads was the least of Borzage's problems. Although the new Breen Code was not yet in place, Borzage faced strong opposition from Will Hays, president of the Motion Picture Producers and Distributors of America. Hays was apoplectic over some of the racier elements of the screenplay, in particular the scenes depicting the couple's intent to have an abortion and Mia Pinneberg's dissolute life. Junior, fearing reprisals, pressured Borzage to tone down these scenes. With Sullavan's encouragement, Borzage remained steadfast in leaving these scenes intact in the finished film. Borzage did make some concessions by eliminating the harsher criticism aimed at the Third Reich as Universal still had a subsidiary crew filming the street scenes for the background projections.

Shooting ended after 36 days of filming in late April. As the film was being prepared for release, Junior waxed effusively, "I am so enthusiastic about this picture, and the talented young woman who has the principal role, that I fear to express myself fully for fear of being accused of exaggeration.... I want the whole civilized world to judge it."[20]

What is unique about this film is Borzage's treatment of Lammchen. In Borzage's hands, the film emerged as something less of a heavily symbolic romance of Depression era lovers and more of a glorious homage to its leading lady. It opens in a German town where a political rally is taking place in wind-driven rain, thus underscoring the country's political unrest. Nearby waits Hans Pinneberg (Montgomery), a pacifist who only wants a life of peaceful co-existence. He is joined by Emma, affectionately called "Lammchen." Sullavan makes her appearance with a charming, luminous close-up and the swelling of music to emphasize her spiritual and redemptive qualities.

At the doctor's office (future gossip columnist Hedda Hopper plays a nurse), Hans meets an angry man (Fred Kohler) and his sickly wife (Mae Marsh, so memorable as the beloved "Little Sister" from *The Birth of the Nation*, but disappointingly shrill here). These two, representing the downtrodden, make more heavy-handed appearances, offsetting the film's tender qualities.

When Lammchen's pregnancy is confirmed, Hans hopes that the doctor will perform an abortion because they are too poor to afford a child. Lammchen persuades him otherwise. Up to this point, the viewer has been led to believe that they're married. Imagine our surprise when, in this pre–Code film (the Breen Code was not enforced until a month after the film's release), they visit the justice of the peace!

Hans keeps their marriage a secret from his cruel boss, Emil Kleinholz (DeWitt Jennings, splendidly mixing the character's comical aspects with sinister malevolence). Kleinholz employs single clerks so he can find a suitable husband for his homely daughter Marie, and he's not above threatening to fire any of them on the spur of the moment. After Marie sets her sights on Hans, Kleinholz begins pressuring the young clerk.

During a Sunday afternoon outing in the park, Lammchen confronts Hans with her suspicions that he's hiding something. As Hans tells her the truth about his work situation, the camera switches to an extremely tight close-up of Sullavan's face. What is remarkable is that Montgomery's face is shoved to the side of the frame so that the audience has an unobstructed view of Sullavan's piquant and expressive face as she undergoes feelings ranging from nagging doubt to unabashed joy.

The entire Kleinholz family, out on their Sunday drive, see the two kissing. Much to Hans' surprise, Kleinholz does not fire him the following day. However, after Marie makes insulting comments about Lammchen, Hans reveals the truth and quits. After weeks of unemployment, he receives a letter from his stepmother Mia in Berlin. She offers them a place to live as well as a job in a prestigious clothing store. Mia (Catherine Doucet) lives with her lover, Holger Jachman, in a well-furnished and spacious apartment. From the beginning, the hard-nosed, financially driven Mia insists they will pay her 100 marks in monthly rent and perform as servants during her "parties."

Despite his jovial demeanor, Jachman (Alan Hale) has a shady reputation. He develops a not-so-innocent interest in Lammchen, who fends him off by revealing her pregnancy.

Through Jachman's influence, Hans gets work as a salesman. He is befriended by Heilbutt (G.P. Huntley), the head salesman. With Hans' subsequent admission of being fond of Heilbutt (a self-proclaimed nudist), there is an element of homoerotic attraction between them. Heilbutt later resigns in protest over the store's new policy of salary based on the percentage of sales.

Through a colleague, Hans learns the true nature of Mia's "parties" in which Mia and Jachman provide young women for lonely, rich men. Enraged, Hans returns to the apartment and breaks the breakfast dishes in front of the party guests. It looks like Hans has finally acquired a backbone, but he stops in mid-tantrum and recoils in shame. That he wimps out illustrates precisely why movie audiences didn't embrace this character. In the era of virile, rugged leading men like Gable and Cagney, Montgomery the Wimp just wouldn't do. Hans takes Lammchen away from the apartment.

A kindly furniture hauler, Puttbreese (Christian Rub), offers a place to live in his carriage house. Their troubles continue when Hans is fired after insulting a vain movie actor (Alan Mowbray). In the next scene, we are treated to the sight of Lammchen in a beautiful, shimmery dress. Jachman had unexpectedly appeared with the dress and an invitation for the couple to dine with him. Arriving home, Hans is awestruck by the sight of Lammchen's overpowering and radiant vision of a divine angel bathed in heavenly light.

When Lammchen goes into labor, Puttbreese leaves to find a doctor. Meanwhile, Hans is minimally involved in a street riot. He is ashamed to realize how far he has fallen. When he arrives home, Puttbreese informs him that Lammchen has given birth. Upon seeing them, Hans undergoes a spiritual transformation and vows to do better as a provider. In a lovely moment, beautifully underplayed by Sullavan, Lammchen tells Hans, "We created life, so why be afraid of it?" With the unexpected arrival of Heilbutt, who offers Hans a job in Amsterdam, the couple have triumphed over the fickle forces of life.

The film was released at the end of May. Despite advertising taglines like "The Greatest Universal Picture since *All Quiet on the Western Front*," the film was not the success that Universal had hoped. As feared, audiences were not in the mood to be reminded of their own struggles. What didn't help was that *Little Man, What Now?* was included in the Legion of Decency Council of the archdiocese of Chicago's list of condemned films because the *woman* had not suffered enough to appease the censors.

Ditzen avoided seeing the film. He was distressed when Universal sent movie stills after the New York premiere. He found them "disgusting. Lammchen in an evening gown in the attic, Lammchen with a new dress in every scene—and no scene which would give you the slightest idea of the social circumstances of the unemployed."[21] It was reported that Hitler's only complaint was that the film was made by a Jewish producer.

Despite its disappointing box office returns, the film fared well critically, and Sullavan earned glowing notices. *Time* magazine judged the film as "not one of Director Borzage's best pictures." The critic continued, "Sullavan's brilliant acting in *Only Yesterday* made her Hollywood's brightest prospect since Katharine Hepburn" and opined that she "makes *Little Man, What Now?* her picture." *Photoplay* magazine noted, "Director Frank Borzage achieved his masterpiece" and that "the production is another triumph for Margaret Sullavan [as] she surpasses the heights of her performance in *Only Yesterday*." The *Baltimore Sun* was equally impressed:

> In her first picture, *Only Yesterday*, Margaret Sullavan was catapulted to fame with a suddenness that has few parallels in screen history. Her second film, *Little Man, What Now?*, serves to confirm the verdict of the public, and to establish her firmly among the leading ladies of the screen…. She plays the courageous young wife with deep feeling and a natural eagerness, and her frank simplicity is a talisman which should carry her a long way on this all too artificial screen of ours.

A dissenting voice, the *Hollywood Reporter* opined, "Margaret Sullavan is very lovely and completely good, but for a gal who rose to sensational stardom in her first picture, her role is hardly big enough for her." The critic missed the point. Although it could be argued that her character is secondary, Sullavan holds the film together and keeps it from settling into a pathetic display of pathos. She plays with a freshness and naturalness that make her performance as relevant today as it was 80 years ago. What is even more astonishing is the frank manner she exudes healthy sexuality. Instead of a "tainted" woman who must pay the price through suffering, Lammchen is a normal woman who is comfortable with her pregnancy. There is a brief scene, when the couple are in bed, in which Sullavan gives a fleeting look of sexual anticipation that is startling. Sullavan's radiant appearance and insightful performance elevate this film into something special. Without her, *Little Man, What Now?* would be considerably more depressing than it sometimes is.

The other cast members give noteworthy performances fully keeping with the film's theme. Pleasure can be derived especially from Hale, who gives the best supporting performance. Montgomery gives a fine performance as long as he is not heavy-handed. There are moments when the actor is too morose and the viewer quickly loses patience. Fortunately, these scenes are brief. Perhaps Borzage was cognizant of the actor's negative impact as many of these scenes are immediately followed by Sullavan's welcome reappearances. As a couple, Sullavan and Montgomery are marvelously suited for each other—a tribute to their acting abilities.

Little Man, What Now? is a dated film, although it is filled with genuine pathos and charm courtesy of Borzage's assured handling of the material. He imbues his film with an abundance of symbolism in reference to spirituality and the power of redemption. As is the case with so many of his films, the delight of *Little Man, What Now?* lies in the eye of the beholder as each person takes something different away. Borzage successfully illuminates the tender qualities of hope and optimism that permeates throughout the couple's spiritual journey. He is less successful in depicting the economic and societal hardships. Here, the political and social unrest are merely a background device. He was more successful in merging the themes of human spirituality and life's tumultuousness in *Three Comrades* and *The Mortal Storm*.

Comparisons between this film and D.W. Griffith's *Isn't Life Wonderful?* (1924) have been made over the years. Griffith's film, however, lacks the subtlety exhibited by Borzage and is overly melodramatic. A better case can be made for *Man's Castle* as both films deal with a couple fighting against oppression and the hero's redemption by the pregnant heroine. While *Man's Castle* is rooted in Depression-era America, *Little Man, What Now?*, despite its German locale, can be regarded as a film with universal appeal. That neither Sullavan nor Montgomery speak with a trace of an accent is due to Borzage's vision of his actors representing the plights of couples all over the world.

In 1967, the film was remade as *Kleiner Mann, Was Nun?*, a three-part television miniseries, in East Germany. Another television version was presented in West Germany in 1973. The following year, Peter Zadek, director of the 1973 version, adapted the novel as a musical for the German stage.

For many years, *Little Man, What Now?* was a forgotten film due to its designation as a blacklisted film courtesy of the Breen Code. It was not until Borzage's neglected films were revived in the 1970s and 1980s that *Little Man, What Now?* was recognized as a film worthy of reevaluation. *Little Man, What Now?* is *not* an anti–Nazi film. This misperception first appeared in Michael Burrows' book *Patricia Neal and Margaret Sullavan* and perpetuated by Steven Scheuer's 1981 book *Movies on TV*. Scheuer called the film "the earliest of all Hollywood's anti–Nazi films."[22] This claim has persisted, despite the fact that there are no incidents that depict the rise of Nazism. There are strong references to Communism, but nothing to support the claim of being anti–Nazi.

Borzage proved he was Sullavan's ideal director and she was his Muse. In the films he made with her, Borzage created the memorable Margaret Sullavan performances that film historians and moviegoers have cherished to this day. More than anyone else, Frank Borzage secured her lasting legacy.

11

Round Two
with Henry Fonda

*I love to roam around where nobody knows me and where I can do what
I want.*[1]

During the filming of *Little Man, What Now?*, Sullavan sat down with William French of *Motion Picture* magazine. "I have no design or pattern for my life," she said. "I am moved entirely by impulse—living day to day, and loving it."[2] This was more than just a momentary lapse into self-reflection as to another reporter, Sullavan vented her discontent as it related to the confining terms of her contract. She continued to loudly reject fame and stardom as the whole Hollywood atmosphere felt superficial to her.

Universal began lining up more projects for their star. Among those proposed were *Strange Roads* (with Robert Montgomery on loan from MGM), *The Left Bank* and *Night Life of the Gods*. The most anticipated project was *Angel* with John Stahl directing; *Angel* eventually emerged as a Paramount Ernst Lubitsch film with Marlene Dietrich in 1937. As Elizabeth Yeaman reported, "Future plans for Miss Sullavan are always vague because no one seems to know whether she will be on hand for any assignment."[3]

In early April, Sullavan decided that she wanted to take a month's vacation in England. As she explained to interviewer Elza Schallert, she had always yearned to go to England. Having saved enough of her own money, she was finally able to afford a trip abroad and made arrangements. However, at one point, it was reported that she might have to postpone any planned trip in order to begin an unannounced project. She then stopped begging and threatened to "disappear" unless she was permitted to make the trip. It was not long before she reported gleefully, "I just won a battle with the studio and will be on my way in a few days."[4]

At the end of April, Sullavan flew to New York City before embarking on a cruise ship for England. She spent a few days with Jed Harris, who, by this time, was behaving more bizarrely. It was widely reported that Harris went as far as to hire private detectives to follow Sullavan in Hollywood and New York City. Why did Sullavan put up with such erratic and unpredictable behavior? According to Ruth Waterbury of *Photoplay*, Harris fascinated her.

When Sullavan made it to England, she felt free from the pressures of stardom despite the fact that she (along with Mae West and Elisabeth Bergner) was among the favorite film actresses in England. For the most part, she managed the feat of traveling incognito throughout the country. She drove along the coast to towns such as Dover, Rye and Winchelsea. At one point, it is alleged that Sullavan took up with a rugged fisherman and disappeared for a week. Such news did not sit well with Universal executives anxious for her return to filmmaking. She continued to shun reporters, but did consent to an occasional interview, such as the one with Gladys Baker, special correspondent for *Picturegoer* magazine. Sullavan remarked of her career ambition: "I want more than anything in the world to be a really fine actress." She also said, "I like a certain amount of solitude. I'm never too certain what tomorrow will bring. My real self isn't at all like my screen self."[5]

After her vacation, Sullavan made a vow to return to England as often she could. Back in New York City, she made an unexpected telephone call to Day Tuttle, director of the Westchester Playhouse in Mt. Kisco. Not ready to return to Hollywood, she was anxious to act in a play, even for one week. Realizing the gold mine of publicity, Tuttle readily agreed to let her perform with the troupe. It was quickly decided that she would star in *Coquette* during the week of July 2. Among her co-stars were former University Players Joshua Logan, Myron McCormick and, appearing as her lover Michael, Henry Fonda.

Fonda was hired by the Playhouse founders, Tuttle and Richard Skinner, not as an actor, but as a set designer for the 1933 summer season. During the course of that season, Fonda secured small acting roles in some of the productions. According to Howard Teichmann, Sullavan had also performed with the Playhouse that summer; this claim is disputed by a June 24, 1934, article in the *Ossining* (NY) *Citizen-Register*, which stated that Sullavan had appeared with the troupe in 1932. Despite being an active member of the summer stock troupe, Tuttle remembered a quiet, almost reclusive Fonda during that season. "I think he had been terribly hurt by Sullavan's success [on the stage and in Hollywood]," Tuttle told Teichmann.[6] After the end of that season, Fonda returned to New York without much prospect of success.

Finally, in March 1934, Fonda struck it big in a musical revue called *New Faces*, which was previously presented as *Low and Behold* in Pasadena, California, in May 1933 with Tyrone Power and Eve Arden among the cast members. The Broadway critics liked what they saw and praised Fonda and a young comedienne, Imogene Coca. After 149 performances, it closed in early July. Fonda had already left the show to make a triumphant return to the Westchester Playhouse at the start of the 1934 summer season. Bolstered by fame, Fonda was more than ready for an encounter with his ex-wife. After the previous season of playing small roles, it is not clear how he inherited the male lead in the new play. Reportedly, Sullavan championed Fonda's cause by telling Tuttle, "That ex-husband of mine is really a very good actor."[7]

With its advance publicity ("Movie Actress to Be Starred at Playhouse"), *Coquette* was presented to a full capacity crowd and proved to be a successful venture during its week's run. Two years later, a magazine writer recounted the impact of the play. "The performance of *Coquette* was the most moving I have ever witnessed," she wrote. "Half of the audience was in tears as the play drew to a close. To me the experience was almost devastating."[8] According to the *White Plains Daily Reporter*, "Last night's opening was a triumph on more than one count." As for the leading lady, "Margaret Sullavan was in her element last night as Norma Besant.... Her characterization was vibrant and finely drawn, shrewdly timed and knowing." (Unfortunately, the microfilm copy of the review is so damaged that comments on Fonda's performance are impossible to read.) With an air of excitement of a bona fide movie star in their midst, the play proved to be one of the more memorable theatrical offerings of that summer.

It was a matter of time before the professional admiration between the two exes evolved into more potent expressions of unresolved issues. It all started rather innocently on the Fourth of July. During the summer season, all of the actors lived in a large inn, the Kittle

House. They ate their meals together in the dining room. Tuttle recalled that he and Fonda wanted to celebrate the Fourth of July with fireworks. Tuttle and Fonda had built a trough out of old scenery and set it on the lower terrace as the place to launch the rockets. The two men decided to collect money for the fireworks. Fonda went around with his hat, collecting money from all those in the dining room. He approached Sullavan and held out his hat. Surprisingly, she shook her head. Thinking that she was teasing him, he moved in closer and held the hat out. Again, she shook her head. At this, Fonda loudly asked if she was not going to contribute any money. Refusing to acknowledge him, Sullavan turned her attention toward her salad.

As Fonda continued to make his way around the dining room, Tuttle remembered, "You could see that he was smoldering." By the time he reached actor Ross Alexander, Fonda was overheard saying in an exasperated tone, "And with the money some people are making." Sullavan rose from her chair, picked up a goblet of ice water (Sullavan and Alexander always insisted that it was a pitcher) and poured it over his head. Fonda played the scene for laughs as he used some napkins to wipe his face. As he exited the dining room, everybody roared with laughter—except for Sullavan, who calmly finished her meal.

During that evening's performance, Tuttle recollected, "Their love scenes were perfect; off stage they didn't speak."[9] The story ends there in Fonda's autobiography; Quirk continued the story. As to be expected, their unsettled feelings for each other quickly turned to renewed interest and eventually passion. A few troupe members noticed that the two were frequently spending more time alone walking through the woods. Alexander reportedly saw Sullavan leaving Fonda's bedroom in the early hours of the morning. It was obvious to many that the exes were again enjoying each other's company.

One night, according to sources close to the couple, Sullavan and Fonda were alone in the woods. Feeling bold, Fonda talked incessantly about his newfound success. Unable to resist cutting him down to size, Sullavan snidely referred to *New Faces* as a small-time revue. Fonda shot back with a sarcastic reply of his own regarding her making silly faces for the movies. Then, he struck a nerve with the following statement: "I understand the makeup department had a hell of a time making your tiny little chinless face look big enough for the camera." Stung by this unexpected attack, Sullavan slapped Fonda across the face. He only grinned and held her tighter. In the heat of the moment, it is heavily implied by Quirk that the two made love in the middle of the woods. "That night, Fonda wasn't tame—for once in his life," Sullavan reportedly told Hedda Hopper.[10]

When the play ended its week's run on July 7, Sullavan returned to New York before departing to Hollywood to begin work on her next picture. Once again, Fonda was left behind to fend for himself. This time, he was not without hope that, eventually, they would get back together again.

12

Wyler's Pet Peeve

We were constantly fighting over the interpretation of her part, over everything. We didn't get along at all. She had a mind of her own and so did I.[1]—William Wyler

Prior to her trip to England, Sullavan remarked, "I'm a normal woman and eventually will want a husband, home and children."[2] In another interview, she threw out a tantalizing teaser that she would be married before finishing her next production, *The Good Fairy*. Hollywood insiders assumed it would be Jed Harris; others thought of John McCormick, whom she'd been seeing a lot of. She not only carried out her promise, but she chose the most unlikely candidate.

The Good Fairy was originally presented by Ferenc Molnar as *A jó tündér*, in Budapest in 1930. Playwright Jane Hilton translated it into English and *The Good Fairy* was presented on Broadway in October 1931. Helen Hayes played Lu, the kind-hearted gold digger, for 151 performances. It was later reprised for an additional 68 performances with Ada May (Hayes had returned to Hollywood).

Junior promoted *The Good Fairy* as a major Margaret Sullavan production, which would offset the disappointing grosses of her last film. Screenwriter Preston Sturges spent months modifying the risqué play to avoid offending the censors. Retaining little of the play's material, he made significant changes. The laundered version had a new opening sequence along with a sweet strain of youthful optimism in place of the play's cynical tone. The leading female character, now an innocent orphan, was tailored to highlight Sullavan's endearing qualities. William Wyler, a 32-year-old director at Universal, was chosen to helm the production. "[*The Good Fairy* was] one of the first important films I was making at Universal," Wyler recalled. "Maggie was a star and I was a very young apprentice director just starting, so for me it was quite a step."[3]

Wyler was born on July 1, 1902, in Mülhausen, Alsace, within the German Empire (located along the eastern border of France). His father Leopold was Swiss and his mother Melanie was of German descent. Leopold was first a traveling salesman and later a successful haberdashery businessman. As a child, Wyler was "something of a hellraiser."[4] After World War I, Wyler worked briefly as a shirt salesman in Paris before realizing he would not make it in the clothing business. His mother contacted a distant cousin, Carl Laemmle, Sr., in the U.S. Laemmle hired Wyler to work at Universal in New York in 1921 at $25 a week. After a few years, Wyler dreamed of being a director in Hollywood. He arrived in Hollywood in 1923 and worked several jobs, including laborer, second assistant editor and assistant director at Universal. He eventually became the youngest director on the lot. In 1928, Wyler became a naturalized United States citizen. He finally achieved notable success directing such films as *A House Divided* (1931) and *Counsellor-at-Law* (1933).

In regards to *The Good Fairy*, Wyler recalled, "The picture was important to me.... I was doing one of Universal's important pictures. The story appealed to me. Preston had written a very good script, and the other actors were marvelous." Also cast were such stalwart actors as Herbert Marshall, Frank Morgan, Reginald Owen, Eric Blore and Alan Hale—an impressive line-up of comedic performers. Wyler also respected Sullavan: "She was a good actress. She had a marvelous voice, something very peculiar in the voice that was very attractive."[5] With her reputation for erratic behavior on the set, Sullavan had met her match in Wyler who had a feisty temperament of his own.

Production began on September 3, 1934; *The Good Fairy* was scheduled for a seven-week shoot. Problems arose immediately, because Sullavan disliked the script. Finding many of her lines unspeakable, she insisted on daily rewrites. Wyler said, "I remember one incident—and there she was probably right. She was this sweet, innocent girl out of the orphanage coming into this fancy restaurant and saying, 'Oh, isn't this wonderful.' She said, 'I'm not going to say that another time.'"[6]

Another reason for the delay was Wyler's directorial technique: He indulged in endless retakes in order to achieve his perception of perfection on the screen. This rubbed Sullavan the wrong way. Perhaps it was his desperation to prove himself in comedy that put her on edge. Whatever it was, she made his life miserable. Frieda Rosenblatt, Wyler's script girl, recalled that Sullavan "did spiteful things to get her way. If she was tired and wanted to go home and Willy had one more scene to do, she would smear the makeup on her face. That would mean that everything had to stop so she could be made up again. Which might take hours. So they couldn't shoot."[7]

Another obstacle was that the unfinished script had not been formally approved by the Hays Office as the original draft was somewhat spicy. Junior asked Sturges to rewrite the script several times after filming began. One objectionable scene was Konrad's attempted seduction of Luisa in his apartment. As rewritten, the scene emerged as amusing, yet sweet. Sturges spent an additional 13 weeks fixing the script.

The biggest disruption was Sullavan's clashes with Wyler. She was constantly testing Wyler to see how far she could go. This often resulted in shouting matches. According to Marshall, "It was the case of the irresistible force meeting the immovable object."[8] Their fights increased in intensity as filming progressed. As Wyler reflected, "I knew more about pictures than she did."[9] One day, Wyler finally had enough and berated her in front of the cast and crew:

> Now you listen to me. You've disrupted this company, you've made this picture—don't interrupt!—last 12 weeks when the shooting schedule was seven and you've all but demoralized me ... now this is the end. You're going to enter left, stand on that chalk mark, and twist that vicious pan of yours into the semblance of a human face and drench this scene in pathos. And you're not going to underplay or suffer silently by gritting your teeth. You're going to cry—get it? Bawl! And like it![10]

With those words ringing in her ears, Sullavan turned and walked off the set (reportedly for the twenty-second time). The executives pressured Wyler to wrap up filming. Eventually, the hostile environment took its toll on Wyler and his star. Watching the daily rushes, Wyler noticed something wrong with Sullavan's appearance. He recalled the following conversation with cameraman Norbert Brodine,

> "The girl looks terrible, what's the matter?" Wyler asked.
> "You two had a fight," Brodine replied.
> "What has that to do with it?"
> "Each time you have a fight with her and she's tense or unhappy, she looks terrible. I can put all the lights on her, she won't look good."[11]

So what did the beleaguered director do? To salvage the situation, he asked her out for dinner. Surprisingly, she accepted. The evening went well and eventually they began to enjoy each other's company.

From then on, things proceeded smoothly and Sullavan was much more cooperative. Soon the lovebirds become openly intimate on the set among hooting and hollering from the crew. It was not long before Wyler fell deeply in love with Sullavan and began to contemplate marriage. A proposal of sorts came about one night when the two were in the projection room watching rushes of the wedding scene. "Do you think," he whispered breathlessly, "there is any law against a star marrying her director?"

Sullavan leaned in closer and squeezed his arm. "I'll tell you tomorrow," she whispered.

After a sleepless night, Wyler sought Sturges' advice the following day. "What do you think of my marrying Maggie?"

"Well, she's not marrying you for your money," Sturges responded, pointing out Sullavan's greater earning power.

That night, Sullavan arrived with her answer. "There is no law against an actress marrying her director. I looked it up." They made secret wedding plans to avoid the onslaught of publicity. The couple intended to circumvent California's mandatory three-day waiting period by eloping to Yuma, Arizona. No one, except their closest intimates, knew of their plans. Imagine their surprise when Jed Harris appeared on the set one day. Frieda Rosenblatt recalled, "I don't know what he knew. But he was there. He took Maggie aside and pleaded with her to marry him right there."[12] Troubled by this, Wyler later surmised, "She desperately wanted to get away from him…. Trying to get away from Jed Harris contributed to the fact that she married me."[13]

On November 25, Harris made one more appeal. Sullavan and Wyler went to Harris' hotel, but it was Sullavan who spoke to Harris alone. After what felt like forever, Sullavan appeared. She calmly said, "Okay, let's go," and that was the end of the Harris situation—for now.[14]

Wyler charted a DC-3 to fly the couple, along with his lawyer, to Yuma, over the California-Arizona border. "The justice of the peace was in his slippers and bathrobe," Wyler recounted, "and he stood there and married us with the radio blaring behind him. He had to get his wife to witness. She was in the bedroom and couldn't come out, so he handed her the papers to sign under the door. It was terrible."[15] After the ceremony, the newlyweds ate at a local coffee shop. The waitress recognized Sullavan and alerted the local newspaper. The couple boarded the plane and headed back to Hollywood. The pilot asked in jest, "Where do we go—Reno?" Reflecting on that remark, Wyler joked, "It was a good suggestion. After that wedding, we should have gone straight up there."

The newlyweds reported to Universal on Monday morning. "Everyone was astonished," Wyler recalled. "Here we had been fighting like cats and dogs and the next thing you know we're married. I was crazy about her."[16]

By Monday evening, newspapers across the nation ran coverage of the elopement. Under a picture, one caption read, "Margaret Sullavan, cinema star, and William Wyler, her director, radiate happiness."[17] According to Robbin Coons, "William Wyler, as befits bridegrooms, referred questions about their romance to his bride. Miss Sullavan, as befits Miss Sullavan, had little to say." What she did say sent all of the columnists back to their typewriters: "We've been in love more than a year. The reason we said nothing about it was that we didn't want ourselves continually talked about and written about as going together."[18] Little did Coons realize that the mischievous bride was playing with him.

Back on the set, the newlyweds basked in the afterglow of wedded bliss and worked in harmony. Complaints arose that Wyler was preoccupied with reshooting Sullavan's close-ups (indeed, Sullavan is afforded some of the loveliest close-ups of her early films). The executives were also dissatisfied with Sturges' "lack of contribution" to the film, so he was fired three weeks prior to completion. (A comic genius like Sturges would not be down for long. Five years later, Sturges gained prominence at Paramount as a successful screen-writer and director with *The Great McGinty*.)

The Good Fairy wrapped on December 17. During the post-production, Wyler was still not off the hook. Long dissatisfied with his career at Universal, he asked for his release. "One of the reasons I had left Universal was to become a bigger director ... and become as big as Maggie," he admitted.[19] According to one source, the studio agreed to his request and terminated his services. However, *Daily Variety* reported that Universal dropped Wyler because they were unhappy with the costly delays due to the constant retakes. Whatever the situation may have been, Wyler was out of a job with no plans for the near future. So he made plans for an European honeymoon.

Universal had other ideas for Sullavan's time and she put up a widely publicized fuss. The *Reno Gazette* reported,

> Margaret Sullavan again is engaged in her regular pre-picture argument with Universal executives.... This time it's over her honeymoon. The actress and her new hubby, William Wyler, wanted to leave immediately on a European honeymoon. Studio officials want her to make another picture first. So the battle is on—with the odds in favor of Miss Sullavan.[20]

As expected, Sullavan emerged victorious and the couple proceeded with their plans. They agreed to attend the *Good Fairy* premiere at Radio City Music Hall in New York on January 31, 1935. This was the first time a film had been booked for the theater sight unseen. It was also one of the rare occasions in which Sullavan attended the opening of one of her films. The original theatrical trailer proclaimed the film as "a major screen event with the exquisite star of *Only Yesterday* and *Little Man, What Now?* A new Sullavan picture!"

The film opens at a playground with a group of young girls chanting and exercising. "Once more, girls, and with more life, more freedom!" encourages an older woman. The camera pans back and a set of bars becomes visible. We are at the Municipal Orphanage for Girls in Budapest. Thus begins this beguiling film replete with Sturges' visual and verbal wit.

Luisa (Sullavan) is chosen by Maurice Schlapkohl (Alan Hale), the owner of the largest movie theater, to be an usherette; among the young ladies he inspects is Ann Miller in a bit. Luisa promises Dr. Schultz (Beulah Bondi) that she will perform her good deed every day outside in the world.

Luisa makes the acquaintance of Detlaff (Reginald Owen), a cantankerous waiter. Leaving the theater, Luisa is approached by an aggressive masher (Cesar Romero). To escape his unwanted attentions, Luisa introduces Detlaff as her husband. Learning that she has just come out of an orphan asylum (not an insane asylum as he feared), Detlaff invites her to an exclusive party at a swanky hotel the next evening.

In the party scene, Sullavan is afforded some lovely close-ups which emphasize her endearing qualities. Luisa attracts the attentions of Konrad (Frank Morgan), president of the South American Meat Packing Company, Inc. Konrad is enchanted by the guileless, innocent Luisa and attempts to seduce her. (With Morgan's befuddled, harmless demeanor, this situation is much funnier and far less sinister than Adolphe Menjou's similar attempted seduction in Universal's 1947 remake *I'll Be Yours*.) The inconveniently present Detlaff, protective of Luisa, sets up a hilarious scene where Konrad is continually frustrated in his awkward efforts at seduction. To escape his increasingly romantic overtures, Luisa tells Konrad that she is married. Undeterred, Konrad offers to make her "husband" rich. Faced with the prospect of performing a good deed, Luisa comes up with the name from a phonebook of a lawyer, Dr. Max Sporum.

The next day, Konrad visits the bearded, impoverished lawyer (Herbert Marshall) and offers him a non-existent position. Although skeptical at first, Sporum accepts the position and is encouraged to refurnish his office. Curious about the recipient of her good deed, Luisa visits Sporum in his newly refurbished office. She is tempted to tell him the truth, but, after seeing how his life has been transformed, she doesn't have the heart.

With Luisa's encouragement, Max buys a new sports car and a new suit, and shaves his beard. Luisa is attracted to the more youthful-looking and handsome lawyer. Finding himself likewise interested in Luisa, Max becomes upset when he assumes that she is another man's mistress after she tells him that she must meet Konrad in his hotel room that night.

Detlaff tries to prevent Luisa from meeting Konrad, but Luisa is determined to follow through. Detlaff will not be dissuaded and vows to protect her from a calamity. While en route, Luisa stops to telephone Max. Every Sullavan film has a definitive Margaret Sullavan moment and this particular scene highlights her "clarity of vision" quality. This scene is a tricky one and could have easily become too sudsy, but Sullavan handles it faultlessly. The halting, husky voice on the verge of choking sobs, the plaintive, haunted look in her eyes, the absolute sincerity and conviction of her acting—these are the qualities that made her such an endearing personality on the screen and stage. This scene easily knocks the socks off of Luise Rainer's acclaimed, but overly lachrymose, telephone scene from *The Great Ziegfeld*.

In his hotel room, Konrad pursues Luisa, but quickly falters. In a rambling, sweetly awkward speech, Konrad reveals that he is desperate to have her in marriage. The room suddenly goes dark and Detlaff hits Konrad and carries Luisa out of the hotel. Konrad goes to Sporum's office to inform him of his "wife's" unfaithfulness. As Max tells Konrad that he has no wife, Luisa and Detlaff arrive. Luisa fabricates another story to protect Max's newfound wealth, but is reduced to tears when faced with the prospect of repeating her improbable tale. Max holds her in his arms as she tearfully reveals the whole truth behind her role as his "Good Fairy." The film concludes with a lovely, soft-focus close-up of the radiant Luisa at her wedding.

The film was not the smash hit the studio expected. Critical reviews were mixed for the film and its star, even though Sullavan won some of her best notices to date. Among the New York critics who found fault was *The New York Times*: "When it is hitting its stride, the film … is so priceless that it arouses in one the impertinent regret that it is not the perfect fantastic comedy which it might have been…. Although Miss Sullavan is not the expert comedienne that her role demands, she is frequently able to persuade us that she is at home in a part for which she is temperamentally unfitted." The *New York Daily Mirror* opined that the film "proves Miss Sullavan to be as fetching a comedienne as she is an impressive dramatic actress."

Upon the film's general release in mid–February, the nation's critics followed the pattern set by New York. The *Boston Globe* critic had high praise:

> The results—thanks to acting such as seldom graces the cinema—are a notable achievement that should rank the film as one of the ranking productions of 1935 … Miss Margaret Sullavan brings a fluttery lovableness that is fairly breathtaking. No more perfect role could have been found for Miss Sullavan.

Seen today, this sparkling comic gem is still a delight. It may be light on plot, but its clever situations and bright lines energize it. Under Wyler's expert guidance, the film is breathlessly paced, which is precisely the right method to elevate the slight plot. *The Good Fairy* stands apart as a unexpected glittering specimen in Wyler's career, which was notable for trenchant dramas such as *The Little Foxes* (1941) and *The Heiress* (1949). The script is pricelessly funny as situations spin deliriously out of control. One is surprised and delighted by Sturges' inspired genius.

The cast is sheer perfection. Marshall, who could be heavy-handed, is in fine comedic form here. The only fault is there are moments when the obvious age difference between Sullavan and Marshall suggests paternal rather than romantic feelings. Owen is splendid, as are Hale and Bondi. The scene-stealer of the film is Morgan. He is alternately hilariously funny and surprisingly touching in his quest for marriage and family. His comic interplay with Owen is worth the price of admission.

As the orphan, Sullavan is delightful. Although made to look plainer than usual, she is still enchanting and endearing. Her voice has a huskier quality, but it is well in tune with her character. One is hard-pressed to imagine any other actress navigating through the potentially sticky role; Janet Gaynor comes the closest, but she would have destroyed the delicate pathos of the telephone scene. Film historian David Shipman had effusive praise for this performance: "In no other film … does she so well demonstrate her ability to find that point at which she could express her own personality or star quality while still offering maximum fidelity both to the script and the rules of human behaviours."[21] John DiLeo was impressed enough to include her performance in his book *100 Great Film Performances You Should Remember—But Probably Don't*. "The undimmed radiance of her Luisa Ginglebusher is a fitting legacy; Sullavan was a good fairy to anyone who loves the movies."[22]

The Good Fairy was remade by Universal in 1947 as *I'll Be Yours* with Deanna Durbin, Tom Drake, William Bendix and Adolphe Menjou in the Sullavan-Marshall-Owen-Morgan roles. It is consistently enjoyable, particularly for Durbin fans since she is given songs to sing. Whereas the original was a screwball comedy, *I'll Be Yours* is more of a sentimental romantic comedy not unlike the romcom of today. The only sour note in all of this pleasantness is Menjou. With his jaded roué looks and mannerisms, he comes across as a creepy old man and the effect is unnerving.

Sturges utilized his screenplay as the basis for a musical, *Make a Wish*, which premiered on Broadway in April 1951 and featured Nanette Fabray and Melville Cooper. It was considered "Sturges past his prime" and lasted 102 performances. In 1956, *Hallmark Hall of Fame* presented *The Good Fairy* on television with Julie Harris, Walter Slezak and Cyril Ritchard. The final version was televised in West Germany as *Die Fee* in 1969.

∼∼∼

While in New York, Sullavan and Wyler went to see her former husband Fonda in the play *The Farmer Takes a Wife*, which provided Fonda with his dramatic Broadway success. Sullavan cajoled her husband into visiting Fonda backstage after the show. As Wyler recalled, "I'm afraid I didn't take it very gracefully.… I was all prepared to hate this former husband, but Fonda turned out to be charming, delightful and attractive." Wyler failed to understand why Sullavan ended her first marriage and it stoked the flames of his own insecurities. In early February, the Wylers sailed for London on the *Ile de France*. In London, they spent time with Wyler's older brother, Robert. Outside their hotel, Sullavan was mobbed by adoring fans. Wyler recounted,

A crowd wanting to see her and get autographs got us separated. I stood and waited for her to get through. One girl felt sorry for me and finally came over and stuck out her scrapbook and pencil. "Here, you, too," she said. I said, "Thank you, very much" and signed "Mr. Sullavan."[23]

The couple traveled from Paris to Wyler's hometown, Mülhausen, before skiing in Switzerland. After Vienna, Wyler took her to Munich to meet some of his relatives, Siegfried Laemmle (brother of Carl, Sr.) and his son Walter Laemmle.

Since Hitler came into power in 1933, the situation had grown worse for those of Jewish faith. Walter related an incident which emphasized their plight. Wyler and Sullavan were staying at the luxurious Regina Palace Hotel. "It was too conspicuous for me to be seen there. A Jew stayed out of places like that even by then. But Willy called us to come see him." The party ate downstairs in the bar, where there was a dance floor. Wyler asked his cousin to dance with his wife. Still fearful, Walter stated that he was Jewish. Not understanding the gravity of the situation, Wyler responded, "Oh, what the hell, you can dance." As Walter recalled, "I danced with Margaret for maybe two minutes. I said to her, 'I feel uncomfortable.'" She understood and they sat back down at the table. "Everything was already under the Nazis," Walter remembered, "and I didn't want to have any difficulties."[24]

Walter's parents fled to the United States weeks before the Nazis rounded up the Jews. After a brief time in Dachau concentration camp, Walter emigrated to the U.S. in December 1938. He was the last member of his father's family to escape the Holocaust.

The Wylers traveled next to Southern France before heading back to the U.S. on the ocean liner *Rex* in late April. Universal had recently finalized an agreement to loan Sullavan to Paramount for the Civil War drama *So Red the Rose*. In exchange, Paramount loaned Carole Lombard to Universal for *Love Before Breakfast*. *So Red the Rose* was scheduled to begin in early May, so the honeymoon was cut short. This was good timing as Wyler had spent an astonishing $10,000; he reflected, "I came back broke."[25] Even though Sullavan had significantly more money, Wyler was too proud to let her pay for any part of their honeymoon. However, as he soon learned, this was the least of his concerns. For the couple, the honeymoon was over in more ways than one.

13

Shades of Scarlett

No Civil War picture ever made a nickel.[1]—Irving Thalberg

While Sullavan was wrapping up her European honeymoon, Louella Parsons reported,

Paramount is viewing with uneasy eye the advent of Margaret Sullavan as a star in King Vidor's first [film for Paramount], *So Red the Rose*. Of Miss Sullavan's ability the studio has no doubt, but during her two years at Universal, from which lot she is being borrowed, she proved to be a difficult person to handle.[2]

Paramount had high expectations for their screen adaptation of Stark Young's novel *So Red the Rose*. Drawing upon his family's experiences in Mississippi, Young had written an emotional account of the long-cherished pre–Civil War days of gracious Southern living. Young later admitted he was not interested in telling a story of the war; rather, he was illuminating the worldview of the Southern aristocracy. "I want it to be a monument in the South of a certain quality of society that was there."[3] The novel was a great success and ranked third among the best-selling fiction books of 1934. It enjoyed widespread popularity for a couple of years until Margaret Mitchell's phenomenally popular *Gone with the Wind* eclipsed its success. Today, *So Red the Rose* is generally regarded by literary scholars as Young's finest and most successful work.

King Vidor, who wanted to make the film as soon as the property was available, was the ideal director to handle such a prestigious project. A director since 1913, he had notable success with such memorable films as *The Big Parade* (1925), *The Crowd* (1928) and *The Champ* (1931). With a budget set at $1 million, Vidor was given free rein in bringing Young's novel to the screen.

In the finished screenplay, historical accuracy was emphasized with information contributed by the United Daughters of the Confederacy. Faithfulness to the book, however, was not: The screenplay differed greatly from its source. The new, sentimental, romanticized theme appealed to Vidor and he felt that "we got a very good film out of it."

For the role of the headstrong daughter Vallette, Vidor wanted Sullavan, because "she was one of my favorite actresses."[4] Paramount approved the casting, made the necessary arrangements, and held its breath.

"When King Vidor invited me to Paramount to see him about the leading part,": Sullavan recalled, "I soon discovered that my awful reputation had preceded me. He was so polite and condescending that I suspected he considered me hard to handle. And just to be different, I agreed to everything he said."[5]

With location shooting at Malibu Lake, near Sherwood Forest, the studio spent a couple of weeks looking for an appropriate lodging for Sullavan. To their surprise, Sullavan insisted she would be happier in a tent. According to Sullavan, "I'm as used to roughing it as any person in Hollywood and I generally make my summer vacations as primitive as possible."[6]

By late May, Sullavan had reported for location filming. Her co-stars included Randolph Scott, Pauline Lord and Walter Connolly. It was Lord who proved to be a thorn in Paramount's side. Having read the completed script, she decided her part was unsatisfactory and walked off the picture. Janet Beecher was brought in and the Lord scenes were reshot.

Sullavan told James Fisher of *Screenland* magazine, "I like [my part]—I think it's swell! It's as exacting and subtle as any I have played." As she explained,

> It is really an interpretation of a composite characters—a young woman who is meant to represent all the coquetry, the romance and the spirit of self-sacrifice which stamped the personality of every young woman of the South at the time of the Civil War. At least that is the significance of the characterization as Mr. Vidor hopes to bring it to the screen. I hope I shan't disappoint him![7]

She didn't. Years later, Vidor told Brooke Hayward, "I was just thrilled with her. I think I would have done any picture if she was going to be ii it."[8]

Sullavan enjoyed her experience on location. "I am having so much fun," she told the wardrobe women. "It's so far away from everything that I can be just as dirty and comfortable as I wish and nobody near to stare at me."[9] On the set, Vidor told an interviewer, "You expect the worst and when your actors turn out to be excellent players with an understanding of the parts, you experience a beautiful thrill…. And then you discover with increasing surprise that Margaret Sullavan really likes the role she has been given, that the story is coming along and that the production will balance the budget."[10]

The director took advantage of an unusual practice of engaging the cast in rehearsals: "It was an opportunity for the actors to have a chance to free their characterizations and a chance for me to talk to them at length about their parts…. It was just like a stage play."[11]

This practice did have its unforeseen consequences as Sullavan memorized the entire script and knew the others' parts better than they did. As a result, she engaged in the annoying habit of telling others how to play their roles. This did not go over well with some of the more experienced actors like Connolly. One day he complained to Vidor that, when Vidor was consulting with the cameraman, Sullavan went around telling the other players how they should react to her in their scenes. In talking with her, Vidor found that Sullavan was unapologetic. As Vidor related, her response was terse and to the point: "Look, Vidor, my performance is just as good as those around me, no better and no worse. Some of them are slipping in their Southern accents. I have to bring them up short." In a quiet voice, Vidor said, "Maggie, you're getting paid to *act* in this picture, and I'm getting paid to *direct* it. So, let's cooperate and keep to our separate functions." To his surprise, Sullavan did not push the issue. "She never gave me any trouble after that," Vidor marveled.[12]

One of the actors most intimidated by Sullavan was Scott, who was playing her romantic partner. Although he had been acting in films since 1928, he had been mostly confined to leading roles in low-budget westerns and an occasional supporting role in bigger productions. With his success as Fred Astaire's pal in *Roberta* (1935), Hollywood insiders predicted that his star was on the rise. Appearing opposite Sullavan was a major step in that direction. However, she was often frustrated by his acting in some of their scenes together. At one point, she asked Vidor what his "issue" was. The answer to her query was in reference to the rumors of his sexual orientation given his living arrangement with Cary Grant.

While filming continued back in Hollywood, Sullavan waged her own battles on the home front. To no one's surprise, the couple could not sustain the euphoria of their intense attraction from the *Good Fairy* set. They were too much alike in temperament and creative artistry to survive for long. The biggest bone of contention was the inequality of their professional standing. Sullavan was a big star and Wyler resented living in her shadow. Not long after she reported to Paramount, Wyler received an offer from Fox to direct *The Gay Deception*. This was his first real chance since Universal and he accepted the one-picture deal. Wyler impulsively bought Sullavan a two-carat diamond ring valued at $1100. His euphoria over earning a substantial paycheck ($25,000 for a ten-week shoot), however, quickly evaporated. "With great pride," he recounted, "I came home and showed her my check for $2500 dollars and she showed me hers for 8500 bucks. That's tough. I couldn't buy her gifts that she couldn't buy herself."[13]

The other problem was Wyler's insecurities, which fueled his jealousy. At that time, Henry Fonda was working under contract to Walter Wanger in Hollywood. Having made a huge impact in the screen version of *The Farmer Takes a Wife*, Fonda was now busy with Fox's *Way Down East*. News items such as the following did not help ease Wyler's feelings: "Margaret Sullivan's ex-husband, Henry Fonda, passes William Wyler, her new spouse, every day on the Fox lot.... Then you wander over to Paramount and there's Henry watching his ex-wife, Margaret, work before the cameras."[14] Playwright and screenwriter Lillian Hellman recalled,

> She made him completely miserable—miserable and jealous. She was very nasty to him.... She saw to it that he would be jealous of her. Because there were a great many other gentlemen along the way to tease him with. I don't know what she did to him about them, nor do I care, but he was in great pain about them.[15]

If that wasn't enough, Jed Harris had reappeared in Sullavan's life, still intent on wooing her back. He telephoned constantly from New York and, if Wyler answered, Harris demanded that Wyler get Sullavan.

Despite all the rancor between the two, there were good times. For his 33rd birthday, Sullavan had a brand new Harley Davidson motorcycle delivered to the Fox lot. According to a news article, "Wyler's boyhood wish finally was fulfilled."[16] They enjoyed riding around on it. But the couple's arguments became more frequent and more intense. Wyler admitted, "She castrates a guy—she makes him feel like two cents—and two inches."[17] Their fighting also became physical. According to Quirk, an actor friend (later identified by Jan Herman as Charles Starrett, who appeared with Sullavan in *So Red the Rose*) recalled an incident in which he and his wife could hear the couple violently fighting from down the canyon. The following day, Starrett noted that Wyler's face looked bruised while Sullavan's appeared unharmed.

By now, Hollywood hosts and hostesses left the Wylers off their invitation lists because the marriage was in trouble and no one wanted to be a part of the spectacle. By early June, rumors of an impending separation appeared in gossip columns. Sullavan bristled, "There is absolutely no foundation to this report. We are having our house repainted, and under those conditions, it would be unhealthful and uncomfortable living there."[18] However, it wasn't long before she admitted that they had separated. "It's a shame a happily married couple can't have a little riff once in a while without a divorce rumor cropping up," she snapped.[19] Her new address was listed as the Chateau Elysee.

So Red the Rose was completed by mid–August but it wasn't ready for general distribution until November. In the meantime, Paramount saw to it that interest would be high due to the vast amount of publicity. With the distinguished literary reputation of Young's novel and the drawing power of its leading lady, Paramount expected a box office smash.

Advertisements had tag-lines such as this one: "All the epic beauty, the gallantry of the men and women who fought 'The Lost Cause' in this great, glowing picture of the Old South."

The opening credits depict slaves working on a cotton plantation with a melancholy strain of a spiritual that has a somber quality. The intended effect, perhaps, is to stir the hearts of those who still lamented the lost days of genteel, gracious Southern living. Rather, one is more likely to be offended by the glorification of slavery as it is depicted in this film.

The locale is the stately Portobello plantation in Mississippi in April 1861. Malcolm Bedford (Connolly) and his wife, Sally (Beecher) await the arrival of their son Edward and his college friend. Sally tells Malcom of a strange dream in which the roses were dripping with blood. She is fearful of an impending war, but Malcolm reassures her that no such war will occur.

Vallette (Sullavan) makes her appearance, looking lovely in her white dress. She makes a "grand movie star entrance" through the door. Vallette has a crush on her distant cousin Duncan (Scott). While he may have feelings for her, he views her as a child. Infuriated by Duncan's lack of interest, she vows that she will set her sights on Edward's friend. "I'll twist him around my finger. I'll have him proposing to me in no time." Shades of Scarlett indeed!

That night, Duncan encounters neighbors with news of war. Duncan, a pacifist, cautions them not to get carried away. They will return later for a donation of 20 horses and any human volunteers. The scene ends with a shot of Scott's face, which is void of any emo-

Left to right: **unidentified child, Sullavan, Walter Connolly and Janet Beecher in** *So Red the Rose* **(1935). The failure of this Civil War drama caused many to question David O. Selznick's sanity when he purchased the screen rights to the novel** *Gone with the Wind.*

tions. Up to this point, Scott displays an easygoing, charming presence. With the strain of trying to act in a serious scene, his limited acting range shows and he looks as if he were auditioning for the part of the great "Stoneface," Buster Keaton.

Meanwhile, Vallette is busy fending off an amorous Archie (Robert Cummings), who is in full throttle mode with passion mixed with the excitement of going off to battle.

The volunteer army arrives. Vallette, swept up in the moment, barely conceals her disgust with Duncan's refusal to fight. Edward (Harry Ellerbe), torn by conflicting feelings of duty to the cause and devotion to his mother, waves goodbye to his friend.

The grim realities of war invade the Bedfords' idyllic lives when Vallette receives word that Archie was killed in battle. In her finest moment in this film, Sullavan manages the shifting moods of this scene beautifully as she reads the letter which bears the sad news. Archie's death prompts Edward to leave for the front. In the movie's most touching scene, father and son say their goodbyes. It's a simple moment of a complicated parent-child relationship that speaks volumes.

Yankee soldiers kidnap Malcolm so he can serve as a guide. Enraged and humiliated, he is determined to go fight. He asks his son, Middleton (Dickie Moore), to round up the slaves for some instructions before departing. The following scene unfolds in an offensive manner and is Vidor's first mishandling of the saga. The slaves enter singing "Let My People Go." Addressing them, Malcolm says, "I've never been a bad master to you and you never been bad slaves. What happens to you, what happens to all of us, will depend on the wisdom of the Almighty God." He departs with great fanfare and jubilant singing of "The Walls of Jericho." Everything about this scene feels phony.

The next scene partially eliminates the bad taste left in one's mouth before the picture goes totally haywire. Mrs. Bedford had a vision of Edward lying dead in a nearby battlefield. Searching for him, she is accompanied by Duncan and the family's faithful butler, William (Daniel L. Haynes). Vidor wisely kept the soundtrack music out, leaving only a chirping bird as the background noise to create a haunting effect. With Beecher's heartbreaking, restrained emotions, it is a deeply moving and affecting scene. With the still smoldering battlefield and Edward's body in the wagon, Duncan does a complete about-face and decides to go off to fight. One wishes for some explanation (like Rhett Butler in *Gone with the Wind*) to justify his change of heart, but there is none. With such ambiguity during a crucial moment, it's no wonder that the film starts to completely unravel and all of its earlier promise fades.

News reaches Portobello that Gen. Grant has taken Vicksburg. Excited by the prospect of freedom, the Bedford slaves revolt and loot the place. In the midst of this uprising, a critically wounded Malcolm returns. As he lies dying, Vallette takes Middleton to the slaves' quarters to stop the revolt. Thus begins the most ridiculously offensive scene in the movie. The damage that ensues is irreparable: Walking through the restless crowd, Vallette confronts the leader of the revolt, who informs her that they are no longer slaves. She tries to reason with them, but it's no use. The notion of a woman quelling a potential riot is ludicrous; Sullavan is unconvincing, as if she knew that the scene was bad to begin with. When called a liar, Vallette slaps the offender and rails against him in fury. This silences the crowd, but they are still uneasy. It is not until Middleton reminds Cato (Clarence Muse) that he has not yet made him a rabbit trap, that the leader finally relents. This is enough to bring the multitude back to their senses.

Back at the house, Malcolm succumbs as the slaves arrive singing another spiritual. Mrs. Bedford informs the singing mass they are now free. Based on the jubilant cheering, it's a safe bet that Middleton won't be getting that rabbit trap any time soon. One night,

Valette finds a wounded Yankee soldier on the porch. She has him brought in before he can be found by Confederates led by none other than Duncan. She dresses the Yankee in Edward's uniform, just minutes before Duncan arrives. Duncan spots the boy, and Vallette pleads with him to spare his life. Duncan has been hardened by war and will not listen to her. A fellow officer arrives and the situation looks hopeless for the Yankee. Then Duncan pretends that the boy is Edward. A stronger actor would have made this moment sizzle with dramatic tension. None of this is plausible given Scott's stilted performance. Duncan runs out to join his soldiers, but is immediately captured by the Yankees outside. The family is forced out of their home as it is burned to the ground.

After the war, the family is living in slaves' quarters. Vallette, apparently blessed with Sally's psychic gifts, informs her mother that she hears Duncan's voice and then wanders through the woods to find him. Vallette spots Duncan on the other side of a river. They cross a bridge and collapse in each other's arms. Just as one waits for the inevitable passionate kiss from the lovers, **THE END** flashes on the screen instead. What is especially needed in the final moments is a sense of hope in the Frank Borzagean manner; without it, the film remains a depressing experience.

So Red the Rose premiered at New York City's Radio City Music Hall in early November before its general release. Eileen Creelman of the *New York Sun* reported that Stark Young was delighted with it and that the author found Sullavan "enchanting." "I can't think of anyone else who could have played her," he enthused.[20]

Upon its national release, the film garnered some excellent reviews. According to the *Boston Globe,* "[It's] not only a charmingly told Civil War romance, but it is an impressively acted and handsomely photographed stellar vehicle for the poignant, exquisitely sensitive Margaret Sullavan…. Helen Hayes has deserted pictures but Margaret Sullavan takes her place as the most honestly affecting and authentically emotional star of the screen." Equally enthusiastic was *Picture Play* magazine: "If you have tears, prepare to shed them now. Tears for the heartbreaking beauty of Margaret Sullavan's acting, tears for a poignantly true picture of life in the South." The critic praised the film for "it furthers Miss Sullavan's reputation as one of the screen's greatest."

There were those who were not impressed. The *Washington Post* found fault with the leading lady: "Margaret Sullavan has been better and looked lovelier than she appears in the feminine role of prime importance. She plays the part rather by rote, it seems to these eyes and ears—a little as if the whole matter bored her a trifle."

Despite the mostly positive reviews, the film fared poorly at the box office. (Predictably, it did better in the South than elsewhere.) This led a few pundits to label the film *So Red the Ink.*[21] With this financial failure, Civil War dramas were declared "box office poison" for several years with the only exceptions being *The Little Colonel* and *The Littlest Rebel,* Civil War musical-dramas starring Shirley Temple.

From today's perspective, *So Red the Rose* is a curious film that has as much to commend it as it does to condemn. Among its assets is the beautiful photography. It's a great-looking film and a good example of quality craftsmanship. The first half is replete with poignant and sharply etched scenes depicting the family's trials. During this portion, the film promises to be a memorably moving experience. On this level, the film is at its best as an intimate drama. Furthermore, it is extremely well acted by a skillful cast. Connolly's performance has humor and pathos. Beecher's portrayal is beautifully restrained. A tempestuous characterization is offered by Cummings. The biggest surprise is Haines, who is dignified and warmly sympathetic as William. This character is markedly different from the mostly awkward and stereotypical African-American portrayals.

Sullavan gives an alternately spirited and tender performance as Vallette, an obvious forerunner of Scarlett. In many of her early scenes, she displays a fetching manner that demonstrates why men found her so irresistibly attractive. Near the end, however, she is bland during the mansion-burning sequence. Fortunately, these scenes are short and do not affect the overall impression of her performance. Scott offers the weakest performance. While fine in some of the lighter moments, he is painfully stolid in the heavier scenes. To give the man his due, however, it must be stated that he received some good reviews and was awarded the Southern Cross of Honor by the United Daughters of the Confederacy for his portrayal. The film's fine qualities, however, cannot overcome its faults and one is left with profound disappointment. This is primarily due to Vidor's gross mishandling of the slavery issue.

Due to the film's failure, studio executives decided against purchasing the screen rights to *Gone with the Wind*. However, Mitchell's novel was such an instant bestseller that Selznck reconsidered. A month after the novel's release, Selznick paid $30,000 for the screen rights. Many insiders questioned his sanity. Selznick proved to be a genius.

The widely publicized search for the actress to play Scarlett O'Hara began early in the fall of 1936. Among the early front runners were Tallulah Bankhead, Miriam Hopkins, Constance Bennett, Jean Harlow (yes, you read that right)—and Sullavan, who was a strong candidate for over a year. As late as December 1937, Walter Winchell submitted this report: "The long-time rumors that Margaret Sullavan would get the Scarlett role will be confirmed any day. I understand she definitely has the part."[22]

When asked if she would like the role, Sullavan told Gladys Hall that she would not as she played a similar character in *So Red the Rose*. That was a face-saving gesture as Sullavan was out of the running in early 1938. Vidor theorized that, with the birth of her first child in 1937, Selznick's interest in her cooled. Vidor believed she would have been wonderful as Scarlett.

By early January 1938, there was a new rumor that Sullavan would play Melanie, Scarlett's competition for Ashley Wilkes. That part, in retrospect, seems a perfect match for Sullavan's appealing screen persona and few people wondered why she wasn't considered earlier. Then came this news: "Maggie Sullavan's out as a possibility for the Melanie role in *Gone with the Wind*, because she's baby buggy shopping again."[23] Selznick, anxious to start filming, would not wait for Sullavan to become available.

Comparisons between *So Red the Rose* and Selznick's film are inevitable: the strong-willed heroine, the male protagonist with anti-war sentiments, the destruction of the Southern way of living. Indeed, one wonders if Margaret Mitchell didn't get some of her ideas from the 1935 movie. In the end, *Gone with the Wind* endures as a masterpiece of American cinema. Furthermore, Scarlett is a formidable figure of strength, courage and determination; Vallette, on the other hand, emerges from her trials a defeated, frightened woman. Audiences in the Depression era did not want their heroines as downtrodden as they were. The comparison holds true today.

14

The "Showmanship" of Margaret Sullavan

I do take issue with this policy of manufactured fame.... The glorifying is pure showmanship, I know, designed to make a player more interesting to audiences. But I am not a showman and I don't suppose I ever will be.[1]

During the *So Red the Rose* shoot, Sullavan vented her frustration: "I didn't come to Hollywood to say silly things for the magazines and pose for silly publicity pictures. I came here to act."[2] As Universal discovered, this was not enough. Promoting her as a versatile actress had not yet reaped dividends at the box office. Audiences did not want actresses who could act, they wanted actresses who *looked good* while acting. As Margaret J. Bailey analyzed, "Audiences of the Thirties sought the escape and glamour that Hollywood provided. They went to the movies to see the stars and the costumes and to feel the excitement."[3] Top stars like Joan Crawford and Kay Francis, presented as high fashion models, were potent box office attractions. So, in preparation for her next film, Universal decided to give Sullavan a glamorous Hollywood makeover in order to widen her fan base. They chose a screenplay based on a highly popular "woman's story," a genre that brought in the paying customers. By the time the resulting film, *Next Time We Love*, was released, it was the unanticipated audience reaction to her pairing with an untested male co-star that ultimately provided the "showmanship appeal" that has withstood the test of time.

Next Time We Love, based on the Ursula Parrott novel *Say Goodbye Again*, was first serialized in *McCall's* magazine from December 1934 to April 1935. The sentimental plot contained autobiographical references, such as Parrott's first marriage to a *New York Times* correspondent and the hidden pregnancy of the couple's only child. At the time, Parrott (the pen name of Katherine Ursula Towle) was a highly popular writer whose romantic fiction novels proved equally successful as screen adaptations (most notably *The Divorcee*, 1930). Parrott's popularity was so great that Universal purchased the screen rights to *Say Goodbye Again* before it was published in *McCall's*. Parsons announced in early November 1934 that Universal intended to pair Sullavan with Roger Pryor. Several screenwriters, including Preston Sturges, worked on the screenplay. According to Stewart biographer Marc Eliot, William Wyler was initially set to direct.

Sullavan was hardly enthusiastic. The film was the lesser of two evils, with the other option of sitting around and not working off the contract. When Sullavan was summoned to re-shoot scenes for *So Red the Rose*, *Next Time We Love* was put on hold. Other projects, such as *Within the Present*, Ernst Lubitsch's production *National Velvet* (produced by MGM in 1944 with Elizabeth Taylor) and *Autumn Serenade*, a Viennese musical comedy (of all things), were considered. A bid to appear in *Pride and Prejudice* on Broadway was rejected.

After a while, plans for the Parrott project resurfaced and Austrian film actor Francis Lederer was slated to be Sullavan's co-star. Then the film was delayed again due to another one of Sullavan's "disappearances" and it wasn't long before Lederer proved to be unavailable as well. The production was temporarily shelved as the studio looked for an acceptable substitute for the leading man.

During this time, James Stewart was in Hollywood working as a $350-a-week MGM contract player. He had received excellent notices for a few of his Broadway performances, and this brought him to the attention of Metro's Billy Grady. Once in California, he moved into a Brentwood farmhouse with his former roommate Henry Fonda and Johnny Swope. Hollywood stardom eluded Stewart as the studio didn't quite know what to do with him. Not conventionally handsome like Clark Gable or Robert Taylor, Stewart did not fit the typical leading man mold. He was a lanky young bumpkin with a hesitant manner of speaking best utilized in small roles. Stewart later explained to *Modern Screen*, "I didn't think I had what it takes. I'd see myself in the mirror while shaving and any little ideas I might have had along the Hollywood way were nipped in the shaving brush."[4] His first few assignments included an uncredited bit in a Shemp Howard short, a small part in *The Murder Man* (1935), and another small part in a Jeanette MacDonald-Nelson Eddy operetta, *Rose Marie* (not yet released). With such an inauspicious start, there was no guarantee that Metro would keep him when his six-months' renewal option came up.

According to Marc Eliot, Sullavan had a chance encounter with Stewart: She saw him walking along Hollywood Boulevard, looking forlorn. Sullavan had the driver pull over and, in short time, he was sitting next to her as they reminisced about their lives back in New York. Sympathetic to his plight, Sullavan decided that he would be perfect as her *Next Time We Love* leading man. Eliot insisted that Lederer was then dismissed in order to accommodate Sullavan's wishes; this claim has not been supported by other sources, but it is worth noting that the announcements of Lederer's departure and Stewart's appointment were only nine days apart.

It took some convincing to get Universal to agree to Stewart's casting. Standard Hollywood publicity offered a variety of accounts of how he was cast. One piece of fabrication came from Jerry Hoffman:

> Never before have so many newcomers been placed in important parts, even featured. Now comes James Stuart [*sic*], Princeton boy, a stranger to movie fans, established in stick and on the stage, who gets the important assignment of playing opposite Margaret Sullavan in Ursula Parrott's *Next Time We Love*. Stuart has E.H. Griffith, the director, to thank. Ed liked his tests and arranged for Universal to borrow him from Metro-Goldwyn-Mayer.[5]

In reality, it was not that easy. Universal was leery about casting an unknown in such an important part. According to co-star Ray Milland, "Margaret Sullavan was the star, and she was a big star at Universal … and they did anything she asked them to do." They had to. Sullavan threatened to raise a major ruckus if she didn't get her way. Metro was contacted and arrangements were made. Stewart recalled, "Universal wanted to use the MGM backlot for three weeks, so MGM said they could if they gave me a part in their film."[6]

Filming began on October 21, 1935. Stewart's nervousness in front of the cameras showed in the early rushes. Sullavan went out of her way to make the neophyte look good on screen. Milland recalled, "Our director initially raged at Jimmy because of his exaggerated stage techniques and if he'd been a better director he could have helped Jimmy." Both

Griffith and Junior Laemmle wanted Stewart replaced before any more footage was shot. When Griffith complained that Stewart was ruining the movie, Sullavan came to Stewart's defense. She vowed that she would prove once and for all that Stewart had what it took to be a major movie star. To accomplish this, she spent a lot of time with him, helping him lose his stage mannerism and developing a more relaxed style of acting. "They spent many hours into the night rehearsing," Milland recalled. "What was obvious was that Jimmy's performance improved with Margaret's coaching…. You just knew that these two people loved each other."[7] Grady doubted anything was going on between the two, but conceded that Stewart "was in love with her, always had been, and everyone around them knew it. It showed so plainly on his face, and on the screen."

"I always felt that much as she loved him, Jimmy just wasn't Maggie's type sexually," said Jerry Asher, a Metro publicity man. "He always got her motherly and sisterly."[8]

With Sullavan's infinite patience, Stewart became much more at ease and relaxed with his role. After shooting a particularly challenging scene, even Griffith had to admit that Stewart could act. Later, Griffith credited Sullavan for making Stewart a star.

The one who did not appreciate Sullavan's above-and-beyond efforts was Wyler. As their marriage continued to deteriorate, he became increasingly suspicious of his wife's professed platonic relationship with Stewart. Upon viewing one of he rushes, Wyler quipped sarcastically that his wife certainly got something special out of Stewart. It did not help matters when Sullavan had revealed to an interviewer a few months earlier that, although she found her husband a lovable man, "I don't love him."[9]

Despite their frequent attempts of patching up their troubled marriage, it was clear that the end was near. "She can hurt a man like no woman I've ever known," an unidentified source revealed to a magazine writer.[10] Yet Sullavan was guilty of irrational jealousy as well. At that time, Wyler was directing Samuel Goldwyn's *These Three* with Joel McCrea, Miriam Hopkins and Merle Oberon, to whom Sullavan took an intense dislike. According to Charles Higham, Sullavan had conceived the irrational notion that Oberon (who was involved with David Niven) was preying on her husband. Sullavan would suddenly appear on the set and deliberately unnerve the actress during filming.

An unforeseen event finally destroyed the fragile bond of matrimony and the two separated for good. According to actress Lupita Tovar, Sullavan made a $1000 wager with Lupita's husband Paul Kohner as to who would become pregnant first. Some time afterward, Lupita became pregnant. "Several years later," Lupita reminisced, "an envelope came in the mail with a check for a thousand dollars and a note to my little girl, Susan. It explained that Maggie had made a bet with me, and now she was paying up."

The truth of the matter was that Sullavan actually became pregnant first, but got an abortion without Wyler's knowledge. According to Wyler's eldest daughter Catherine, "He told me she got pregnant with their child. She didn't feel like having it. I imagine career reasons. She told him after she aborted the child…. He said that's what ended their marriage, getting rid of it without telling him. She knew he would have wanted it."[11] It is likely that Sullavan chose to abort not out of career reasons, but out of her desire not to bring a child into a rocky marriage.

As she was dealing with the fall-out of another failed marriage, Sullavan had to contend with unwanted scrutiny by the press. According to the writer of the article "Margaret Sullavan Still a Problem; Won't Conform to Hollywood Ideas!," "Hollywood's speculating these days whether Margaret Sullavan, the firebrand of the picture colony, can be tamed. Will Margaret, the query goes, eventually be brought to do the things the cinema capital expects of its movie actresses, or will the former Broadway star reserve the right to her independence to the last?"[12] Stories like these caused Sullavan to grouse, "What conceivable interest could my purely personal affairs have for strangers?"[13] With such a reluctant subject, what did enterprising writers do to fill up space? They started talking to those who worked with her. According to one source, the unpredictable star could be easily angered by thoughtless actions by those she trusted: "She's intolerant but not arrogant. Abrupt, blunt, frank and stubborn." However, he quickly added, "But if I were suddenly flat on my back, broke, alone and in trouble, I'd find in her the one true friend a man needs when he's down." According to another anonymous source, "Sullavan is kind to people on the set, the prop boys, electricians, and so forth, but she's hell to the boys in the front office."[14]

Griffith offered his perspective on Sullavan's professionalism: "[She] is far too intelligent not to understand the value of cooperation.... Though she is firm in her conviction of how she interprets a part, she never refuses to listen to another's point of view if she feels something constructive is being offered."[15]

Next Time We Love chronicles the lives of a couple as they navigate through the demands of marriage, parenthood and high-powered careers. The film opens in New York City in 1927. Chris (Stewart), a struggling, small-time newspaper writer, impulsively marries his college girlfriend Cicely (Sullavan). Chris' friend Tommy (Milland) serves as the best man. During the wedding luncheon, Chris steals away to call the newspaper office. In his absence, Cicely confides to Tommy that she is not going to be a burden to Chris. She intends

Left to right: Ronald Cosbey, Ray Milland and Sullavan in *Next Time We Love* (1936). Universal tried something different to entice the fans, but it was her pairing with little known James Stewart that elevated this sudsy weepie.

to pursue a career in acting. Tommy, who has some connections with theatrical producers, offers to help her.

Before long, Chris is promoted to bigger stories and Cicely lands a small part in a Broadway play. Their first fight involves their conflicting career goals, but both vow to work through their difficulties. When Chris is offered a management job at the newspaper office in Rome, Cicely refuses to go with him: She has made a good impression in her current play and doesn't want to give that up. Her refusal leads to a heated exchange of words in a restaurant and Cicely leaves. After reflection, Chris realizes that he should not stand in the way of her career.

Up to this point, it is Sullavan and Stewart's real-life friendship that permeates their characterizations and the movie shows promise of being something special. Unfortunately, as the characters continues to display their less-than-noble motivations, the viewer loses interest despite the excellent performances.

On the way back from seeing Chris off at the cruise ship bound for Rome, Cicely confides to Tommy that she is pregnant. Chris was not told because she didn't want to interfere with his career. When the landlady sends a telegram to Chris after Cicely gives birth, Chris deserts his job. As a result, he is fired from the paper. Chris takes a low-paying job with the city news bureau and Cicely stays home to take care of Kit. When Cicely lands a six-months' contract at $150 per week salary, Chris is determined to find a way to provide for his family without his wife's assistance.

Cicely visits Chris' former managing editor, Mr. Carteret (Robert McWade), and pleads with him to hire Chris back. Impressed by her act of self-sacrifice, Carteret offers Chris a correspondent job in Russia. During their long separation, Cicely reaches "stellar heights in the theater" (according to a magazine caption) and is in the process of moving out of their apartment. She receives a letter from Chris who will be coming home for a brief time before heading off to another part of the world. Rather than being overjoyed, Cicely is oddly subdued. Cicely shares with Kit's nursemaid, Madame Donato (Anna Demetrio), that she doesn't feel married to him any more. Madame Donato offers some ineffective advice that does not help lift Cicely out of her funk. One wonders how spunky Hattie McDaniel (briefly seen a few minutes prior) would have changed the dynamics of this scene with some of her own no-nonsense advice.

Chris arrives at the apartment and the two are uneasy in each other's presence; it is somewhat surprising to see Sullavan chain-smoking like a high-strung Bette Davis in this scene. The couple head off to Cicely's Connecticut house to see Kit, who is about two years old. While there, the couple have a frank conversation about their loneliness. The sexual tension percolates as Chris prepares to catch the train back to the city. They embrace and kiss. Fast-forward to 1935. After years of waiting on the sidelines, Tommy confesses his love to Cicely. It seems he has loved her since Day One. Caught off guard, Cicely is not sure how she feels. Although she is terribly lonely, she doesn't want to hurt Chris. Tommy tries to convince Cicely to divorce Chris so she can marry him (what a faithful friend he turned out to be). While deeply fond of Tommy, Cicely does not love him the way she once loved Chris. She vows to wait for Chris, no matter how long it takes.

By this time, Chris has resigned from his foreign correspondent job under the pretense that he's writing a novel. However, Carteret suspects there's a different reason and he asks Chris outright if he's going to die. Chris admits that he had contacted a fatal disease while in China. He keeps this bit of news from Cicely. Cicely joins Chris in St. Anton, Switzerland. Cicely is shocked by Chris' haggard appearance, but he shrugs off her concerns. In a sacrificial mood, Chris tells Cicely that he no longer loves her and wants her to divorce him so she can marry Tommy. Cicely sadly agrees that perhaps that is the best option. "Maybe next time we live, we'll have time for each other," she wistfully tells him. Regardless, she still wants to spend the next few days together like old times. This is too much for Chris, so he leaves behind a note telling her that it's over.

Cicely catches up with Chris at the train station on his way to the sanitarium. He still lies to her about not loving her, but she doesn't believe him. As sappy as this scene turns out to be, the intense display of emotions between the two electrifies this sequence. Chris finally confirms her worst fears. He also confesses that he still loves her. Relieved to hear this, Cicely draws Chris close to her at the final fade-out.

Released at the end of January 1936, *Next Time We Love* got mixed reviews. *The Baltimore Sun* opined, "Margaret Sullavan is the most promising of the younger stars, and deserves better vehicles than she has been getting." However, it conceded that "[m]any persons will find the charm and skill of Miss Sullavan's performance sufficient compensation for the weakness of the story." Even the more charitable *Variety* had trouble recommending the film: "Margaret Sullavan has been dealt a weakish, rambling narrative and a part that doesn't seem to be up her alley…. Smothering the elfin quality that has helped lift the girl to prime attention is a thick cloak of ultra-sophistication, and the possibilities are that this off-key characterization will cause disappointment among a portion of her femme following…. Miss Sullavan's uncannily effective break in her larynx does the usual damage on the tear duct."

Many critics found much to praise in the film. The *Rochester Democrat and Chronicle* was enthusiastic: "They've made a fine-textured, utterly true and quite tenderly moving little drama…. We're not astonished by the delicate, eloquent playing by Miss Sullavan as the wife. She has stirred us before with her vibrant emotional strength and persuasiveness, her smile through the tears."

The film was profitable enough to make Universal happy. However, seen today, *Next Time We Love* must be ranked as one of Sullavan's worst films. Although both she and Stewart give multi-layered performances and the film has been gorgeously produced, there is very little else to like. Its sudsy plot is based on a series of sentimental situations that would have played better in a serial format on daytime soap opera. Taken as a whole in one sitting, it is too much talk and too little connection to reality. Perhaps if the characters had spent more time saying what they really meant, we could have avoided much of the tearful nonsense. Griffith's unimaginative and pedestrian direction keeps the film firmly rooted in its "women's weepies" formula. *Next Time We Love* might have been something special with a more perceptive director at the helm.

With some reservations, the main performances are excellent. Stewart comes across as natural as we have come to expect. Sullavan gives a finely nuanced performance that displays Cicely's evolution from a naïve girl to a renowned stage actress. Her best scenes occur near the end in the St. Anton sequences when she gives a breathless display of the emotional aspects of her role. She is heartbreakingly real here. In addition, the transformation in her appearance is well delineated. The early scenes emphasize her elfin lovability, and in the later scenes she projects a mature, refined sophistication that is extremely flattering. Unfortunately, there are times when her character (and Stewart's) come across as selfish and immature. It seems that their penchant for sacrifices is rooted in self-centered narcissism rather than being altruistic. It is due to their artistry and appealing screen personalities that we don't find them unlikable.

Of the supporting cast, only McWade fares well as he managed to find some humor and dignity in his role. The rest of the performers are simply not up to snuff. Milland suffers the most in an ambiguous role of the "friend." One never shakes off that sneaky suspicion that he is just biding his time before he preys on Cicely's loneliness for his own benefits.

The film does boast two notable "firsts." Number one, it featured Stewart in his first important leading role. This was the lucky break he needed. Largely unknown to moviegoers, Stewart's unexpectedly fine performance proved to be the sensation of the film. As the *New York Times* observed, "James Stewart … promises in this his first picture to reach New York to be a welcome addition to the roster of Hollywood's leading men." *Time* magazine opined, "The chief significance of *Next Time We Love* in the progress of the cinema industry is likely to reside in the presence in its cast of James Stewart." Equally remarkable was the impression he made on female moviegoers. As Gladys Hall of *Modern Screen* put it, "You can't compare him with anyone, past or present. He can't be 'typed' because there is no prototype." Still puzzled by his physical attraction to female filmgoers, Hall posed her question to a female companion. The response was quick and insightful: "He promises tenderness with strength underneath. He isn't obviously any one thing. It's just that he seems to promise—everything!"[16]

Back at Metro, Grady noticed that Stewart came back changed. Due to Sullavan's assistance, Stewart showed more confidence and a greater command of film technique than before. Both Stewart and Grady have always credited Sullavan for helping Stewart to be his unique and inimitable self on screen—the very qualities that has enabled him to remain one of the greatest film actors of all time.

The other "first" was the teaming of Sullavan and Stewart; they would make four films together. Not since the team of Janet Gaynor and Charles Farrell had a couple seemed so closely linked to real life. There was no touch of the slightly-out-of-reach immortal aura, but rather two normal individuals who might have well lived next door. According to Parish, their appeal as a screen couple is easily understood:

> She can effectively be at once both naïve and posed, egotistical and benevolent, while his range moved from the gangling hickish to the resolutely mature…. As a team they radiated a reserved warmth which made moviegoers believe that viewing into the characters' private lives was not a salacious event but a delicately shared experience, revealing not just company best manners, but honest to goodness real emotion.[17]

Noted *New Yorker* film critic Pauline Kael had a special fondness for the Sullavan-Stewart team: "[They] are magnetic together. This first pairing of Sullavan and Stewart is memorably romantic."[18]

Quirk once asserted that Stewart never performed better than opposite Sullavan in their films together. While that may be arguably the case for Stewart, it is certainly true for Sullavan. While she was always sincere and convincing with her other male co-stars, she was at her most piquant opposite Stewart. There's that extra sparkle in her eyes, as if to say, "See, I told you that he'd become a big movie star."

15

Final Round with Henry Fonda

Breaking up with her the second time was not the tragedy it had been originally.[1]—Henry Fonda

For Sullavan's next picture, she was loaned out to the Walter Wanger Production unit at Paramount. Her leading man was none other than Henry Fonda. The prospect of a former husband and wife working together sparked tremendous publicity—as well as their once dormant feelings, thus signaling the complete demise of the Sullavan-Wyler union.

The Moon's Our Home was based on a Faith Baldwin story which was first serialized in *Cosmopolitan* magazine from September 1935 through January 1936. These installments were compiled into a novel bearing the same name. Baldwin was a highly successful romantic fiction novelist; *Time* magazine noted her addition to the ranks of best-selling female authors like Kathleen Norris and Edna Ferber.

Wanger made this one of his top productions of the year. Cinematographer Joseph Valentine, who photographed Sullavan in *Next Time We Love*, was borrowed from Universal to continue the "Beautification Project." Her outfits, designed by Helen Taylor, included the most expensive and elegant gowns she ever wore in films. Wanger assembled a top-notch supporting cast (Beulah Bondi, Charles Butterworth, Margaret Hamilton and Walter Brennan). Wanger's budget exceeded $400,000, quite a sum for an independent production.

Veteran comedy director William Seiter was brought in to direct. With Sullavan and Fonda's limited experiences with comedy, Seiter was a perfect choice as he patiently guided the two comic neophytes through their parts.

Early on, Sullavan demanded that the script be rewritten as the original screenplay, like Baldwin's original work, was weak and sentimental fluff. Sullavan reportedly insisted that Dorothy Parker and her husband, Alan Campbell, be hired to punch up the dialogue. Parker, a writer with a caustic wit, is best remembered for her devastating comment that Katharine Hepburn "runs the gamut of emotions all the way from A to B" after seeing her in *The Lake*.[2]

In early January, the film crew reported to Lake Tahoe for location shooting. It was during this time, Seiter recalled, that one could see the Sullavan-Fonda sparks surface and become a flame as filming continued. Separated from Wyler, Sullavan acted upon her new-found respect for Fonda.

By then, Fonda was doing quite well as a leading man. For the first time since Sullavan achieved stardom on Broadway, Fonda's career was on the ascent. With his self-esteem restored, Fonda was more than a match for Sullavan in every possible way. It wasn't long before the former husband and wife were intimate once again.

Seiter noted that the love scenes became much hotter than what would be accepted under the Breen Code. Upon seeing the rushes, Wanger was not amused and ordered Seiter to reshoot many of the scenes. Some of the spicier dialogue also had to be toned down. Despite pressure from the Breen Office and Seiter's admonitions, Sullavan insisted on injecting her own unique take. "Take a little of the gaminess out of it if you have to," she suggested, "and I'll let my innuendos do the rest."[3] Viewing the finished film, Seiter saw that she was right. "That was her wonderful light touch. She had it both ways with the script and that performance."[4]

By the time the cast and crew returned to Hollywood, things had gotten so serious between Sullavan and Fonda that they began looking for a house together. In the meantime, they vehemently denied rumors of romance. For *Photoplay*, Fonda presented his case in the article, "Why I Will Not Re-Marry Margaret Sullavan." "They're not in love any more," wrote George Stevens. "They don't want to live together any more. They're swell friends, they make a good screen team, and they like to play checkers on the set. And that's that."[5] Sullavan told an interviewer, "I want everyone to know that I'm interested in Henry's career. I believe in him. I think he's a wonderful actor, and I want him to have his chance."[6] It was not long before insiders suspected something more than mutual professional courtesy was fueling this friendship.

According to columnist Donna Risher, "La Sullavan, who in real life is Mrs. William Wyler, wife of the director, shot Hollywood eyebrows up another notch when she appeared at a preview of *Rose Marie* on the arm of her ex-husband, Fonda, thus making a field day for the news cameramen."[7] While the couple continued their joint public appearances, it was not long before the rumor mill worked into heated overdrive. Those close to Sullavan and Wyler were not surprised when Jimmy Starr reported, "Those old debbil divorce rumors are cropping up again between Margaret Sullavan and William Wyler. This time, gossips claim, she'll file papers—and any minute!"[8] What was not known was that Sullavan had long ago moved out of their Bel Air home.

Those rumors were laid to rest when it was reported on March 13 that the couple was already divorced. The divorce was granted on the basis of "incompatibility." When questioned, Sullavan revealed, "I've been divorced for some time…. My attorney knows all about it. I don't know just how it was all arranged, but I'm happy—very happy." When asked about the oft-repeated rumors of remarrying Fonda, Sullavan played coy. "Marry Henry Fonda, my former husband?" she asked. "I can't say just now—maybe."[9]

Henry Fonda was married to Sullavan from 1931 to 1933. By the time this photograph was taken in 1936, the exes were seriously contemplating re-marrying.

Sullavan later told *Modern Screen*. "[Wyler is] a great talent—one of the greatest, and he has a strong distinctive personality." As to why their marriage failed, she admitted they clashed all the time due to their strong personalities. "There are only two exits for a situation like that—jump in a lake or get a divorce." Wyler also mellowed in his recollection of their marriage as he reflected that their relationship may have been salvaged if they had done another movie together. He added, "Maggie never really exploited her full potential as a dramatic actress though she did many fine things."[10]

Upon completion of *The Moon's Our Home*, Sullavan was scheduled to begin *Money from Heaven* with Joel McCrea. However, Universal received a frantic request for another loan-out from Paramount. Taking advantage of the situation, Universal got the better deal. In exchange for Carole Lombard for Universal's *My Man Godfrey* opposite *her* former husband, William Powell, Sullavan remained at Paramount to replace Marlene Dietrich in the troubled production *Hotel Imperial* opposite Charles Boyer. *Money from Heaven* became *Two in a Crowd* with Joan Bennett opposite McCrea.

When Sullavan reported to the *Hotel Imperial* set, the production was already in shambles. The project, previously entitled *I Loved a Soldier*, was based on a 1917 Hungarian play. It had been made twice as a silent film, first as a 1918 Hungarian film and then as a 1927 Paramount film with exotic Polish star Pola Negri. During the shooting of the Negri film, Rudolph Valentino died unexpectedly in New York. Negri, reportedly having an affair with Valentino, left the film in mid-production to fly to New York. There, she created quite a media sensation with her melodramatic display of grief, thus starting the widely believed speculation that Negri used Valentino's death to further her career. Despite the costly delays, *Hotel Imperial* turned out to be one of Negri's biggest film successes.

In January, 1936, filming on the sound remake began. Early on, an accidental discharge of a gun injured a crew member and narrowly missed killing Boyer. Dietrich and director Henry Hathaway were in constant disputes over her appearance as a poor chambermaid. Dietrich insisted on maintaining a glamorous image, even though it was at odds with the early phases of her characterization. Dietrich also insisted on rewrites as she was not satisfied with how her part was conceived. As Hathaway recalled, Dietrich "has become a monster of her own making." With the escalating crisis, producer Ernst Lubitsch was forced to shut down the production for several weeks until the issues were resolved. After the production resumed, Lubitsch was fired from the film after a blow-up with an executive. This caused Dietrich, whose contract stipulated Lubitsch's personal supervision of her films, to walk off the set in mid–February. With nearly $1 million already invested, Paramount was in a bind and Sullavan was their salvation.

In the early days of filming, Hathaway was delighted with Sullavan's cooperation. "She was marvelous," he recalled. "She didn't care how ugly she looked," he added in reference to the early scenes. Then, disaster struck. Sullavan was injured in an on-set accident which left her with a fractured right arm. As Hathaway remembered that fateful day, Sullavan and Fonda (a visitor on the set) were being "very playful":

> She'd have a water pistol and she'd squirt him in the face with it, and he'd scream laughing and squirt her and they'd fall over. He'd rib her about her ugly hair and face and costume, and she'd chase him and he'd chase her in and out of the scenery! They fell over a pile of wires, which we call a spider, and rolled over on the floor, and she found she'd broken her *arm*![11]

With her arm set in a cast, Sullavan was instructed not to return to filming for at least six weeks. Executives scrambled to find yet another replacement. After Paramount's Claudette Colbert turned down the role, there were reports that Bette Davis would be borrowed from Warner Brothers, but nothing came of it. The film was finally abandoned when Boyer had to leave for France for a film commitment. Paramount, however, was not going to let $1 million go to waste and the project was eventually resurrected as *Hotel Imperial* in 1939 with Ray Milland and Isa Miranda. The film apparently was under the same jinx as Milland suffered a near-fatal accident which resulted in a four-week hospital stay. The plagued film flopped at the box office. Despite this, the material was trotted out for yet another version in 1943. This time, however, the brilliant Billy Wilder served as co-screenwriter and director. *Five Graves to Cairo* with Franchot Tone, Anne Baxter and Erich von Stroheim is a well-crafted, mesmerizing World War II drama.

Convalescing at home, Sullavan continued her romance with Fonda and new rumors circulated of an impending re-marriage. According to Louella Parsons, "I don't believe anyone can say for a fact that such a marriage will take place. I don't believe Margaret herself knows. Henry has said again and again that any time she wants to say 'yes' will suit him. But Maggie says that she will never marry again until she is sure."[12] Universal, sensing that something would happen, decided to cast Sullavan and Fonda in a picture tantalizingly called *Reno in the Fall*.

The Sullivan-Fonda romance quickly unraveled. Fonda recalled the incident that led to the final break: "There was a party at the West End Tennis Club.... Johnny Swope and Jim Stewart were there, and I took Sullavan. At one point during the evening, I cut in on another girl. And that triggered it. Sullavan blew. She wouldn't even let me take her home."[13]

According to Quirk, the situation was more complicated than Fonda's ambiguous version. As reported by several eyewitnesses, Fonda had gone off to dance with another woman while Sullavan was in the rest room. When she returned, she found the two dancing closely together. Angered, she went over and yanked the girl away from him by the hair and ripped the front of her dress. She turned around and slapped Fonda across the face, then she stormed out.

Fonda's account gives the impression that this episode occurred during the filming of *The Moon's Our Home*, but various newspaper reports indicated the couple were still involved in late April, long after the shoot. An April 21 column in the *Los Angeles Examiner* reported on the couple's appearance at a party given at the Westside Tennis Club. More interesting is this little tidbit in the April 22 edition of the *Los Angeles Evening Herald Express*: "Another star with a big florist's bill these days is Henry Fonda. You guessed it. They are for Margaret Sullavan since she broke her arm."[14] One assumes that these flowers were of the "Forgive Me" variety rather than "Get Well Soon."

Regardless of how it happened, Fonda recalled that Sullavan told him, "This is a mistake, Hank. This thing between us—it's not going to work." In hindsight, Fonda admitted, "She was smart enough to realize that we could not make it happen again."[15]

By the break-up, *The Moon's Our Home* was released. After the April Fool's preview, the *Hollywood Citizen News* predicted the film would be a box office hit.

The film opens in Hollywood as glamorous screen star Cherry Chester (Sullavan) is in the throes of a tantrum complete with flying vases and other knick-knacks. The cause for all the commotion: Cherry's (*née* Sarah Brown) wealthy grandmother Lucy Van Steedan has sent numerous telegrams requesting her return to New York City. Cherry resents her interference and vows not to go, declaring to her beleaguered assistant Boyce (Bondi), "I am an actress. First an actress, then a woman. My art comes before everything else." This is just one of the many delightful examples of the film's ironic twists of the stars' real-life circumstances.

During an interview, Sullavan pokes fun at the Hollywood image by assuming a glamorous, aloof and slightly bored demeanor; clearly, she is taking swipes at Hepburn. There is a sweet, melancholy moment where Cherry describes her ideal romance. The moment is shattered by the latest telegram, which indicates that Lucy is gravely ill. With a shriek and a flurry of activity, Cherry and her entourage depart for New York via a cross-country train.

In Chicago, Anthony Amberton (Fonda), a famous adventurer and novelist (inspired by American traveler-author Richard Haliburton), boards the train. His idea of a perfect woman? Certainly not a "marshmallow-faced movie star" like Cherry Chester. In an inspired split screen set-up, Cherry and Anthony speak disparagingly of the other although they have never met. As the two proceed through their bedtime rituals, we realize how compatible these two lonely personalities are, down to the last cigarette.

Once in New York, Cherry discovers her grandmother (Henrietta Crossman) has deceived her. Lucy insists she gives up the Hollywood nonsense and marry her distant cousin Horace (Charles Butterworth), whom Cherry finds insufferable. At a book signing in a department store, Anthony becomes seriously ill when he smells the scent of "Cherry Blossoms" perfume, a fragrant made specially for Cherry. He narrowly escapes a mob of lovestruck fans by jumping into Cherry's horse-drawn carriage on a busy city street. They are instantly attracted and find they share similar views of life. Impetuously, Anthony urges Cherry to go away with him to the mountains. As her head begins to swirl with romantic notions, her reverie is cut short when Anthony realizes that his watch has been stolen. (The film is filled with such abrupt, screwball scenes like this, which give it a contemporary feel.) He gives Cherry a card with an address of his favorite winter hotel. Intrigued, Cherry decides to journey incognito to Moonsocket, New Hampshire.

The Simpson's Inn is run by the no-nonsense Mrs. Simpson (Margaret Hamilton, who steals the film from the other supporting players). Cherry is joined by Anthony and they introduce themselves by their real names, Sarah Brown and John Smith. Alternately irritated by his brash nature and intrigued by her feelings of love, Cherry quickly falls for Anthony.

Over time, Cherry becomes enamored of the simple, anonymous life. There is a wonderful scene when she gives Mrs. Simpson her frilly, unpractical nightgown. It's a moment that speaks volumes in emotional depth due to the delightful interplay between the two. Mr. Simpson's (Spencer Charters) look of surprise as he discovers his dour wife in this nightgown in the subsequent scene is worth the price of admission.

Romantic feelings between Cherry and Anthony continues to grow until, one day, they decide to get married by the justice of the peace. The elopement does not go off without complications during the film's funniest sequence. Realizing that Anthony has had a marriage license in his possession for several days, Cherry takes offense and begins an argument as the hard-of-hearing justice (hilariously played by Walter Brennan) proceeds with the ceremony. Throughout their argument, he mistakenly interprets their words of anger as declaration of love.

The wedding night is derailed when Cherry uses some of her perfume, thus making Anthony violently ill. Misunderstanding, Cherry angrily flees back to New York and agrees to marry Horace. Why Cherry would succumb to this defies logic even in a madcap romp. This is the exact moment when the movie starts to deflate. But it is almost over and the effect is minimal.

There is a chance encounter between Anthony and Horace (who knows him as John) in New York and Anthony is invited to a New Year's Eve engagement party to meet his fiancée. Cherry and Anthony meet up and realize that they still have feelings for each other. They even reveal their celebrity identities and vow to be happy together—as long as she gives up her screen career. This, of course, sets the stage for another round of name-calling

Sullavan and Walter Brennan, one of the many excellent players who supported the sparkling leads in the forgotten comic gem *The Moon's Our Home* **(1936) (courtesy Gary Combs).**

and harsh words before engaging in a knockdown, drag-out fight. Horace (with impeccable timing) comes upon them and, without missing a beat, says, "By the way, have you two met? Johnny Smith, this is my fiancée." This should have been the final line of the film. Instead, we have to sit through ten more minutes of illogical plot development until the final kiss at the fade-out.

Many critics found the comedy to their liking. The *Literary Digest* magazine opined, "It is very possible that the last six months of picture-making have not resulted in any comedy, high or low, to excel *The Moon's Our Home*, a delicious, sly prance concerning nothing much at all, but doing it with spry madness.... Whatever Miss Sullavan and Mr. Fonda may make of their personal problems, the picture definitely will establish them as a high-comedy team without compare in Hollywood." The *Hollywood Spectator* magazine called the film "one of the brightest comedies we have had in a long time." There was high praise for Sullavan as she "proves herself a great trouper ... and generally conducts herself with physical vigor that is captivating. She is equally at home in the mental phases of her role, giving one of the most appealing and amusing characterizations the screen has shown us of late."

A rare negative review came from the *New York Herald-Tribune*: "[T]he unfolding of the narrative ... is laborious and far-fetched, where it should have been foolishly gay." Despite that, though, there was commendation for Sullavan as she succeeded in creating "an arresting characterization of a spoiled heiress and screen star.... Although it verges on burlesque, her performance is assured and diverting."

The Moon's Our Home has been unfairly relegated to forgotten film status despite some positive remarks from contemporary sources. Fonda told John Springer, "It was fun. It has pace and charm, and I found myself laughing and enjoying it, too. It has held up much better than a lot of those pictures of the '30."[16] The heartiest endorsement comes from an unexpected source. In a 2008 televised interview with Elvis Mitchell, sublime funnyman Bill Murray raved about one of his favorite actresses and film on Turner Classics Movie's *Under the Influence* series:

> MURRAY (referring to Sullavan): Wow, so watchable … what a beautiful … what a creature she was.
> MITCHELL: It's weird, because of all those actresses of that period, she has disappeared. Nobody talks about her.
> MURRAY: I thought that movie was really…an unusual film.[17]

Seen today, *The Moon's Our Home* is a delightful, zany romp, full of inspired screwball slapstick and a surprising, tender romantic undertone. There are also great lines and sharp observations about human nature. The film has a contemporary feel and stands as a fine early example of the modern-day romcom. It is easily one of Sullavan's most enjoyable comedies, comparing favorably with *The Shop Around the Corner* and *The Good Fairy*. Even the last ten minutes of extraneous footage fail to put a dent in its madcap spirit.

Devin McKinney believed the screenplay was specifically tailored to capitalize on Sullavan and Fonda's history as the film has that rare real-life feel. "The movie itself—that third mind that comes alive when film egos interact—senses the history of intimacies in play," McKinney wrote. "The air between the two stars crackles with the camera's suspicion that something is up."[18] It is this potent element that kicks the film into overdrive. Had the leading roles been played by another pair, the film would not have succeeded as well as it did.

The supporting players are all superb and contribute greatly to the merriment. However, they do not detract from the leads. Fonda displays his flair for comedy and it is refreshing to see him play the aggressor for a change. He is extremely handsome, frisky, and quite sexually charged. In the most challenging role of her career, Sullavan is fabulous as she manages the extreme ranges of her character's emotions, yet keeps her a likable human being. In other hands, Cherry Chester might have been a burlesque of a shrew. Sullavan is lovingly photographed in several soft-focus close-ups and looks beautiful in her gowns. Film historian Ted Sennett made an off-kilter remark when he wrote that Sullavan's "wistful, throaty voice is somewhat at odds with the character."[19] Nothing could be further from the truth as Sullavan deftly uses the wide range of her voice to denote the character's many moods. Rarely has she demonstrated her vocal prowess so effectively.

The biggest surprise is Seiter's direction. His handling of the combination of madcap nonsense and sweet romance is astoundingly good. A search revealed that Seiter is best known for Laurel and Hardy's comic gem *Sons of the Desert* (1933), which is regarded as their best film as well as one of the top 50 comedy films of all time by the American Film Institute. Seiter is also known for *Roberta* (1935), an unimaginative bore redeemed only by Astaire and Rogers' dancing. Other than that, Seiter must be considered a director who is only as good as the material he has to work with. *The Moon's Our Home* serves as a shining example of what Seiter could accomplish with the right producer, script and cast. A later Sullavan comedy, *Appointment for Love* (1941), is a lackluster effort which painfully reveals Seiter's inability to surmount a trivial script.

With a critically well-received movie and the bright stars, the film should have been a smash. It wasn't; it lost a little more than $110,000. With everything in its favor, what went wrong? First of all, in 1936, movie theaters were saturated with screwball comedies. Every studio had major contributions to this film cycle, with *Libeled Lady* (MGM), *Theodora Goes Wild* (Columbia) and *My Man Godfrey* (Universal) being the most popular and well-represented in Oscar nominations.

The bigger issue had to do with the fact that Sullavan's films had been steadily losing money. Despite the amount of publicity generated by the reunion of the former husband and wife and the general excellence of the film, moviegoers were losing interest in Margaret Sullavan just as they were losing interest in Hepburn. The truth of the matter was that her drive for independence and strong dislike for the "Hollywood system" were jeopardizing her career and Sullavan knew it. Even Fonda had his own opinion on this situation: "Personally, I don't think they have given Margaret Sullavan any picture roles yet as big as she is capable of playing."[20]

Frustrated with her stagnant film career and growing restless with her broken arm, Sullavan decided to take charge of the situation. In mid–May, it was announced that she was leaving for New York "to get some special treatments for that broken arm which hasn't healed as rapidly as she hoped. It's out of the splints, but still pretty stiff, and rather than take the chance of having it disabled for life, she will not start work [on a film] for several weeks longer."[21] Little did Universal realize that their unhappy star would get more out of her visit to New York City than just a fixed arm—and that it would be a little more than four years before she would set foot on the Universal lot again.

16

The Best of Both Worlds

*The human response I get out there in the theater from the audience each
night is worth more to me than all the acclaim which comes from movie
critics and movie fans.*[1]

By mid-summer, Sullavan returned to Hollywood after her New York sojourn. There
were those who doubted the legitimacy of her broken arm as judged by this news item's
assertion that she was "claiming a broken arm," thus making her unavailable for any film
work.[2] With this "inconvenience," along with Fonda's film commitment in England, Universal postponed the filming of *Reno in the Fall*. That project eventually reached the screen
as *The Road to Reno* in 1938 with Randolph Scott and Hope Hampton.

Bored with her self-imposed respite from film work, Sullavan began seriously considering a return to Broadway. As she later told an interviewer, "You learn to act in the presence
of an audience."[3] After three years in Hollywood, she was anxious to return to a profession
she loved.

While waiting for something to come her way, Sullavan reunited with ex-husband #2,
spending a considerable amount of time offering feedback and assisting William Wyler
with the daily rushes of *Dodsworth*. However, Wyler was not easily baited like Fonda,
because nothing came from their time together. Another possible reunion with Fonda was
preempted by Fonda's engagement to socialite Frances Seymour Brokaw in September.

Restless, Sullavan turned her sights toward a new conquest—her agent, Leland Hayward. This development was not lost on Hollywood gossips. Jimmy Starr reported, "With
her arm full of books (the other is still in a cast, you know), lovely Margaret Sullavan was
seen in a very close conversation with Leland Hayward."[4] What was notable about this
development was that Hayward was still romantically linked to Hepburn, but more about
that in the next chapter.

Hayward was born William Leland Hayward II on September 13, 1902, in Nebraska
City, Nebraska. He came from an affluent family of rich heritage and notable names. His
grandfather was Monroe Leland Hayward, a well-known Nebraskan Senator. The Senator's
son (William Leland's father), Col. William Hayward, was a celebrated World War I hero
who had commanded the 369th Infantry Regiment, now known as the "Harlem Hell Fight-
ers." When Leland was nine, his father and mother, Sarah Coe Ireland, divorced; both married other people.

Young Leland attended prep school in the East before attending Princeton University.
However, he did not take his studies seriously and flunked out after freshman year. Much
to his father's annoyance, Leland took on a number of menial jobs, such as a New York
City newspaper reporter, a screenwriter for First National, and a press agent for United

Artists at a weekly salary of $50. After an unsuccessful attempt to produce his own motion pictures, Leland became a Hollywood talent agent in the mid–1920s. In this capacity, he discovered his true calling and made a tremendous success of it. Very much his own person, Leland did not fit the widely accepted stereotypes of a talent agent. Not only that, he was considered to be one of the most attractive men around. After the success of the part-talking film *The Jazz Singer* (1927), Leland realized that there was a gold mine in stage actors with cultivated voices suitable for the talkies. He moved back to New York to work as a motion picture talent agent for the prestigious American Play company. By the mid–30s, he combined his New York agency with Myron Selznick's California agency.

Ginger Rogers recalled a charming story involving Sullavan and Hayward. Clients from both agencies were brought in to sign new contracts. Reportedly, Sullavan joked, "I'll sign if you write into it that Leland has to marry me as part of the deal."[5] Amused, Hayward signed the contract.

Leland had a reputation as a ladies' man who enjoyed the company of many famous women, including Greta Garbo and Myrna Loy. It has been stated that he was on the rebound from a long relationship with Katharine Hepburn when Sullavan entered into his personal life. The impact she had during this critical period was immense. Hayward recalled to Brooke that Sullavan was "the most enchanting, wonderful, delicious human being in the world."[6]

Meanwhile, Broadway playwrights Edna Ferber and George S. Kaufman were developing their newest project, *Stage Door*. The pair previously collaborated on two highly successful plays, *The Royal Family* (1927) and *Dinner at Eight* (1932). *Stage Door* was based on the experiences of Ferber's niece, actress Janet Fox. Ferber considered *Stage Door* a "touching play" that paid homage to the "gaiety and indomitable courage [that] would make the beholder marvel at the tenacity and fortitude of the human race."[7] For Kaufman, it was an opportunity to extol the virtues of live theater as superior to motion pictures.

The play details the lives of the young women who live together in a shabby New York City boarding house called the Footlights Club. They yearn for fame on Broadway, but struggle to land that elusive lucky break. Roommates Terry Randall and Jean Maitland are good friends, despite fundamental differences in their goals. Terry devotes herself to the stage while Jean takes the chance to go to Hollywood, much to Terry's barely concealed disgust.

As the play continues, these two diverse viewpoints provide dramatic tension. Terry remains true to her dreams while Jean becomes a successful movie star. Terry's playwright boyfriend, Keith, also went to Hollywood even though he once ridiculed the motion picture industry. Keith comes back to New York as a Hollywood celebrity and proposes to Terry. Rejecting his proposal, Terry stays in New York. Her persistence pays off when she stars in a Broadway play which promises to be a hit. She also finds true love with a man who supports her stage career. Unfortunately, Terry's newfound success comes at a high cost after a fellow actress, Kaye, commits suicide after being fired.

The role of Terry was tailor-made for two actresses at the time: Hepburn and Sullavan. Kaufman thought Sullavan would be ideal, "despite her slight madness."[8] When Sullavan visited New York that summer, Kaufman, with Ferber's reluctant permission, approached her. Realizing that a Ferber-Kaufman play would be her long-awaited Broadway hit, Sullavan readily accepted. What she did not know was that Leland had earlier promised the part (without Ferber or Kaufman's knowledge) to Hepburn. Sullavan signed a contract with producer Sam H. Harris for the full run of the play and the national touring production. When word got back to Hollywood via newspaper columns, Universal was livid. Sullavan managed to appease Universal by promising to star in the film *Wings Over Honolulu* after the play.

Ferber had misgivings about Sullavan, but Kaufman, as director, had the final say. He also hired many little known actors: Frances Fuller, Lee Patrick, Phyllis Brooks, Mary Wickes and Tom Ewell. During that summer, Kaufman was involved in the Mary Astor Diary scandal, which indicated that they were having an adulterous affair. Unsavory gossip involving a well-known person did significant damage to his career. But Kaufman emerged relatively untouched, while Astor's film career took a hit. She did, however, garner a Best Supporting Actress Oscar for *The Great Lie* in 1941.

While Kaufman was under the stress of the negative publicity, his efforts was less than his usual and *Stage Door* suffered accordingly. During the last days of rehearsals and the try-out tour, both Ferber and Kaufman constantly rewrote the play. *Stage Door* opened on

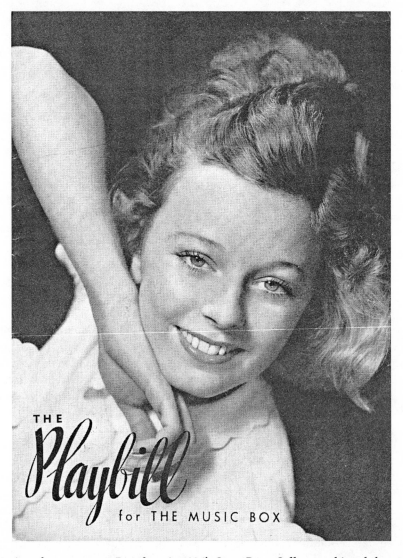

With her triumphant return to Broadway in 1936's *Stage Door*, Sullavan achieved the rare feat of earning glowing personal notices in a glittering box office success.

September 28 in Philadelphia. Throughout the try-out tour, the general consensus was that it lacked the rollicking sense of humor that graced Ferber and Kaufman's previous plays. Thus, the authors kept rewriting the play up until opening night on Broadway. The end results, according to Ferber, was "rather good, but not frightfully good."[9]

The play opened on Broadway at the Music Box Theatre on October 22. The critical consensus was that Sullavan made a sensational return to Broadway. The *Newark* (NJ) *Evening News* reported, "She still is an attractive young woman with tremendous sincerity on the stage, with a simple and therefore powerful way of performing dramatic scenes. Her touch of comedy is graceful and I, for one, regret that she cast her lot with Hollywood." The *New York Daily News* enthusiastically wrote that Sullavan "brings Terry Randall splendidly to life. The throaty, emotional voice; the dash of tears in the throat and eyes; the fire of defense and the exultation of conviction are finely realized."

The comments among the drama critics were that the Ferber-Kaufman play had fallen short of the mark. As the *Syracuse Herald* perceptively noted, *Stage Door* "may not be a great work, but the majority of playgoers, I venture, will find it great entertainment." As for Sullavan, there was high praise: "She is superb, defying that theme that her Hollywood career has not have made her a unique talent." The most insightful comment came from columnist Jack Gaver:

> Take Margaret Sullavan out of *Stage Door* and you would not have much left…. This vivid young actress with the long bob and slightly husky voice is the saving grace of the play…. This will probably be a financial success, too, but that does not alter the fact that it is a low-quality script, padded with semi-vaudeville clap-trap and reeking of a maudlin quality.[10]

Sullavan managed to achieve what few movie actresses was able to accomplish at that time: a glittering Broadway success that was a box office smash along with personal raves. Miriam Hopkins, Nancy Carroll and Elissa Landi failed in their attempts. Even Hepburn was reluctant to return to New York, so she toured the country in *Jane Eyre* rather than face a repeat of the withering critical reviews for *The Lake*.

Things could not have been any better for Sullavan: a hit play, a revitalized career, a new man in her life, and a baby on the way. When she told Hayward, he was elated and proposed marriage; later, he maintained that the proposal was *her* idea. The engagement was kept a secret; news of her pregnancy would have to wait even longer.

Included in her circle of New York friends were Frances Fuller, who was appearing in *Stage Door*, and her husband Worthington Miner, a future pioneering television producer. Years later, Miner recalled, "Fran and I had been unusually close to Maggie and Leland…. She was a wonderful and loyal friend…. Maggie had one of the most inquisitive minds I had ever encountered. It was, for me, one of her most irresistible charms." Of their friendship, Miner noted, "It was the kind of association that breeds a lasting intimacy that even years of separation can do little to tarnish."[11]

Now that Sullavan achieved her dreams of a certified Broadway hit, rumors began circulating that she would retire from the screen. This prompted columnist George Ross to state, "The host of Margaret Sullavan's cinema fans may have seen the last of her comely features and heard the last of her quaintly husky voice on the screen…. She has told friends that she is giving up her motion picture career to pursue a theatrical one." Sullavan told Ross, "Working in the films is definitely not acting. Sitting in a chair for two hours on the set and then walking up to the cameras for a short 'take' to say 'My baby just died' or something like that isn't my idea of giving a performance." While conceding Hollywood made her a household name, Sullavan admitted a special fondness for the theater. "It's the first time I've been in a bona fide hit right from the start," she continued. "And the thrill, the excitement and heart-warming satisfaction is so terrific, too!"[12] To another interviewer, she elaborated on her views about film acting: "Making movies is the dullest going I know. I've never had a moment's thorough satisfaction at the studios."[13]

On November 16, Louella Parsons announced, "Hollywood, over its coffee and grape-fruit this morning, is due for a little surprise."[14] The previous day, Sullavan and Hayward were married at St. Paul's Episcopal Methodist Church in Newport, Rhode Island. Hayward's father stood as a witness. Sullavan wore a gray ensemble suit, with a red handbag and a corsage of orchids. After a lunch reception at Col. Hayward's residence, the couple returned to New York.

Ginger Rogers recalled Sullavan calling her Malibu Beach house. Among Rogers' visitors that day was Jimmy Stewart. Stewart, who must have been crushed by the news, hid his hurt from Rogers. Others found out when they read the newspapers. Though shocked, people were not surprised by this unexpected news. According to columnist Robbin Coons, Sullavan

> has consistently refused to run true to form as prescribed by Hollywood gossip. When she married her agent, Leland Hayward, in the east the other day, she delivered the knock-out blow to those who would have charted her—and his—course differently.... When she was playing in a picture with Fonda, the gossips insisted these two would make a second attempt. So Fonda married an eastern society girl, and Margaret Sullavan married Leland Hayward the young agent who (a few months ago) was the reported fiancée if not the secret husband of Katharine Hepburn.[15]

Although Sullavan made *Stage Door* a financial success, Ferber had become increasingly irritated with the actress' erratic behavior. It had started during rehearsals when Sullavan became difficult. After the Broadway opening, Ferber found that Sullavan was "really very trying."[16] Although Ferber was Hayward's client, she could not resist a petty gesture when she gave the newlyweds a wedding present of a set of Steuben glasses. Ferber was known for giving nothing less than Baccarat.

Ferber's attitude did not bother Sullavan in the least. Everything in her life was gloriously in sync with her dreams. When the screen rights to the play were bought by RKO, several actresses, including Marion Davies, vied for the plum role, but it became a vehicle for Hepburn. Sullavan's response was decidedly pointed: "Hepburn got the role, but I got the guy—and the baby to go with him!"[17]

In this 1936 publicity photo, Sullavan radiates a beguiling combination of vulnerability and mature sexuality that was tremendously appealing to both moviegoers and theatergoers.

Sullavan and Hayward kept her impending motherhood a closely guarded secret as they pondered the timing of revealing this news. Ferber was not fooled. She long suspected something was up as it became clear that Sullavan wanted out. With greater frequency, Sullavan showed up late at the theater. She also was ill and skipped performances now and then. Unable to hide her advancing condition any longer, Sullavan and Hayward told Ferber and Kaufman during dinner one night. Ferber was livid, writing in her diary: "As I feared, she announced she was going to have a baby. As I had predicted some such charming trick before *Stage Door* ever opened, I wasn't surprised. But what a miserable little double-crossing wench it is." Sullavan and Hayward assured the playwrights she would tour with the play after October, but Ferber doubted that Sullavan would follow through. As Ferber wrote in her diary, "The Sullavan situation about *Stage Door* is now insane. She and Leland evidently will do anything to get out of her touring. I am completely fed up with the whole thing."[18] Ferber carried a grudge for some time as evident in her autobiography, in which she wrote that the play "was a success, and in the midst of the success Miss Margaret Sullavan left it, throwing about 40 people out of work, and over that we draw a veil, dear readers."[19]

Kaufman took the situation better. Even though he was disappointed by Sullavan's desertion, he maintained his friendship with Sullavan and Hayward and visited the couple in Hollywood during the late 1930s and early 1940s.

Now that Sullavan and Hayward had come clean, it was a matter of time before the news reached the gossip columns. "Margaret Sullavan is going to have a baby!" Parsons crowed. "At least we get a big rumor that says so. Hayward, back in Hollywood, dropped a broad hint."[20] Despite this, Sullavan still tried evading the issue. Parsons recalled Sullavan approaching her a few days after Parsons' announcement. "Please, Louella, do be careful what you print about me in the future," cautioned Sullavan. "When you wrote I was going to have a baby, I wasn't going to—as far as I knew. Right afterward I found I was pregnant, after all."[21]

Still the rumors persisted as Sullavan would not confirm nor deny the facts. One columnist caustically noted, "The betting odds today seemed to be that Broadway is due for another 'Act of God' baby and that this time the mother will be Margaret Sullavan, star of *Stage Door*."[22] The theatrical use of the phrase "Act of God" originated back in 1928 when Helen Hayes had to withdraw from *Coquette* due to her pregnancy. Her departure caused the play to close down in the middle of its phenomenal run. Normally, the other actors were given severance pay. Not so with Jed Harris, who attempted to avoid paying them by claiming that Hayes' reason for leaving was an "Act of God." He argued unsuccessfully that, since he couldn't control the circumstance, he should be exempt from paying.

Once the baby rumors were confirmed, the producers decided to close the play in mid–March or early April. The producers entertained the notion of replacing Sullavan with either Joan Bennett or Jean Muir, but they realized that it was Sullavan's reputation and talent that made the play a hit. Although it was their decision to shut down, Sullavan bore the brunt of the blame. Perhaps out of guilt, Sullavan agreed to appear with the cast in the radio broadcast on the Kate Smith radio program on March 12. *Stage Door* closed on March 13, after 169 performances. Afterwards, Harrison Carroll reported, "Universal insists that Margaret Sullavan still is committed to them for several pictures." Of course, Universal was being foolish. Carroll realized that Sullavan would not make things easy as he prophetically noted, "There have been hints that Margaret may have other plans."[23]

RKO's film version of *Stage Door* was released in early October. Starring Hepburn, Ginger Rogers, Adolphe Menjou, Andrea Leeds and a notable cast of lesser-known players such as Lucille Ball, Eve Arden and Ann Miller, it garnered positive critical reviews and earned a moderate amount of money. Adapted by Morrie Ryskind and Anthony Veiller, the film bore little resemblance to the play, causing Kaufman to quip that it should have been titled *Screen Door*. Directed with finesse by Gregory LaCava and expertly acted by the well-chosen cast, the film stands as an enjoyable, sparkling comedy considered by many to be vastly superior to the original work.

In 1946, the play *Stage Door* was presented in London. It also provided the source for two television productions. The first was televised in 1948, the second in 1955. Gore Vidal adapted the play for a 60-minute television production for *The Best of Broadway* television series. It boasted an impressive cast: Rhonda Fleming, Peggy Ann Garner, Elsa Lanchester, Victor Moore, Charles Drake, Dennis Morgan and Diana Lynn as Terry Randall. There was also a short-lived 1950 evening soap opera series which differed greatly from the play.

Despite the status of the 1937 film, the play has been infrequently revived over the years. Some critics have called the play as one of Ferber and Kaufman's best joint work. Still, it is generally considered inferior to the 1937 film, and perhaps this is the reason for its lack of theatrical prominence.

As for Sullavan, the experience of *Stage Door* reconfirmed her dedication to the stage and gave her ego a much needed boost. Personally, she was deliriously happy for the first time. She had finally achieved everything she always dreamed of.

17

Time Out for a Feud

The only thing that dikey bitch and I ever had in common was Billie Burke, who supported both of us in our first pictures.[1]

With her film debut, Sullavan was instantly compared to another overnight sensation, Katharine Hepburn, who made her film debut the previous year. Many called Sullavan the new "Hepburn." It was not long before a rivalry between the two was set up by the publicity department and gossip columnists. In the *Los Angeles Post-Record*, George Lewis offered this tidbit: "All Hollywood studios other than the one which basks in the worldwide success of Katharine Hepburn are busily searching for rivals to her."[2] Warner Brothers had Jean Muir, Fox had Loretta Young, and Universal had Sullavan. Sullavan must have been further annoyed when Parsons reported, "Universal … has hopes of making Miss Sullavan another Hepburn."[3]

Hollywood had long engaged in the practice of building up new stars as rivals to established ones. In the 1910s, Mary Miles Minter was billed by Paramount as "America's *Newest* Sweetheart" to replace Mary Pickford, who just defected to form United Artists. In the early days of the talkies, Marlene Dietrich was brought from Germany by Paramount as a rival to MGM's Greta Garbo. One of Hollywood's more ludicrous attempts was Fox's remaking a 19-year-old singer named Alice Faye into a peroxide, singing Jean Harlow.

Sullavan and Hepburn had a lot in common. They both came from well-bred families (Hepburn's from the northeast). They loved the theater and despised filmmaking. They lived by their own rules in a town that celebrated conformity. They both eschewed glamor for a comfortable pair of worn jeans. However, as Hepburn biographer William Mann noted, "The two were destined to be rivals. Both were iconoclastic, headstrong, and upper-class, but Sullavan was infinitely more feminine and sympathetic. On-screen and onstage, she'd be known for heart-searching emotion, while Hepburn was revered for outward strength."[4] What really set them apart, according to Quirk, was that they had profoundly different views of what was important in life. Sullavan was strongly attracted to men, while having few female friends. Hepburn, on the other hand, had a close-knit, intimate circle of female companions. Quirk theorized that it was the loudly whispered hints of Hepburn's lesbian tendencies that set Sullavan on edge. While both were known for their compassion toward homosexual men (director George Cukor was a close friend of both), it appeared that Sullavan had a difficult time reconciling with homosexuality in women. Sullavan openly mocked Hepburn's close relationships with women. Sullavan believed that Hepburn was shirking her responsibilities as a wife and mother as her own Southern upbringing dictated. Still, that does not justify the open hostility Sullavan felt toward Hepburn.

It was not all one-sided, though. It has been suggested by many that Hepburn resented

Sullavan's professional success on the stage and screen. Sullavan was an overnight sensation in her Broadway debut, whereas Hepburn endured several years of failures and lost jobs before her breakthrough hit with *The Warrior's Husband* in 1932. She must have been further rankled when Sullavan's film debut took some of the attention away from her film *Little Women*, which was released a few weeks later.

Still, there is little to suggest anything more than mere irritation with each other. What was it about the Sullavan-Hepburn rivalry that made it so personal as to endure beyond Sullavan's death? The answer related to two men: Jed Harris and Leland Hayward.

Hepburn had known Harris since 1928, when he was a top-ranking Broadway producer and she was a struggling actress. By her own accounts, his only interest in her was her ability to drive him around in her car. By the time she became a big film star, his career was foundering. When Hepburn returned to New York, Harris enticed her with the prospect of starring in *The Lake*. Harris, ever the master manipulator, proved so convincing that Hepburn imagined he was in love with her. Flattered by the attention, she accepted his offer. Big mistake. Harris was known for the cruel manner he treated his actors and crew. He also had the habit of seducing his leading ladies only to discard them after opening night. Hepburn simply was not prepared to deal with what happened next.

When rehearsals began, it was apparent that Hepburn was wrong for the role. Harris recalled, "I could see she was hopeless. I fought with her—I begged her to stop posing, striking attitudes, leaning against doorways, putting limp hand to her forehead, to stop being a big movie star and feel the lines, feel the character. I was trying the impossible, to make an artificial showcase of an artificial star."[5]

Hepburn's ego took a beating when she realized that Harris was banking on her movie fame rather than her talent. She was demoralized when she found out that Sullavan was Harris' first choice. It was a further shock when she discovered that Harris and Sullavan had been romantically involved for a few years.

Hepburn opened in the play to mostly disastrous reviews, but the play managed a profitable run due to her movie fame. Wishing to further capitalize on this, Harris decided to send Hepburn on a national tour. Mortified at the idea of exposing herself to further ego-deflating reviews, Hepburn tried to reason with Harris. His response was cold: "The only interest I have in you is the money I can make out of you."[6] Salvaging whatever shred of self-esteem she had left, Hepburn paid Harris $13,675.75 to break her contract. *The Lake* closed in early February after 55 performances and Hepburn went back to Hollywood.

According to James Robert Parish, the humiliating situation with Harris and the play fueled Hepburn's anger. From that point on, her irrational feelings toward Sullavan extended to those who were associated with her. She turned down Wyler as a prospective director for *Alice Adams* in 1935, because he was married to Sullavan. Many years later, Hepburn snubbed Sullavan's daughter Brooke. When a mutual friend introduced Brooke to Hepburn, it was recorded that "she looked the young woman up and down, ignored her outstretched hand, and made a guttural sound in her throat as a reply. Possibly the reminder of Margaret Sullavan was enough to put Kate in a bad mood."[7] Brooke recalled thinking Hepburn "a very strange woman."[8]

After winning the Oscar for *Morning Glory* (1933) in March 1934, Hepburn was again a hot Hollywood commodity. One of the projects RKO lined up was a screen adaptation of James M. Barrie's *The Little Minister*. Hepburn initially turned the project down, so RKO contacted Universal about borrowing Sullavan. The *Portsmouth Times* reported, "Universal has signed an agreement that Sir James Barrie's *The Little Minister* will star Margaret Sullavan."[9] When Hepburn caught wind of that, she had a sudden change of heart. She recalled,

"I really didn't want to play it until I heard another actress was desperate for that role. Then, of course, it became the most important thing in the world for me that I should get it. Several of my parts in those days I fought for just to take them from someone who needed them."[10] Hepburn was ill-suited for the role and the movie was a financial failure. When Hepburn got *Stage Door*, she must have expressed her joy in taking yet another part away from Sullavan, because Sullavan reportedly sniped to Johnny Swope that it was Hepburn who desperately needed good parts in light of her four-year string of flops.

As Sullavan's relationship with Harris fanned the flames of Hepburn's hostility, it was Sullavan's marriage to Hayward that cemented the bitter rivalry between them once and for all. Hepburn and Hayward began their relationship when she arrived in Hollywood in 1932. Hepburn was still married to her only husband, Ludlow Ogden Smith, while Hayward was still married to his first wife. After both of their divorces in 1934, Hepburn and Hayward moved into a Benedict Canyon house that once belonged to director Fred Niblo. Hepburn later described Hayward as "a really charming human being ... he was fun. He wasn't complicated. He was easygoing. Not too set in his ways. Loved the ladies."[11] Hayward proposed to her several times. She repeatedly turned him down, because she wanted to focus on her acting career. That did not stop the engagement rumors. At one point, Hepburn consented to an engagement; Edna Ferber recalled throwing a lavish bash in their honor.

All that changed in 1936 when Hepburn carried on an adulterous affair with director John Ford during the filming of *Mary of Scotland*. Hayward was crushed when he found out. According to Parish, Hayward had a long-time crush on Sullavan, so he began reciprocating her romantic overtures. News of their romance in New York trickled back to California. As Hepburn recalled, "Oh, I can see it all. The play was a hit. Maggie was a hit. Everything was glorious. He found her fascinating." As she continued her account, Hepburn's words took on more of a "woe-is-me" tone: "Joy was life. Life was joy. Me, far away, became a sort of unreality. She was there. He was there with her. Oh, live in the moment! And they did."[12] Considering Hepburn had turned down Hayward's repeated proposals so she could focus on her career, her pity party is a bit much.

After Sullavan became pregnant and a marriage date was set, Hayward attempted to tell Hepburn the news in person. Unbeknownst to her, Hayward flew his own plane from New York to Los Angeles. He never made it past her driveway in his car. At the last minute, he decided he just could not tell her. Hayward left to return to New York. He sent her a telegram instead. Hepburn was stunned when she got the message and took the news hard. Even more insulting was the headline in the following day's *Los Angeles Times*: "Margaret Sullavan weds Katharine Hepburn's Manager."[13]

This Harrison Carroll news item reflected the Hollywood Publicity Mill at its finest: "If Katharine Hepburn cares a whoop about the marriage of Leland Hayward to Margaret Sullavan, she isn't showing it."[14] According to Carroll, Hepburn was in such high spirits that she played football with the director and crew of *Quality Street*. Nothing could have been further from the truth. Hepburn behaved like a grieving widow. Many who were close to her, including George Cukor, were puzzled by her extreme reaction. On the set, Hepburn often felt sick to her stomach. She confided to co-star Joan Fontaine that she was deeply hurt by Hayward's betrayal. Eventually, Hepburn's mother reminded her that she had refused to marry Hayward on numerous occasions. According to William Mann, "What put Kate in such a dander was the media's implication that Sullavan had stolen her beau. That was simply intolerable."[15] Brooke Hayward agreed: "I don't think [the marriage] particularly bothered her. She had other things she was up to. But she was afraid of what the world would think."[16]

With her mother's admonitions and the opportunity to save face, Hepburn sent the couple separate congratulatory telegrams. Hepburn's message to Sullavan was brief: "Dear Maggie, You have just married the most wonderful man in the world. Blessings, Kate."[17] Accounts of Sullavan's reaction vary, but Brooke Hayward tells of her father's version: "Mother was so incensed that she burned the cable right in front of Father. He loved it. He told that story all the time."[18] Sullavan must have been disgusted by the hypocrisy of the gesture.

Their professional rivalry persisted for many years. One of the rare times both were under consideration for the same role was Scarlett O'Hara. Hepburn, who desperately wanted the role, must have been miffed when Sullavan's name frequently turned up as a leading contender. Despite her fervent campaigning, coupled with Cukor's influence with Selznick, Hepburn was unable to live up to Selznick's conception of Scarlett.

By mid–1938, Sullavan experienced a revitalized film career and renewed public interest courtesy of the critical raves for *Three Comrades*. Hepburn, on the other hand, was declared box office poison. Fortunately for Hepburn, she encountered playwright Philip Barry and the career-rejuvenating play *The Philadelphia Story* the following year. When the play was adapted for the screen by MGM in 1940, it emerged as a complete triumph as well as a vindication for Hepburn. *The Philadelphia Story* was Metro's second highest grossing film of the year and its success brought Hepburn an exclusive contract. During her MGM period, a new Hepburn image emerged: a strong, independent woman who succumbs to the rhapsody of love, thus becoming a vibrant, luminous woman. It is this image that has endured the test of time.

During their joint years at Metro, it must have irked Sullavan to see her nemesis' career soar, while hers was stagnant. Supposedly, Sullavan was too busy with her growing family to care, but one suspects there was still some resentment.

In later years, the actresses' paths crossed occasionally. In 1949, Sullavan took her children to see Hepburn in Shakespeare's *As You Like It* in New York. It was Sullavan's practice to take her children to the theater, so they could learn about their parents' professions along with seeing a great performance. Sullavan's motives for seeing Hepburn was different. "Tonight," she told her children, "you'll see an example of a really horrible performance."[19]

Despite being deeply wounded by Hayward, Hepburn maintained his services as her agent. She carried a torch for him even while she was involved in a 25-year affair with Spencer Tracy. According to Hepburn, Hayward "tried to explain it to me and he really couldn't—any more than I could explain my refusal to marry him." Still, Hepburn held onto to the illusion that she was the great love of his life. As Hayward lay dying, his wife Pamela contacted Hepburn and reportedly told her, "He loved you more than he loved any of us."[20] Many close friends of the Haywards found Hepburn's assertion absurd, insisting that it was Sullavan who was his great love. However, as Brooke said, "There was no bitterness with Kate, no rancor, so of course he could keep his feelings intact for her."[21]

In the end, despite their many similarities, the two woman were unable to overcome basic human emotions.

18

Broken Promises

The minute I have nothing to do, I go crazy.[1]

By early summer of 1937, Sullavan had everything she long desired: theatrical glory; a husband who was as successful in his career as she was in hers; and the cherished dreams of motherhood realized. "I'm happier than I've ever been in my life.... I'm at peace with myself."[2] The time was ripe for retirement from the acting profession as she had threatened on so many occasions. One would have assumed that she would stay in New York. Instead, the unpredictable star headed back to California.

The Haywards moved to Los Angeles and made preparations to build their house in the Brentwood section before the baby's arrival. On July 5, Sullavan gave birth to a healthy girl at the Cedars of Lebanon Hospital. Using Sullavan's middle name, they named their daughter Brooke. As she settled into motherhood and domestic life, many columnists predicted that she would finally retire from acting. However, Sullavan became restless and needed to be doing something in the acting profession.

Within a month of Brooke's birth, this news item made the round of the newspapers: "La Sullavan will go touring in *Stage Door* in October."[3] This must have annoyed Universal as they believed that she would soon be back to work for them.

Despite this announcement, Sullavan received many film offers from different studios. Among the prospects was RKO's adaptation of a Broadway hit, *Having Wonderful Time* with ex-husband number one as her co-star and ex-husband number two as her director! According to Harriett Parsons, "Pan Berman is so anxious to get Margaret Sullavan and Henry Fonda for co-star spots in *Having Wonderful Time*, he's willing to hold up production to fit in with their schedules."[4] Ginger Rogers and Douglas Fairbanks Jr. took over the roles with Alfred Santell handling the directorial chore.

Waiting in the sidelines was Universal, practically waving her 1933 contract and reminding her that she still owed one movie. Since the release of her last Universal film, the studio had undergone a major upheaval in its leadership. The studio was on the brink of bankruptcy in early 1936. Junior hoped that a lavish musical version of Edna Ferber's *Show Boat* would save the day. However, the studio stockholders would not approve the project unless the Laemmles (father and son) secured a loan of $750,000 from the Standard Capital Corp. The Laemmle family's controlling interest in Universal was put up as collateral. When *Show Boat*'s production costs exceeded the budget by $300,000, Standard called upon the Laemmles to pay back the loan. When they failed to do so, Standard foreclosed on the loan and seized control of the studio on April 2, 1936. The Laemmles were forced to leave the studio. Although *Show Boat* emerged as a critical and financial success, it was too late for the Laemmles. In their place, J. Cheever Cowdin of Standard Capital took over as the studio's president and chairman of the board of directors. Cowdin instituted drastic cost-saving cuts in production budgets and the studio began to focus its efforts on low-budget films.

What brought Universal back into prominence was the unexpected but overwhelming popularity of a teenage singer from Winnipeg, Deanna Durbin. Under the careful guidance of producer Joe Pasternak, Durbin created a sensation in her debut, *Three Smart Girls* (1936). Its financial success put the studio back into solvency due to its ranking as Hollywood's sixth most popular film. Durbin's second film, *One Hundred Men and a Girl*, made even more money and ranked third most profitable film in 1937. Due to the continued success of the Durbin-Pasternak musicals for several more years, Durbin has often been credited with saving Universal from folding.

Feeling that Universal only cared about the Durbin musicals and B films, Sullavan doubted that she would be well served. Universal tried to work with the uncooperative actress. The studio resurrected its plan to produce *The Road to Reno*. This time, however, the project was being promoted as a "super special" to be produced by Pasternak. As further proof of their good intentions, negotiations to secure Fonda as her leading man began. When it turned out that Fonda had just committed to filming *Jezebel*, the executives were willing to postpone the start date until he was available. It appeared that Sullavan (and her agent-husband) must have made some kind of initial commitment as it was announced, "It has been practically agreed that her next starring vehicle will be *The Road to Reno*, for Universal."[5] In reality, Sullavan was simply biding her time as she entertained other suitable offers.

As September came around, Sullavan thought twice about the *Stage Door* tour. As Ferber had predicted, she eventually asked to be released from this commitment. It is conceivable that she used the excuse that being away from Brooke, who was around two months old, would cause both mother and baby undue stress. Whatever the reason, the producers probably decided that an unhappy star would not be worth the trouble, so they granted her release. Joan Bennett inherited her part in the production when it opened in Hartford, Connecticut, on October 16. While it is likely that Bennett's lack of star power made her a dubious choice for Broadway, it was hoped that movie fans across the nation would turn out in droves to see her in person. Unfortunately, Bennett's reputation as an uninspired screen actress, coupled with Ferber and Kaufman's inferior script, preceded her, and the tour was not successful as it might have been with Sullavan. It shut down on February 2, 1938, in Chicago.

In October, Louella Parsons reported: "The deal between Hal Roach Studio and Margaret Sullavan grow hotter and hotter. All that now remains is for Maggie to okay the *Road Show* script.... If she feels that the story is suited to her, she will play it."[6] The Hal Roach of the "Our Gang" series and the Laurel and Hardy slapstick comedies? By this time, Roach had begun to concentrate on producing more sophisticated feature films and experienced tremendous success with *Topper*, starring Constance Bennett, Cary Grant and Roland Young. With the instant recognition of Roach's name to the average filmgoer, it might be just the auspicious re-entry back into her film career.

As she was pondering the Roach offer, Sullavan appeared in the pilot program of Tyrone Power's new radio program, *Jergens Hollywood Playhouse*. The 30-minute program featured a condensed version of *Her Cardboard Lover* with Sullavan and Power in the leads. Reviewer Paul Danai noted, "Margaret Sullavan taking advantage of the fat *Cardboard Lover* femme role to steal most of show from Power."[7] Sullavan then appeared in a 60-minute version of *The Petrified Forest* for Cecil B. DeMille's *Lux Radio Theatre* program, in which she gave a sensitive reading as Gaby opposite Herbert Marshall's rather wooden performance as Alan Squire.

By this time, there were more developments in the Hal Roach deal. Sullavan signed a contract with Roach for two pictures a year for three years. However, the contract gave her the right to approve her scripts and she was not happy with the first draft of *Road Show*. To appease her, Roach offered Sullavan the female lead in *Fancy Free* opposite Ronald Colman. The news of Sullavan's contract with Roach was something of a big deal. According to an *Oakland Tribune* news item, "Addition of Margaret Sullavan to the roster of contract stars and featured players places Hal Roach Studios among the foremost ranks of Hollywood producers, according to reports from the movie capital."[8] Under contract were Colman, Constance Bennett, Brian Aherne, Roland Young, Laurel and Hardy and Patsy Kelly.

Universal contended that she was still legally obligated to complete her original contract and considered legal proceedings. In the midst of all this between the Roach contract and the Universal commitment, there was this surprise announcement by columnist Sheilah Graham, which apparently slipped past the watchdogs: "Margaret Sullavan is being urged to leave Roach to star in *Three Comrades*."[9]

Three Comrades was a project in the works at MGM, one of Hollywood's most prestigious studios. Any association with this studio would be a tremendous boost to Sullavan's career and she was certainly interested. Leland was put in charge of working out some kind of picture deal. Prior to Christmas, Parsons excitedly announced that Sullavan accepted Metro's offer despite the fact that she had promised to do *Road Show* for Roach. Her *Three Comrades* co-stars were announced as Robert Taylor, Spencer Tracy and Robert Young, a better line-up than anything Roach could offer.

Universal finally had enough. Legal proceedings were started, but did not reach the courts as Yeaman reported in early January that Sullavan and Universal had patched up their differences. Not only did she agree to make the one picture which was owed under her old contract, but she signed a new deal where she would make two additional pictures for them. About ten days later, the *New York Times* picked up on the story and offered this piece of information: "Margaret Sullavan has settled a year-old dispute with Universal and is returning to the studio to make three pictures, the first of which probably will be *The Road to Reno*." To accommodate Sullavan's one-picture deal with Metro, it was noted, "Under the new arrangement she is permitted to freelance between assignments if she so desires."[10] Universal would regret agreeing to that stipulation. Within days of the *Times* article, Parsons revealed the shocking news that Sullavan had actually signed a long-term contract with Metro. Leland had worked out a sweetheart of a deal for his wife: a contract that called for six pictures at the rate of two pictures a year as well as script approval.

What happened to the Roach contract? That was swept under the rug.

19

Triumphant Return to the Screen

I don't know why I'm on the screen except that I have to be doing something.[1]

In terms of star power, production output and box office returns, Metro-Goldwyn-Mayer was the most prestigious studio during Hollywood's Golden Age. It was founded in 1924 when movie theater owner Marcus Loew (of the Loew's Theater chain) gained control of Metro Pictures, Goldwyn Pictures and Louis B. Mayer Pictures and combined them into one company. Mayer became the head of the renamed Metro-Goldwyn-Mayer with Irving Thalberg as head of production. Under their leadership, MGM set the standard for quality filmmaking and prospered. During the 1930s, the company had the most number of films in the top ten lists along with more Oscar-winning films than any other studio. Many of the top ten money-making stars were from Metro. Among the top male actors were Clark Gable, Robert Taylor, Spencer Tracy, Robert Montgomery, Nelson Eddy and William Powell; the top actresses were Norma Shearer, Greta Garbo, Joan Crawford, Jeanette MacDonald, Myrna Loy, Rosalind Russell, Eleanor Powell and two-time Oscar-winner Luise Rainer. Clearly, Metro lived up to its motto as having "more stars than there are in Heaven."[2]

When Sullavan arrived on the Culver City lot, she was assigned the late Jean Harlow's dressing room. Superstitious, Sullavan asked for a different one room. According to Jimmie Fidler, "A few weeks later, Luise Rainer, boasting of her complete disbelief in any superstition, moved in…. I wonder, now that she has had a nervous breakdown, and a marital row that wound up in the divorce courts, if she hasn't changed her mind."[3] If that wasn't enough, Rainer, despite her second consecutive Oscar win in March, was in a real career rut and soon left the studio.

Sullavan also had an obsession about not starting any film until it rained. Reportedly, after waiting six days, Mayer directed the special effects department to manufacture rain to appease Sullavan.

Three Comrades was based on the 1937 novel *Drei Kameraden* by German writer Erich Maria Remarque, who had lived in exile in Switzerland since 1933. This book was the third book by Remarque to deal with Germany's involvement in World War I. The first book was *All Quiet on the Western Front. Three Comrades* was a sequel to the second novel *The Road Back* as it dealt with soldiers readjusting to life in post–World War I Germany. Due to the overwhelming critical and financial success of the film version of *Western Front*, Metro bought the screen rights to *Three Comrades* in July 1936 before the novel was published. Remarque's story appeared in serial format in *Good Housekeeping* from January to May 1937, before an English version was published in April 1937. The German edition was published in 1938.

While filming *History Is Made at Night* (1937), Charles Boyer told Frank Borzage about the novel and thought it was a possibility for a film. Borzage, who had a non-exclusive contract with MGM, was selected to direct the film by producer Joseph L. Mankiewicz. "I have always had very high regards for Frank Borzage as a director," Manciewicz wrote to Herve Dumont. "I was impressed by the sensitivity he demanded from his actors."[4]

It was a difficult task to turn Remarque's novel into an acceptable screenplay. Not only did Remarque's lovers live together without the benefit of marriage, but there was the strong anti–Nazi undertone to contend with. Set in Berlin during the late 1920s and early 1930s, the novel reflected the political climate preceding the Nazi party takeover. Dr. Georg Gyssling was the Third Reich's diplomatic representative in Los Angeles. As "Hitler's Hollywood consul," he monitored the studios' activities so negative references to Germany were not found in its movies. Germany's political clout was so great that the Hollywood studio moguls (most of them Jewish) bent over backwards to avoid offending Hitler. Many films perceived as inflammatory were either revised or scrapped altogether. It has been recently written by scholars like Ben Upward and Thomas Doherty that Hollywood's catering to a ruthless dictator was solely motivated by financial profits found in the German entertainment market.

As soon as MGM announced its intentions of filming the novel, Gyssling went into action. There was no need to pressure Breen as there were strict rules regarding the depiction of other countries on film. The script would be subjected to heavy scrutiny before Breen *and* Gyssling expressed their approval.

By May 1937, an original treatment was completed, but Gyssling found it objectionable. Breen tried to persuade Mayer to cancel the picture, but too much money had been invested. Mankiewicz sought out F. Scott Fitzgerald, one of the most celebrated writers of the 1920s' "Lost Generation" novels, notably *The Great Gatsby*. Regarded as the finest writer of the 20th century, Fitzgerald was then a hopeless alcoholic struggling to earn a living. He agreed to come to Hollywood to write screenplays at Metro. As Mankiewicz later recalled, "Scott was one of my idols. I hired him personally for this film, and I had to fight, while everyone in the studio said he was finished."[5] Mankiewicz told Aaron Lathan, "I thought that [Fitzgerald] could capture the European flavor and the flavor of the '20s and early '30s that *Three Comrades* required. I also thought that he would know and understand the girl."[6] Fitzgerald was given a six-month contract at a weekly salary of $1000, making him Hollywood's highest paid screenwriter. He was also given sole authorship. Abstaining from alcohol, Fitzgerald worked diligently, but his first script proved to be a major disappointment as it read like a wordy novel with very little concession for the movie camera. In addition, Fitzgerald not only kept in most of the racier elements, but much of its anti–Nazi sentiments as well. After several conferences with Breen, Mayer, Eddie Mannix (Mayer's right-hand man) and Mankiewicz, a compromise was reached. Based on Breen's suggestion, the movie was set in 1920, so they the moviemakers could "get away from any possible suggestion that we are dealing with Nazi violence or terrorism."[7] Additionally, all sequences referring to the Nazi government, incidents of book burning, and the treatment of Jewish citizens were eliminated.

Mankewicz faced opposition from Fitzgerald, who insisted on remaining faithful to the novel. To address this problem, Mankiewicz hired Edward Paramore to work with Fitzgerald to revise the script. This did not sit well with Fitzgerald since he despised Paramore. After one heated argument, Fitzgerald wrote to Paramore, "Your job is to help me, not hinder me."[8] Other writers were engaged to handle further revisions. Even Mankiewicz rewrote some of Fitzgerald's passages. According to Dumont, "In comparing

Fitzgerald's script and the finished screenplay, it was obvious that Mankiewicz's misgivings were justified: the writer did not have dramatic flair; his scenes lack verve, vividness, and his dialogue, while perhaps beautiful to read, are artificial to listen to when spoken."[9]

One of the most important changes Mankiewicz implemented was the heroine's death. In the novel, Pat succumbs after a long battle with tuberculosis. As a child, Mankiewicz underwent a life-saving operation in which a rib was removed. This was perhaps the inspiration for a similar operation for Pat in the film. According to Fitzgerald, Mankiewicz "wanted Margaret Sullavan to live. He said the picture would make more money if Margaret Sullavan lived. He was reminded that Camille had also coughed her life away and had made many fortunes doing it."[10] Not to be outdone, Mankiewicz interjected that *Camille* would have done better at the box office had Garbo lived! Cooler heads prevailed and Sullavan's death remains one of the most poignant death scenes projected on the screen.

By mid–January, Mankiewicz had given Fitzgerald a look at the approved screenplay. Fitzgerald was aghast at the changes made without his knowledge and fired off that infamous follow-up letter to Mankiewicz. Pointing out all the faults, Fitzgerald prophesized, "I think you now have a flop on your hands."[11] Fitzgerald was particularly upset by the transformation of Pat from a sophisticated European woman into a "graduate of Pomona College." "There were tears in my eyes, but not for Pat—for Margaret Sullavan." Fitzgerald finished the letter with this message, which has become legendary within the Fitzgerald cult: "Oh, Joe, can't producers ever be wrong. I'm a good writer—honest. I thought you were going to play fair."[12]

Mankiewicz later sardonically remarked, "If I go down at all in literary history, in a footnote, it will be as the swine who rewrote F. Scott Fitzgerald."[13] In the end, Mankiewicz felt justified as he commented, "He was a marvelous novelist but he wrote 'unspeakable' dialogue for the movies."[14] Despite this, Metro extended Fitzgerald's contract for one year at a new weekly salary of $1250. Fitzgerald worked on screenplays such as *Gone with the Wind, The Women* (1939) and *Madame Curie* (1943), without success. His contract was not renewed after that. *Three Comrades* was the only film for which he received on-screen credit. In 1978, the Southern Illinois University Press published Fitzgerald's screenplay in book form.

By mid–January 1938, the script was approved by Breen, although he had some lingering concerns. "The story, while dramatically sound and entertaining, is, inescapably, a serious indictment of the German nation and people, and is certainly to be violently resisted by the present government in that country."[15] Mankiewicz put pressure on Borzage to modify the offensive scenes.

As the drama of the screenplay played out, the casting had its own issues. In January 1937, Spencer Tracy and Luise Rainer were announced for the coveted leads; they appeared in *Big City* instead. By July, Robert Taylor, Joan Crawford and James Stewart were slated for the film. Feeling her part would be lost in a male-oriented film, Crawford opted out, much to Fitzgerald's relief (he thought that she was grossly ill-suited). Even Taylor tried to get out of the picture as, being pro–American, he was hesitant to appear as a German. Second-stringers Alan Curtis and Dennis O'Keefe were mentioned as replacements for Taylor, but neither was in serious contention. Mayer needed Taylor's drawing power as box office incentive as he doubted the commercial viability of the project, especially since Universal's filmization of *The Road Back* received mostly negative reviews upon its release in June 1937. Mayer finally convinced Taylor the film would be good for his career. The final cast boasted Sullavan, Taylor, Franchot Tone (replacing Tracy) and Robert Young (replacing Stewart). Filming began on February 4, the day Hitler became commander in chief of Wehrnacht.

During the shoot, studio publicity emphasized the "transformation" of Sullavan's personality. In one story, "Not a Problem Child!," Gladys Hall worked overtime in promoting this image. "She's quieter," Borzage told Hall. "She's tamed down" due to her new priorities as a wife and mother.[16] Sullavan said, "There's one thing in life I want more than anything else in the world—to have my marriage stay as it is…. My home comes first with me."[17]

Years later, Taylor stated he had fond memories of working with Sullavan, whom he found "enchanting." He said, "[H]er talent warranted a much bigger career than Hollywood ever allowed her" (curious since Sullavan was responsible for her career).[18] Sullavan had kind words for her leading man as she reported that he was a swell person to work with. In private, however, she confided her doubts he would be able to correctly play the part.

To another interviewer, Sullavan said of her role. "I want so much to do it well," she declared. She also expressed her newfound happiness: "I like being content—not too content—but more so than I ever dreamed." What came next out of her mouth would send chills down one's spine: "I was going to commit suicide at 30, now I'll wait till 40."[19]

Despite stories about the relative calmness on the set, there was still tremendous tension. The main bone of contention was Fitzgerald's dialogue. Mankiewicz recalled, "Maggie Sullavan pulled me off into a corner of the sound stage and said, 'You've got to do something

Her first MGM film *Three Comrades* (1938) not only gave Sullavan a top-ranking box office draw (Robert Taylor, pictured) as her co-star, but also a career revitalizing role which continues to inspire critical raves today.

about this dialogue…. I can't speak it!'"[20] When she did not get the desired results from him, Sullavan tried a different approach with her director. According to Borzage, Sullavan believed there was too much dialogue. She suggested improvising and cutting as filming progressed. By the time Sullavan, Borzage, and a new co-conspirator, Tone, cut many of Fitzgerald's lines, only a third of his original screenplay remained. Ironically, an unintended victim ended up being Tone as many of his lines were cut, thus reducing his footage.

After 52 days, the production wrapped on April 2. By early May, the film was previewed for Breen and Gyssling prior to its May 22 Hollywood premiere. Both were satisfied with the film and okayed it for release. After its preview, *Variety* panned the film. "Just what Frank Borzage is trying to prove in *Three Comrades* is very difficult to fathom," the reviewer sniped. "It's in for a sharp dive at the box office." These were words Mayer did not want to hear, so the ads proclaimed the film "One of the industry's next great box office hits!" Such ads drew the patrons into the theaters, but it was Sullavan's highly acclaimed performance that made critics and audiences cheer.

The film focuses on the three comrades of the title: Erich Lohkamp (Taylor), the youthful romantic; Gottfried Lenz (Young), the political activist; and Otto Koster (Tone), the pragmatic one. Having served in the Great War together, they struggle to adjust to life in Germany amidst constant political unrest. One night, they make the acquaintance of Herr Breuer (Lionel Atwill) after a high-speed chase. We are treated to a lovely shot of Pat Hollman (Sullavan), an impoverished aristocrat, as she emerges from the car bathed in softfocus lighting and swelling music. She asserts that she and Breuer are only "friends" (we know better). Erich is immediately smitten.

The next day, Erich works up the courage to call Pat to ask her out. However, he is all nerves and it is Pat who sets up the date. They dine at a bar owned by Alfonse (Guy Kibbee). They are soon joined by Otto and Gottfried—thus ushering in a new comradeship.

After their taxi is vandalized, Gottfried reluctantly disassociates himself from his political organization so his friends do not suffer from the consequences of his activities.

When Pat invites Erich to the opera, he hopes he can fit into her world, so he borrows Otto's pants and Gottfried's tails. After the opera, Pat and Erich join Breuer and his party at a fancy restaurant. It is not long before Erich's misguided efforts to fit into her world literally falls apart when his too-tight jacket rips at the seams. A humiliated Erich leaves Pat behind with her mocking friends.

After a drinking binge, Erich finds that Pat has fallen asleep waiting on his doorstep. She is cold and has a brief coughing spell. Nestling in his arms, Pat breathlessly tells Erich, "This is a lovely time of day … the edge of eternity. Let's stay right here forever." Pat coughs again with the romantic music striking an ominous chord. Erich thinks she's cold, but the viewer knows that it's more serious than that.

Abandoning the life of luxury with Breuer, Pat settles into life with the comrades. Otto tries to convince Pat to marry Erich, but she's curiously evasive. He doesn't buy her ambiguous excuses and persists in the matter. Finally, she confesses that she has been in poor health in the past and it may come back. Understanding that she has tuberculosis, Otto convinces her it is still worth taking the gamble at finding happiness—as long as Erich doesn't find out. Sullavan is heart-wrenching as she conveys her conflicting feelings, thus offering the best evidence that she would have been ideal as Daisy from *The Great Gatsby*.

Erich and Pat's wedding takes place in Alfonse's bar. Borzage intercuts the separate close images of all four friends to symbolically seal their spiritual union. For a brief moment, all the stars are aligned in Borzage's magnificent heaven. While on the honeymoon, Pat collapses. Pat's doctor, Prof. Jaffe (Monty Wooley, crotchety without the trademark twinkle in his eyes), is summoned. While Pat (looking frighteningly frail) is being attended to, Otto reveals the truth about Pat's condition to Erich. Dr. Jaffe tells Otto that Pat must be at the sanitarian by early fall.

It is mid–October and Dr. Becker (Henry Hull) is speaking at a rally, when a mob enters the scene and begins fighting with the demonstrators. Gottfried rescues his former mentor and they hide in a warehouse with his supporters. Meanwhile, Pat and Erich are at home. She's unnerved by the wind, but Erich reassures her that his life is much enriched by her presence. "I thank God for you," he tells her in the most outspoken expression of Borzage's religious faith. Erich receives a phone call from Dr. Jaffe, who insists that she leaves for the sanitarian that day.

At the train station, Erich and Pat are joined by Otto. As Pat says goodbye, she is painfully aware of the train whistle blowing and the sound of the pulsing train engine. The haunted look in Sullavan's eyes succeeds in adding poignancy to the moment. She leaves, unaware that Gottfried is in the middle of a riot. Erich and Otto arrive back at the riot in time to see Gottfried gunned down as he and Becker's supporters flee. Wracked by grief, Otto and Erich sell their repair shop so they can devote all their time to searching for Gottfried's killer. On Christmas night, Otto spots him. In one of Borzage's most stunning visual sequences, Otto follows the man through snowbound, deserted streets. As the frantic man arrives at a church, with the "Hallelujah Chorus" from Handel's *Messiah* filling the soundtrack, he attempts to enter inside to safety. But there is no mercy for the man who killed the innocent Gottfried without just cause. As a final touch of this symbolically religious moment, he is shot dead in self-defense by Otto, with the church looming behind him, and "Alleluia" is heard multiple times.

Pat learns that she needs a potentially risky operation. She is concerned about the cost and becomes rather fatalistic in her outlook of life without Erich. She invites him to the sanitarian for the Christmas holidays. Erich learns that Pat's operation will cost them over 1000 marks. Otto decides to sell his prized car "Baby" to cover the cost. After the operation, Pat is given strict instruction to lie very still for two weeks; to do otherwise would put her life in danger. When Otto visits Pat, she learns that he sold the car. Saddened, Pat becomes morbidly philosophical about her purpose in life. "Can't you see, Pat, what you've given us?" Otto asks. "For me, happiness I never thought I'd known. For Erich, his life...." Pat interrupts him. What has she given Gottfried? When Otto falters, this confirms her suspicions that Gottfried is dead. "How did he die?" she inquires.

"Bravely ... proudly ... for what he thought was right," Otto answers. As he continues, the camera focuses on Pat's pensive face during her "clarity of vision" moment. She knows what she needs to do, so that she, too, may die with honor.

The next few minutes are Sullavan's finest on the screen and bear close analysis. When Erich leans into a tight close-up, she becomes upset. "It ticks so loud," she tells him. "Your watch, it's so threatening." After Erich throws the watch across the room, Pat, in radiant close-up, whispers, "Now time is standing still." This is the moment she will carry into eternity.

Pat is left alone after Erich leaves to see Otto off. With pulsing music and a camera that hovers over her (suggesting that her self-sacrificial act has been sanctioned by God), Pat gets out of the bed and, bathed in light from a window, walks out to the balcony. Seeing Erich down below, she reaches out to him as the music comes to a crescendo. Suddenly, the only sound heard is the wind as she collapses. To Sullavan's credit, she resists the temptation to overact this sequence and plays it with simplicity and honesty, thereby making it all the more haunting.

As Pat lies dying in Erich's arms, she whispers, "It's right for me to die, darling. It isn't hard ... and I'm so full of love." Their love remains pure and untainted by the grim realities of their bleak existence. Dumont says this of Sullavan's death: "The sparseness of the effects, the concision of the gestures and editing border on the miraculous: Borzage captures the most beautiful death in film history."[21]

Erich and Otto plan to leave for South America. As they walk away from Pat's grave, they are joined by the ghostly figures of Pat and Gottfried walking alongside them. Near the end of this scene, all four figures are seen in the same manner, indicating they will remain bound together in life and death.

When the film was released nationwide at the end of May, moviegoers flocked to see their idol Taylor in his latest movie, thus dispelling Mayer's fears of a flop. It was well received by the public despite the varying critical reviews. It was not surprising to read crotchety Amy Croughton's dismissive assessment in the *Rochester Times-Union*: "The heroine of Patricia seems rather strained, at times, because of her background and past history are so vague and unsubstantial. Nor does Miss Sullavan's delivery of her lines make them any more convincing." According to *The Hollywood Reporter*, there was much to praise as well as to condemn:

> *Three Comrades* is a combination of the magnificent and the deeply disappointing. The superb performance of Margaret Sullavan as the Camille-like heroine is one of the gems of screen history…. The poignant romance is beautiful. There are moments of splendid dramatic intensity…. [But] its screenplay is too determinedly dramatic and philosophical. Its pace is so pedestrian as to become definitely tedious at times…. Miss Sullavan imparts to the girl a ringing sincerity with a delicacy of lights and shades, which makes her interpretation always entrancing.

The *Syracuse Post-Standard* wrote, "*Three Comrades* is one of the finest pictures that has ever come out of Hollywood…. It does have real depth … a cast that reaches new heights of sincerity and conviction; and direction by Frank Borzage that can't be beaten…. [Sullavan] returns to the screen in complete triumph." The National Board of Review praised Sullavan as "the memorable person … who creates one of those rare and beautiful things that no ordinary words can describe. It is like a spell that comes back in full force every time you think of her, and tempts you to the conviction that there is no better actress on the screen."

Three Comrades managed a respectable profit of $472,000, due to Taylor's drawing power with the female patrons. The film graced many Ten Best Films lists for such publications as *The New York Times* and *Film Daily*. The big winner in all of this was Sullavan, whose performance was hailed as one of the year's best. Sullavan received the British National Award and the *Picturegoer's* Gold Medal. In addition, the National Board of Review rated her performance as one of the year's ten best performances. On January 2, 1939, Sullavan won the New York Drama Critics Award for best actress, winning 13 out of 17 votes. James Cagney of Warner Brothers won for his mesmerizing performance in *Angels with Dirty Faces*.

Speculations ran high that Sullavan would win the Academy Award. Most of the early polls favored Bette Davis for her performance in *Jezebel*. With the New York Critics' Drama Award, however, speculations shifted to Sullavan. Columnist Wood Soanes predicted: "Unless something extraordinary happens at the polls, it is quite possible that two of Hollywood's stormiest of stormy petrels [Sullavan and Cagney] will march hand in hand to the rostrum at the American Academy of Motion Picture Arts and Sciences dinner and get the coveted gold statuettes."[22]

When the Academy Awards ceremony was held in February 1939, Davis and Spencer Tracy (his second consecutive Oscar win for *Boys Town*) emerged as victors. There are two possible explanations for Sullavan's loss. First, she was a rebel who repeatedly and loudly proclaimed her disdain for Hollywood and filmmaking. More damning was Sullavan's total disregard for her Universal contract, to say nothing of the Roach contract. It was unthinkable among the industry executives that any star should disregard a legally binding contract. This was Sullavan's only Oscar nomination, despite widespread consensus that she was one of the screen's finest actresses.

In recent years, many film historians and critics have offered their own choices in the Best Actress category. Interestingly, Davis' *Jezebel* performance is often set aside in favor of other actresses, most notably Hepburn in either *Bringing Up Baby* or *Holiday*. Sullavan manages to make it on a few lists. In the book that sparked the re-assigning award craze,

Alternate Oscars, Danny Peary made his own arguments for Sullavan: "Her every expression moves us; her graceful and thoughtful delivery makes Fitzgerald's most romantic lines seem like poetry. Sullavan is wistful, haunted as one listens to her distinctly throaty voice, one immediately gets the uneasy feeling that Pat already has one foot in heaven."[23] In the blog "Fritz and the Oscars," there is much in favor of a Sullavan win. "There is something about this visibly intelligent and thoughtful actress that enabled her to create something very tragic, disturbing, moving and captivating," 'Fritz' wrote.[24] In his critique, Dan Callahan of *Slant Magazine* opined that this was Sullavan's best performance. "She brings the film to life gradually, delicately, making full use of Fitzgerald's wistful little poeticisms, and dying like nobody has ever died on screen before or since."[25]

What is it about Sullavan's performance that has withstood the test of time? Simply, Sullavan avoided the temptation to give flash to her role. In her own distinctive, sublime manner, she transforms Pat into a living emotion through her intelligent and expressive face. One is instantly drawn into Pat's mysterious world from the start and marvel as her character's layers are revealed. We become a privileged member of Pat's inner world and it is she who gives the film its poignant appeal. It is inarguably Sullavan's finest screen portrayal and it haunts one's memories long after the film's conclusion.

Over the years, criticism has been launched at the film's "unwillingness" to address the Hitler issue. In fairness to Metro, Hitler's fascist regime had not yet emerged as a dangerous situation. Hitler was perceived as a dictator who could be cajoled into "playing nice" as long as the international community did not exert any pressure. When Germany invaded Poland in September 1939, the world was forever changed. In that context, one cannot look at this film as a failed attempt to publicly out Hitler. Nor is the film even an early example of anti–Nazi films. Rather, the film spotlights the story of a time of changing political atmosphere in Germany after the humiliating defeat of World War I. To Borzage, the enemy which threatens the lovers is the cruelty of fate and shortened time. In this manner, it is ironic that the film pulses with a palpable dose of the Fitzgerald's "lost generation" sentiments, despite the loss of much of his material.

Three Comrades endures as a haunting, romantic film that is in need of serious re-evaluation as its "forgotten film" status is unwarranted. Ultimate credit for its beauty can be attributed to Sullavan's performance and Borzage's direction. The film is replete with Borzage's stunning visual imagery that compels repeated viewing as the viewer inevitably notices something new that was missed earlier. The religious motif based on Borzage's Roman Catholic upbringing is particularly noticeable here. Most importantly, the film remains as a sterling example of one of the most mature, thoughtful works of the great Hollywood romanticist. His handling of a potentially mawkish theme and the clunky Fitzgerald dialogue is miraculous. One cannot underestimate Borzage's genius considering the film might have been handled by some of Metro's other directors, whose lack of understanding and insight into its theme and Sullavan's special personality would have rendered the film "dead on arrival."

The performances of the three male leads are worthy of praise and well matched to Sullavan's work. As familiar as one may be as the affable characters Young played in films and television, one is touched by the sincerity, depth and angst he exhibits. Tone, equally remembered for being likably glib in his light comedies, is superb in one of his best roles from the 1930s. Taylor, despite some of the mixed reviews he received, is perfectly cast. Borzage managed to elicit sensitivity from Taylor that is both extremely appealing and natural. He makes a fabulous partner for Sullavan and the two radiate just the kind of on-screen chemistry that only exists in Borzage's romantic vision.

Three Comrades is a superlative and soul-searching love story enhanced by two people who shared a beautiful cinematic rapport: Frank Borzage and Margaret Sullavan. Their collaboration here is the finest work either had ever achieved and stands as an enduring testament to their supreme artistic talents. This film is a fitting tribute to two long-forgotten artists who deserve to be better known and appreciated among today's film audiences.

20

Jimmy and Hot Apple Pie

It embarrassed Jimmy to have so many people whispering that he was carrying this eternal torch for Maggie, and certainly she encouraged it.[1]
—Billy Grady

In his James Stewart biography, Marc Eliot referred to the term "doubling." Originated by French film critic Andre Bazin, "doubling" refers to a cinematic phenomenon "wherein the characters in a film mirror the relationship between the characters in real life, with the resultant sparks supercharged—the reality of the actors' lives off-screen adding depth to the lives of the characters they portray."[2] While Eliot used this term in reference to *The Shop Around the Corner*, a stronger case could be made with Sullavan and Stewart's second teaming, *The Shopworn Angel*.

The film was based on Dana Burnet's short story "Private Pettigrew's Girl," which appeared in *The Saturday Evening Post* in 1918. According to online sources, the story was the basis for a play which apparently never reached Broadway. In 1919, the story emerged as a film entitled *Pettigrew's Girl*. Produced by the Famous Players-Lasky Corp. (later Paramount), it starred Ethel Clayton as Daisy Heath and Monte Blue as Private William Pettigrew. It told the simple story of a lonely soldier who falls in love with a Broadway chorus girl. Although dating a rich man, Daisy falls in love with William and rejects her long-time suitor. William returns from the war to find Daisy waiting for him.

In 1928, the story was resurrected by Paramount as *The Shopworn Angel* with Nancy Carroll (as Daisy), Gary Cooper (as Bill Tyler) and Paul Lukas (as Bailey). This time, the story had a harder, more cynical tone than the original. In this version, Daisy is a jaded chorus girl involved in a steamy affair with Bailey, a man with a dangerous reputation. Although the basic premise of the story remained the same, a different ending, in which Bill dies overseas, was improvised. It was produced near the end of the silent film era; Paramount added a song and a wedding scene in which both Carroll and Cooper were heard saying "I do." The film was a tremendous success. As with the case of many silent movies, this film was lost for many years. A 35mm print (minus the talking sequences and the final reel) was found and currently resides in the Library of Congress film archives.

In 1937, Metro bought the rights from Paramount as a vehicle for Jean Harlow and James Stewart. After Harlow's death in June 1937, Joan Crawford and Dennis O'Keefe were announced as the leads. When Crawford bowed out, Rosalind Russell was her replacement. A short time later, Russell was scheduled to appear in the studio's British-made production *The Citadel*. Sullavan was then assigned the role. Producer Joseph Manciewicz decided that Stewart would appear opposite her. Sources indicate that Melvyn Douglas was initially cast as Bailey, but Walter Pidgeon was selected in the end.

Assigning a director was no easy task. According to various reports, Richard Thorpe was the initial choice. Then newly signed French director Julien Duvivier was considered. H.C. Potter, borrowed from Samuel Goldwyn, was brought in as director and production began on March 29 just as *Three Comrades* wrapped up.

The first task Mankiewicz faced was developing a script that would meet the standards of the Breen Production Code and satisfy Mayer's insistence on providing wholesome family entertainment. Mankiewicz instructed novice screenwriter Waldo Salt, who later won the Academy Award for his *Midnight Cowboy* (1969) and *Coming Home* (1978) screenplays, to make the necessary changes. Many of the seedier elements were toned down. Daisy's occupation was elevated from chorus girl to musical star. Her hard edges were softened and her spiritual redemption was greatly emphasized. The gangster lover, Bailey, became a respectable producer who has unrealized feelings for Daisy. Most important of all, Daisy's feelings for Bill would be mostly platonic on her part and there was no hint of sexual impropriety.

Since their first teaming two years earlier, Stewart had made steady gains at Metro, although it was mostly in supporting roles. The part of Bill Pettigrew was tailor-made and Sullavan was determined to showcase his acting. As the actor's wife Gloria Stewart reflected, "Jim told me that she gave him more direction than the director, that he learned a little something more about screen acting every time he worked with her."[3]

Others on the set and around the studio lot noticed the potent chemistry between the two. According to Grady, Mayer himself proclaimed that the two were red-hot when together on the screen. Co-star Pidgeon found that it was clear that Stewart was deeply in love with Sullavan. He believed that Stewart never played with as much sincerity and conviction with other leading ladies as he did with Sullavan. Both Pidgeon and Potter believed that Sullavan was flattered by Stewart's unabashed attention as it boosted her self-image.

Shooting progressed smoothly, despite Sullavan taking the occasion to be difficult. According to Jimmie Fidler, "If studio workers balloted for the most uncooperative star in Hollywood, Margaret Sullavan would pull an almost unanimous vote."[4] Apparently, the "transformed" star of *Three Comrades* had not changed much at all. In a later interview, Sullavan justified her distaste for interviews:

> When I was working in *The Shopworn Angel*, I refused all press interviews. It was not because I don't like them, but simply because I thought it unfair to my work and to the actors with whom I was working. It's easy to say anything about staying in the correct mood, but if one talks about his childhood for an hour and then tries to get back into the real feeling of a scene, it's very difficult.[5]

There was still an atmosphere of fun on the set. On one occasion, Sullavan arrived on the set sporting a bad case of sunburn after several days at Palm Springs. Although the studio forbade its stars from sunbathing during production, Sullavan was hardly the kind to follow such mandates. Still, she felt uncomfortable—and it wasn't just the sunburn's painful effects. In an impish mood, Stewart could not resist playing a practical joke by plastering dozens of pictures of her with her face and hands colored with red ink on the walls of the set. "An old Stewart touch," laughed Sullavan. "The art is Stewart's idea of heaping coal fire on my fevered brow."[6]

A tremendous amount of publicity extolled Sullavan's dancing skills acquired as a child (interesting since she does very little dancing in the film). What was not revealed was her lack of a singing voice. Mankiewicz recalled a story when Sullavan was directly asked if she could sing. She assured Mankiewicz and composer Franz Waxman that she most certainly could. "Don't you want to hear me?" she innocently asked them. The three went to

Left to right: **James Stewart, Margaret Sullavan and Walter Pidgeon in** *The Shopworn Angel* **(1938). The dated tale of a showgirl regenerated by love was energized by the "doubling effect," courtesy of the unique Sullavan-Stewart friendship.**

a nearby sound stage and Waxman played a song at Sullavan's request. Out of her mouth came what Mankiewicz referred to as caterwauling. "There was nothing approaching a note that was anywhere near true," he recalled. "Franz and I just stared at her incredulously." Sullavan explained she had learned that the only way to convince people that she really couldn't sing was to give a demonstration. As Mankewicz marveled, "That's the day I realized that this marvelous, offbeat delivery that Maggie had was because she was utterly tone deaf and couldn't hear herself talking."

An unknown singer was hired to provide Sullavan's singing voice. The 24-year-old girl was trying to break into show business via motion pictures and had recently secured a bit part in Universal's *The Rage of Paris*. Potter recalled the day they recorded her voice. Due to budget restraints, there was little time for extensive rehearsals. "So, in ten minutes," Potter remembered, "the poor girl had to absorb not only the whole storyline but also *how* the song should be sung, where she should choke up, falter, convey the 'show must go on' spirit, *move* an audience with her bravery, etc. After only one rehearsal with the orchestra, she did it magnificently, and we printed the first take."[7]

Potter was so impressed that he tried to convince the executives to sign her to a contract. Unfortunately, everyone declared that she was just a singer and would never amount to anything.[8] After providing the voice for Louise Hovick (Gypsy Rose Lee) in 20th Century–Fox's *Battle on Broadway* (1938), the dejected girl went back to New York. There she scored a sensation singing Cole Porter's "My Heart Belongs to Daddy" in the hit show *Leave It to Me*. This success led her back to Hollywood with a Paramount contract. After appearing in nine films with little impact, she headed back to Broadway to star in the first of many hit shows, *One Touch of Venus* (1943). Her other notable successes included *South Pacific* (1949), *Peter Pan* (1954) and *The Sound of Music* (1959). Hollywood's loss was Broadway's gain. By now, you should have figured out that it was the future legendary Broadway star, Mary Martin, who provided Sullavan's singing voice.

Principal filming was completed by May 6 and, after two months of post-production work, the film was previewed at the Westwood Village Theatre in Hollywood in early July. The ads proclaimed "Margaret Sullavan tops *Three Comrades* triumph and clinches top stardom!"

The film opens in early April 1917 in New York City, as America prepares to enter World War I. A military parade rouses a hung-over Daisy Heath (Sullavan) from her sleep. A cynical woman with a jaded view of love, Daisy is loved by Sam Bailey (Pidgeon), who is more invested in this relationship than she.

That night, Private Bill Pettigrew (Stewart) steps out in front of Daisy's car and is knocked down. A policeman orders Daisy's chauffeur to give Bill a ride back to camp. The scene that follows delightfully highlights the two contrasting characters: a hard-boiled, practical woman (humorously played by Sullavan in a sassy Jean Harlow mood) and an innocent, naïve man (as only Stewart can play him without inviting ridicule).

Bill pretends Daisy is his girl to his friends at the base. They find out the truth and decide to teach Bill a lesson. At the back door of the theater, Bill and the boys meet Daisy, who quickly catches on and carries on with the pretense. The two then go to the corner soda fountain, where Bill confesses the whole ruse. In the film's best scene, Bill tells her about hot apple pie. "My mother used to bake the best hot apple pie you've ever tasted. But when she died, I couldn't have any. So when I couldn't have any like that, I didn't want any at all." He tells Daisy that she's like hot apple pie. This entire exchange serves as the potent example of the "doubling" concept. Bill falls hopelessly in love with Daisy, while she softens her attitude toward Sam.

Sam arranges for a show at Bill's camp. Daisy makes a hit with her rousing rendition of "Pack Up Your Troubles in Your Old Kit Bag and Smile, Smile, Smile." After the performance, Bill takes Daisy on a tour of the camp. The grim reality of war slowly invades their conversation as Bill talks about the uncertainties of a soldier during wartime. Daisy is touched by Bill's beliefs in the finer things in life and her cynicism dwindles as she assumes a maternal attitude towards Bill.

When Daisy arrives home after her day at Coney Island with Bill, she finds Sam in an irritable mood. Sam insists Bill is in love with her, but Daisy doesn't believe it as Bill knows how she feels. After an argument, Daisy realizes that Sam is jealous. She assures Sam that she loves him. What is remarkable is the wide range Sullavan reveals in her voice: the wonderment of a girl who just experienced simple pleasures she has never known; the ferocious denials of a woman who should not have encouraged Bill's "pretending"; and the tender woman awakened by her love for Sam. Rarely has Sullavan managed the shifting voice inflections and intensity with such perfect ease.

The next night, the troop is being deployed overseas and Bill goes AWOL. He meets Daisy at the theater to tell her he's leaving. Against her better judgment, she leaves the show to spend the rest of the day with Bill.

Bill finally reveals his love for her. Not wanting to hurt him, Daisy implores, "You can't be unhappy. It'll be all right, just go on pretending…. Just pretend, Bill, you're good at that." This potentially laughable moment is blessed by Sullavan's absolute sincerity.

Bill can't pretend any more. He tells her that he wants the real thing—her. One imagines the pain Stewart was in to say this to the unrequited love of his life. This scene resonates with poignant power. Back at her apartment, Bill gazes upon Daisy, who is a vision of loveliness in soft focus lighting and a shimmering white dressing gown; her appearance signals that the regeneration has begun. Bill suggests they could be married at the chapel near the base. Before she gives him an answer, Sam arrives. Bill announces his intentions to marry Daisy. When Sam starts to tell Bill the truth about Daisy, she stops him. In private, she tries to explain the improbable situation to Sam. This is the moment when the film spirals out of control at this illogical plot development; not even Sullavan's acting can salvage the situation. Sullavan speaks her lines fast and furiously as if she's hoping we won't catch on that it's utter nonsense. While she professes her love for Sam, she somehow feels compelled to marry Bill. She will tell him the truth when he comes back. She asks Sam to put their love on hold, so they can loan Bill all the happiness he will ever know. While this trite set-up does not destroy the overall impact of the film, it does inflict some damage which the actors cannot overcome.

As Bill's regiment heads out, he promises to write to Daisy every day, rain or shine. He means it, too. In the war montage, it seems that every third frame shows Bill writing a letter to his beloved. Even as bombs fall around him and the bugles sound, Bill will not put that damn pencil down.

Back in New York, Sam visits Daisy at the nightclub where she appears. Daisy is literally aglow in warm sentiment as she shares Bill's latest letter. Her appearance suggests that her redemption is almost complete, but it will come at a terrible price. While performing a reprise of "Pack Up Your Troubles," Daisy (now blinding against a background of sparkling chorus girls' outfits) sees her maid, Martha (Hattie McDaniel), arrive with a letter from the War Department. When Sam opens the letter, Bill's identification bracelet falls out and Daisy realizes that he is dead. The film ends with a satisfying close-up of Daisy's grief-stricken face as tears flood her eyes while finishing her song. This is the perfect "Margaret Sullavan" ending and does much to erase the bad taste left by the recent sequences.

Released in mid–July, the film was met with mixed reviews. The *New York Times* carped, "There really ought to be a Margaret Sullavan act" which would prevent her "from having to speak such forced insincere lines, from growing finally to look almost spooky herself because of the maudlin unreality of the character she is trying to portray." *Liberty* magazine had unqualified praise as the film was "blessed … with such a delicate, sweetly humorous performance by Margaret Sullavan as to be lifted into the distinction of importance of living character portrayals…. Miss Sullavan so bringing the role of the girl up to the ranks of art that you will remember her and her story with understanding fondness for months after the film has faded away." The *Boston Globe* had this to say: "The love story is unbelievable, but effective, because so ably delineated…. One suspects that Margaret Sullavan could make any characterization convincing, no matter how illogical the plot and the dialogue. She is one of the finest emotional actresses in film, and a picture such as this invariably adds to her laurels."

With the renewed interest in Sullavan after *Three Comrades*, *Shopworn Angel* managed a tidy profit of $146,000. The *Film Daily* rated the film as one of the "notable productions" of 1938. In the end, it solidified Sullavan's standing in Hollywood and Stewart's career received a needed boost before he attained full-fledged stardom the following year.

After three versions, Burnet's story should have been left on the shelf. However, some genius at Paramount had the bright idea of resurrecting the story for its fourth outing in 1959. Entitled *That Kind of Woman*, the film's source was officially listed as Robert Lowry's short story "Layover in El Paso," but there is little doubt that the essential elements of Burnet's story made it into the final screenplay. The film starred Tab Hunter (the cinematic equivalent of white bread here), sultry Italian actress Sophia Loren, and George Sanders. Although the film boasts some stunning black-and-white photography, location footage and some interesting touches by director Sidney Lumet, it ended up a dull gab-fest that was hurt by the lack of chemistry between Loren and Hunter.

Without access to the 1928 film, the 1938 adaptation remains the best, albeit flawed. Despite its dated qualities that harken back to an earlier time, it is an enjoyable movie in which Potter's direction is efficient in keeping things moving at a brisk pace. It is unfortunate that he allows the film to lose its bearings in the last portion and overdoes the symbolic visualization of Daisy's redemption. It must be admitted that the stars are not able to completely hurdle the contrived plot development near the end. What ultimately transcends the film is the marvelous simpatico between Sullavan and Stewart. This film would be considerably less effective were it not for the warm and tender relationship they shared. Frank Miller said it best: "Their emotional openness together gave audiences a privileged look at two souls sharing an intimate connection."[9] The "doubling" effect is evident is many delightful scenes and keeps the viewer emotionally invested.

Sullavan gives a magnificent performance in the most complicated role she ever essayed on the screen. She gives full display of the character's range of evolving emotions and manages the subtle changes in her character's moral development beautifully. For the most part, Daisy comes across as a very real person. The thought of Crawford handling Daisy's transformation is unnerving to say the least. Crawford's forte was that of a sophisticated and glamorous star; her mega-watt personality would have rendered this part and the movie unconvincing. In Sullavan's hands, it is quite an impressive performance that, were it not for *Three Comrades*, would certainly have garnered an Oscar nomination.

As Bill, Stewart has the trickier role. It would have been an asinine part if played by anyone else, but Stewart's inherent sincerity makes it work (until the final moments). His gifts as an actor and his barely disguised affection for Sullavan make us believe in him despite contrary feelings. With the combination of Sullavan and Stewart, one is able to accept even the most trite set-ups.

The supporting cast fits snugly in their roles according to their screen types. As Daisy's long-time suitor, the third member of the triangle, Pidgeon gives a nicely nuanced and intelligent performance. It reveals the easygoing, relaxed style that would eventually propel him to stardom, especially when he was paired with Greer Garson in the 1940s. Hattie McDaniel, one year away from her award-winning role of Mammy in *Gone with the Wind*, is amusing as Daisy's put-upon maid as it allows for an opportunity to provide a level-headed contrast to Daisy's mercurial nature. Additionally, she is afforded a great moment in which she contemptuously brushes off an unwanted remark as she enters a posh night club. Given racial segregation at that tune, it's a daring moment.

Appearing in the uncredited role of Jack, the elevator boy, is Jimmy Butler. After a promising debut in *Only Yesterday* and a noteworthy performance in Borzage's anti-war allegory *No Greater Glory*, Butler should have been on his way to stardom. But as he grew older, important film roles dwindled to smaller, non-billed walk-ons. Given Sullavan's fondness for the boy and propensity for helping those in need, it is conceivable that she helped Butler secure the small speaking role. Butler continued playing small roles in various films until mid–1943. He then went off to fight in World War II. He was killed in action in France on February 18, 1945, two days prior to his 24th birthday. He left behind his young wife Jean and two boys, one three-years-old and the other only six months. Sullavan was reportedly greatly saddened to hear of his death.

∽∽∽

Many years after making *Shopworn Angel*, Potter shared with Quirk his views that, had Stewart not been so shy about expressing his deep love for Sullavan, they may have married. Stewart, however, never did press his suit. Instead, he pined for her in the background, while maintaining a close friendship with her until the day she died. Stewart dated several of Hollywood's most beautiful stars, including Ginger Rogers, Dinah Shore and Olivia de Havilland. A few times, he was even engaged. Yet he was not able to commit to marriage. Sullavan's divorce from Leland Hayward in 1948 may have given him the long-awaited opportunity to actively pursue her. Actress Myrna Dell, who was engaged to Stewart in the late 1940s, recalled to Donald Dewey, "Everyone in Hollywood knew the stories about Jimmy and Margaret Sullavan … [and] he was still clearly in love with her in the late 1940s." She elaborated:

> Sometimes when I was at his house, she would call from New York or Connecticut, and suddenly he had this tiny puppy dog voice talking to her. I might as well have not been there. She really manipulated him, even long distance. Anything she said was right, anything said against her was absolutely wrong. I got the feeling that she'd call him whenever she was in need of a little adoration.[10]

A Valentine's Day item in Frank Neal's syndicated column in 1949 revealed Stewart as one of Hollywood's most eligible bachelors: "Jimmy Stewart still insists to his buddies that he won't stand still for a cutie and be rushed into matrimony. Some of Jimmy's pals think he might eventually wind up getting hitched to Margaret Sullavan."[11]

What prevented Stewart from acting upon his feelings? For one thing, Sullavan had become seriously involved with an Englishman, Kenneth Wagg, by 1949. Perhaps Stewart finally realized the futility of the situation. At a dinner party hosted by the Gary Coopers, Stewart was introduced to a divorced mother of two, Gloria Hatrick McLean. The two had a lot in common and things became serious quickly. On August 9, 1949, the 41-year-old actor married Gloria. Among the wedding guests were Sullavan and Wagg.

Although Sullavan and Stewart maintained their close friendship, Gloria claimed that she was never worried. "He never gave me cause to be suspicious or jealous in any way," she told Michael Munn. "I could never be jealous about Sullavan…. Despite their history way back when, he was never going to have an affair with her because it was against his principles."[12] Not long after his marriage, Stewart was quoted as saying, "My definition of love is being devoted to one another unselfishly."[13] All the pretending in the world could not have convinced him that Sullavan was capable of reciprocating that kind of love.

What set Gloria apart from Sullavan was fundamental: self-confidence. A friend, Gloria Winants, elaborated, "Nobody had a great sense of self [than Gloria], and probably nobody had appreciated it more or depended on it more than Jimmy."[14] Jimmy and Gloria Stewart remained married until Gloria's death from lung cancer in 1994.

21

Balancing Motherhood and Career

I've never really thought seriously of a "Baby vs. Career," because there was
never the decision involved that there must be with an important star.[1]

When Sullavan was in between film shoots, she reveled in her role as a mother. Though she had previously made infrequent visits to her parents' home in Norfolk, Sullavan made more regular trips to Norolk after Brooke's birth. During these trips, Sullavan often hired a nurse to help care for her young daughter. One trip she had made in July of 1938 generated a considerable amount of publicity. However, after she had two more children, she began to view the publicity associated with her home town trips as an intrusion upon her family's privacy.

With highly regarded performances in her two newest films, Sullavan's future at Metro-Goldwyn-Mayer looked promising. The timing could not have been better as a few of Metro's high-ranking actresses were dubbed box office poison by Harry Brandt, president of the Independent Theatre Owners of America, in early May. Among the Metro actresses named were Greta Garbo, Norma Shearer, Luise Rainer and Joan Crawford. As Hollywood reeled from the unexpected attack, it became imperative that Metro build on Sullavan's momentum. Some proposed film projects included *Too Hot to Handle* with Clark Gable and *Northwest Passage* with Robert Taylor and Spencer Tracy. The most interesting project was a musical called *Ziegfeld Girl*, with Crawford (in a highly anticipated debut as a singer), Eleanor Powell and Virginia Bruce. Not to be outdone was Hal Roach with its attempt to lure Sullavan back to honor her contract. This ambitious project, entitled *Robbery Under Arms*, was released as *Captain Fury* in 1939. Universal grew impatient with her refusal to honor *her* commitment with such films as *Service de Luxe* (made with Vincent Price and Constance Bennett) and *Letter of Introduction* (made with Andrea Leeds).

Then there was a bombshell of a rumor: She was pregnant. According to Parsons, this caused her to withdraw from *Northwest Passage*. "Miss Sullavan may deny she and her husband, Leland Hayward, are expecting the stork as she did when she had a similar 'exclusive' a few years ago, but we get our news from such an authentic square that we are printing it as a fact."[2]

Such unexpected news put Hollywood in a lather over their prediction that Sullavan's career would be irreparably harmed by having a second child. Sullavan didn't care what people thought. "Had I known for sure that having a baby would end my so-called picture career," she confided to Radie Harris, "I'm afraid I would have behaved just as badly! … I have an old-fashioned theory about careers for actresses—that they are wonderful in their proper place—and their proper place is *not* in a happy home. So long as acting can remain a side issue with me, I am very grateful for the excitement, activity and income it affords."[3]

In another interview, she spoke candidly about her attitude toward life: "I want to get all the fun I can out of life and so I make my own rules. I respect other people and their rights, but I don't see why I should be bound by a lot of silly rules that have no bearing on my happiness."[4]

Sullavan's next assignment came from an unexpected source: Joan Crawford. Under contract to Metro since the mid–1920s, Crawford was one of the studio's highest ranking actresses since the early 1930s. Not only was she among the top box office stars, she was the studio's top-drawing actress for three consecutive years (1933 to 1935), earning the title "Queen of the Movies" from *Life* magazine in 1937.[5] However, her career began to fade starting in 1936 due to a few poorly received films, namely *The Gorgeous Hussy* (1936) and *The Bride Wore Red* (1937). Despite her box office rating falling to sixteenth place, Crawford's contract was renewed in early 1938 for another five-year period at $1.5 million per year. Her last film, *Mannequin*, had done better at the box office when released in December 1937. Crawford believed that a

Throughout her life, Sullavan made periodic visits to her hometown and her parents. This newspaper photo was taken in July 1938. The unidentified nurse was most likely engaged for Sullavan's daughter Brooke (courtesy Sargeant Memorial Collection, Norfolk Public Library).

new pet project of hers, a screen adaptation of a play called *The Shining Hour*, would be the vehicle to put her back on top.

The Keith Winter play, which opened on Broadway in February 1934 to good notices, was a modest success; it did better in London in early September. Crawford had seen the play in New York and desperately wanted it for herself. Producer Edmund Goulding had other ideas as the play was purchased for Crawford's rival, Norma Shearer, in 1935. By mid–1938, the property was available. Long having admired Sullavan's professionally, Crawford reasoned that a co-starring stint with her would pay off at the ticket window. Mayer approved her request for Borzage as director, but had reservations when she also requested Fay Bainter and Sullavan as her co-stars. As Crawford related, Mayer said, "Joan, don't you realize that these three women's roles are equal? Those two talented actresses could steal your picture!" Still, Crawford was determined to have her way: "I'd rather be a supporting player in a good film, than the star of a bad one."[6] Unfortunately, Crawford got the worst of both as evident in the final film.

Scenarist Jane Murfin and poet Ogden Nash were assigned to revise the play. The locale was transferred from England to rural Wisconsin (to avoid a repeat of the critical drubbing Crawford received for the English drawing room comedy *The Last of Mrs. Cheyney*). The character of Marcella was renamed Olivia and her character was rewritten in alignment with the familiar Crawford persona of the working-class girl who makes good. A 15-minute prologue set in New York City was added to highlight Olivia's background. The final change was to allow Judy (Sullavan) to live rather than die as she did in a house fire at the end of the play. After a few months' work, the final screenplay was submitted to producer Mankiewicz. He could not resist the temptation to rewrite the script even though Nash had done what he thought was a "respectable job."[7] This time, Mankiewicz's interference did not save the picture as it had with *Three Comrades*. Crawford told Quirk, "When it finally sank into me that we'd put so much into a movie that offered the public so little in terms of story value, I was ill. We should have thrown the script into the fire instead of Maggie Sullavan!"[8]

With Melvyn Douglas (replacing Charles Boyer, whose French accent would have been incongruent in the role of a Wisconsin farmer) and Robert Young handling the male roles, the production began on August 22. From the beginning, there was rampant speculation that there would be problems between the two headstrong women on the set. "We disappointed them," Crawford recalled. "We met, and hit it off together from the start."[9]

Quirk claimed that Sullavan did not feel the same way about Crawford. Reportedly, she told Leland that Crawford was so caught up in a Hollywood fantasy that she continued acting even after the cameras stopped rolling. In her desperation to salvage her status as box office queen, Crawford became more obsessed with how she looked on screen, from costuming to lighting. Sullavan, who never cared an iota of this aspect of filmmaking, found Crawford's anxiety annoying. What drove Sullavan to further distraction was Crawford's nervous habit of knitting between scenes. With such opposing personalities and temperaments, how on earth did Crawford and Sullavan manage to complete the film without a blow-out?

What may have ultimately worked to their advantage was that both were in different emotional states in their lives. Not only was Crawford consumed about her floundering career, she was in the process of divorcing husband number two, Franchot Tone, after catching him in an act of infidelity. She herself engaged in extramarital affairs with many on the lot, including Mankiewicz and Borzage, but Tone's act was deemed as unforgivable. Sullavan, on the other hand, was blissfully content with a happy marriage, growing family and a successful film career. Perhaps if Sullavan had been in a different emotional place, she might have felt compelled to vent her frustrations on Crawford.

There are conflicting accounts from several sources about their real life relationship. Quirk maintained that Sullavan did not like the high-strung Crawford, while other biographers claimed that the two became lifelong friends. What is known is that Crawford was extremely fond of both Sullavan and her daughter Brooke. Perhaps it was due to Crawford's affection for Brooke (as she could not have children of her own) that softened Sullavan's attitude. As Crawford revealed, "The baby and I were devoted to each other and I confess I had permitted her what I never later permitted a child of my own—she wrote on my dressing room walls with lipstick."[10] It has been stated that Crawford's feelings toward Brooke inspired her to adopt children. Whatever it may have been, the actresses maintained a friendship that went beyond filmmaking as Brooke recalled Crawford's first adopted daughter, Christina, as a guest at her birthday parties. According to Crawford in an interview later that year, she and Sullavan had "seen each other several times since the picture, and I like her very much and she likes me."[11]

While all of this was going on behind the scenes, the publicity department went to considerable lengths to paint a much more playful atmosphere where members of the cast and crew frequently enjoyed ice cream parties on the set! Crawford recalled a time when she was the victim of one of Sullavan's spur-of-the-moment pranks. "In one scene, I had to carry Maggie out of a burning house," she reminisced.

> Maggie was pregnant, I thought three months, but just before the fire scene, they told me *seven* months.... Now that I knew, I was urgently concerned. I carried this girl out of the burning house, trying to watch for falling timbers, trying not to slip on the gravel. I'm strong, heaven knows, but I wasn't strong enough. I fell on the gravel, on my elbows and knees to break the fall, so Maggie wouldn't get hurt. My elbows and knees were bloody, but I didn't know. I was hysterical over Maggie. She had her eyes closed, and they didn't open. "Maggie, dear, are you all right? Maggie!" I screamed. She waited until I was frantic. Then she opened those wide eyes of hers and grinned. She was just fine. She never played jokes unless she adored you—but what a time to show it![12]

Production wrapped up in early October. To generate interest, the five stars appeared on the studio's *Good News of 1939* radio program and re-enacted key scenes from the movie on November 17. According to *Variety*, "The listeners got a fancy exhibition of one actress trying to outdo the other in emotional understatement.... The strung-together snatches of dialog sufficed to stimulate interest."

The film was released the following day. Interestingly, *The Shining Hour* did not receive the advance publicity accorded the studio's other movies, like *Sweethearts* and *The Hardys Ride High*. The film did not even reach New York City until mid–January, 1939; this should have been the first indication that it was a failed enterprise, but some curious spectators insisted on seeing Crawford in her "comeback film."

Olivia Riley (Crawford) is a popular nightclub dancer in New York. Perhaps it's Olivia's beauty or seductive allure that makes her front page news when it is reported that she plans on marrying a wealthy Wisconsin farmer, Henry Linden (Douglas). It certainly isn't her dancing as displayed during her number (set to variations of Chopin's "Valse, Opus 64 No. 2"). Crawford demonstrates nice versatility, but it's not clear why she has achieved such fame. There's a scene from an earlier Crawford movie, *Dance, Fools, Dance* (1931), that is more sexually charged than this lame number, courtesy of the Breen Production Code.

In her dressing room, Henry proposes marriage, but she puts him off again. As Olivia recalls her tough upbringing, Crawford displays touching vulnerability as she expresses her fear that she may never measure up in his world. "I was too busy all day dipping shirts in the laundry and busy all night picking up my old man out of the gutters," she ruefully reveals in a Crawford-inspired piece of improvisation. When she says, "If only I liked you a little less and loved you a little more," it rivals that other great "kiss-off" line from Kay Francis' *Secrets of an Actress* when she tells Ian Hunter, "I love you, Peter, but I'm not in love with you."

Henry won't take no for an answer and she finally relents even though she doesn't love him. Cue David (Young), Henry's brother, who strongly opposes the marriage. When the newlyweds arrive at the Linden estate (in a fleeting but daring "anti–Jim Crow" moment, Olivia hugs her maid, Belvedere), Olivia is coolly received by her sister-in-law, Hannah (Bainter). But David's wife Judy (Sullavan) forms an instant bond with Olivia. Alone in her bedroom, Olivia confides to Judy that she is frightened of Hannah. The scene between the two actresses illustrates the difference between Crawford the *actress* and Sullavan *as* Judy.

Although Hannah promises Henry she will be respectful to Olivia, she gets her digs in as often as she can. In the meantime, David has done a complete about-face. Romantic

On the set of *The Shining Hour* (1938) with Director Frank Borzage, the man who best captured the piquant, enchanting and timeless Margaret Sullavan screen persona.

tension percolates between Olivia and David, who admits he wants what he doesn't have and is bored with what he does have (Judy).

Hannah, suspicious, broaches the subject with Judy, who doesn't want to hear it. There is a minor verbal skirmish between the two, with Judy getting the last word. What's remarkable is that it is the frail-looking Judy who's best equipped to put Hannah in her place. It's a neat twist on the conventionally drawn neglected wife character and Sullavan handles her little zingers with beguiling charm.

Henry and Olivia start building their own home on the outskirts of the estate. By now, Judy suspects that Olivia and David have romantic feelings for each other. From this point on, the film is concerned about Judy, the "brave wife nobly suffering" (to paraphrase David Shipman), rather than the predictable development of the affair.

During Olivia's housewarming party, Henry finds Judy alone in the garden (Sullavan is not particularly well gowned nor coifed in a misguided attempt to highlight her girlishness in contrast to Olivia's sophistication). She has a heart-to-heart talk with Henry about her love for David. She says, "David might look at me and suddenly knows that he loves me … so that he might hear a song and think of me … that he might walk into a room that I just left and know I'd been there." It's a breathtaking emotional moment because we know her heart is breaking over the knowledge that her husband no longer loves her. Meanwhile, Olivia is having a tough time of it as she gets into another skirmish with Hannah, fends off a drunken farm hand with a right hook, and ends up locking lips with David.

One night, a disheveled Hannah tries to talk Henry out of going away. In a heated moment, she declares, "I love you the way sisters have always loved their brothers and wives who don't love their husbands but their husband's brothers!" The incestuous tone and further rants finally jolt Henry out of his complacency and he jumps to his feet in anger. At the end of his tirade, he puts his pipe back in his mouth, sits down and calmly resumes his bookkeeping work. It's hard to say what's more unnerving: Hannah's incestuous obsession or Henry's ability to so quickly spin 180 degrees on his emotions. Freud would have salivated over this dysfunctional family.

That night, Judy has an honest discussion with Olivia; she's willing to sacrifice her happiness for David's. Sullavan's exquisite, no-frills approach elevates this into a riveting scene. They are interrupted by the news that Olivia's house is on fire. Olivia and Judy arrive to find it engulfed in flames. Wild-eyed Hannah pleads with Henry to let the house burn. As she slips further into hysteria, Henry realizes that she set the fire. Judy decides to run into the burning house to free David for Olivia. Olivia runs in to rescue her. As the house collapses in total ruins, this excessively melodramatic movie does the same.

Olivia, who sustained minor burns to her hands, clears things up with David the next morning. David, who has seen the errors of his ways, finds Judy lying in bed, wrapped in bandages from head to toes with only an opening for her expressive, tearful eyes. (If Judy is that badly burned, wouldn't she be better off in a hospital?) These two reconcile.

Olivia is still confused as to what she wants. She realizes that she loves Henry, but can't stay in the house. As she walks out, Hannah implores Henry to go after her. He jumps into Olivia's moving car. Henry takes her into his arms and kisses her, thus pulling her away from the wheel. With a whoop, Belvedere (Hattie McDaniel) leans in from the back seat to take over the driving. After all that overheated melodrama, we end with a Keystone Cops gag? Ridiculous.

The film received mostly negative reviews. One of the few positive notices came from *Screenland* magazine: "Joan Crawford's fans are already probably hoarse from cheering their star's performance in this picture. It's undoubtedly her best in a long, long time." Surprisingly, this critic found fault with Sullavan's performance: "Even the magnificent Miss Sullavan can't make this wifely paragon plausible." Most of the other critics took the opposite stance as Crawford got most of the critical drubbings and Sullavan the lion's share of the praise. The *Syracuse Post-Standard* opined, "Not that Miss Crawford gives a poor performance—it's just that the rest of them … have such meaty roles that they overshadow her for the most part." Sullavan was singled out as being "especially fine…. [She] steals most of the scenes in which she appears." The *Detroit Free Press* was more enthusiastic: "It is Margaret Sullavan—who has been going hot in her recent movies—who has the most sympathetic and believable role and walks away with the honors."

The film proved to be a disappointment for Crawford and it lost $137,000. As Douglas told Quirk, "I didn't think Joan really appeared to advantage in it. She was challenged by the superior acting skills of Maggie and Fay and to her credit she did try to rise to the challenge. But Borzage, fine director that he was, was not the director to bring out the best in her."[13] Fortunately, Crawford proved her resiliency with her fabulous performance in *The Women* in 1939. Her Oscar-winning performance as *Mildred Pierce* laid to rest the "Box Office Poison" label and the legend of Joan Crawford, Ultimate Movie Star, endures to this day.

The Shining Hour must be ranked as Sullavan's worst movie. For a film that held so much promise with its star-studded cast, a literate, witty script, and fine production values, it's painful to watch it fall apart in a welter of melodramatic foam. The film does not hold up with repeated viewing and closer scrutiny as its numerous faults become more obvious; in none of Sullavan's other movies does this hold true. Borzage, who has shown his gift in elevating the most mundane situations into gems of emotional impact, is at a loss here. While there are some interesting Borzagean touches, the artificiality of the scenario is too much for him to overcome. The movie starts out well enough with its cosmopolitan setting in New York and some zingy lines; once the setting transfers to Wisconsin, the film unravels.

Crawford does better than one would expect and she has some fine moments. Unfortunately, when Sullavan is in the same scene, Crawford's acting technique suffers in comparison to the sublime Sullavan. At least she is still the glamorous clotheshorse that diehard Crawford fans expect. Bainter has some nicely etched moments, but she becomes monotonous before the midway point. When she loses her sanity near the end, it comes across as ludicrous rather than dramatic. Of the actors, Young performs slightly better in an unsympathetic part. Douglas suffers the most in the underwritten, standard role of the duped husband. There are times when one wants to reach in and smack him.

The movie is not a total loss as long as Sullavan is on the screen. In her quiet, unassuming manner, her character becomes the emotional centerpiece of the overwrought saga. She is heartbreakingly real, particularly when she realizes that she's losing her husband. She's no simpering wife, however. With the exception of the foolish decision to toast herself in the fire, Judy is the most level-headed, clear-eyed character and knows what needs to be done to remedy a bad situation.

The play was rehashed *six* more times for television: twice for English (1951, 1958) and four for American television (1950, 1951, 1954 and 1956).

As *The Shining Hour* was trudging its way through the movie theaters, Sullavan landed the coveted role of the second Mrs. de Winter ("the Scarlett O'Hara of 1938") opposite Orson Welles in the radio adaptation of Daphne du Maurier's best-selling novel *Rebecca* on December 9, 1938. This was the debut program of the CBS radio series *The Campbell Playhouse* (the continuation of Orson Welles' *The Mercury Theatre on the Air*). In its review, *Variety* noted, "Miss Sullavan was superb throughout."

At that time, David O. Selznick was going to produce the film version of *Rebecca* as soon as *Gone with the Wind* was finished. In another highly publicized search, Selznick hunted for an actress to play the second Mrs. de Winter. With her well-received performance, Sullavan was one of the first actresses tested. This was Selznick's third and last attempt to cast Sullavan in one of his productions (the first being *A Star Is Born*). Although it is not clear when Sullavan actually made the screen test, it is likely that it was done prior to her second child's birth in February as her test was done entirely in close-up; screen tests of the other actresses were filmed from the waist up. Others tested were Anne Baxter, Loretta Young, Joan Fontaine and Vivien Leigh. For a time, Sullavan was a recurring favorite as many of these actresses, especially Fontaine, failed to impress either Selznick or director Alfred Hitchcock. But Selznick could not conceive of Sullavan in the part. "Imagine," he remarked, "Margaret Sullavan being pushed around by Mrs. Danvers right up to the point of suicide!"[14] Fontaine, who had appeared mainly in B-movies with an occasional supporting role in bigger productions, won the part and became a movie star.

Sullavan's screen test is available for viewing. According to Andrew Sarris, Sullavan "was too assured, too confident, for the part of a socially intimidated bride, hopelessly out of her depth. She would have had Judith Anderson's Mrs. Danvers doing windows in no time flat."[15] Sarris may have something here. Although Sullavan displays a fine understanding of the role, one cannot help but question if her inner strength would have mitigated against her.

Sullavan turned to more urgent matters: the impending birth of her second child. On February 10, 1939, a second daughter, weighing in at six pounds, 11 ounces, was born. She was christened Bridget.

22

At the Peak of Her Artistry

I have a mind of my own and it deserves the respect of dictating my actions.[1]

After Bridget's birth, Sullavan remained out of the spotlight for a long time. Her only professional engagement was the radio broadcast of Edna Ferber's *Show Boat* for *Campbell Playhouse* on March 31, 1939. Throughout the broadcast, one cannot envision Sullavan as an innocent girl buffeted by fate. Among the highlights were Helen Morgan's singing of a Stephen Foster song, "Why, No One to Love?" and the acting debut of Ferber in the role of Parthy Ann Hawks. The mind boggles at the notion of Ferber resolving her animosity towards Sullavan as her Parthy had a hostile edge to it.

Movie fans were eager for another appearance. They were partially satiated when a compilation film, *Land of Liberty*, premiered on April 30, 1939, at the New York World's Fair and the San Francisco Exposition. Sponsored by the Motion Picture Producers and Distributors of America, the film told the story of America with clips from Hollywood films. A scene from *So Red the Rose* featuring Randolph Scott and Sullavan was used. *Land of Liberty* was shown daily from April to October 1939 and from April to October 1940. The *New York Times* reported, "It is a remarkably fine [film]. For all its gaps, it is a fascinating record and tribute to Hollywood as well as to our democracy." *Land of Liberty* was re-edited and released for national distribution in January 1941. The *San Francisco Chronicle* opined, "Stars of the box office magnitude of Margaret Sullavan, Fredric March, Walter Brennan, Walter Huston, Randolph Scott, Basil Rathbone and Henry Fonda make appearances during the running of the picture; enough of an all-star cast to please the most exacting."

This wasn't enough to appease her fans as Parsons noted, "Why hasn't Margaret Sullavan made a picture since the birth of her daughter six months ago? That's what the fans all over the country are asking."[2]

Meanwhile, the MGM publicity department announced several projects: *Ziegfeld Girl*, with a script revised so that Hedy Lamarr and Lana Turner could replace Joan Crawford, Eleanor Powell, and Virginia Bruce (*Ziegfeld Girl* reached the screen in 1941 with Lamarr, Turner and Judy Garland); *Ruined City*, which was to be filmed in England with Robert Donat; and *Remember the Day* (made by 20th Century–Fox in 1941).

With *The Shop Around the Corner*, not only was Sullavan reunited with Stewart, but was also given an insightful and gifted director, Ernst Lubitsch. The German-born Lubitsch, along with Borzage, recognized her unique artistry. This fortunate collaboration resulted in an enduring reputation of a film that has cemented her Hollywood legacy for today's moviegoers.

A successful and prolific motion picture producer, director and writer, Lubitsch began his career as an actor in 1912 in German short films. He achieved international acclaim with a series of German historical films starring Pola Negri in the late 1910s and early 1920s. Lubitsch found American success with his inaugural film, Paramount's *The Patriot* (1928), which earned five Academy Award nominations including Best Direction. With the advent of talking pictures, Lubitsch's career received a tremendous boost with his suave and masterful handling of early musical films, such as the groundbreaking *The Love Parade* (1929) and *The Smiling Lieutenant* (1931). Today he is highly revered for his sophisticated sex comedies, notably *Trouble in Paradise* (1932), generally regarded among scholars and critics as one of the greatest comedies of all time.

The Shop Around the Corner was based on an obscure play, *Ilatszerarl* (*The Perfumery*) by Nikolaus László, which premiered in Budapest in 1936. Lubitsch was intrigued by the play as it recalled his childhood in his father's clothing store. As he reflected to a newspaper interviewer at his film's New York City opening,

> It has a universal theme and tells a simple story. I have known just such a little shop in Budapest. The feelings between the boss and those who work for him is pretty much the same the world over, it seems to me. Everyone is afraid of losing his job and everyone knows how little human worries can affect his job.[3]

In 1938, Lubitsch purchased the screen rights for $16,500 and tried negotiating an independent "share the profits" deal with Myron Selznick under his own company, Ernst Lubitsch Productions. This was to be his first film since leaving Paramount after an unsuccessful tenure as production chief. German actress and singer Dolly Haas and Janet Gaynor were among the earliest contenders for the female lead. Lubitsch tried to interest Paramount, RKO and United Artists in releasing the film. There were no takers (no surprise, after the dismal box office results of his last two films), so Lubitsch abandoned the project in late October 1938. When he signed a two-picture deal with Metro at the end of 1938, he included the László play (which cost the studio $62,500) with the understanding that he would direct and produce the film. MGM insisted he begin production on *Ninotchka* with Greta Garbo and Melvyn Douglas first. Since Lubitsch's personal choices for the leading roles, Stewart and Sullavan, were unavailable (Stewart was committed to Universal for *Destry Rides Again*), he conceded to the demand.

After completing *Ninotchka*, Lubitsch and his frequent collaborator Samson Raphaelson put finishing touches on the *Shop* screenplay. According to Raphaelson, there was little left of the play. "Nothing, not one scene, not one line of dialogue, coincides with the film," he recalled.[4] The setting was even switched to a leather goods store. While the basic premise remained the same, some of the other plot threads involving Hugo Matuschek were relegated to the sidelines and the story of the lead couple was emphasized. The most significant change was the attention paid to the lives of everyday people trying to survive in an uncertain world. In a *New York Sun* interview, Lubitsch declared, "We cannot make pictures in a vacuum now. We must show people living in the real world.... [Audiences] want their stories tied to real life."[5] The film was a throwback to the "shop comedies" Lubitsch directed and acted in, in the mid–1910s. In fact, the character Lubitsch played in *Shoe Salon Pinkus* (1916) bears a strong resemblance to the Pepi character played by William Tracy. Years later, when Raphaelson reflected on his work on *Trouble in Paradise*, he stated:

> I much more enjoyed and had much more respect for *Heaven Can Wait* ... and *Shop Around the Corner* [which] dealt with sentiments, with emotions, with backgrounds, clerks—their slavishness, the tensions between them, their insecurity, romance on a level that I felt and respected.[6]

Lubitsch assembled a well-balanced group of seasoned performers in support of his leads: Frank Morgan, Joseph Schildkraut, Felix Bressart, Sara Haden, Inez Courtney and

William Tracy. Lubitsch always claimed that Stewart had occurred to him in the initial phase of the project. Since *The Shopworn Angel*, Stewart starred in the popular films *You Can't Take It with You* (1938), *Made for Each Other* (1939) and *Mr. Smith Goes to Washington* (1939). His career was definitely out of the apprentice phase and into the "leading man" category.

According to Gloria Stewart, the casting of Sullavan was a foregone conclusion. Sullavan was a mother of two and Stewart was dating a lot of other women at that time. Gloria reasoned Lubitsch knew that, by casting them together, there would be the on-screen chemistry that was always there. Their private lives would provide a level of detachment that the story required. To achieve maximum effect of this tension, Lubitsch shot all of the scenes in the order in which they occur in the narrative. This method was effective as the abrasive aspects of Sullavan's on-set behavior was perfect for the early portions of her characterization. Gloria Stewart confirmed, "Margaret was always good at saying and doing things to make people mad and she was even able to get Jim mad." Due to his unabashed affection for her, Jimmy Stewart conceded, "I could never be angry with Margaret for long, even though she said and did a lot of things that riled a lot of other people."[7]

Through it all, Stewart marveled at her talent and considered himself fortunate to play opposite her. As he recalled to Michael Munn, "You never quite knew what she might do when the cameras rolled, and that made the work so interesting." He recalled that, during a scene, she would say a word or give him a look differently than she had before. "Although they were just small things, with her they were major because it made all the difference to a scene ... and that's partly what made her so good."[8]

Principal photography ended at the beginning of December. When the film was shown in New York on January 25, 1940, Lubitsch said, "It's not a big picture, just a quiet little story that seemed to have some charm."[9]

Lubitsch's sentimental ode to the everyday man begins with the arrival of the employees of the Matuschek and Company leather goods store in Budapest: the brash, street-smart errand boy Pepi (Tracy), the mild-mannered clerk Pirovitch (Bressart), clerks Flora (Haden) and Ilona (Courtney), and the head clerk, Alfred Kralik (Stewart). The last to arrive before Mr. Matuschek is the well-dressed, duplicitous Vadas (Schildkraut), who is disliked by his co-workers. When Mr. Matuschek (Morgan) arrives, the workers are ready to begin another day. They all function as one unit in an environment of safety and complacency.

In the stock room, Alfred shares with Pirovitch a letter he received from an anonymous female pen pal. "My heart was trembling as I walked into the post office and there you were, lying in Box 237. I took you out of your envelope and read you, read you right there, oh my dear friend," he reads. They have already exchanged several letters.

Into the shop walks an out-of-work clerk, Klara Nowak (Sullavan), who is desperate for a job. She's persistent despite Alfred's best efforts to dissuade her. She is hired by Matuschek after she takes it upon herself to sell a much-maligned item (a cigarette box that plays "Ochi Tchornya") as a candy box to an unsuspecting customer.

Flash forward to six months later. Klara's presence has complicated Alfred's once peaceful life. When he addresses a concern that Mr. Matuschek had with her blouse the previous day, she takes offense and this leads to a heated argument between the two which has become the new mainstay of their lives. Alfred confides to Pirovitch that he's finally going to meet his anonymous pen pal that night at a local café. In an endearing moment in which Stewart is an expert, he reveals his insecurities about his chances with the opposite sex. They will identify each other with him wearing a red carnation in his lapel and she using hers as a bookmark in Tolstoy's *Anna Karenina*.

Mr. Matuschek arrives and already is in a crotchety mood. He announces that they will stay after hours tonight to decorate the store windows for the Christmas holidays. Klara tells Ilona that she has an engagement that night at 8:30. One quickly realizes that Alfred's secret pen pal is none other than Klara. However, can they overcome their mutual dislike to accept each other as the writer of their cherished letters? The genius of Lubitsch's film is that the question is not easily answered as we have come to expect from so many recent romcom films.

That night, Alfred intends to ask for a raise; instead he is unexpectedly fired. The sequence in which Alfred reads his letter of recommendation and the close-up of his trembling hands as he places his sales book, pencil and key on the counter is heart-wrenchingly played by Stewart. With minimal dialogue, the scene packs an emotional wallop. After Mr. Matuschek receives a mysterious phone call, he dismisses the employees. Within minutes, a private detective enters and confirms Mr. Matuschek's suspicion that his wife is having an affair with an employee: Vadas. After the detective leaves, Mr. Matuschek goes into his office. His attempted suicide is foiled by the unexpected return of Pepi from his errands. It's a jarring moment that highlights the frailty of life and love.

From this somber turn, the film moves into its best sequence. Pirovitsch accompanies Alfred to the café to deliver a note explaining his absence. Pirrovitch discovers that the anonymous pen pal is none other than Klara. Disbelieving, Alfred takes the letter back and walks away. Inside, Klara anxiously waits. We see the lonely desperation in her eyes. It's an illuminating moment that is a tribute to Sullavan's talent. Alfred returns to the café, but keeps his identity a secret. According to David Thomson, "The café conversation may be the best meeting in American film."[10] It is not long before the two begin bickering.

> ALFRED: There might be a lot we don't know about each other. You know, people seldom go to the trouble of scratching the surface of things to find the inner truth.
>
> KLARA: Well, I really wouldn't care to scratch your surface, Mr. Kralik, because I know exactly what I'd find. Instead of a heart, a handbag. Instead of a soul, a suitcase. And instead of an intellect, a cigarette lighter ... which doesn't work.

Sullavan and James Stewart's sublime performances in Ernst Lubitsch's beguiling comedy *The Shop Around the Corner* (1940) are still relevant today in this age of Rom.Com.

Despite Klara's distress over his unwanted presence, Alfred cannot resist annoying her. After engaging in more mindless bickering, Alfred, fully exasperated by a woman who will not back down, launches into a verbal assault. "Now, let me tell you something, Miss Nowak," he fumes. "You may have very beautiful thoughts, but you certainly hide them. As far as your actions are concerned, you are cold and snippy like an old maid and you're going to have a tough time making a man fall in love with you."

"*I* an old maid? So, no man could fall in love with me," Klara counters without flinching. "Why, I could show you letters that would open your eyes, but no, I guess not. You probably wouldn't understand them. They're written by a man that's so far superior to you that it isn't funny. I have to laugh when I think of you calling me an old maid. You, you little, insignificant *clerk*."

The look of anguish on Alfred's face is startling. It's not the impact of Klara's comment that affects us (after all, he did call her an old maid). Rather, it's the implication that the two are unable to surmount their petty grievances and insecurities long enough to see that the love they have been longing for may never be realized. What cements this feeling is that Sullavan does not show any regret for her remarks as shown in other adaptations.

The next morning, Alfred is summoned to the hospital room where Mr. Matuschek is recuperating. Mr. Matuschek asks for forgiveness for having suspected him and puts Alfred in charge of the store while he rests. Alfred's first task is to fire Vadas discreetly.

A subsequent scene in the post office is haunting in its raw emotions. It is Thomson's favorite scene: "The shot of Sullavan's gloved hand, and then her ruined face, searching an empty mail box for a letter is one of the most fragile moments in film. For an instant, the ravishing Sullavan looks old and ill, touched by loss."[11]

Later that evening, Alfred visits Klara in her apartment after she has taken ill. She appears painfully frail and defeated as she sits in bed. An unexpected letter arrives and suddenly Klara comes to vibrant, radiant life as she reads the letter from her pen pal. Alfred wrote the letter with the premise that the pen pal came to the café and found the two of them sitting together. In a delightful scene, beautifully acted by Stewart, Klara reads this excerpt from her letter: "Who is this very attractive young man who's just the type women fall for?" Andrew Sarris had high praise for Stewart in this scene: "It is a dangerously delicate moment. It would have been very tempting for a flickering triumphant expression to have passed over Stewart's face, but instead an intensely sweet and compassionate and appreciative look transfigures the entire scene into one of the most memorable occurrences in the history of the cinema."[12] With her spirits buoyed, Klara promises to return to work the next morning.

When Mr. Matuschek arrives at the store on Christmas Eve, he is thrilled by the brisk business. In a touching monologue, Morgan displays fine dramatic power as Mr. Matuschek expresses his sentiments that the store is his home and his life. Just when we thought that we couldn't be more choked up, Lubitsch has another surprise as Mr. Matuschek, without his wife, seeks a Christmas Eve companion. He talks to the newest errand boy, Rudy (Charles Smith—one of the Barbershop Quartet singers in *In the Good Old Summertime*), who is also alone. Their delight over the prospect of a fancy dinner and companionship brings tears to one's eyes.

Back in the store, Klara admits to Alfred that, early on, she had found herself attracted to him. Despite this revelation, Alfred continues his deception by telling her that her "fiancé" came to see him. Sullavan's confused reactions to Alfred's descriptions of her dream man as overweight and something of a dolt is utterly beguiling. Her beau ideal quickly descends into a depressed, unemployed and, worst of all, an unimaginative plagiarist.

Alfred cannot stand it any more. He holds her in his arms and tells her, "Please take your key and open Post Office Box 237 and take me out of my envelope and kiss me." As her face shows a flicker of recognition, he puts a red carnation in his jacket lapel.

As Klara reels from the shock, Alfred tentatively asks, "Are you disappointed?"

Klara admits, "Psychologically, I'm very confused." Then she elatedly looks at him. "But personally, I don't feel bad at all." They finally embrace.

Upon its release, the critics were mostly unanimous in their praise. *Photoplay* called it

> a gem of a movie, packed with charm, finely drawn characters, and superb acting.... It is unlikely that you will roar with laughter or burst into tears, yet throughout the film you will struggle with a desire to cry a little and catch yourself chuckling instead. It takes something approaching genius to get an effect like that.... Stewart turns on his usual brand of boyish charm with enormous success while Miss Sullavan plays to perfection the almost drab Klara Novak.

Variety praised "the outstanding characterizations by Margaret Sullavan and James Stewart.... Picture is certain to lift both players higher in audience popularity." The *Syracuse Post-Standard* was equally impressed: "It would be hard to imagine two people better suited for the roles of Kralik and Miss Novak than James Stewart and Margaret Sullavan. It's just another proof of the fact that these two are such fine actors that they can make any part live for their audiences."

For some, there were the inevitable comparisons to *Ninotchka*. According to the *New York Herald-Tribune* reviewer, "The characters and the incidents have been so brilliantly treated that the film becomes a disarming and beguiling comedy." However, he cautioned that

> you will be making a mistake if you look in this film for the same Lubitsch magic which made *Ninotchka* one of the most eminently satisfying exhibits of last year. The material is not as good. And Margaret Sullavan, although she turns in a splendid performance in the leading feminine role, is no Garbo.... Miss Sullavan has been away from the screen far too long. Once more she shows that she has few colleagues who can match her for crowding a line or a scene with emotional intensity, even when it is just a minor situation. She portrays the naïve shop girl ... with captivating conviction.

In later years, Tony Thomas thought it was unfortunate that Lubitsch was "attempting to tell a Hungarian story with American actors."[13] What Thomas failed to realize was that, during Hollywood's Golden Age, it was a rare occurrence when foreign characters were actually performed with accuracy. While there were exceptions like Greta Garbo, Maurice Chevalier and Marlene Dietrich, foreign-born actors were often overlooked by the American public. Recall Anna Sten or Ferdinand Gravet? Audiences were willing to overlook the lack of a foreign accent as long as the actor met the other qualifications of the role. Furthermore, at that time, a character with a heavily pronounced foreign accent was someone whose motives could not be trusted. This was particularly noticeable after the United States entered World War II.

Another argument could be made in what can be described as the "Universality of Character." Stewart and Sullavan were performers whose screen appeal transcended ethnic stereotypes. In this context, *The Shop Around the Corner* is really a tribute to the middle-class workers everywhere in the world, not just Budapest.

The film was successful in New York. However, outside of major cities, it did not do well as Lubitsch fans did not want to pay to see a "gentle" comedy when they were expecting a sly, sassy comedy. There was no shortage of zesty comedies like *His Girl Friday, My Favorite Wife* and *Road to Singapore* that year. However, the film was an unexpected hit among the European markets and ended up with a profit of $380,000 worldwide.

On September 29, Sullavan, Stewart and Morgan reprised their roles in an abbreviated radio broadcast for *Screen Guild Theater*. While a pleasant program to listen to, one cannot help notice that Sullavan and Stewart are overly strident at times; in the later scenes, Stewart is hammy as he fishes for laughs. Interestingly, Kralik's name was changed to Martin, no doubt in deference to the war in Europe.

In 1947, Lubitsch wrote to world-renowned critic Herman G. Weinberg, "As for human comedy I think I was never as good as in *Shop Around the Corner*. Never did I make a picture in which the atmosphere and the characters were truer than in this picture."[14] Around the same time, Lubitsch told the *Los Angeles Times* that *The Shop Around the Corner* was the "best picture I ever made in my life."[15]

Sullavan was pleased with the film, which was rare for her. According to her daughter, "She thought it was her best film. Mother was a natural comedian, and I think she felt that was a film that showed off her comedic talents best of all."[16]

The Shop Around the Corner has been adapted successfully many times. It was first remade as a musical, *In the Good Old Summertime*, in 1949 with Judy Garland and Van Johnson in the leads and Buster Keaton sadly underutilized in a supporting role. The original Raphaelson screenplay was reworked to accommodate Garland's screen persona. With the locale changed to a Chicago music store at the turn of the 20th century, this is a pleasant Garland vehicle—and that's the problem. With Garland singing and dancing all over the place (her performance is particularly manic, being either too abrasive or earnest), she crowds every other player out. It is more of a Judy Garland songfest than an ensemble piece and bland Johnson doesn't stand a chance. Another problem is that, with Robert Z. Leonard's "Heavy Underlying of the Obvious" style of comedy, the delicate story has been reduced to stock musical comedy situations biding its time between musical numbers. Nonetheless, *In the Good Old Summertime* was a critical and commercial success and is fondly revered by the Garland cult today.

In 1963, the László play was produced as a Broadway musical, *She Loves Me*. Utilizing much of the Raphaelson screenplay with some newly developed characters, it centered around Budapest parfumerie employees Georg Nowack and Amalia Balash as the bickering pen pals. *She Loves Me*, which ran for 302 performances, received five Tony nominations, including Best Musical. A London production opened a year later for 189 performances. *She Loves Me*, revived a few times in award-winning productions on Broadway and London stages, was recently revived in 2015 to critical acclaim and multiple nominations.

In 1970, there was talk of producer-director Blake Edwards filming the play as a vehicle for his wife, Julie Andrews. That project was never realized, but there was a 1978 BBC-TV production. It's a delight to watch as the songs are memorably catchy. There is genuine humor and pathos in the plight of the two clerks. Most of all, the telecast succeeds because it focuses on the development of all of the characters in an ensemble piece, thereby avoiding the mistake of the Garland musical.

Another television production, *Illatszertár*, was shown in Hungary in 1987. In 1998, the Raphaelson-László script provided the inspiration for *You've Got Mail*. The plot was updated by Nora Ephron, who achieved success with superbly crafted comedies like *When Harry Met Sally* ... (1989) and *Sleepless in Seattle* (1993). The plot was considerably revised (the pen pals correspond via the Internet) and the essential premise is different: Kathleen Kelly (Meg Ryan) owns a small bookstore, The Shop Around the Corner, in New York City. Joe Fox (Tom Hanks), the owner of a large bookstore chain, puts her out of business. There is the inevitable encounter in the coffee shop, the only hold-over from the original screenplay. While frequently amusing and entertaining, *You've Got Mail* lacks the tension and touching insight which made the original such an emotional experience. For-tunately, the teaming of Hanks and Ryan strikes the same kind of on-screen sparks as the Sullavan-Stewart team; Ryan is particularly adorable in her quirky style as the girl-next-door type. *You've Got Mail* received generally favorable reviews and was commercially suc-cessful.

In 2001, the Raphaelson screenplay was faithfully adapted as a straight play entitled *La Boutique au Coin de la Rue* (translated as *The Shop at the Corner of the Street*) in Paris. A critical and commercial success, it garnered five Molière Awards, the French equivalent of Broadway's Tonys. In 2009, László's original play was produced for the first time in the United States as an English-language version called *The Perfume Shop*. With a new adap-tation by E.P. Dowdall, László's nephew, the play returned to its origins as it dealt with the story of the young lovers and the troubled marriage of Mr. Maraczek with equal emphasis. The play premiered at the Asolo Repertory Theatre in Sarasota, Florida, in December 2009. A simultaneous Canadian production premiered in Toronto.

The Raphaelson-László script surfaced once more as a 2012 television movie, *Christmas in Boston*. The largely revised and updated plot concerned Gina (Maria Sokoloff) and Seth (Patrick J. Adams), who have been pen pals for 13 years and now have the chance to meet for the first time when he goes to Boston for an important business deal. However, both have sent their best friends' pictures to each other, so they have to convince their friends to pose as them. Everything works out in the end in a predictable manner. The leads are pleasant enough, but the subplot involving their friends' escapades shoves them out of the limelight.

Given the various reincarnations, it is easy to understand why *The Shop Around the Corner* does not mean much to the modern-day moviegoer in this age of crowd-pleasing entertainment where subtlety has become a lost art. Fortunately, many scholars and critics have appreciated (and continue to appreciate) the original film. In her review, Pauline Kael raved that the film is "close to perfection—one of the most beautifully acted and paced romantic comedies ever made in this country." She found Stewart and Sullavan's perform-ances as "full of grace notes; when you watch later James Stewart films, you may wonder what became of this rather deft, sensitive, pre-drawling Stewart. As for Sullavan, this is a peerless performance; she makes the shop girl's pretenses believable, lyrical and funny."[17]

In recent years, the film has won additional honors. In 1986 and 1987, it played for 66 weeks at Paris' Cinematheque Francais, making it the most successful reissue at that time. The American Film Institute rated the film #28 in its listing of the 100 greatest romantic films. Richard Schickel of *Time* magazine included the film in his listing of the "All-Time 100 greatest films made since 1923."

Lubitsch's reputation is deservedly based on his sexually sophisticated comedies in which the famed "Lubitsch touch" is evident to the delight of moviegoers and critics. What's lacking, however, is the touch of humanity which is the reason *The Shop Around the Corner* moves us so deeply, as Lubitsch allows us to share in his personal experiences. As Scott Eyman assessed, "Ernst gives the people at Matuschek and Company the full measure of his respect and affection. Through the dignity with which he treats them, the film becomes a celebration of the ordinary, gently honoring the extraordinary qualities that lie within the most common of us."[18] The fact this film was made in the early days of war in Europe makes it all the more poignant as one man's tribute to a way of life that was rapidly disap-pearing. Through the violence and horrors of war, Europe would be transformed forever and Lubitsch was paying his last respects.

This tender undertone, however, does not detract from the film's humor. There are several bright lines and comical scenes that are played in a gentle manner. We may not laugh out loud, but there are times when we are so charmed that we realize we are grinning from ear to ear.

According to Donald Dewey, Lubitsch once reported that Stewart and Sullavan "were the only actors whom he had directed who not only didn't try to upstage one another, but who went out of their way to make the other look good."[19] In the true spirit of cooperation, these two maintained an atmosphere of ensemble acting. In none of their other joint films are the two so well suited in terms of character impact as both are on equal footing here. Stewart is wonderful as a young man whose full range of emotions makes him endearing. We care very much for Alfred Kralik as he embodies the ordinary man's struggles to find meaning in his daily existence. Likewise, we are concerned about Klara Nowak. Through Sullavan's sublime performance, we experience her anguish and admire her resolve to rise above her circumstances. This Klara Nowak is no simpering ingénue: She's feisty, fiercely independent, and very capable of holding her own when dealing with the opposite sex— while never losing our sympathies in the meantime. The beauty of Sullavan's brilliant performance is that she conveys so much heartfelt emotions through her eyes and body expressions. If she had begun her career during the silent film era, she would have been marvelous.

What is also astonishing about her performance is the transformation of her physical appearance. Without the tricks of photography, clothing or hair style, Sullavan is ravishing. In the beginning, she is rather dowdy as if we were looking through Alfred's eyes. However, as Klara lets go of her anxiety, she acquires a luminous, radiant glow as an indication of her feelings of love. This transformation is done without special effects—relying on Sullavan's instincts as an actress— and the effect is mesmerizing.

Most importantly, we are deeply touched by the impact her character has on us. At no time do we feel that we are watching an actor giving a performance; instead, we are given a rare treat of developing a personal connection to the character as if they existed in our own world. In what could have been a "throwaway" role, Sullavan is unforgettable.

Sullavan's performance as Klara Nowark in *The Shop Around the Corner* (1940) proved to be most revealing as it mirrored her true self, of a head-strong woman who harbored deep insecurities about love.

The most striking character, however, is Matuschek as splendidly brought to life by Morgan. In many ways, Matuschek mirrors Lubitsch's personal life as Lubitsch's first marriage ended when he discovered his wife's affair with a trusted friend.

During the filming, Lubitsch was married to his second wife, but it was generally believed that this couple was ill-suited for each other.

According to Raphaelson, "His life outside of work was an increasingly empty one. He had … a wretched, meaningless home life. His whole life was his work. He was a sad man to contemplate."[20] Given this insight, Matuschek becomes a touching tribute to one of our greatest film directors and Morgan is fully up to the task. His comic performances may have escalated into a buffoonish caricature in other films, but that is never evident here.

Of the rest of the supporting cast, Bressart, Schildkraut and Tracy make their indelible marks. Tracy is especially memorable in his breakout role as Pepi, but this did not lead to a bigger career. Perhaps, he was too similar to Mickey Rooney to be allowed to make that much of an impact at MGM.

The Shop Around the Corner endures not only as one of the greatest romantic comedies of all time, but also as a fitting example of Margaret Sullavan at her absolute best. Even if she had done nothing else, her impact would still be a haunting and lasting one today.

23

The Approaching Storm

There are two ways of meeting difficulties: you alter the difficulties, or you alter yourself to meet them.[1]*—Phyllis Bottome*

After the release of her fourth Metro film, Sullavan became restless under the confines of her contractual obligations. What complicated matters was her dislike for Mayer, who was a stronger executive than was "Junior" Laemmle and not as easily put off. His "interference" in her career irritated Sullavan to no end. Reports of temperamental behavior on the set became more frequent as she became increasingly "unavailable" to the press. When she spoke, she extolled the virtues of motherhood while managing to rub Hollywood the wrong way: "The important thing in Hollywood is to be a mother. There is nothing else here to occupy the mind."[2]

Sullavan became more difficult with the selection of her next film. As Billy Grady recalled, "She wanted a top star vehicle, yet was happy to subordinate her own personality for the greater good of a picture where many performances needed equal pointing-up and emphasis."[3] Many projects were announced: *Wyoming*, another attempt to team her with Robert Taylor; *Escape*; and *To Own the World* with James Stewart (released as *We Who Are Young* with Lana Turner). There was even talk of Sullavan returning to Broadway to star in *Young Man with a Horn* with Burgess Meredith under Jed Harris' direction.

It was finally announced that Sullavan, Stewart and Morgan would appear in the screen adaptation of English writer Phyllis Bottome's international best-seller, *The Mortal Storm*, to be directed by Frank Borzage. This announcement was a surprise as *The Mortal Storm* was decidedly anti–Nazi in its tone. It wasn't that long ago when Metro had to contend with all of the political hullaballoo with *Three Comrades*. Despite the declaration of war against Germany by Britain, France, Australia and New Zealand after the invasion of Poland in September 1939, the United States wished to remain neutral. There were those in the film industry who were no longer willing to keep silent. Warner Brothers was the first to produce an anti–Nazi propaganda film, released in May: *Confessions of a Nazi Spy* caused considerable concern among Washington politicians that it would provoke Germany into retaliating against the United States. Despite its highly sensationalized theme, the film was not successful as Americans did not want to consider the grim prospects of war. In response to the film, the Hays Office enforced a ban on all anti–Nazi films from mid–September 1939 to January 1940. As Joseph Mankiewicz recalled, "Warner Bros. had guts. They hated the Nazis more than they cared for the German grosses. MGM did not. It kept on releasing its films in Nazi Germany until Hitler finally threw them out."[4] The film that triggered Hitler's ban: *The Mortal Storm*.

Bottome had won fame in the U.S. when her 1934 novel *Private Worlds* was made into a highly regarded 1935 film. While living in Germany during the mid–1930s, Bottome was troubled by the rise of the Nazi Party and their overt persecution of German Jews. She wrote *The Mortal Storm* as a searing indictment against the Nazis' twisted ideology. It was also intended to be a wakeup call to Britain and the U.S., two counties whose practice of appeasement greatly concerned her. Bottome had a difficult time finding a London company willing to publish such a provocative novel. She was grateful when Farber and Farber accepted it in 1937. For the American publication in 1938, Bottome wrote three more chapters which deepened her attack on the treatment of the European Jews. *The Mortal Storm* was also serialized in the *New York Post* throughout April in 1938.

Finding a studio to film the book proved to be another daunting task. Politically charged movies, like *Blockade* (1938) had proven failures. The novel eventually reached the desk of a Metro synopsis writer, Helen Corbarely. With her comments ("The author has not taken sides on the question of Nazism ... this is not a book of propaganda, but a fair picture of the situation in Nazi Germany"), Corbarley clearly misunderstood Bottome's message.[5] William Dozier and Kenneth MacKenna of the Story Department read the screenplay synopsis and tried to convince Mayer to make the film. At that time, only three Hollywood studios remained involved in distributing films in Germany: 20th Century–Fox, Paramount and MGM. However, as the situation worsened in Europe, Mayer was pressured to speak out. Based on Colbarely's misguided comments, Mayer believed that he had found the vehicle in which he could make a "safe" political statement that would not incite harsh criticism. In April 1939, Mayer purchased the rights to the novel for $25,000.

By early summer, one of the studio's top screenwriters, Claudine West, completed the first draft of the screenplay. While it was faithful to Bottome's anti-fascist message, several changes were made to satisfy the censors. Of particular concern was that Freya, the novel's female protagonist, was impregnated by her communist lover, Hans. Another revision was the transformation of Hans, who is killed, into Martin, a pacifist. The character of the Jewish father, Prof. Roth, was more developed than it was in the novel. Jewish characters were now referred to as "non–Aryan." The screenplay was further revised based on the recommendations of the executives who were anxious over political backlash. Three more writers, including German emigrants George Froeschel and Paul Hans Rameau, were charged with modifying the general structure of the story and verifying accuracy. Even after producer Sidney Franklin submitted a finished draft to the Breen Office and Mayer, revisions were conducted throughout the shoot as Breen applied additional pressure to soften its stance on the brutality of the Nazi Party. Bottome and West fought to leave in many of the Jewish references, but their efforts proved futile. Mayer was too nervous about making such a bold statement and nothing could persuade him otherwise.

The finished script inspired a different controversy after the film's release. In August, 1940, Al Rosen filed a lawsuit against members of the Loew's Corp., including Borzage, West, Froeschel and Anderson Ellis (Rameau's pseudonym). Rosen claimed that various plot elements of his screenplay *Mad Dog of Europe* were used in the film. By March 1943, *The Hollywood Reporter* reported that Rosen was still seeking an injunction, damages and impounding of the film. It is unclear if the lawsuit was ever resolved.

Prior to filming, Bottome contacted Franklin to offer her suggestions, many of which were not welcome. She continued to provide unsolicited input throughout the shoot. Despite this snub, Bottome remained optimistic. In a letter, she wrote, "I have a most wonderful cast.... I think they have kept the spirit of the book, in spite of the necessary changes for screen purposes."[6] The studio did concede to one suggestion when, in the original script, both Martin and Freya die crossing the Austrian border. Bottome offered that Martin should live and carry Freya's body across the border as a message of hope. There was some discussion about reshooting the ending to allow Freya to live, but nothing came of it.

Principal photography began on February 8, 1940, with additional location shooting at Salt Lake City and Sun Valley, Idaho. An impressive cast was chosen in support of Sullavan and Stewart: Robert Young, Frank Morgan, Maria Ouspenskaya, Bonita Granville, Robert Stack and British stage actress Judith Anderson. However, after two weeks of filming, Anderson (Mrs. Roth) and Scotty Beckett (as the youngest son, Rudi) were dismissed. Silent film star Irene Rich and Gene Reynolds substituted.

When production began, the Battle of Karelia had been raging for a few days. As each day brought updated news of the situation in Europe, a somber mood enveloped the set. There was a noticeable lack of the usual horseplay and pranks as cast and crew were quietly unnerved by changing world events. The constant strain eventually caused Franklin to excuse himself from the film, so British producer Victor Saville was brought in. According to Saville, "It seemed to me that what had been done had little reality to the harshness that the conflict demanded. Both the cast and director seemed to have approached the subject as though it was a strong political disagreement between the Republicans and Democrats in Arkansas." Saville quickly got to work. "After three days of work on the script and rehearsals with the cast, I was able to get rolling and then I hit another problem." That problem was Borzage, who had "suddenly collapsed." As Saville explained,

> Later, I found this was partially a private disturbance. I liked Frank and did not want to do anything to disturb him further. So, instead of seeking another director, I went on stage and directed the film. I set up the camera, rehearsed the cast, then handed the whistle to Frank and retired to the back of the stage to wait for the next set-up. The unit, the cast, and all concerned were very discrete over the whole operation, and I had managed to smooth out a difficult situation with hurt to no one.[7]

Borzage's marriage of 24 years was deteriorating after the revelation of his wife's affair. Even though Borage engaged in his own extramarital affairs (Crawford and Lamarr, to name a few), he took this news hard and began drinking heavily. Later, Saville caused considerable controversy when he claimed he took over direction because Borzage was drunk on the set. Many have disputed Saville's assertion. In a letter to Herve Dumont, Stack wrote, "I was only in about ⅓ of the movie and I don't remember Saville being on the set, let alone directing. I met him once or twice, but certainly Frank Borzage was the director of *The Mortal Storm* when I was around." Stewart also wrote to Dumont: "Frank Borzage directed all of the picture, *Mortal Storm*. No one but Frank Borzage directed *Mortal Storm*."[8]

In his autobiography, Stack recalled an unusual incident on the set:

> About two weeks in filming, an official-looking gent arrived on the set and was seen talking to the producer Victor Saville. By the expression on Victor's face, I knew that the news wasn't good. Then I saw Robert Young pacing back and forth, his hands behind his back, mumbling, "My children, what about my children?" It took a while for the news to filter down to me. The Swiss consulate had received word from Germany that everyone connected with *Confessions of a Nazi Spy* and *The Mortal Storm* would be "taken care of" when Hitler won the war.... The threat seemed more than mere hyperbole.[9]

On another occasion, Stack stated he didn't care about what Germany would remember. "And that was the attitude of Jimmy, Maggie, the director Borzage, and most everybody else.... Nobody had the brains to take what the Swiss guy said seriously."[10]

The situation became more serious as the local German-American Bund, a pro–Nazi organization in America, protested loudly. The atmosphere on the set was tense as fights between the pro–Nazi group and members of the film crew broke out. The book-burning sequence almost got out of control with the fighting.

Borzage defended the film as a story of a family's disintegration. He elaborated:

> It just happens to have Nazi Germany as its background. Our film won't have any "heavies" and it's not an attack on Germany. It's just a picture of what happens when a force like that arises.... We don't condone the brutality, naturally. We try to show the fanatic fervor the motivates it, but we don't excuse it.[11]

Despite the turmoil on the set, Sullavan was deeply proud of her association with this film. Faith Service reported Sullavan liked her role better than any she had played because the character held principles that mirrored her own. As Sullavan explained, Freya "realized that the side she chose was not the popular one.... She took it and didn't look back. It is one of the commandments I have made for myself."[12]

Borzage later remarked to Quirk, "She was one of the most generous and unselfish people I knew when it came to other actors; she boosted them, encouraged them, always wanted them to give their best."[13] This was particularly true of Morgan, whom Sullavan felt was giving the best performance despite his reputation as a buffoonish comedic actor. When Borzage was asked to comment on Sullavan's qualities as an actress, he replied, "She gives herself over wholly to the scene, the dialogue, the emotional colorations of the scene.... Not one wasted emotion, not one false gesture. She gave the impression of living the woman she played, not acting her."[14]

Saville was likewise pleased with Sullavan. "Film stars are not just stars because the publicity department says so," he reflected.

> They have something loosely called "star quality" and, strangely enough, this quality is as distinct in each personality as fingerprints are different in ordinary mortals. Margaret Sullavan shone with winsome appeal, yet had such integrity that it made her work strong and believable. The role of the professor's daughter, Freya, in *The Mortal Storm* was a perfect example of why she was a star.[15]

Filming was completed on April 9, nine days after Hitler invaded Norway. Upon seeing a rough cut in May, Bottome wrote to Franklin and Claudine West. "*Mortal Storm* magnificent. Warmest congratulations. Whole cast, production and script 100 percent of the novel." To Bottome, the film was the "final message to the hearts and mind of America; by it we had hoped, not to drag them into war, but to awaken them in time to what must happen to humanity if the swastika took the place of the cross."[16] But the studio was still nervous about the movie's strong anti–Nazi theme, so the publicity department played it safe by promoting the film as "The Most Exciting Picture! The Love Story of Today! With the popular sweethearts of *The Shop Around the Corner*."[17] The movie trailer proclaimed the movie "as something you must see, not only with your eyes, but with your whole heart."

When the film was previewed in Hollywood on June 10, Hitler had just occupied Paris. This prompted the *Motion Picture Herald* to report, "A few months or weeks ago this Hollywood press audience would have used the word 'propaganda' to describe the film and speculated on the policy prompting its manufacture. This word was not heard in the auditorium or foyer on June 10th."[18] The sobering reality of the European War could no longer be ignored.

After the film's credits, a solemn voice fills the soundtrack. At the conclusion of the monologue, the narrator intones: "The tale we are about to tell is of the mortal storm in which man finds himself today." The camera pans over mountains and focuses in on a small town. A title slide reads: "January 1933. A small university town at the foot of the Alps in southern Germany." (Many scholars have pointed out that such a location is geographically

In Frank Borzage's masterpiece *The Mortal Storm* (1940) starring Jimmy Stewart and Sullavan, the anti–Nazi subject matter was beautifully explored.

non-existent.) The occasion is Prof. Viktor Roth's (Morgan) sixtieth birthday. He is surrounded by his loving family: wife (Rich), daughter Freya (Sullavan), son Rudi (Reynolds), and his two stepsons, Erich (William T. Orr) and Otto (Stack).

Walking across the university campus, Roth is warmly greeted by students and colleagues. In the lecture hall, he is greeted by a crowd of cheering and clapping students, faculty, and family. Fritz Marberg (Young) is the first to speak, praising the professor's accomplishments. Martin Breitner (Stewart), a veterinary student, offers his heartfelt appreciation on behalf of those in the lecture hall.

At the professor's birthday dinner, Fritz announces that he and Freya are engaged. The maid rushes in with exciting news of her own: Adolf Hitler was elected chancellor of Germany. It is not long before this announcement divides this family. Fritz, Otto and Erich are energized as Germany will return to its former glory. Others are concerned for the safety of the professor, a non–Aryan.

The scene switches to the Breitners' mountain home. Tending to a newborn colt are Elsa (Granville), who works for the Breitners, and Mrs. Breitner (Ouspenskaya; this tiny, troll-like, thickly accented woman is the mother of tall, angular and American-sounding Stewart?). Martin has given up his studies in animal science at the university due to the changing political scene. Freya arrives and invites Martin to a local inn to join Fritz and her stepbrothers.

At the inn, the mood is momentarily joyful, but the arrival of two people reveals the underlying tension: Mr. Werner, Rudi's non–Aryan teacher, and Nazi Youth leader Holl (Dan Dailey … *the* charming Dan Dailey of the Betty Grable musicals, who gives a truly disturbing performance in his film debut). Members of the crowd rise to their feet and raise their arms in salute as they sing a song extolling the virtues of the New Germany. Martin and Freya stand, but do not raise their arms—alone in a sea of raised arms. Holl notices Mr. Werner is not standing. He nearly slugs the elderly man. Avoiding a brawl, Martin walks Mr. Werner to the door and then returns to his table. Fritz and the brothers are furious. They want to know where Martin stand politically. Before Martin answers, word spreads that Mr. Werner is being attacked outside the inn. Martin and Freya rush out to Mr. Werner's aid.

Fritz warns Freya about the consequences of her actions and its impact on her father. "Your party threatens men like my father. We disagree more than I realized," she rebukes him. "I don't think I shall ever be heart and soul with your convictions."

At the university, Roth is now shunned by everyone. In the lecture hall, he faces a seething crowd of Hitler's Youths. Holl challenges Roth on the theory there are no differences between the blood of Aryans and non–Aryans. Holl declares the class as banned. The entire class, including Fritz, walks out.

Freya breaks the engagement, even as Fritz protests as if it were a silly squabble. It's over, she mournfully tells him, sad to lose a man she no longer recognizes. One night, after Martin walks Freya home, he is attacked by Nazi Youths. After Mrs. Roth stops the fight, the brothers decide to leave the house. When Erich tells Roth that the family's safety is in peril, Roth counters, "I've never prized safety, Erich, either for myself or my children. I prized courage."

One night, Freya visits Martin. While looking at the family's collection of bridal cups, Martin shows her one that has no name painted on it. It's his. Martin reveals that he wants something he doesn't deserve. Looking furtively at her, he asks, "Freya, have I a chance?" It's a poignant moment of raw emotions, courtesy of the "doubling effect." They are interrupted by Mr. Werner, who has come to their house to avoid arrest. Martin offers to accompany him through rugged mountain terrain to the Austrian border.

After they leave, the Nazi patrol, headed by Franz (Ward Bond), arrives. Franz questions Freya and Mrs. Breitner, but notices that Elsa is jittery. The scene where he interrogates her is truly harrowing. Franz fails to get the information from her, so he demands that Martin report to headquarters by the next day. Martin can never come back home without fear of arrest.

In early spring, the professor is arrested and sent to a concentration camp. Freya asks Fritz, now an officer, to help them locate her father. Fritz, still having some feelings for Freya, offers to make arrangements for her mother to visit the professor. When Mrs. Roth sees her husband, he looks tired and much older, despite reassuring her he is fine. He implores his wife to take Freya and Rudi out of the country. Their reunion is heart-wrenching and masterfully played by Morgan and Rich, thus embodying the transcendent love that knows no age limit or physical barriers. Not even the off-screen interruptions of the guard can diminish the power of their love.

After Roth dies, Mrs. Roth takes Freya and Rudi to Austria. Freya is detained at the border because she has her father's last manuscript in her possession; her passport is confiscated. She goes to the Breitner home and discovers that Martin has returned to take her to Austria. The Gestapos learn of the plan after Elsa is tortured. Against his will, Fritz is put in charge of the ski patrol that will intercept Martin and Freya at the border. The commander reasons that Freya will hold Martin back and he's right. The scenes depicting their climb up a steep mountain show Freya frail and unable to keep up.

By early morning, Austria is within sight. However, Martin notices the patrol approaching. Despite the danger, Martin and Freya ski down the mountain. The patrol is unable to catch them, so Fritz gives the orders to shoot. Freya is hit. Martin, injured, carries her across the border. The viewer is privileged to witness one of Sullavan's sublime death scenes. Cradled in Martin's arms, Freya whispers, "We made it, didn't we? We're free."

Martin replies, "Yes, we're free. You can hear the church bells from the village." He wants to continue their trek. Freya: "No, wait ... let me rest a little ... dear Martin, I'm tired ... yes ... very, very tired."

One can actually see her spirit leaving her frail body as she dies in his arms. What's remarkable about this scene is its simplicity: no surge of music, just a tight close-up of the two with the wind blowing through her hair. It's amazing how much emotion Borzage can evoke with such minimum effects.

Back at the Roth home, Fritz tells Otto and Erich about Freya's death. Shocked, Erich mutters, "Freya killed, it doesn't make sense. And Breitner goes free."

> OTTO: "Yes, free to think as he believes. Wasn't that what he said?"
> ERICH: "Free to fight against all we stand for?"
> OTTO: "Yes, thank God for that."

Angered, Erich slaps Otto before rushing out. Otto walks through the house, listening to the voices of those who once inhabited it, before running out the front door. As the camera pans back, a narrator is heard: "And I said to the man who stood at the gate of the year: 'Give me a light that I may tread safely into the unknown.' And he replied: 'Go out into the darkness and put your hand into the Hand of God. That shall be to you better than light and safer than a known way.'" This comes from the first lines of Minnie Louise Haskins' 1908 poem "The Gate of the Year"—a fitting tribute to Bottome's passionate plea for humanity's call to action.

After the movie's release, Bottome enthusiastically remarked in a cable from London to the *New York Times* that the film would live in her mind "as the best possible medium for a message that the hour has made more poignant now than ever. Without liberty there is no human life. Without the individual's complete acceptance of moral responsibility, there is no such thing as human decency; there is only a shameful slavery enforced by inhuman cruelty."[19]

The Mortal Storm was released on June 12 and received mostly favorable notices. The *New York Times* was unstinting in its praise:

> At last and at a time when the world is more gravely aware than ever of the relentless mass brutality embodied in the Nazi system, Hollywood has turned its camera eye upon the most tragic human drama of our age.... *The Mortal Storm* falls definitely into the category of blistering anti–Nazi propaganda.... It is magnificently directed and acted. James Stewart and Margaret Sullavan bring to vibrant and anguished life the two young people who resist the sweeping system.

Not all reviewers felt as strongly. The *Oakland Tribune* had some harsh words: "Sitting through its enactment is a grueling experience, and I feel a rather unnecessary one; for I still feel that the theater is not the place for propaganda films or sociological lectures." Some of the actors were not spared from the diatribe: "Frank Morgan, who gives the best performance of all, is little more than a funny man in a beard and serious mein; [and] Margaret Sullavan attempts nothing in the way of characterization."

For every bad review, there were two or three with overwhelming praise. According to the *Bismarck* (ND) *Tribune*, the film was "characterized by brilliant performances upon the part of an outstanding cast. [Sullavan,] who may always be depended upon for a sterling performance, surpasses anything she has done previously."

The Mortal Storm earned a small profit of $108,000. According to columnist Frederick Othman, "The moviemakers are learning by sad experience these days that people go to the picture shows for fun." As proof, Othman offered that *The Mortal Storm* "was an exceptionally fine picture, with good plot, actors and direction. It should have been one of the studio's top moneymakers of 1940 but it had the anti–Nazi sting and reports indicate it is doing so-so business."[20] That the film eked out a profit at all was due to the Sullavan-Stewart names on the marquee. Still, it was a critical success and won such honors as the Blue Ribbon Award Badge of Merit (Best Picture of the Month, June 1940); *Film Daily's* Ten Best Pictures, *New York Times'* Ten Best Pictures, and the Canadian Critics Best Selection of 1939–40.

As feared, there was an uproar from Berlin. In Washington, D.C.,, the German ambassador was alarmed by the film's anti–German propaganda. In early July, Goebbels banned all MGM films in Germany. Metro closed its Berlin office shortly afterwards. Latin American countries, including Venezuela and Costa Rica, refused to show it. Another controversial film released by Metro in October, *Escape*, caused Hitler to ban all MGM films in German-occupied areas. In 1942, *The Hollywood Reporter* reported that *The Mortal Storm* was the first anti–Nazi film to be presented in Brazil and proved an overwhelming success, breaking attendance records.

The film is undoubtedly one of Borzage's most trenchant masterpieces and deserves more recognition than usually attributed to it. In this instance, Borzage fully developed his favorite theme—a force that puts its lovers in peril. The force is often perceived to be the fascist government and its effect on a subgroup of humanity (the Roth family). Given this concept, there has been much criticism which downplayed the film's powerful message. Borzage utilized his anti–Nazi theme not so much as a warning call to the world, but rather to depict, through the rise of Nazi Germany as its background, the deterioration of the individual's spiritual nature. The film is less of an indictment of Hitler and more of a personal look into man's soul. It abounds in strong religious references from the utterances of God by various characters to Elsa praying in front of a shrine to the Virgin Mary. The film's real power stems from the rift between friends and family as characters choose sides on an urgent moral issues. It is frightening when Fritz commits to a cause that is spiritually and morally corrupt. We are grateful when Otto renounces his party, because this implies that there is still hope in a deeply troubled world.

No one else but Borzage could have made a film that resonates with such emotional power, despite Saville's claim. It is, perhaps, his most mature work in that he demonstrates extraordinary insight into the individual's perspective of a terrifying world situation. As he did in *Little Man, What Now?*, he uses severe weather conditions, such as snow, lightning and wind, to create a sense of overwhelming oppression.

Borzage was gifted with a strong cast of natural, subtle performers. To imply that Sullavan, Stewart and Morgan are merely mouthpieces in a dramatization of global events, as some critics have stated, underestimates the film's potent message of individual choices. The most successful movies are those in which important issues are presented through characters with whom one can identify. Here, the cast's lack of German characteristics allows for the universal acceptance that what's happening "over there" can happen anywhere. We all know that Stewart could never pass for anything other than "Apple Pie American," but it doesn't matter given his masterful performance. His Martin is a deeply felt, heroic figure, who faces the ultimate challenge to be true to himself and his convictions.

Sullavan's Freya ranks among one of her top five performances. She displays integrity and resolute determination; yet, there are times when she appears so vulnerable that we want to protect her. We are deeply moved by her desire to maintain normalcy in a chaotic world that has turned her life upside down. We are also impressed by her display of courage as the storyline progresses. Had Freya lived, she undoubtedly would have become a freedom fighter along with Martin. Her memorable performance deserved an Academy Award nomination as columnist Frederick Othman predicted back in 1941.

Stewart and Sullavan do not stand alone. Morgan is splendid as he displays unexpected depth and subtlety. It's a shame that the Academy did not to nominate him, either. Young is fine cast against type as a Nazi zealot—a keen portrayal of a man in deep spiritual conflict and a definitive demonstration of his often overlooked gifts as a dramatic actor. Many other members of the cast, particularly Rich, Granville and Ouspenskaya, made fine impressions. Only Stack fails to impress with his wooden performance.

In the years since its release, critical opinions have not always been particularly favorable, but there has been some renewed interest. David Thomson included the film as one of the 1000 films moviegoers should see in his book *Have You Seen*? He noted, "Frank Borzage does not shirk showing us the mounting brutality of fascist Germany."[21] Not to be outdone was Steven Schneider with his book *1001 Movies You Must See Before You Die*. According to Schneider, "I don't know of any other actor who could so expertly play the moral center of a film like Jimmy Stewart. *The Mortal Storm* is probably one of Stewart's most nuanced good guy portrayals ever." While admitting that he was "not a huge fan of Sullavan, she is markedly compelling as Freya." Schneider judged that the film "did something that most Hollywood films didn't—it exposed the destructive nature of the Nazi Party in Germany—not as a war movie with soldiers and tanks, but as a film about the destruction of a family."[22]

Sullavan's next film, which also dealt with anti–Nazi sentiments, elicited the same type of critical reception at the time of its release and in subsequent years as well as inciting another political firestorm.

24

Taking a Bold Stand

The alliances with Remarque were friendly and professional. She was the perfect type for his heroines, but to my observance was never involved in his theories.[1]—Audrey Christie

So Ends Our Night was based on Erich Maria Remarque's 1939 novel *Liebe deinen Nächsten* (*Love Thy Neighbour*). An English adaptation first appeared in a serialized version in *Collier's* magazine in April 1939. In May, Metro purchased the screen rights, intending it as a vehicle for Robert Taylor, Spencer Tracy and Sullavan. With Sullavan's maternity leave, the project was put on hold. The novel was released in English and German versions in 1941 after Remarque revised it to reflect changing events. (The English translation, *Flotsam*, was released in March 1941, after the film's release.)

In January 1940, the project was resurrected by the newly created producing team of David L. Loew and Albert L. Lewin for their first feature. Loew was the son of one of Metro's founders, Marcus Loew. After several years as an MGM producer, he left to launch an independent career. Lewin, like Loew, was a former associate producer at Metro. Their production company was called the Loew-Lewin Productions. *Flotsam* was specifically chosen in an effort to aid Britain in the early days of the European War. Since both men were Jewish, they were disturbed by the spread of Nazism in Europe. After the Nazis occupied France and Denmark, Lewin helped friends and associates living in Europe. Eventually, he succeeded in bringing Jean Renoir to Hollywood.

With a budget of $401,000, the production crew included notable names associated with MGM, like award-winning set designer William Cameron Menzies and cinematographer William Daniels—no doubt the Loew connection did much to ensure *Flotsam* would be a well-crafted, grade-A film. The book was adapted by Talbot Jennings in a fairly faithful manner and director John Cromwell was delighted with the finished script, declaring, "It was one of the best scripts I've ever had."[2] As production assistant, Stanley Kramer, later a renowned director and producer of memorable films (*High Noon*, 1952; *Judgment at Nuremberg*, 1961), received his first screen credit.

The producers set out to assemble a cast worthy of the film's subject matter. In January 1940, Louella Parsons announced Luise Rainer was in negotiations to play the part of Ruth Hollander. However, Rainer soon left her stalled film career behind to try her luck on Broadway.

Meanwhile, Metro planned several projects for Sullavan's final film under contract. Among those considered were *Equilibrium* with Spencer Tracy and an untitled project which would have reteamed her with Stewart. Sullavan said she needed time to rest after completing two films in succession.

By early June, Sullavan was loaned by MGM to join Fredric March in two of the three leading roles in *Flotsam*, the film's working title. It was later reported by Harriet Parsons (Louella's daughter) that Sullavan agreed to commit to another Loew-Lewin production, *Night Music*, based on a Clifford Odets play.

The casting of the third lead, Ludwig Kern, proved to be an ambitious task. Kramer claimed responsibility for a little-known actor, Glenn Ford, being cast: "I saw one of his screen tests and was impressed. He was an open-faced young man, good-looking, and with an appealingly direct screen style. I recommended him to the producers and championed his cause."[3] Ford, under contract to Columbia, was in the programmer *Babies for Sale*; two more low-budgeted features, *The Lady in Question* and *Blondie Plays Cupid*, had not yet been released. Ford was invited to read for the part. Arriving at Loew's Santa Monica beach house for an interview, Ford was surprised to find March and Sullavan there as well. As Ford recalled,

> I managed to read as ably as I could in front of these two legendary actors. March started teasing. He'd say, "Margaret, doesn't he remind you of a young Hank Fonda?" … It was just in fun. Later, when I was getting ready to leave, March patted me on the back and said, "Congratulations! We all agreed you'll be perfect in this part." I mumbled, "Th-thanksss, Mr. March," and then I drove home in a daze.[4]

Filming began in early August on an Universal sound stage. It was not long before Sullavan's age-old fight with Universal came to a head. Now that Sullavan was not safely confined within Metro's studio gates, Universal was ready with legal action. The studio obtained a court order that prevented her from appearing in *Flotsam* on the basis that she was breaking her original contract. According to a news report, "Universal charged … it wants to start filming *The Invisible Woman* with Miss Sullavan in the title role."[5] She was ordered to appear in court by mid-week. It was announced a few days later that Sullavan and Universal came to an agreement. Sullavan was allowed to appear in *Flotsam* as long as she reported to Universal for the one picture she owed; according to Quirk, Sullavan was court-ordered to make two films. At least Sullavan could claim a small victory as she was excused from *The Invisible Woman*. Virginia Bruce had the honor of "appearing" in her place.

There were other issues back on the set. One of the more delicate problems was that Sullavan was a 31-year old mother of two toddlers. Could she be photographed to look young enough to be realistic in love scenes with her 24-year-old leading man? Fortunately, photographer Daniels did his job well. "I was glad he succeeded," Cromwell recalled. "As Daniels managed it, they came out looking like a couple of kids the same age."[6]

Ford was energized by his association with Sullavan and March as they treated him with respect. Ford believed that Sullavan was instrumental in helping him with his big chance in film. He maintained that Sullavan allowed him to be favored in some important scenes, an act of professional courtesy for which he was eternally grateful. After one successful day's shoot, Sullavan presented him with an expensive necktie in appreciation. According to his son Peter Ford, "Dad prized [this gift] and wore it for many years as a good luck charm."[7]

Despite an atmosphere of mutual good will and camaraderie, Cromwell recalled that Sullavan could be argumentative and temperamental, especially when she felt her performance was compromised by other actors. Cromwell remembered a time when they were filming a love scene, in which he had instructed Ford to behave in a sophisticated manner. Sullavan challenged him on this matter, stating it wasn't in character and would upset the effect of the scene. When Cromwell viewed the rushes, he saw that she was right and reshot the scene.

In his autobiography, Kramer wrote,

> I most fondly remember Margaret Sullavan. She was a beautiful blond whose almost tubercular fragility did not conceal an exceptional talent.... She was very kind to me, perhaps because I was so young and inexperienced. She talked seriously to me about the picture and even asked my advice about various aspects of her performance. It took me awhile to realize that she wasn't asking because she actually needed my advice. She simply wanted to make me feel good, to build my self-confidence.[8]

In the cast was Erich von Stroheim, by then a director and actor from the silent film era, who was appearing in a small but pivotal role. She befriended von Stroheim, whom she believed was badly treated by the hypocritical Hollywood establishment. It is not known if she extended the same courtesy to Anna Sten of the infamous "Goldwyn's Folly" fame, who was attempting a comeback as a supporting actress.

Despite her professionalism, Sullavan could not resist giving her producers a few gray hairs. "Producers of *Flotsam* practically had a stroke when they found out Margaret Sullavan took her first solo flight last week," Harrison Carroll reported. "Margaret won't fly any more now until the end of the picture."[9] If the producers thought that was the end of their worries, they were sadly mistaken. George Howard wrote of the time when the makeup man arrived on the set on a power scooter. Intrigued, Sullavan asked if she could take it for a ride. "In a moment, she was roaring over the set, her skirt tucked under her, making a tremendous racket."[10]

Principal photography was completed by mid–October. By mid–January 1941, the film was ready for the Hollywood and Miami, Florida, premieres. Despite the poor box office reception to other "anti-Nazi" films, Loew and Lewin were optimistic that their film would prove the exception.

It opens melodramatically with lightning flashes between the opening credit transitions and thundering music. Against a dark sky, shadowy human figures walk across the screen. The foreword states it is not afraid to deal with the crisis in Europe.

The story begins in Austria in 1937 before the German occupation. Two refugees are arrested as they flee from a hotel. These men have no passports. Without passports, refugees have been stripped of their rights as citizens. While Ludwig Kern (Ford) is questioned by Austrian customs officials, the older man, Josef Steiner (March), is interrogated by Gestapo official Brenner (von Stroheim). Steiner is a German political dissident who escaped from a concentration camp two years prior. Brenner offers him a passport in exchange for the names of those who helped him. Steiner stands firm in his refusal. This results in a fascinating cat-and-mouse game which generates suspense as Brenner coolly plays with Steiner's emotions. The actors play brilliantly off one another and the effect is mesmerizing.

While in jail, Steiner senses Ludwig's youthful confusion and befriends him. The two men are released together into the woods near the Czechoslovakian border. When asked why he is a refugee even though he's an Aryan, Steiner tells Ludwig, "I'm simply an ex-soldier who hates the gang who rules Germany"; overtly obvious references like this caused consternation among the government officials. This sets the stage for a flashback as Steiner, escaping from the concentration camp, risks his life to see his wife Marie (Frances Dee) before fleeing the country. In a moving scene exquisitely played by March and Dee (who has rarely been as good as she is here), they struggle to say goodbye without attracting attention in the crowded marketplace. In a scene worthy of Borzage, the couple shares one last heartbreaking look before he disappears into the crowd.

Back to the present: The two men separate. Steiner returns to Vienna to learn about his wife in Germany. He uses his newfound skills at cards to earn money for an Austrian passport. Ludwig, arriving in Prague, searches for his father. One night, he wanders accidentally into Ruth Holland's (Sullavan) bedroom. Smitten, he strikes up a conversation with her the following day in the hotel lobby. An innocent remark sparks an unexpected reaction and she leaves.

Alone in her room, Ruth looks out the rain-soaked window as she recalls a painful incident. (Despite the overuse of this technique in film, it still generates sufficient emotions.) Ruth, a chemistry student, is confronted by her angry fiancé, who tells her that their relationship is over because a newspaper item has caused him embarrassment as she is Jewish. With cold finality, he informs her, "It's a pity that you're not dead like your father and mother." Anger flashes across Ruth's eyes as she delivers a well-deserved slap to the cad's face.

Ludwig appears to apologize for whatever he may have said. Later that week, Ruth informs him she's leaving for a lab job in Vienna. The two share one last dinner together, and then have their first kiss; Sullavan and Ford play this potentially mawkish scene with such sincerity and naturalness that it is a breathtakingly *real* moment. The couple's reverie is interrupted by the birth of a baby—and the mother's death. The drunken husband is bitter and Ruth contemplates the futility of their situation as refugees. Ludwig hands Ruth a lilac blossom, as if to remind her (and the viewer) that life, while fragile, can still be cherished. Cromwell neatly captured the essence of the eternal "Circle of Life." The cynic may shake his head at Ludwig's seemingly illogical action; the romantic embraces it for its simple truth.

After learning that his father committed suicide, Ludwig heads to Vienna where he finds Steiner working as a carnival barker. Steiner enlists the aid of his sympathetic boss, Potzloch (Joseph Cawthorn), to hire Ludwig as Lilo's (Sten) assistant in the shooting gallery.

Meanwhile, Ruth is told by Prof. Meyer (William Stack) that she can no longer safely work at the college. Ruth tracks Ludwig down through his address on his letters. She arrives at the carnival and Potzloch, sensing the two are in love, hires Ruth.

One night, Ludwig gets into trouble after placing a weighted bullet in a gun when an Austrian police chief was enjoying a winning streak. Suspicious, the chief demands to see his passport. Ludwig attacks him after he insults Ruth, calling her a "filthy little Jew." In jail, Ludwig is visited by Lilo, who informs him Ruth has fled to Zurich.

Ludwig finds Ruth living at the luxurious apartment of a friend. Ruth reveals that she hasn't written him for fear she'll bring him bad luck. Now that he is here, she is comforted by his presence and decides to travel with him to Paris. Back in Vienna, a large poster announces **Nazis Invade Austria!** as newsreel footage shows the Germans' entry into the city. Spotting Brenner in a motorcade, Steiner narrowly escapes when the Gestapos arrive at the carnival. Lilo pulls a gun on them—an act of bravery which will cost her her life.

Ludwig and Ruth cross the Swiss Alps toward the safe haven of Paris. (During production, the Germans occupied that city, thus evoking a bittersweet sense of irony.) The couple's journey is stalled when Ruth falls seriously ill and is sent to a nearby hospital. As bad luck would have it, Ludwig is picked up by the police. When he is released, the couple move on to Paris. They are joined by some of their friends, including Steiner, who finds construction jobs for his friends. One day, Steiner receives word that his wife has only a few days left to live. Despite the grave danger, he decides to go back to Germany. Before departing, he leaves an envelope of money with Leo and instructs him to give it to the young couple after ten days.

One night, Ruth learns Ludwig has been picked up by the police and will be deported to the border. This time, Ruth is determined to do something. Over Leo's cynical objections, Ruth berates him: "Before I knew him, I felt old and full of suspicions. And he made me young and he made me laugh again. It was hopeless without faith, kindness in humanity. He made me cheerful and full of life. Yes, and he's done it with his simple, straightforward instinct … with his love, if you must know!" Sullavan's breathy, rushed delivery, coupled with careless diction, makes it a challenge to hear her monologue clearly as few critics at the time noted.

Ruth tries to enlist the help of a friend's uncle. When he refuses, she threatens to marry his nephew. Admiring her resolve, he agrees to help Ruth obtain a passport, but warns that Ludwig's situation is not as easily fixed. In Germany, Steiner is arrested. He makes a plea to see his wife but is rebuffed by the colonel. Brenner intervenes and makes a proposal that Steiner be allowed to visit his wife in exchange for the names of those who helped him escape. Steiner visits Marie in the hospital. Her happiness, however, is tempered by fear for his safety. He assures her that there is no danger. In extremely tight close-up, March radiates warmth and tenderness as Dee exudes wifely devotion. When Marie finally succumbs, we see the life drain from Steiner's face. It is a well-played scene done with subtle and light pathos to maximum effect. Afterward, Steiner is met by Brenner. Walking down a glass-enclosed staircase, Steiner pushes Brenner through a window and they fall to their deaths.

Leo gives Ruth the money, which is used to secure a passport for Ludwig. They plan to marry and travel abroad to South America or the United States. **THE END** appears with the final footage of the darkened figures walking across the landscape, dashing any hope of basking in the warm glow of the couple's future. Clearly, the producers are reminding us there are still many who must trudge through uncertain times. Although the impression of this moment is initially depressing, enough of the film's beauty remains in one's memories to counteract this effect.

Upon its general release, *So Ends Our Night* (renamed before its release) was met with mixed praise. The *Boston Globe* raved that Remarque's novel

> has been made into a magnificently directed and acted film. *So Ends Our Night*..is a gripping, powerful and very human tale…. A really superb group of players has been assembled for the leading roles; stars with box-office appeal but more performers who bring artistry and integrity to their characters. Outstanding are Fredric March and Margaret Sullavan, who have never done anything shoddy or artificial on the screen.

The *New York Herald-Tribune* conceded that, while the film "has great sincerity and considerable random power [and] has been unstintingly produced, ably directed and performed, [it] is episodic, overlong and singularly unmoving." The cast was uniformly praised and Sullavan was complimented for bringing "all her artistry and emotional intensity to the romance." The *Rochester Times-Union*'s Amy Croughton reported, "With a long cast of gifted, experienced players, careful direction for details by John Cromwell, and artistic setting and photography, *So Ends Our Night* is interesting and engrossing entertainment without quite becoming a great picture…. [Sullavan's] mannerisms and her nasal voice prevent her characterization of Ruth from being as appealing as it might have been in other hands."

Variety noted that the "picture, decidedly overlengthy and filled with repetitious episodes, is a box office problem…. It may hit par in a few metropolitan areas, but is dubious fare for general bookings." This assessment proved accurate. Despite this disappointment, Remarque reportedly enjoyed the film and praised the performances of March and Sullavan, who, he felt, beautifully captured Ruth's strength of character.

So Ends Our Night is not an easy film to evaluate as its many fine qualities are somewhat offset by its length (close to two hours) and convoluted plot. The final impression of this somber film is similar to *Three Comrades*: You either are moved by its powerful emotional impact or you are bored to tears. To maximize the viewing experience, one needs to be willing to embrace the "Borzagean-type" sentiments. One also needs to watch the film in its entirety without ill-timed commercial interruptions, which disrupts the cumulative effect and lessens its emotional power. Keeping this in mind, one encounters a film that resonates with dramatic power and emotional impact. Cromwell's direction rivals Borzage's as his best. The photography, background music, settings—all are fine examples of Hollywood's craftsmen at their peak. The film was nominated for an Academy Award for Scoring of a Dramatic Picture.

The performances are splendid. March gives the haunted Steiner immense sympathy and power. Ford is terrific as Kern. It's hard to reconcile this youth with the hard-boiled characters he played in movies like *Gilda* (1946). Some of the supporting players are even better than the distinguished leads. Dee is the revelation for, long after the film has ended, one has a vivid memory of her heart-wrenching portrait. The other great performance is given by von Stroheim. He's not on the screen much, but his very presence causes the film to sizzle with dramatic excitement. The only disappointment is Anna Sten's lackluster performance. She seems oddly out of place and does not make much of an impression.

Given the overall excellence of the cast, it's understandable why Sullavan sometimes gets the short end of the stick with the critics. Dan Callahan cynically noted that "she offers a sort of 'Sullavan's Greatest Hits' performance," with references to *Three Comrades* and even *The Moon's Our Home*.[11] It is likely that Dee's memorable appearance overwhelms one's memory of Sullavan; after all, it's not often that anyone is able to steal the film from the supreme Sullavan. Let it be said, though, that Sullavan is as fine here as she is in her other great roles. She invests her character with honesty and simplicity as to make Ruth tremendously appealing. One shudders to think how the heavy-handed Luise Rainer would have destroyed the delicate, fragile nature of the character.

On January 17, 1941, the day the film premiered, an interesting news item appeared:

> Moviemakers indicated today that there'll be few propaganda pictures in the future, not because of possible governmental bans, but because theatergoers simply won't buy tickets.... Charges of Senator Burton K. Wheeler that the movies were helping lead America into war therefore have fallen on indifferent ears in Hollywood.[12]

Still, the anti–Nazi propaganda was a hot topic in Washington, D.C., and, in September, a Senate subcommittee began an investigation into whether Hollywood had intentionally campaigned to bring the U.S. into war through its anti–Nazi, pro–British and pro-interventionist themes in such films as *I Wanted Wings* and *Dive Bomber*. Senator Gerald Nye charged Hollywood with producing "at least 20 pictures in the last year designed to drug the reason of the American people, set aflame their emotions, turn their hatred into a blaze, fill them with fear that Hitler will come over here and capture them."[13] Among the "highly inflammatory" films on the list were *The Mortal Storm* and *So Ends Our Night*. Several executives and producers, including Saville, Lewin and Loew, were brought in to defend their actions before the House of Representatives. Hired to defend the film industry, noted lawyer Wendell Wilkie told the five-member committee, "If you charge that the motion picture industry as a whole and its leading executives as individuals are opposed to the Nazi dictatorship in Germany, if this is the case, there need be no investigation. We abhor everything Hitler represents."[14] Later, it was discovered that, not only were there very few anti–Nazi propaganda films released in 1940, but that the members of the committee had not seen the films they were investigating. In October, the hearings were suspended with Senator D. Worth Clark's promise that they would resume at a later time. After the December 7, 1941, attack on Pearl Harbor, the investigation was dropped for good.

25

No Small-Time Affair

*If this new picture really does send her skyrocketing, write her down as one
of the few who ever won the Hollywood game while flouting its rules.*[1]
—*Jimmie Fidler*

Fannie Hurst's phenomenally successful novel *Back Street* was first serialized in *Cosmopolitan* as "Grand Passion" in the fall of 1930. Its theme of an ill-fated love affair between a married, prominent New York businessman and a vibrant socialite, who is content to become his "back street" mistress, struck a responsive chord among the female readers. Hurst must have drawn upon her own experience of an extramarital affair with Arctic explorer Vilhjalmur Stefanssonas.

After the installments were compiled into a novel, Universal paid $30,000 for the screen rights. *Back Street* reached the screen in 1932 with Irene Dunne as Ray Schmidt and John Boles as Walter Saxel. Despite some negative critical reviews, it was a tremendous financial success and put director John M. Stahl, Dunne and Boles in the forefront of Hollywood's notables. While faithful to Hurst's novel, this version is dull and dated. The screenplay is sophomoric and often induces unintentional laughter due to Stahl's listless direction. The cast members do not fare any better. As the likable cad, Boles struggles with a part that is ill-conceived. Dunne's performance is likewise stilted and lacks the warmth of her later dramatic performances. What is interesting is its frank, pre–Code sexual attitude. This *Back Street* is no tragedy; rather, it's about two people who should have known better, but can't help themselves.

Like most pre–Code films, *Back Street* could not be reissued in 1935 because the Breen Office found it objectionable. Of particular concern was that the heroine's stepsister was a happy mother of two, even though the first child was conceived out of wedlock. Even more damaging was when the heroine asks her married lover for a child. Breen sermonized, "[T]he portrayal of the 'kept woman' theme, and of the adulterous relationship between the two sympathetic leads … does not contain proper moral values to measure up to the requirements of the Code."[2] Universal's request for reissue was denied again in 1938.

Bruce Manning, one of Universal's prolific screenwriters, gave Deanna Durbin several box office successes, In 1940, he was given his first assignment as producer. With a budget of $1 million, Manning's *Back Street* remake was earmarked as one of the studio's important productions of the year. The first hurdle Manning and his frequent collaborator, Felix Jackson, had to surmount was updating the original screenplay to meet the tighter Production Code regulations. Breen wanted the screenplay to convey the message that the adulterous relationship was morally wrong and the lives of the lovers were worse off due to the affair. Ray had to be depicted "in a state of total degeneration caused by poverty and loneliness."

There could also be "no suggestion that Walter had any sort of official appointment" as his means of employment. Additionally, there could be no "intimate love scenes" between the couple.[3] The final script was approved by Breen and production could begin. In deference to the European War, some of the characters' German names were changed: Ray Schmidt and Kurt Sheindler became Ray Smith and Curt Stanton.

English director Alfred Hitchcock, who made a sensation with *Rebecca*, was the initial choice to direct. Another well-regarded English director, Robert Stevenson, was eventually chosen. Stevenson, under contract to David O. Selznick, was loaned out to Universal. How Sullavan became involved in what is generally regarded as her masterpiece is something of a mystery due to conflicting stories. The most likely account comes from the newspaper columns of 1940. After her overnight acclaim with her performance in *Rebecca*, Joan Fontaine was sought for *Back Street*. Negotiations between Selznick (to whom Fontaine was under contract) and Universal were completed. However, by late September, Fontaine raised eyebrows by walking out on her commitment. She then went to RKO for Hitchcock's *Suspicion*—and the Best Actress statuette.

Universal had no other female star on the lot who could handle the prestigious assignment. Sullavan was contacted by Manning and on October 4 Louella Parsons announced, "There was rejoicing indeed today on the Universal lot for Margaret Sullavan has agreed to play the role in *Back Street*."[4] Parsons also reported that Sullavan would report to Universal upon the completion of *Flotsam*. Sullavan later stated,

> When the opportunity to play in a good story directed by a master of his craft presents itself, any star or feature player can regard herself as a very fortunate individual. Such an opportunity presented itself when Universal studios asked me to star with Charles Boyer in a plcturizatlon of Fannie Hurst's great novel, *Back Street*.

Likewise, she was enthusiastic about the director. "The choice of Robert Stevenson as director was all that either Mr. Boyer or I could wish."[5] Sullavan's words may have been the handiwork of the publicity department as her statement about being asked to star with Boyer is refuted in Parsons' October 10 column: "Today Charles Boyer put his name on a contract to play opposite Margaret Sullavan in *Back Street*."[6]

According to Larry Swindell, Sullavan requested Boyer. Boyer and Sullavan admired each other's work and wanted to work together ever since the ill-fated *I Loved a Soldier*. Boyer had a non-exclusive contract with Universal, so acquiring him was easy. The only issue was that Boyer's contract stipulated top billing. Sullavan's contract had the same stipulation, but she was willing to give him top billing in the credits. With Boyer's "French Lov-air" reputation and brooding bedroom manner, women would line up en masse at the movie theaters.

The one person who was not happy was Fannie Hurst, who was miffed when the executives rejected her suggestions for the revised script. She also objected to Boyer as she felt that Walter was decidedly Midwestern and the French actor was all wrong. Despite the film's popularity, Hurst remained vocal about her dislike for it.

The shoot progressed relatively smoothly. The studio bent over backwards to accommodate Sullavan. William Daniels was borrowed from Metro as cinematographer. Period costumes were designed by Muriel King to conceal her advancing pregnancy with her third child. Sullavan got along well with Boyer. Although he had been warned about Sullavan being difficult to work with, they worked harmoniously. The only challenge was that she had to contend with morning sickness. Boyer recalled teasing her about the sex of the child. Sullavan was adamant it would be a boy. After the birth of her son William, Boyer marveled at the notion of how Sullavan could be so certain.

Sullavan also got along with her director: "Both Charles and myself were enthusiastic about Bob's direction of *Back Street*, for he showed a meticulous care in minor details which would appear to be trifles to a less experienced or less understanding director. In the big dramatic moments in *Back Street*, he was capable of wringing every emotional moment from his story."[7] Likewise, Stevenson enjoyed his experience with his notoriously difficult star: "Margaret Sullavan is an extraordinarily intelligent woman. She is very easy to direct if one just treats her as an intelligent woman."[8]

When *Back Street* was in its post-production stage, Universal executives announced their plan to premiere the film in Miami on February 4. Many of the principal players, including the two stars, would attend, along with the producers. Prior to the premiere, Jimmie Fidler, reporting from Miami, commented, "Universal studio heads … are unanimous in predicting that it will make Margaret Sullavan one of the screen's ranking box office draws."[9] The rest of his column provides a fascinating insight into Sullavan's career to date; that information will be revisited at the end of this chapter.

Early on, Ray Smith (Sullavan) tells her persistent suitor, Curt (Richard Carlson), "If I ever do fall in love, it has to be all the way or nothing," setting the tone for this "woman's picture." It begins in Cincinnati at the turn of the 20th century. Vibrant, progressive-thinking Ray aspires to go to New York City. At the train station, her friend Ed Porter (Frank McHugh), a traveling salesman, introduces her to Walter Saxel (Boyer), one of "those Louisiana Frenchman." There is an instant mutual attraction and Ray falls in love. Near the end of his stay, Walter tells Ray that he must leave the next day for his job. He also has a fiancée waiting for him in Louisville.

The next day, Walter calls Ray and asks her to meet him at the boat landing. Walter arranges for a minister to marry them. Ray, waylaid by a crude salesman (Frank Jenks), arrives at the boat landing only to see the steamboat leave the dock.

Five years later, Ray and Walter have a chance encounter in New York City. Walter is an important New York banker in his wife's uncle's firm and Ray has become a clothes designer. During dinner, Walter tells of his plans of marrying her on the boat years ago. The pained look on Ray's face bears her aching loneliness. With only her expressive eyes, Sullavan conveys far more emotions than any screenwriter's words could have mustered. Ray tells Walter of the events that transpired on that fateful day. They grapple with the realization of their lost chance at happiness. Despite the fact he's married, Walter flashes his dark, brooding eyes at our heroine, who is doomed. Sullavan continues to work her magic in spite of Ray's stupidity as we believe that she will eventually come to her senses.

The subject of divorce is broached once. Ray, who is only concerned for Walter's career and happiness, is content to remain as his "back street" mistress as long as he loves her.

On New Year's Eve, Uncle Felix offers Walter an opportunity to take a six-month business trip in Europe—on the condition he takes his wife. He is aware of the affair and his calm demeanor suggests the double-standard it is acceptable for a married man to have a mistress as long as he is discreet. In the fall, Curt, who is successful in the automotive manufacturing field, makes a surprise visit. Before he leaves, he announces his intentions of proposing to her. As she has done in the past, Ray makes light of it.

The following sequence signals a shift in the movie's romantic mood. Arriving home, Ray finds Walter waiting for her. Their joyous reunion is tempered when Ray realizes that he has been back for five days. She is crushed to learn that Corinne had given birth to a daughter in Spain. She is troubled by this revelation and the viewer experiences renewed hope that she will come to her senses and ditch the bastard.

Hurt, Ray accepts Curt's proposal and heads back to Cincinnati. Walter finds Ray at

Sullavan in *Back Street* (1941) with Charles Boyer. Universal spared no expense making this woman's weepie (often regarded as Sullavan's finest), one of the studio's big hits of the year.

the station as she is boarding the train to Detroit. Ray tries to be strong, but she's wavering. Sullavan's sincerity and understatement makes this a breathtaking moment.

When Walter says, "I'm not going to let you go, Ray," she caves once again and the scene ends with a close-up of Walter's smug, conceited face. At this moment, the film ceases to be a romance and becomes a drama of a futile, frustrated relationship controlled by a selfish man. Up to this point, Sullavan has created a poignant portrait of a woman struggling to find her moral compass. The viewer has been rooting for her to emerge victorious. When Ray gives in to Walter, the last shred of the once vibrant spirit of Ray Smith as well as audience sympathy die. For Sullavan fans who have been inspired by her triumphs over daunting obstacles, this is a bitter pill to swallow.

The year shifts to 1928. Walter and his family board a luxury liner to Europe. Walter is now an important public figure as indicated by the intense press coverage. Gossips notice the elegantly dressed woman coming up the gangplank. Ray is an older, sadder and downtrodden woman. It seems that everyone, including Walter's adult children, know about Ray—everyone except their mother. Their son Richard (Tim Holt) vows to take care of the situation.

That night at a casino, Ray finds Walter's children glaring at her from across the table. Unnerved, she leaves and returns to her apartment. Richard follows and confronts her. Walter enters the apartment and is surprised to see his son. He attempts to reason with his son, but Richard will not hear his excuses and storms out.

The next morning, Ray reads that Walter has suffered a paralytic stroke. As he lies dying, Walter implores his son to telephone the number 2–6–7–9. Richard recognizes Ray's voice and the tension builds as he struggles to do the right thing for his father. He finally holds the phone up to Walter. Hearing his lover's voice, Walter then dies. As she overhears the doctor pronounce his death, Ray frantically cries into the phone, "Walter, don't leave me! Walter, you can't! Walter, don't go!" This is prime tear-jerking stuff at its most mawkish. However, Sullavan and Boyer beautifully underplay the scene and it pulses with intensity and packs an emotional assault to the tear ducts.

Days later, Richard visits Ray at her apartment to offer her passage back to New York. When he realizes that she is ill, he leaves to summon a doctor. "Your son was just here, Walter," Ray says to his picture. "He was so kind to me…. He might have been my son … our son. I wonder what would have happened if I met you that Sunday at the boat?" After a brief montage, we find that Ray has died, her head near Walter's picture. Along with the telephone scene, this is Sullavan's big moment. She displays such naturalness and restraint to suggest powerful emotions. Many other actresses of that era would have destroyed this tender moment (including Dunne in the original and Susan Hayward in the second remake), but not Sullavan. So, dear Margaret, you are hereby forgiven for some of the artificial moments during the latter sections.

The Miami premiere was a huge success with an overflow of curious spectators. Stevenson remarked to Eileen Creeland of the *New York Sun*, "Bruce Manning and I made it exactly as we wanted it to be…. I've never had a happier time on a picture."[10] Unfortunately, the film's stars were among the missing as Boyer was ill with influenza and Sullavan, eight and a half months pregnant, was advised against flying. Universal sent their top star, Deanna Durbin, instead.

The Hollywood Reporter called *Back Street* an "absorbing, beautifully done film, with deep human appeal." Boyer was "at his supreme best," while Sullavan "again scores one of her dramatic triumph." A sour note came from Joe Fisher, who felt, "There is much to bring women into the theater, but little to keep them there." Fisher sniped he "got awfully tired of Charles Boyer's overly romantic attitude." Nor was Sullavan spared: "Usually, I consider Margaret Sullavan one of the three best actresses in Hollywood, but after *Back Street* she'll have to take a back seat to some others."[11]

When the film was released nationally, there wasn't much variation in critical opinions. The *Rochester Democrat and Chronicle* noted, "The new picture is considerably superior to the first one, admirable and highly popular as that was." While conceding that "Miss Dunne is a fine player," the critic felt, "Miss Sullavan has even more warmth and resourcefulness. Her portrayal is one of the finest, most delicately shaded and most emotionally stirring the screen has had in a long time." One of the few negative comments regarding Sullavan's performance came from the *Syracuse Post-Standard*. The critic despaired, "If only Miss Sullavan could overcome that annoying nasal quality in her voice, she would gain even deeper praise for her abilities." Could it be that Crotchety Croughton was pinch-hitting for another newspaper that day?

As predicted, *Back Street* emerged as one of Universal's most popular film of the year. In mid–March, *The Hollywood Reporter* reported that the film was being held over at 26 of 50 key engagements.

Twenty years later, Hurst's novel was resurrected for its third screen incarnation. This time, Ross Hunter transformed the outdated melodrama into box-office gold. As a producer, Hunter had tremendous success with *Magnificent Obsession* (1954) and *Imitation of Life* (1959), his remakes of two popular John Stahl films. If any film could embody the term "eye candy," Hunter's *Back Street* certainly fills the bill. With the handsome leads, glamorous clothes, on-location footage and warm Technicolor, it is a beautiful film. Several changes were made to update the material. The film's time period was set from post–World War II to 1960 to capitalize on current fashion style. The film loosely followed its predecessors' plots and there are significant changes to reflect the new moral standards of the early 1960s. The male protagonist, Paul Saxton, is married to bitter alcoholic Liz, who refuses to grant him a divorce. This twist preserved John Gavin's popularity as a likable, masculine leading man. Additionally, the ages of the adult children were dropped, so Paul Jr. is around ten years old; it is implied at the end that the orphaned children (Liz is killed in a car crash) will be adopted by a grieving Rae Smith (Susan Hayward). For the most part, this movie is fairly enjoyable in a predictable way and much more romantically engrossing than the earlier versions. The only weakness, outside of an occasionally silly plot development, is Gavin's stiff performance. Then again, one imagines the average female viewer was more concerned with gazing at his handsome visage rather than his limited acting skills.

Of the three adaptations, the Boyer-Sullavan film is considered the best. There are many fine qualities to commend it: sumptuous production details, fine screenplay, exquisite photography, and Frank Skinner's Oscar-nominated score. Stevenson displays intelligence and restraint in his handling of the material. Rarely does he overstep the boundaries of good taste. *Back Street* remains his finest work in terms of overall craftsmanship.

Some members of the cast are excellent. McHugh shines in the serio-comic role of Ed Porter, displaying surprising depth underneath the glib salesman banter. Right behind him is Holt as Richard Saxel. He could have succumbed to the priggish nature of the part like William Bakewell in the earlier version. Instead, Holt reveals traits which preceded his splendid characterization as George Amberson in *The Magnificent Ambersons* (1942). Carlson is sincere and pleasant in the typical male juvenile manner. Few of the actresses stand out with the exception of Esther Dale as Ray's crotchety stepmother and acerbic Cecil Cunningham as the sharp-tongued landlady.

At the center is Sullavan, who dominates the film. Gorgeously gowned in the period costumes and becomingly photographed, she has rarely looked as beautiful as she does here. Her Ray in the early scenes is tremendously appealing and sympathetic; her performance during the New York segments displays emotional intensity that is heartbreaking in the best Sullavan manner. Based on her acting here, one could easily make a case that her Ray Smith is the definitive Sullavan performance. So, why do I feel let down?

While Sullavan does wonders with the part, she is not temperamentally suited to play the role. She has to work too hard against the odds. Watching a vibrant woman subject herself to a tortured existence of loneliness and despair is frustrating. Not only that, the role also goes against the grain of the Sullavan screen persona—an independent, intelligent and free-spirited woman in charge of her own life.

Boyer's characterization is likewise problematic. He does so well in conveying Walter's innate selfishness that he is something of a heel. His palpable Gallic charm does not go far enough in saving the day for him.

Back Street is widely accepted by some as Sullavan's finest film and her performance among the best she's given on the screen. When Quirk interviewed the actress in 1952, he told her *Back Street* was his favorite Sullavan film. As for the effectiveness of her performance, Sullavan revealed, "I applied 'E.E.'s' [Clive] technique in that. There was a terrible loneliness in Ray Smith; an outsiderish element that I often had known in my own life."[12]

∼∼∼

In the aforementioned Fidler column, he provided this insight into Sullavan's career at that time: "Margaret Sullavan, though successful, has never won the full measure of popularity she deserves. I fully believe—I've said so before—that she is not only one of the three or four best actresses in pictures, but also the most consistent." He continued:

> The others have their ups and downs. I've seen Bette Davis, for Instance, when she was positively "hammy." Garbo, who can rise to inspired heights, can also flounder as helplessly as a high school drama student. Rosalind Russell, usually deft and subtle, at times overacts ridiculously. But Miss Sullavan is always as smooth as silk. I've never seen her make a false move on the screen. The fact that she isn't a bigger star is due primarily, I believe, to her own attitude. Afflicted with stubborn independence, she launched her career with a bold declaration of her dislike for Hollywood and her scorn for many of the industry's most sacred taboos.[13]

Evaluation of Sullavan's film career at that time demonstrates the truths of Fidler's comments. In Theda Bara's biography, Eve Golden made this statement which rings true today as it did back in the early days of film: "The true definition of a 'star' is someone who will pack the theaters no matter what the vehicle is."[14] Given that litmus test, Sullavan has not yet reached the level of popularity that was enjoyed by many of her peers—Davis, Francis, West, to name just a few. What these actresses had was personality that audiences could associate with: Davis was the hard-working actress, Francis the elegant clotheshorse, and West the naughty but funny sex symbol. While these actresses were at their peak, moviegoers flocked to the theaters. Once their studios had discovered the "formula" that guaranteed box-office results, it was repeated with slight variations until that formula dried up. Unfortunately, once a star was past his or her prime, they experienced decline along with public apathy. Some became long-neglected and forgotten names.

On the other hand, Sullavan's popularity had to do with her high reputation with the critics. Her more popular films (*Only Yesterday*, *Three Comrades*, *The Shopworn Angel*) confirmed the public's perception of the "Sullavan Personality." However, since she was not typecast, she did not achieve the coveted status as a high-ranking box-office draw. It was hoped *Back Street* would push Sullavan's career forward into that realm.

The combination of the Boyer-Sullavan team and Hurst's popular story made *Back Street* a box office winner. Has the little rebel finally beaten Hollywood at its own game? The answer came with the release of her next picture.

26

Farewell to Universal

It may be very proper to be conventional, but it would be very dull.[1]

While *Back Street* was playing around the country, Sullavan prepared for the birth of her third child. She reveled in the role of motherhood and took the responsibility of parenting seriously. Brooke, four and a half, and Bridget, two, were described as "blond, pretty, pert and independent." Brooke was the "mischievous item. She's always prowling around and investigating the curiosities of nature," and Bridget was "her mama in miniature."[2]

On March 27, Sullavan gave birth to an eight-pound boy named William Leland Hayward. According to Parsons, "Leland said he didn't care whether it was a boy or a girl but he was wearing a smile that wouldn't come off when William Leland Hayvard put in an appearance."[3]

Parsons also reported Sullavan's next film for Universal as *The Man Who Lived Alone*. Taking a swipe at *Back Street*, Parsons informed her readers that Sullavan, "who is at her best as a modern, intelligent girl of the present period," will be playing a reporter in the Joseph Pasternak production.[4] However, in early May, Parsons updated her readers with the news that "the Margaret Sullavan-Charles Boyer combination in *Back Street* was sufficiently potent to warrant an encore." While divulging the correct title, *Heartbeat*, Parsons mistakenly described it as "a highly dramatic story in which Maggie and Mons. Boyer will have a chance to tear out the hearts of everybody, including the exhibitors, who just love these two in sob stories."[5] *Heartbeat* was actually a romantic comedy written by Hungarian playwright Ladislaus Bus-Fekete. In 1938, this story was proposed as an Otto Preminger production. That deal fell through and the script was peddled to a few studios, including Warner Brothers and Twentieth Century–Fox. Universal purchased the screenplay for $50,000. With his success with *Back Street*, Bruce Manning was chosen to produce and adapt Bus-Fekete's story with Jackson.

Later, Boyer recalled that, during the filming of *Back Street*, "I mentioned to Maggie that I was about to drown in all the tears my pictures were causing, and that I would like to do a comedy just for a nice change." Sullavan agreed to *Heartbeat* as her final film for Universal.

William Seiter, with whom Sullavan had worked in *The Moon's Our Home*, was Sullavan's choice for director. She told Boyer that Seiter "is a wonderful person for comedy."[6] Filming was delayed until mid–summer, due to Boyer's need for rest after just completing *Hold Back the Dawn* at Paramount. The Universal project was renamed *Appointment for Love* during production.

This film had a relatively short shooting schedule of four weeks and the two stars again enjoyed their association. Seiter appreciated the professional dedication of the stars, even though he understood that comedy did not come naturally to either one. Boyer enjoyed describing an incident which occurred early in production. He had just completed a scene with Eugene Pallette when Seiter yelled, "Hey, Charlie, you just said that line as if you really believed it." Boyer recalled stating, with some pride, that he always tried to believe everything he played, which is the essence of a good dramatic performance. He was taken aback by Seiter's response. "Well, that's wrong," the director explained. "The essence of farce is disbelief, and this isn't high comedy, it's farce. Here we have some very tentative dialogue that sure won't be funny if it's played straight. In a farce, you have to be suspicious of every syllable." Taking Seiter's advice, Boyer worked hard to improve his comedic performance. After a successful shoot, Seiter complimented Boyer: "Now, come on, Charlie, what's all this great lover crap anyway? You're a born light comedian!"[7]

Seiter also worked with Sullavan on her comedic techniques. "Talented actress that she was," Seiter recalled, "I didn't feel that comedy came as easily as the drama—the approach and timing are altogether different—but she worked at it."[8] Sullavan was cooperative on the set and Seiter did not put much stock in the reports of the famed Sullavan temperament. He learned that dealing with Sullavan in a no-nonsense, frank manner did much to curb her tendency for perfectionism. Rita Johnson, cast as the scheming other woman, found Sullavan was supportive of her co-stars. Johnson noted that there was a lack of diva behavior on the set; Sullavan patterned her performance to facilitate mutual cooperation among all of the actors as she believed it benefited the film as a whole.

During the filming, Sullavan spoke to an interviewer regarding her dislike of watching herself on the screen. "When I'm through with a picture, I'm through," she explained. "To see it wouldn't change my feeling about it. Not even the hackneyed suggestion that I should view my work on the screen in order to 'study my technique' will not change my feeling about the matter." During filming, she likewise had no desire to see herself in the rushes.

> While I'm at work, my producer, my director and my fellow players are my guides. Personally, I generally feel that I am wholly inadequate for the part. I doubt that I could walk into a theater, see myself in a picture, and tell whether I am good or bad.... I don't believe I could be "my own best critic."[9]

When filming was completed, Seiter was pleased with the film. As he told Quirk, he believed *Appointment for Love* came out as well, if not better, than *The Moon's Our Home*. Everybody is entitled to their own opinions. The Universal executives, on the other hand, apparently didn't think as highly as the film had its preview in Glendale, California (instead of Miami or New York City), on October 22, 1941. The smaller venue would soften the inevitable critical lambasting. To further hedge their bets, the publicity department plastered Boyer's name all over the ads to draw the female customers.

The film opens promisingly with a couple kissing in a bedroom. Then the curtains fall and we realize that we are at a play. A beautifully gowned woman (Sullavan) is roused from her sleep by enthusiastic applause. As playwright Andre Cassil (Boyer) gives a speech at the curtain call, she quickly falls back asleep. Andre assumes that she has fainted and asks if there's a doctor in the house. Rousing once again, she reveals that she herself is a doctor, Dr. Jane Alexander. When Andre questions her, she admits that she had fallen asleep because his play was terrible. Embarrassed, she exits the theater hastily, leaving her purse behind.

At Andre's opening night party, the play is hailed as a hit. Andre is in the process of romancing Edith (Ruth Terry) when he is interrupted by a long-distance phone call from actress Nancy Benson (Johnson), one of his current flings. Jane arrives to retrieve her purse.

Andre is intrigued by her approach to love being "so logical that you can prove it in a laboratory." (Jane's assertions are a bit strange, but Sullavan manages to make it plausible.) Despite the fact that she continues to give him the brush-off, Andre remains infatuated. Eventually, he wears down her resistance and they dine together. The time is cut short when she leaves for an emergency at the hospital.

The following scene, the only honest one in the film, is a lovely moment courtesy of Sullavan's deeply felt emotions. As Jane leaves the hospital, she finds Andre waiting for her. "How did you know I wanted you to be waiting here?" she asks as the romantic background music swells. She is exhausted, but elated with the fact that she saved two lives, a mother and her infant child. She then impulsively kisses Andre, before expressing her joy over this miraculous event. "And you were waiting right here," she tells him as she falls in his arms.

"I'll always be waiting," he replies in a clever reversal of their roles in *Back Street*.

Swept up in the moment, the two get married and leave for a two-week honeymoon at his hunting lodge. Their blissful wedding night is interrupted when Nancy calls Andre from the train station. Not wanting to make his bride jealous, Andre pretends that he needs to help "Old Fire Chief Benson" put out a fire at the depot. (Why he doesn't come clean with his relationship with Nancy makes for a pointless, tedious plot development all too typical of marital farce.)

Having told her on the phone about his marriage, Andre is not surprised to find a dejected and wounded Nancy at the depot. He suspects that she is only acting, which sets off an amusing bit where a train rumbles pass the station, thus drowning out her angry tirade. Nancy manages to guilt Andre into casting her in the lead of his new play. Her complete about-face and enthusiastic response reveal that she has been putting him on all along.

Andre arrives back at the lodge and discovers that Jane has been aware of the true nature of the "fiery situation." She explains that she is not jealous, because jealousy "is a hangover from the caveman days and has no place in the civilized mind." As the two finally settle in for a warm, cozy night, Jane is called back to New York for another emergency.

Back in the city, Andre is shocked to learn that his wife has rented an apartment five floors above his. Jane's rationale for their separate living arrangement: Since they have incompatible schedules, it makes sense that they have their own places. After Andre's producer, George (Pallette), learns of the unusual living arrangement, he tells Andre to live his own life, so Jane will become so jealous that she'll come to her senses. The tedious business of Andre trying to arouse jealousy in his wife begins.

Andre's first attempt comes about when he instructs his leading man on the proper art of kissing his leading woman, who happens to be Nancy. As he expects, Jane arrives in time to see the two kissing. Andre acknowledges his wife and confirms the effectiveness of his stage kiss technique. To his chagrin, Jane is unfazed. However, a chance encounter with an old suitor, Michael (Reginald Denny), during lunch manages to arouse Andre's jealousy. Andre is particularly perturbed when Michael vows to do everything to break up their marriage.

That evening, Andre invites Edith to his apartment with the hope of Jane interrupting their "date." (as played by Terry, Edith is such a personable young lady that it's a shame that Andre callously sets her up as a stooge in his plans; this is supposed to be funny stuff.) As she demonstrated earlier, Jane's reaction is not what Andre was hoping for. Making matters worse, Michael is staying up in Jane's apartment. For unclear reasons, Michael is under Jane's observations as part of his treatment. It's this kind of phony plot contrivance that continually dampens the film's fun spirit.

Sullivan in *Appointment for Love* (1941) with Charles Boyer. This marital farce gave Sullavan a rare opportunity to be glamorous on screen, but otherwise offered little entertainment value for Sullavan fans.

One night, both Andre and Jane separately plan a romantic evening in the other's apartments. The problem is that neither knows it. Morning arrives and Andre is furious when he learns that Jane was not at the hospital as he had hoped. Unable to reach her at the hospital, Andre finds out that she is at a local radio station as part of a panel on a medical program. Andre confronts her during the live broadcast. Inexplicably, this incident becomes national news. It must have been a really slow news day if that makes front page news. Instead of a simple heart-to-heart talk that would have cleared up the matter, Jane tells the eager newspaper reporters that she spent the night in the apartment of one of the "most charming, romantic men in all of New York City." Of course, such an ambiguous answer only fuels more gossip and newspaper headlines. It's not long before the doctor plans to file for divorce, while on an expedition with Michael in Mexico. Nancy, of course, has set her sights on Andre once again.

Jane is relieved when the elevator operator tells her that Andre stayed in her apartment during the night in question. That evening, Jane makes an unannounced appearance at Andre's party. The party stops dead in its tracks as Nancy maliciously puts Jane on the spot. The scene is set for a confrontation that sparkles with feminine witchery.

"Don't you worry about him. He's well on the road to a speedy recovery, aren't you, Pappy?" Nancy taunts.

"Will you kindly take your hands off my husband and stop calling him Pappy?"

"Now, honey," Nancy purrs, "don't start getting jealous."

This elicits an unexpected reaction from Jane, who gives Nancy a resounding slap. On the way out, Jane announces that she is not pursuing a divorce.

Andre follows Jane back to her apartment and she finally tells him the truth about that night. They embrace and kiss. As the elevator operator leaves the building, he finds Jane's apartment keys on the sidewalk. Smiling, he drops them down the storm drain.

Upon its release at the end of October, the film was met with surprisingly good notices; in some cases, the reviews exceeded those for *Back Street*. There were those critics who disliked the film. The *New York Herald-Tribune* was disappointed:

> With Charles Boyer and Margaret Sullavan as the embattled husband and wife, the film has a rare quality of acting brilliance. It has been handsomely produced under William Seiter's direction. All that is lacking is the sustained merriment and distinctive treatment that might have made the photoplay irresistible entertainment.... At the Music Hall they are at their best in material which is no more than second best.

Film Daily stated that the film "will find strong favor at the box-office." The critic cautioned, "The acting talents of Boyer and Miss Sullavan overcome a lightweight script that literally strains out loud to reach its objectives.... [Sullavan's] appearance on the screen is always a welcome one. She is a talented actress of great charm and can even appear convincing as a woman doctor. Her performance is a standout." *Variety* enthusiastically proclaimed that, with the stars "generating double-power marquee voltage, *Appointment for Love* is a neatly constructed piece of bright entertainment for adult attention. It's an 'A' attraction from every angle, and due to spin the key run wickets at a merry pace." Boyer's performance was acclaimed as he "carries a gay charmer role to catch attention of the women," while "Miss Sullavan's exceptional charm and ability sock over her performance for strong influence on the men—resulting in double-barreled appeal which will pay off at the b.o."

Despite the overabundance of marital comedies in current release, *Appointment for Love* generated a tidy profit. Moviegoers were willing to pay to see Boyer and Sullavan together in another movie, despite the inferior quality of the film. Perhaps the timing of its release helped as there were still uncertainty about the United States' involvement in the war in Europe. Any form of escapism was sufficient in helping moviegoers forget about their problems. According to Swindell, more people saw *Appointment for Love* on December 7, 1941 (the day Pearl Harbor was attacked), than any other film in release.

To answer the question posed in the previous chapter: "Was Margaret Sullavan considered a box office draw of high ranking?" I am of the opinion that Sullavan never quite made it to that level. Too many factors played into the box office results of her films—her co-stars, the genre, and the audience's perception of the "Margaret Sullavan vehicle." When one of these three factors is missing, the profits suffered accordingly.

It is not often that one forgets a Margaret Sullavan film—or even the actress herself—so quickly after watching it, but it is the case in this circumstance. Despite her chic, upswept bob and some stylish dresses, Sullavan fails to make much of an impression. Indeed, there are times when she appears plain and dowdy. The main problem lies with the fact that the part has its roots in far-fetched and unrealistic behavior. While Sullavan has some moments of charm, it is not enough to overcome the obstacle of trying to breathe realism into an illogical character. The role could have been played by any other actress of her caliber without noticeable differences. How many of Sullavan's other roles could that statement be made?

What is even more surprising is that two female supporting players manage to steal the film. Terry, who made a name for herself first as a singer for the Paul Ash Chicago Theater Orchestra and later as a leading lady in several minor Western films, is a treat with her fresh beauty and personality. More memorable is Johnson, a former MGM contract player who was often relegated to B movies. Not familiar with her body of work, I was caught off-guard by her multi-faceted comic performance. Whether playing the ambitious actress, the sensible friend of Boyer's, or the scheming, catty Other Woman, Johnson is something of a revelation. A second look at her career is certainly warranted.

Boyer fares a little better than Sullavan. At least he is able to capitalize on that inimitable Gallic charm. Still, there are times when he flounders in the poorly written role. It is obvious that he is not a natural comedian and is working overtime to compensate. The other male players, Eugene Pallette, Reginald Denny, Cecil Kellaway and Gus Schilling (as the elevator operator), have the benefit of wittier lines and better parts.

Despite the film's production values and an excellent supporting cast, *Appointment for Love* must be deemed as the most insignificant movie of Sullavan's career. The producers presented the film as if it were vintage champagne, when, in reality, it's nothing more than sparkling grape juice which has gone flat. The blame for this can be attributed to the Manning-Jackson script and Seiter's direction. With the artificial premise set up by the script, it's all very illogical and Seiter is hardly the kind of director to overcome the script's deficiencies. It is hard to believe that this is the same man who directed the inspired foolishness of *Sons of the Desert* and the sweetly romantic, madcap romp *The Moon's Our Home*.

Prior to the film's release, Columbia released the marital comedy *You Belong to Me* starring Barbara Stanwyck and Henry Fonda. There are many striking similarities between the two films. Stanwyck is a doctor who is very serious about her medical practice; interestingly, both Sullavan and Stanwyck's characters bear the names of future actresses—the esteemed stage, film and television actress Jane Alexander, and the award-winning film and television actress Helen Hunt. Dr. Hunt impulsively marries a wealthy playboy (Fonda), but cautions him that her career is still very much of a priority. This is proven when she answers an emergency call on their wedding night. There is the patient-suitor who arouses the husband's jealousy. There is even the sequence when the whereabouts of a spouse during the night is in question. What sets these two films apart is that *You Belong to Me* is a tiresome attempt at comedy compared to *Appointment for Love*. Stanwyck is her usual personable self, but Fonda is terrible in the most abrasive character he ever had the misfortune to play. His neurotic, insanely jealous character casts a different light on the meaning of the film's title.

Appointment for Love was one of the first American movies to be shown to German civilians after the end of World War II. For Sullavan, the film was the end to the long-embattled commitment to her former studio.

27

Fulfilling Her Obligations

During the past four years, I managed to make several pictures while bring-
ing three babies into the world. If continuance of such a program demands
I make less frequent screen appearances, I am content to do so.[1]

Disregarding the picture she owed Metro, Sullavan looked forward to time with her growing family. Metro must have been unnerved when it was reported that Sullavan said, "I think that six children will be about right." Regarding their philosophy of child rearing, she divulged, "We believe the children shouldn't be hampered by and have their lives cluttered up with doting parents and visitors. They're entitled to privacy, plenty of freedom and opportunity to pursue their childhood wills." To accommodate this, "We are now completing a separate, though connected house expressly for the children." The children's residence resembled an old red barn with a big playroom, bedrooms and a kitchen. "Living this way, the children will learn early on home responsibilities and privileges."[2]

This arrangement allowed Sullavan flexibility in resuming her career after her sabbatical. Until then, she was committed to provide her children a childhood she never had. Her brother Sonny, a frequent visitor, recalled, "The three children were … her reason for living…. They were really a happy family."[3]

In October, it was reported that she might go to London to play the feminine lead in *This Above All* opposite Tyrone Power; Joan Fontaine took over the role. In December, the United States declared war on Japan, Germany and Italy. Several close friends joined the military service: Fonda enlisted in the Navy, Swope the Army, and Stewart became a military flyer. Hayward and Jack Connelly continued their association with Southwest Airways, which served as a wartime air cargo line and provided pilot training for the military. Sullavan went on war bond tours, like "Stars Over America."

Hollywood suffered a terrible loss in January 1942 when Carole Lombard was killed when her plane crashed after a bond tour. It was rumored that Sullavan would replace Lombard in *They All Kissed the Bride*; Joan Crawford, who donated her salary to the Red Cross, was cast instead.

Sullavan turned down so many film offers that Jimmie Fidler scolded, "Margaret Sullavan should be reminded that idols should never be idle too long."[4] He tried a different tactic the following week: "I'm sorry that Margaret Sullavan doesn't see fit to resume full-time activity on the screen. Few stars are as well suited to play the serious roles that are in demand today."[5] That didn't work either as Sullavan rejected roles in *Watch on the Rhine*, *Claudia* and Lubitsch's *Heaven Can Wait*. The most interesting proposal was Warner Brothers' request that she play opposite Bette Davis in John van Druten's *Old Acquaintance*. Warner executives sent someone to meet with her in New York, but Sullavan balked at the idea of playing the bitchy friend. It has been reported that Sullavan denounced the studio's efforts on Brock Pemberton's radio show, irritating those involved—except van Druten.

In November 1942, Fidler included this intriguing item: "Is it true that Margaret Sullavan and Leland Hayward, hitherto rated one of Hollywood's happiest couples, have rifted?"[6] If this was true, it's conceivable that Sullavan resisted bringing more children into the family.

Then came the surprise announcement. "Screen Star Margaret Sullavan today had announced her retirement from the movies to devote her full attention to her children," Parsons breathlessly proclaimed. "'I have three children,' she said, 'and I wish to dedicate myself to them.'"[7] The only problem was the one picture she owed. Unlike Universal, MGM was powerful and not put off so easily. Sullavan turned down several scripts before settling on *Cry "Havoc."*

The Allan R. Kenward play was first presented at Hollywood's Beachwood Studio Theatre in late September 1942. Russian actor Vladimir Sokoloff directed a small cast including Ann Dere, Flora Campbell, Maxine Stuart and Eugenia Rawls. Inspired by the recent incidents of American forces fighting Japanese armies on Bataan, the plot dealt with courageous women serving as nurses at an army camp. The play opened without much fanfare, but word of mouth quickly made it the must-see theatrical event of the season. Two weeks later, MGM purchased the play for $20,000. At the same time, Lee Shubert wanted to produce it on Broadway. Due to a Dramatists Guild Council rule that stipulated that a play purchased for the screen cannot be performed on stage until one year after its sale, Shubert applied for a waiver. Shubert argued that he should be allowed to produce the play due to the timeliness of its subject matter. Otherwise, the play would date and be unprofitable after a year's time. The Guild granted Shubert's request. Helen Hayes and Ingrid Bergman were among those who wanted to appear in the Broadway production.

Meanwhile, at Metro, top stars vied for a role in the film. Glamour girls Hedy Lamarr, Lana Turner, Donna Reed and Ann Sheridan were among the many under consideration. By November, an impressive cast was assembled: Fay Bainter as Captain Marsh, Joan Crawford as Pat, Greer Garson as Smitty, Ann Sothern as Grace and Marsha Hunt as Connie. *Cry "Havoc"* was earmarked as one of the studio's biggest attractions.

The play, retitled *Proof Thru the Night*, opened on December 25, 1942, with Katherine Emery, Florence Rice, Ann Shoemaker and Carol Channing as Steve; the mind boggles at the notion of Dolly Levi playing a Russian sniper. The play proved no Christmas gift and was roundly panned by the critics. The play's title changed to *Cry "Havoc"* on December 30, but it did not matter and it folded after 11 performances.

Now that the play was a bona fide Broadway flop, all of the lovely ladies who desperately wanted a part in the movie were nowhere to be found. Crawford had long bowed out of the film after stating "It should have been called *The Women Go to War*."[8] Merle Oberon, recently cast as Smitty, became unavailable due to illness.

With the play's failure, Mervyn LeRoy, the original director, was re-assigned to the prestigious *Madame Curie* with Greer Garson and Walter Pidgeon. In early April, veteran director Richard Thorpe was hired. Usually associated with B or "lesser A" films, Thorpe was regarded as a director who could complete a film on schedule. This feat was credited to his rare use of retakes. Theorizing why the play flopped on Broadway, Thorpe said, "In Hollywood, the audience felt like it was inside the dugout with those girls. The customers suffered with the actors. In New York the performers seemed too far away, too artificial, too hard to believe."[9] The Paul Osborn screenplay retained much of the plotline of the play, but the set-up with Pat as a suspected Nazi spy was eliminated. Filming was conducted in the same jungle set used for *White Cargo* (1942) and *Bataan* (1943). Still, there was the feeling *Cry "Havoc"* was doomed to repeat its Broadway failure. Thorpe later admitted he was not enthusiastic about the project, but did what he was told by the studio.

In early May, Parsons announced, "Margaret Sullavan who retired to be Mrs. Leland Hayward and take care of her three children, is returning to the movies. After much persuasion, she has agreed to play Smitty in *Cry 'Havoc,'* one of the leading roles in this widely discussed motion picture.... Maggie seems perfect for the part. It is right up her alley and she'll do a swell job."[10]

The six-week shoot began on May 13 and, as expected, there were many challenges, especially since the main cast consisted of 13 women. First, Thorpe addressed the deglamorization of the women. They had to do their own hair. The makeup department had their own special assignment. "The idea was for the nurses to look like their faces were scrubbed clean," Thorpe continued. "We had to give 'em a little plain makeup for lighting purposes." The final touch: "We smeared 'em with oil so they'd look hot and sweaty."[11]

Thorpe recalled he had been warned about Sullavan's erratic temperament but, to his surprise, he "found her a sweetheart to work with—which is more than I could say for some of the others."[12] Sullavan enjoyed working with Bainter, cast as her superior, and resumed their friendly association from *The Shining Hour*. Still, Sullavan could not refrain from telling others how to play their scenes. Thorpe recalled that Joan Blondell, as Grace, often took offense to her unwanted interference.

Daniele Amfitheatrof, who wrote most of the music, offered this comment: "[Sullavan's] personality is very clearly expressive in music, and she is easy to write for. She has a sweet, appealing and clear-cut personality."[13]

Filming concluded on June 30. Sullavan's opinion was pointed: "That picture stinks!"[14] The bright side was she completed her obligation to Metro-Goldwyn-Mayer.

Sullavan reveled once again in domestic life. Brooke remembered her mother seemed happiest in baggy old pants puttering around the house. The trappings of Hollywood stardom was more than annoyance and she stayed far away from it all. The only concession she made was hosting elaborate birthday parties for the children. "I suspect that ... she felt obligated, more for the sake of her children than herself, to overcome her disapproval of the life around her."[15]

How does one promote a film (*Cry "Havoc"*) with a grim story and a Broadway flop? The answer was quite simple. Mislead the audience. In the trailer, the viewer is told, "It's the Mighty entertainment with 11 *glamorous* stars!" There are lovely shots of the cast—including Connie Gilchrist, who hardly qualifies as glamorous. Against the background of New York City, we're told that "it's the startling stage hit that rocked the theatrical world!" A bit of an overstatement if there was one.

The film centers on the efforts of Lt. Smith, or Smitty (Sullavan), to find nurses for a military hospital in Mariveles. Her superior, Captain Marsh (Bainter), believes Smitty is overworking herself to exhaustion, alluding to a mystery illness that is a part of Sullavan's repertoire. She wants to send Smitty to a hospital in Australia. Smitty won't hear of it as she has too much work to do.

Returning from Manila, Flo (Hunt) brings back a group of stranded American women, a varied bunch with little medical training: Pat (Sothern), a hard-boiled sort who takes an immediate dislike to Smitty; Connie (Ella Raines), a wealthy Philadelphia girl; Steve (Gloria Grafton), a Russian; Nydia (Diana Lewis), a scatterbrain from Alabama; Luisita (Fely Franquelli, who, in real life, hailed from Manila), a Manila peasant; Sue (Dorothy Morris) and Andra (Heather Angel), sisters from England; Helen (Frances Gifford), a switchboard operator; and Grace (Blondell), a burlesque dancer from Brooklyn. "Burlesque? What did you do in burlesque?" asks Smitty. Grace quips: "You know what you do to a banana before you eat it? Well, I do it to music."

Leaving the girls in their underground bunker, Smitty steals away to call her sweetheart, even though it's against regulations. Her sweetheart is none other than Lt. Holt, whom Pat has already set her sights on. Despite her extreme fatigue, Smitty is beautifully radiant during their conversation. "Nothing short of Death can keep me away," she says at the end. Hanging up, exhaustion overcomes her once more. Sullavan is a pro at a scene like this and she is magnificent.

Capt. Marsh meets with the girls to express her gratitude for their service. She warns, "Any time now, a hell worse than you ever imagined will break loose," thereby setting the tone for the movie. As the girls settle in, Sue offers her insights into what she says is a simple war. (Throughout, many of the characters are given the opportunity to reflect on

The stars of *Cry 'Havoc'* (1943). *Left to right*: (*top row*) Fay Bainter, Marsha Hunt; (*bottom row*) Ann Sothern, Joan Blondell, Margaret Sullavan. Based on a Broadway flop, this film was a deeply moving tribute to courageous nurses fighting Japanese forces.

the war.) Afterwards, she leaves to explore the camp. The rest of the girls are left with frayed nerves. It's not long after a Japanese air raid that they are immersed in caring for the wounded men after a raid. Among the missing is Sue.

From the start, Pat disregards Smitty's direct orders and Smitty becomes frustrated with her. The girls alternate their time between caring for the wounded, clearing out the debris from the bombed hospital, and working at the switchboard. Pat looks forward to the switchboards as it gives her an opportunity to pursue Lt. Holt. As the film progresses, the viewer gains an insight to the girls as they share their fears and hopes. The most touching one is Connie as she struggles to deal with her fears; later, we admire her transformation into a self-assured nurse's aide. On the other hand, we never really get to find out Pat's story underneath her abrasive, tough-girl swagger. When Pat softens and shows a tender side, she quickly reverts back to the hard-boiled act. Any insight into her character might have made for a stronger emotional impact, but the screenwriters have cheated us.

After days of searching, Andra learns that Sue has been found alive. However, the experience of being trapped in a shelter with several corpses has unhinged her. Sue and her sister are transported to Corregidor.

One night, Flo reports that the Japanese had sunk the U.S. supply ship that would have brought them more medical supplies and food. As the news sets in, there is another air raid. The hospital is bombed again. After the all-clear siren sounds, the girls are dispatched to aid the wounded. While outside, they are under direct enemy attack. The siege ends when the enemy plane is brought down. An uncredited Robert Mitchum is shown dying in Connie's arms.

Grace's leg is injured during the second raid and Smitty takes out the shrapnel. Delirious with pain, Grace reveals that they know about Lt. Holt, and Pat is stealing him away from her. Smitty leaves the room and breaks down. She is momentarily buoyed by Holt's phone call checking on her. Despite his profession of love, nagging doubts cloud her face as she fights back tears. It is another sublime "Margaret Sullavan Moment" that is played with admirable restraint.

Smitty tells the girls that the situation is dire. There will be no more supplies. Furthermore, Gen. Douglas MacArthur has ordered the Army to stay put. As volunteers, the girls are free to leave. Despite the inherent dangers, all of the girls decide to stay. Six weeks later, they are disheartened to hear that MacArthur has been sent to Australia. Pat goes into Lt. Holt's office to get the inside scoop. Meanwhile, Connie is killed by a Japanese gunner when she and two of the girls go swimming. The girls grieve Connie's death and begin to despair. Pat attempts to bolster their spirits by revealing details of an U.S. attack strategy. The girls are filled with hope. Listening in, Smitty realizes Pat got her information from her sweetheart and warns Pat to leave him alone. Smitty orders Pat off to her assignment, before being overcome by that mysterious illness. Flo forces the feverish Smitty to lie down. Smitty confesses her secret marriage to Lt. Holt. She also admits to having attacks of malignant malaria. Smitty implores Flo not to reveal the news of her illness or her marriage to anyone.

The situation becomes desperate as the Japanese begin to close in. Pat receives word that Lt. Holt has been killed in battle. Smitty arrives and barks orders at her. Nydia tells her that Pat just heard that her boyfriend has been killed. Cue the music as Smitty reels from the shock. (I am eternally grateful that Oberon opted out of the part as she would have ruined the scene with melodramatics.) After Pat and Nydia leave, Smitty is left alone. Sullavan is afforded a lovely scene as she enters her husband's office, picks up his pipe, and finally puts the hidden wedding band on her finger. Sullavan's sensitive, subdued handling of this scene makes it a memorably heart-wrenching moment.

Back at the bunker, the girls are anxious as they await orders to move out. When Pat confides to Flo that she never did anything with the lieutenant, Flo tells Pat about Smitty's marriage and illness. Although initially angered, Pat admits being impressed by Smitty's courage.

The Japanese invade the camp. Smitty arrives and tells the other girls there won't be any trucks to take them away. When Smitty is alone, Pat tries to talk to her, but ends up chastising her for withholding the truth. The girls are discovered by an unseen Japanese soldier. As they exit the bunker, Smitty admits she was wrong to withhold the truth. Touched by Smitty's apology, Pat tells her that her husband has remained faithful. The two, arm in arm, walk out of the dugout to "The Battle Hymn of the Republic" (which makes for a stirring if incongruous ending).

Cry "Havoc" had its New York premiere on November 23, 1943. The *Herald-Tribune* endorsed it as "well-written, brilliantly performed and grimly realistic.... [T]he virtues of the production are bright and unmistakable. For one thing, it has Margaret Sullavan in a leading role, lending nobility and eloquence to every scene in which she appears.... Miss Sullavan..is as magnificent as ever." The *Times'* critique was along the same lines:

> In certain aspects, it is moving—as any picture is likely to be which shows in agonized detail the ugly horrors of war and death—and it does draw a grim and plausible curtain upon that battle so heroically lost. But it is also another one of those pictures ... which is heavy with theatricality and the affectations of an all-girl cast.... Margaret Sullavan has what is probably the most credible and revealing role.... And she plays it in a manner which makes it certainly the most affecting one.

The London Times had unqualified praise: "There are one or two false notes, but the film as a whole is a triumph of imaginatively realistic statement and the acting is worthy of it. Miss Sullavan ... gives a study of mind in control of an intolerably strained body which is brilliant in its restraint and understanding."

Cry "Havoc" is an unexpectedly powerful and poignant film, far surpassing my expectations. While certain elements are predictable and dated, it is an engrossing war drama with intervals of comic relief to alleviate the grim outlook of the foregone conclusion. Thorpe handles the material with a sure hand. Under his guidance, it is well-paced and builds up to its suspenseful climax with convincing realism. Thorpe uses tight close-ups among the claustrophobic settings to convey the futility of the women's mission. Background music is likewise used effectively throughout; the only complaint is the inclusion of "Battle Hymn" as it conveys hope even though the women are doomed.

Most members of the cast are excellent. There are times when Sothern over-emphasizes the hard-boiled Pat as if she were auditioning for a role as Leo Gorcey's sister in a *Bowery Boys* movie. She is much more effective in the softer moments, including a touching scene as she catalogues a dead solder's possessions. Equally problematic is Diana Lewis. Although cute and perky, Lewis often reminds one of a younger version of Betty White's *Golden Girls* character. This was Lewis' last film as she retired to become Mrs. William Powell. Blondell does well, providing much-needed laughs with her snappy one-liners. She also has a terrific scene in which she talks to a dying soldier—a real heart-tugging moment. With the sole exception of Fely Franquelli, all of the other actresses (most notably Ella Raines) manage to shine in their individual moments. Since many of them are either young starlets being groomed by Metro or lesser-known actresses from other studios, this allows the viewer to identify with the characters instead of admiring performances of recognizable actresses.

Sullavan is superb as the overtaxed Smitty. She is believable as the no-nonsense commander, yet she is luminous in her quieter scenes. She is particularly touching in the telephone scenes and when she finds out that her husband was killed. Her performance easily rates as one of her finest. On a side note, this is the first time we see the hairstyle that Sullavan adopted for the remainder of her life. Its style is similar to the look she sported in *The Mortal Storm* and *So Ends Our Night*, but it's shorter. In her memoir, Hunt discussed its impact: "It was exactly right for the winsome actress with the foggy voice, who broke all our hearts at will. It helped the impression of a waiflike child, which she countered with a strong screen presence."[16]

Cry "Havoc" is often compared to Paramount's *So Proudly We Hail!*, which was released earlier in 1943. *So Proudly* is a blockbuster of exciting action, comedy and romance. With its strong religious undertone, it offers a more patriotic and hopeful outlook in contrast to the grimly realistic *Cry "Havoc."* *So Proudly* boasts a large cast of well-known actors (Claudette Colbert, Paulette Goddard, Veronica Lake, George Reeves, Sonny Tufts) who give excellent performances. However, by the end, we are impressed by the performances even though we fail to connect with the *characters*. The opposite is true with *Cry "Havoc."* The actresses are so realistic, we forget we are watching a performance, which creates a highly emotional impact. This is why Crawford and Oberon would have overwhelmed the movie with their mega-watt glamor. *So Proudly We Hail!* was a huge moneymaker and garnered four Academy Awards nominations, while Metro's little war drama made a moderate profit due to its topical subject matter.

With the release of both films, Hollywood embarked on a cycle of "Women at War" pictures. Some of the more "notable" productions, such as 20th Century–Fox's *Four Jills in a Jeep*, Universal's *Ladies Courageous* and Metro's *Keep Your Powder Dry*, are not worth the time nor space to discuss in any detail.

In 1947, *Cry "Havoc"* was remade as a telefilm in the United Kingdom with Joyce Heron as Smitty and Elizabeth Hunt as Pat. Kenward's play has been revived in small theatrical venues such as Syracuse and Anaheim Hills without much success. The consensus on Kenward's original script is that it's "remarkably tame" and plays like a "war-story cliché"[17]

This news item appeared in late July: "Margaret Sullavan is lending an ear to John van Druten's plea she take the lead in a new play he has written."[18] This time, he had an offer that she could not refuse.

28

The "Voice"
That Rocked Broadway

By the time I am 35, I will have a million dollars, five children, and I will have starred on Broadway.[1]

As Margaret Sullavan reportedly informed Charlie Leatherbee, once she reached this goal, she would retire to devote herself to her family. With her phenomenally successful return to Broadway in John van Druten's *The Voice of the Turtle* in 1943, Sullavan was in the position to do exactly that.

Van Druten was a prolific English playwright and screenwriter with many notable successes. While he was writing the first act, it occurred to him that Sullavan would be ideal as Sally. From that point on, there was no one else he would consider although he realized he had only seen her in *Chrysalis* and *Stage Door*. Of the latter, he failed to recall any details of her performance despite the fact he thought she was good. The only screen work he had seen was the trailer for *The Mortal Storm*. He wondered if she would leave her family behind in California.

The producer, Alfred de Liagre (Delly), agreed that Sullavan was the perfect choice. A completed script was sent to Sullavan, who immediately wired she would love to do it. She first suggested they should cast Dorothy McGuire instead. "She is free and she is really 22," she wrote.[2] Columnists reported rumors that Sullavan wanted to return to Broadway, but many doubted anything would come of it.

Leland set up the terms of the contract: ten percent of the gross and 15 percent of the profits. With her own investment of $2000, Sullavan was entitled to royalties from the purchase of the rights for motion picture, radio and additional theatrical adaptations. She committed to the play until June 1, 1944.

There was considerable excitement when it was reported that Sullavan signed for the play. (Cynics who remembered her "Act of God" from *Stage Door* warned van Druten she would never do it.) Once Sullavan's commitment was finalized, the search was underway for a leading man. Many prominent actors were away at war and those who were left turned down the role. Under strong consideration was a young stage actor, Gregory Peck. Exempt from military service due to a back injury, Peck was in high demand. However, a newly signed film contract with Selznick took Peck to Hollywood.

One day, Sullavan ran into a neighbor from the Brentwood area, Elliott Nugent, who was an multi-faceted performer. Nugent, who just completed a Broadway run in *Without Love* with Hepburn, was in Hollywood to direct *Up in Arms* for Goldwyn. Sullavan asked him, "How would you like to play a 32-year-old sergeant, with me as a 22-year-old girl?"[3]

When Nugent read the script, "I was never more captivated by any script, but I did not fall over myself to accept immediately." First, he had promised to direct a *Road* picture with Bob Hope and Bing Crosby. Second, he wanted to be amply compensated for his services. "I knew that there were not many stars available, and if I did the play I would want much better terms than I had gotten with the Theatre Guild." Hayward drew up Nugent's contract and he received the same deal as Sullavan.

Audrey Christie, who also appeared in *Without Love*, was cast in the third role. With van Druten assigned as director, Delly set a budget of $20,000 and the single set, three-character play began rehearsals. However, Delly did not like the title, which came from a verse in the Song of Solomon: "The voice of the turtle [dove] is heard in our land," representing the birth of spring. Delly urged van Druten to change it. Nugent's wife Norma suggested the title sounded intriguing. "There, you see," said van Druten, "The women like it. The title stays!"[4]

The part of Sally is a demanding one, because "she's on the stage when the curtain rises, and she's there when the last curtain falls. In between those points, she has 125 'sides' or pages of dialogue, compared with around 65 for the leading part in the average three-act play."[5] Nugent recalled, "After a morning of rehearsals, John van Druten often took Delly and Audrey Christie and me to lunch at Dinty Moore's or Sardi's, but Maggie Sullavan refused to leave the stage. The stage manager would bring her a sandwich while she worked endlessly over her own scenes, several of which were solo and required extensive 'business' with props, tables and cushions."[6]

When the play opened in New Haven in early November, it was well received. However, the script required cutting after opening night. "The laughter was so frequent and sustained that we went 45 minutes over the usual running time," Nugent remarked.[7] The rewrites required additional rehearsals.

Increasingly, Sullavan was missing domestic life and resented being away from her children. According to Nugent, "[O]n opening night in Boston, when I went into her dressing room at the Wilbur Theater to congratulate her on her beautiful performance, she only sighed and said, "Oh, Elliott—will it ever be any fun any more?"[8]

Despite this, Sullavan continued to strive for perfection in her performance. Van Druten found she required special handling as her major fault was "an excessive self-mistrust. Direction is largely a matter of encouragement and of enhancement of her self-confidence in what she is doing."[9] He found praise for a specific piece of business or line reading resulted in the opposite effect. Once told that she handled a certain passage well, she became self-conscious and unable to repeat it for a while. Despite this, he found her obsessively eager for criticism in her quest for perfection.

The company completed its successful try-out run in Philadelphia on December 4. Preparations were finalized for the December 8 opening at the Morosco Theater. On the afternoon of the opening, Sullavan and van Druten strolled along Fifth Avenue. She tugged at his arm and said, "Now, John, even if we're a flop, you will make Delly keep the play running over Christmas, won't you? I've promised my children that they can come east and spend Christmas in New York."[10]

She need not have worried, for *The Voice of the Turtle* proved to be a critical and box office smash. There were some critics who disliked the play and Sullavan's performance. The magazine *The Nation* called the play a "pleasant light comedy." With the exception of Christie, the cast received some harsh words: "Miss Sullavan is too darned adorable at times, and it is hard to believe that the sergeant, as Nugent depicts him, has ever been a playboy in Paris." The critic offered this assessment:

I for one should like to see Margaret Sullavan in [an adult] play because I think she has the makings of a good actress. In her present role, she makes a few valiant attempts to turn a type into a character, but she doesn't get much help from the script and falls back on prettiness and charm. She possesses a great deal of both—so much, indeed, that if she wants to be a legitimate actress with more than one role in her repertory rather than a stereotyped star in the streamlined Hollywood daydream money—she had better watch out.

These reviewers were in the distinct minority as critical raves and record box office attendance drowned out the negative words. The *Journal-American* enthusiastically wrote, "*The Voice of the Turtle* is a well-nigh perfect play…. And, as acted by [Sullavan, Nugent and Christie], it is a well-nigh perfect evening of acting…. [Sullavan was] wistful, humorous and just plain superb." The *Daily News* praised the play as "the first wholly satisfying, completely captivating comedy of the season…. [Sullavan] is proof that Hollywood can't be such a bad place, after all—for she gives a thoroughly right performance." The *Sun* raved, "Miss Sullavan could not have chosen a happier part in which to visit Manhattan. Throughout she brings to the role of Sally warmth and humor and charm in abundance."

The play begins on a Friday afternoon in early April. Sally Middleton (Sullavan) has moved into her new apartment in the East Sixties. Like most struggling actresses, Sally had come to find fame. She also came to be with her married lover, a producer. He, however, dumps her when she ruins their "fun times" by falling in love. Heartbroken and confused, Sally confides to Olive (Christie), a promiscuous, worldly woman always on the make. Olive advises Sally to avoid serious talks of love with men. Unbeknownst to Sally, Olive had planned a date with Bill Page (Nugent), an army sergeant on leave for the weekend, but stands him up when she gets a better offer from another man. Bill arrives at Sally's apartment and discovers Olive had ditched him. To complicate matters, there are no available hotel rooms in the city, so Sally offers to share her apartment for the weekend. It is not long before the two fall in love.

As described, the play doesn't sound like much. What elevated it into something special was the sophisticated dialogue and the manner in which van Druten explored Sally's sexual struggles as she tries to reconcile her childhood teachings of chastity with her growing affection for Bill. The element of "Will she or won't she?" gave *The Voice of the Turtle* the necessary ingredient to lift the slight plot out of the ordinary. In addition, Sally, presented as the "girl next door" type, was in perfect alignment with the "Margaret Sullavan Persona." The play, controversial for its time, gave war-weary audiences the escape they needed.

One imagines that Sullavan was thrilled by the terrific reception of the play. However, her mood was hardly jubilant. Nugent recalled that on the second night in New York, "Maggie pinned up a calendar beside the door of the set. Each night when the performance was over she would check off a day as if the year of her contract were a prison term."[11] Sullavan detested long-term commitments as it was difficult to remain fresh in a part that is repeated night after night. She always claimed a repertory company that presented new plays each week would have been the ideal situation for her. Deep down, she was conflicted between her desire for an acting career and being home with her children. It wasn't long before she began to hate the play.

Reports of her temperamental behavior were legendary among the Broadway community. Harold J. Kennedy, who later directed Sullavan in summer stock, recalled hearing that one day she broke a mirror over the head of her company manager, Sammy Schwartz, before a matinee of *The Voice of the Turtle* in New York "and then sent her maid at intermission to find out if he was going to take her out for dinner as usual."[12]

"She was a strange girl," Nugent reminisced, "but a fascinating one—on stage or off."

He found it odd that, although she was happily married and a mother, "she did not hesitate to talk quite frankly of her previous husbands and love affairs. I do not believe that any man who had once been in love with Margaret Sullavan ever quite got over it." He theorized that this attraction extended to the men in the audience as evidenced by the large number of males in attendance. Nugent continued, "Women admired her, too, and swarmed to see the play." He further noted, "The ones who knew her seemed to be a bit afraid of her because at a party she spent little time talking to wives." While his wife established a rapport with Hepburn, she had a hard time warming up to Sullavan. Norma "felt a bit put off at the short shrift Maggie gave her in social conversation."[13]

Nugent told Quirk that working with Sullavan was a "symphony of interplay. She had the most complete concentrational capacity of any actress I ever worked with, and she had the knack of getting the best out of her fellow players."[14] Still, Sullavan had a mischievous

THE PLAYBILL

FOR THE MOROSCO THEATRE

Sullavan's 1943 return to Broadway *The Voice of the Turtle* was a sensational critical and box office success, thus ensuring financial security for years. But she resented being away from her children.

side as Nugent thought she got some kind of sadistic pleasure when she used any number of scene-stealing techniques during the performance just to keep him off guard.

Christie found Sullavan pleasantly professional, but felt that Sullavan was "quite a lonely girl and woman." As she elaborated to Michael Burrows, "Despite three children, exciting marriages and a career, I feel she was always looking for a more routine way of living." Of Sullavan's ability, Christie stated, "She had such a rare quality and talent, but was not that impressed with herself."[15]

Analyzing why Sullavan made such a terrific impression, van Druten mused that she seemed "like a real girl, which is … the quality that has pervaded all her work and endeared her to the public." However, he quickly pointed out that this "may have damaged her career in pictures, stopping her from reaching the topmost ranks of box office stardom, where a certain artificiality of glamor and a larger-than-life stature of personality are the first requirements."[16] On the stage, van Druten cited her strengths: "She moves exquisitely, handling her whole body with plasticity and freedom. She never speaks on the stage without thinking, and she has the great gift of being able to listen."[17]

Despite her growing frustration, Sullavan appeared to take it in stride. To an interviewer, Sullavan remarked that one of the challenges she faced was that "in a play like this, you start cold; and the play builds as you boost yourself over one comic or dramatic hurdle after another. By the time the curtain calls come, you're all wound up like a top. You can't unwind in a hurry either. Too much nervous tension."[18]

In another interview, Sullavan's true feelings were revealed as she voiced her opinion that any patriotic woman realizes that running her home and raising her family was the best way to support the war effort on the home front. As friend Sara Mankiewicz, Herman J. Mankiewicz's wife, assessed, "She had a very romantic concept of motherhood and marriage—incurable romantic, she was—and very much involved with it." The trouble started when "her career started to be an interruption to her, to her duties and home."[19]

As her dissatisfaction grew, rumors circulated she would vacate the play. In early February, Fidler asked the question that was on everybody's minds: "Is Margaret Sullavan leaving the hit play *Voice of the Turtle* in June because she has a new date with the stork?"[20] Fearing that her departure would shut down the play, columnists suggested some possible replacements: Betty Field, Geraldine Fitzgerald and Martha Scott.

In early March, there was a collective sigh of relief when Parsons reported the cast would close the play on June 24 for eight weeks during the summer. The cast would return in the fall, with Sullavan's final appearance set for December 15. Perhaps a full year's run would help her achieve more financial security, so she could enjoy a longer retirement from acting?

Later in the spring, *Voice of the Turtle* was chosen for a command performance in Washington, D.C., at the request of the First Lady. The cast did not meet the president, who was ill with influenza, but Mrs. Roosevelt met cast members in their dressing rooms after the performance. At *Billboard*'s first annual Donaldson Award in July, *Voice* received four awards: Outstanding Play, Best Actress, Best Supporting Actress and Best Setting. Nugent lost to Paul Robeson in *Othello*. The play also scored big at the New York Drama Critic Poll: best play, best direction and best male and female performances. "This was my biggest success as an actor," recalled Nugent.[21]

As a patriotic gesture, the play was performed free for a week in June for all men in uniform. The cast donated their services, van Druten waived his royalties, and the management suspended rental fees. Delly paid the house and stage staff out of his own pocket. Over 800 men were released from area hospitals to attend the first night's performance.

During the summer, Sullavan returned to California. Movie roles were offered and promptly rejected. The most intriguing role was the schoolteacher in *Tomorrow the World* opposite Fredric March. Nugent owned a share of the property and was slated to direct. Betty Field played the part and Leslie Fenton directed.

Meanwhile, Delly was fielding offers for the film rights at the asking price of $3 million. It was expected that the cast would recreate their roles under Nugent's direction. Since Sullavan and Nugent had an ownership in the play, they were involved in negotiations. One offer came from 20th Century–Fox. Hedda Hopper reported, "Twentieth Century is being tempted to pay the exorbitant price asked for *Voice of the Turtle*, but only if Margaret Sullavan remains with the New York cast as long as the play lasts."[22] It's likely Sullavan had a few choice words in response. Warner Brothers won the bid for an undisclosed amount. The film was released in 1947 with Ronald Reagan, Eleanor Parker and Eve Arden playing the main roles. Van Druten adapted his play by adding situations and characters (enacted by Wayne Morris and Kent Smith) to flesh out the plot. The film is regarded today as a pleasant wartime comedy, well-played by an engaging cast.

On August 28, the cast reopened the play. Sullavan remained until December 16, 1944. By the time of her departure, she was the highest paid actress on Broadway at a weekly salary of $4000. She topped Mary Martin (*One Touch of Venus*), Ethel Barrymore (*Embezzled Heaven*) and Mae West (*Catherine Was Great*) for the 1943–1944 season.

Before Sullavan's exit, several replacements were again considered, with Jean Arthur, Florence Rice and Betty Field the most prominent names. Field stepped into the role and, according to Nugent, was very good. Martha Scott and Florence Rice assumed the role later; John Beal replaced Nugent on January 1, 1946.

The show remained highly profitable and enjoyed an astounding run of 1557 performances before it closed on January 3, 1948. Along with the musical *Oklahoma!*, the comedy was one of the few hits of the 1943–44 season. Today, it ranks tenth for the longest running straight (non-musical) Broadway play. Despite this distinction, revivals have been scarce. Outside of a few summer stock performances, including the well-received summer stock production with sultry screen siren Veronica Lake (of all people) in 1951, the play did not have a major revival until the 2001 Off-Broadway production. Nor were there any television productions. Perhaps the play's theme of sexual frustration was considered too risqué for the 1950s and 1960s.

The play's phenomenal success solidified Sullavan's reputation as a legitimate stage star. For those who were fortunate enough to see it, her appearance was an indelible memory. Andrew Sarris wrote, "It is only because I happened to have seen Margaret Sullavan's poignantly bubbly performance in *The Voice of the Turtle* that I can bear witness to her stage magic."[23] Sullavan held a minimalist view of this play. In 1954, she told a *New York Times* interviewer, "The play was adored so. People would come back starry-eyed to tell me how much they liked it. It was the most adept job of playwriting I've ever known in my life. It's a most remarkable play because it's about nothing."[24]

With the completion of her commitment, Sullavan retired to assume the role of mother and wife.

29

Period of Uncertainty

I came out here to get away from all that and not to be Margaret Sullavan, but Mrs. Leland Hayward.... I love this life, and the privacy and to be completely myself.[1]

In late 1944, Sullavan pursued her dream life away from the public eye and bought a house in Connecticut without Hayward's consent. In love with the secluded life in the area, Sullavan believed raising children there was preferable to California. She also began despising Hayward's job as a talent agent and felt he could be equally successful as a Broadway producer. When his first production *A Bell for Adano* (1944) was a big hit, it was logical to relocate to the East Coast. After Christmas, the family moved to Brookfield, Connecticut, Sullavan quickly embraced the rural lifestyle from gardening to raising farm animals. Hayward did not. Used to the fast-paced lifestyle, he became restless. The children also had difficulty adjusting.

In late May 1945, Hedda Hopper reported, "Leland Hayward says Maggie (Margaret) Sullavan has absolutely nothing on her mind—no play, no picture, no baby. She's settled into her Connecticut home and is divinely happy." Cynically, Hopper added, "Knowing Maggie, I wonder how long that is going to last."[2] Sullavan continued turning down offers of movie and stage roles, including Leland's production *State of the Union*, which proved another tremendous hit.

Success came at a steep price as Hayward spent more time away from home. Along with producing, he was still involved with Southwest Airways and managed a small roster of celebrities in Hollywood. Lauren Bacall recalled, "He was a demon worker"; his career reduced his presence at home to sporadic weekend visits.[3] Sara Mankiewicz blamed Sullavan for the situation: "She wanted him to be a husband and father.... He was never cut out for that role." Mankiewicz believed Sullavan was conflicted between her career and motherhood. "She liked the money and she was glad to make it, but she really regarded it as an imposition."[4] She believed Sullavan would have been content in the traditional role of a mother.

Sullavan considered a return to Broadway in plays like *Dream Girl* and *Mary Rose*. There was also talk of a London engagement of *The Voice of the Turtle*, and she was most agreeable. In the meantime, she made the surprise move back to California to accommodate Hayward's career. While maintaining the Connecticut farm, Sullavan bought another house in the mountains overlooking the Pacific in the Catalina Island area. The children were thrilled to be reunited with Jane and Peter Fonda. Both Brooke and Jane were old enough to suspect there was something behind the Sullavan-Fonda friendship, but could not imagine how. "They had a look of naughtiness when they came together.... They seemed so inseparable that for years Jane and I would wonder what might be going on between them."[5] Eventually, the girls found out the truth. Brooke mused, "I can't remember how or when we discovered that once upon a time … our mother and their father had been married and very much in love."[6] Brooke continued, "My mother thought that Henry was the best actor she knew and told us so very often. She was enormously loyal to him."[7] Jane Fonda remembered Sullavan as a "petite, talented, flirtatious, temperamental, Scarlett O'Hara–style Southern belle."[8] "What impressed me most about her was how athletic and tomboyish she was," Jane recalled. "Dad had taught her how to walk on her hands during their courtship, and she could still suddenly turn herself upside down—and there she'd be, walking along on her hands." One person who did not have fond memories was Fonda's wife Frances, whose mental illness worsened

By 1945, Sullavan, having adopted the pageboy hairstyle (her enduring trademark), had announced her retirement from acting to devote herself to motherhood.

after Peter's birth in 1940. Jane noted, "I intuited that something in Dad became more alive when Sullavan was around, and if I picked it up, Mother must have."[9] A friend recalled that Frances had "always hated her" and cynically referred to her as "Madame H."[10]

By early 1946, Sullavan was restless. Periodic, extensive stays at the Brookfield farm did not alleviate the strain of an unraveling marriage. It was reported in March 1946 that Sullavan agreed to do *Voice of the Turtle* in London. There was also talk of playing in Paris and Moscow prior to the London engagement. Richard Carlson was briefly considered for Bill Paige before the role was accepted by Joseph Cotten. However, a film commitment kept Cotten from making the scheduled July date, so Carlson was back in the running—until *he* had to report for a film commitment. To accommodate Cotten's schedule, plans were reset for a September opening. By mid–August, however, the engagement was called off. The official excuse was that Cotten was still working on *Katie Goes to Congress* (retitled *The Farmer's Daughter*). Parsons gave another reason: "The London producer wanted an assurance that Maggie and Joe would remain in London for the run of the play, which could be one year, two years, or even longer."[11] Sullavan would never agree to be separated from her children for that long.

There were more disappointments. Warner Brothers was casting the role of Sally for the film version of *The Voice of the Turtle*. Ronald Reagan was already cast, so it was a matter of finding the actress to appear opposite him. Early contenders included Jean Arthur and Olivia de Havilland. When Sullavan's trip to England was cancelled, she was in the

Sullavan's children (left to right front: Brooke, Bridget, Bill; with "Kitty" Hawks in the back) (Brooke Hayward Papers, 1911–1977, Billy Rose Theatre Division, The New York Public Library for the Performing Arts).

running to reprise her stage role. The issue was that, while only three years older, would she look young enough opposite the youthful-looking actor? To resolve this issue, she made a screen test with him. Some people championed Sullavan. Parsons pointedly wrote, "Margaret Sullavan, more than any actress I know, has the gift of looking like a teenager."[12] An earlier comment from Jack Gaven, however, illustrated the reality of Sullavan's advancing age: "Still the most appealing looking of the stars is Margaret Sullavan despite the fact that she's going to have to do something about a burgeoning double chin."[13] When Eleanor Parker inherited the part, it was a devastating blow to Sullavan's self-esteem as she had to abdicate a role she created to a younger actress. To add insult to injury, an offer from Metro required she'd play 14-year-old Elizabeth Taylor's *mother* in *Rich, Full Life*.

There was an intriguing prospect of a mini–University Players reunion on Broadway with Stewart, Fonda, Kent Smith and Mildred Natwick with Joshua Logan and Bretaigne Windust directing and producing. Conflicting film commitments prevented this from happening. Sullavan's professional activities were limited to appearances on radio programs such as "I Give You Maggie" with Van Heflin on March 8, 1947. That program was a highly sentimental account of a woman whose insecurity led her to suspect her husband of infidelity. Sullavan was miscast in a role that did not allow for her intelligence and sensibility.

While Sullavan's career was foundering, she spent more time in Connecticut. Hayward remained in California. As Millicent Osborn asserted, the blame was mostly Sullavan's: "It was really an essential arrogance … of wanting things the way she wanted them without regard for what Leland wanted."[14] As rumors of their marital woes circulated, Sullavan discovered that he had been seeing Nancy "Slim" Hawks in California. Hawks was still legally married to director Howard Hawks, even though they had separated. This revelation hit Sullavan hard as, from all appearances, she had been faithful to Hayward during their marriage. When confronted, Hayward was contrite—but only because he got caught. Hating the idea of subjecting the children to the nasty business of divorce, Leland and Margaret agreed to seek individual counseling in an effort to save the marriage. Then came the proverbial straw that broke the camel's back.

Back in April, Delly again approached Sullavan about bringing *The Voice of the Turtle* to London in the summer of 1947. This time, Sullavan was not compelled to stay longer than six months. Her psychiatrist advised her to go in the belief that a brief separation might rekindle the love between husband and wife. Hayward begged Sullavan to reconsider. In a decision she later regretted on many levels, Sullavan chose London.

Wendell Corey played Bill and Audrey Christie was back as Olive. They rehearsed briefly before appearing at the Morosco in New York for a four-day run. Then the cast, along with van Druten, sailed for England. The pre–London provincial tour would begin on June 16 in Manchester for one week, followed by one week in Edinburgh and Glasgow before opening in London on July 9.

Sullavan's stay in England got off to the worst possible start. As she recalled, "A friend greeted me with the news that Leland had gone right off to Hawaii with Slim for a lovely two-week vacation—quite openly, so that it hit all the stinking gossip columns immediately."[15] Columnist Dorothy Kilgallen reported, "The Margaret Sullavan-Leland Hayward break is Hollywood's biggest 'open secret.'"[16] With his ultimate betrayal, any chance at reconciliation was gone.

The one bright hope was the triumph the play promised to repeat. However, during the Manchester engagement, Sullavan, sensing the difference in English audiences, became apprehensive. Reportedly, she wailed to Delly, "Is this what we came to England for? Where, oh where, is our slick little play?"[17]

At the Piccadilly Theatre in London, *The Voice of the Turtle* "managed to lay a large egg."[18] The reviews dashed all optimism. The *London Times* set the tone: "It is essentially childish entertainment…. Those who like it at all will like all of it, but others may feel that such virtuosity deserved a better subject…. Miss Margaret Sullavan's trick of emphasizing points by a guttural rasp or a sudden slow distinctness is very striking in its artificiality, but it only just stays the evening." The *Daily Telegraph* found Sullavan's acting "artificial," while the *Daily Mail* declared she played "sotto voice and spasmodically: she has a somewhat fixed charm."

The play's failure can be attributed to its inappropriate timing as England endured several years of harsh wartime conditions. Audiences were in no mood for a breezy, light comedy on a subject matter they wanted to forget. Another long-running American comedy, *Life with Father*, fared just as poorly. However, other imported plays, like *Oklahoma!*, *Annie Get Your Gun* and *Born Yesterday*, proved popular. Van Druten's play closed on August 30 after 69 performances. "It was the greatest disappointment in John van Druten's career," Christie reflected.[19]

After this disappointment, Sullavan was restless, miserable and lonely. Surprisingly, she stayed in England for a couple more months. Perhaps she needed more time away to plan her next move. "Nobody in the world would be as hurt by infidelity from a husband as Maggie," reasoned Osborn. "To her it was a most shattering blow."[20] In mid–October, she flew back to California to tell Hayward the marriage was over. He begged her not to leave him. What about the children?, Leland asked. To Sullavan, it was better to end the marriage than perpetuate a lie.

It is illuminating to read Leland's account to Brooke:

> What the hell did she expect? I implored her not to go [to England] ... I told her how vulnerable I was. She knew. There was no big deal.... I was a damned attractive man. Women adored me, I adored them, but that didn't mean I was behaving like Don Juan.... After years, I started having an affair. Nothing original about that. I honestly didn't know what the hell I was supposed to do next. She decided for me. Chose exactly the wrong course of action.[21]

Walter Saxel would have been proud. Sullavan, however, was no Ray Smith, so she asked Leland to leave. A few family friends sided with Leland. Osborn told Brooke, "I thought a great deal of the divorce was Maggie's fault.... It was the most needless divorce, because they were crazy about each other."[22]

The divorce was granted in late April 1948. Sullavan testified in court that Hayward "found their marriage very irksome. Miss Sullavan ... testified that Hayward, on the day he left their home, said, 'I'm not meant for marriage. I'm not meant for home life.'"[23] Sullavan maintained custody of the children with $900 per month in child support along with alimony. Sullavan was given their Los Angeles and Brookfield homes. The following year, Leland married "Slim."

Sullavan took the divorce hard. "She was always madly in love with your father," Mankiewicz told Brooke. "The divorce came as a most terrible shock to her." Mankiewicz surmised that "was the beginning of the end."[24]

Sullavan took the children back to Connecticut and tried to re-establish her acting career. She was hopeful when she was asked by Irene Selznick to read for the part of Blanche DuBois in Tennessee Williams' *A Streetcar Named Desire*. As Williams recalled, "She didn't seem right to me, I kept picturing her with a tennis racket in one hand. I doubted that Blanche had ever played tennis."[25] Jessica Tandy landed the part and scored a triumphant success. In 1949, Sullavan declined the offer to replace Tandy during the summer months.

An offer came from Bette Davis, who wanted to film *Ethan Frome* with Henry Fonda as the husband, Sullavan as the invalid wife, and she as the interloper. It was a much delayed project that never made it beyond some costume tests in Technicolor.

After these setbacks, Sullavan started dating again. Of one suitor, Parsons asked, "What goes with Margaret Sullavan and Kenneth Wagg?" Parsons had seen this couple dancing at a popular New York nightclub and observed, "Maggie looked happy for the first time since she and Leland Hayward separated."[26]

Erskine Johnson made a plea for Sullavan "to come out of retirement and return to the screen [as] Hollywood needs some good actresses," but she had no desire to make films.[27] Film offers dwindled as Sullavan refused to consider a return to filmmaking. King Vidor wanted Sullavan for *The Fountainhead* (1949). The role was played by a newcomer with her own unique husky voice, Patricia Neal. In mid–1948, Parsons lamented, "I don't know whether it is because Hollywood holds unhappy memories for Margaret Sullavan, or because she has developed more inhibitions like Greta Garbo—but we aren't going to get her back."[28]

What few realized was that Sullavan was losing her hearing in her left ear. She was suffering from otosclerosis, a form of deafness caused by the growth of bone over the middle ear. She contacted the foremost expert, Dr. Julius Lempert, in New York City. Lempert had perfected a technique in which a new opening was bored through the mastoid bone and a new eardrum was grafted over the aperture. Sullavan was scheduled to undergo this procedure at Lempert's private hospital, the Institute of Ontology, in mid–November.

Prior to the operation, Sullavan made her first television appearance. Worthington Miner was directing a pilot episode called "The Storm," for a new drama anthology series, *Studio One*. He knew she was having a rough time of it personally and professionally and wanted to throw a life line. She accepted his offer within 24 hours of receiving his wire.

The challenge of performing live television is that actors have to be on their toes as there is no room for big mistakes. Forgotten lines or business can be covered up, but an actor is on edge that they will embarrass themselves in front of millions of viewers. In 1954, Sullavan admitted, "It's absolutely awful. It combines the worst features of all the media. You stumble over the crew, just like in the movies. You have opening night jitters all the time, just like on the stage. You have to worry about the microphone, just like in radio."[29] According to Miner, "She was no half-assed amateur. She was a professional. She worked like a dog and without complaint."[30] Things progressed nicely—until the dress rehearsal when all hell broke loose.

Much of the last act was done with a voice recording in which Sullavan had to react as if in her own thoughts. "All was going well," Miner recalled, "until I saw her hesitate." After a few confusing seconds, "she let out a frightened sound, beat on the piano with her bare fists, and raced out of the studio to her dressing room, screaming, 'I can't do it! I can't do it!'" The stage manager approached Miner and offered this observation: "The sound on that recorder was too low, but not all that low. It was still audible. But for a deaf person, it would have been incomprehensible."[31]

When Miner arrived at her dressing room, Sullavan threw herself in his arms and sobbed. "I can't do it! I can't hear one word. Not one!" Miner asked if she was going deaf. "Yes, I've got to have an operation," she replied.[32] Miner managed to convince her the recorder was not working properly. It was not her hearing that was the issue. Calm once again, Sullavan returned to rehearsals.

The hour-long episode aired on November 7, 1948. *Variety* carped, "*Studio One* got off to a start that left the viewer both confused and bewildered." Sullavan rated a favorable comment for her "fine, sensitive portrayal."

Dr. Lempert's procedure was a success and Sullavan was deeply grateful. News was withheld from the press, but after Parsons noted "[Sullavan's] hearing is greatly improved" a few weeks later, it was no longer a private matter.[33]

Sullavan was considered for Clifford Odets' play *The Big Knife*, opposite John Garfield, until she received a more intriguing offer from William Taub. *People Like Us*, written by English playwright Frank Vosper in the 1930s, was based on the sensational, true-life story of a British couple executed for the murder of her husband in 1922. The play was banned by Lord Chamberlain after a performance at the Strand Theatre in the mid–1930s. The play was performed at the Wyndhams Theatre in London again in 1948. Its success prompted Taub to purchase the rights for Broadway. Despite Taub's lack of experience as a producer, Sullavan signed the contract. The play was scheduled to open on February 23, 1949.

Before rehearsals, Sullavan was not satisfied with the play as it was highly reminiscent of an earlier Vosper play, *Spellbound*. Taub assured Sullavan that the play had been rewritten, but she thought otherwise. Further requests for modifications were ignored and she left the play. Taub was not going to let her get off that easily, so their personal battles became public. "Like a bolt from the blue," reported the *New York Times*, "came word last night that Margaret Sullavan has for some mysterious reason changed her mind and isn't interested anymore in appearing in *People Like Us* despite the fact that she is under contract to do so."[34] Taub asked Actors' Equity to intervene. Furthermore, Taub wanted Sullavan to pay $75,000 in damages for breach of contract. He then sought an injunction to prevent her from working elsewhere. Four months later, the matter was settled when an arbitrator sided with Sullavan on the basis that Taub misrepresented the play. Taub vowed to take the matter to court. Later, there was talk of recasting the part, but the play never made it out of the planning phase.

During this challenging time, Sullavan became serious with Kenneth Wagg. By January 1949, their relationship was fresh fodder for gossip. Pundits charmed their readers by stating that Sullavan would someday become "Maggie Waggie."

On April 11, 1949, Sullavan made her second television appearance for *Chevrolet on Broadway Presentations* of "The Twelve Pound Look." The telecast was deemed outmoded in its appeal. *Variety* opined the program "seems too static for proper video presentation, despite excellent enactments." Sullavan was commended for being "charming." Incidentally, Ethel Barrymore had appeared in a short-lived production of *The Twelve-Pound Look* on Broadway in 1911.

Next, Sullavan turned down an offer of $5000 per week for ten weeks of summer stock. After an absence of six years, the unpredictable actress decided to return to Hollywood.

30

Long-Awaited Return
to the Screen

If I didn't need the money I wouldn't be working.... I don't think it's particularly important that I work. I'd rather be with my children.[1]

Based on the 1944 novel by Ruth Southard, *No Sad Songs for Me* had been languishing at Columbia since the studio purchased the screen rights at the time of its publication. The plot (a housewife with cancer has a short time left) was considered risky. Ironically, Southard, who never published another book, died of colon cancer in her mid-eighties. Victor Saville was originally slated to direct. In 1946, it was announced that Casey Robinson would produce and write the screenplay with Irene Dunne as the star; she, like Loretta Young, Claudette Colbert and Joan Crawford after her, turned it down. In early 1949, producer Buddy Adler sent the final screenplay by Howard Koch to Sullavan, who immediately wired "When do I start?"[2] In an interview, Sullavan revealed that the film and character intrigued her.

> I flatly refuse to play namby-pambies and Mary Scott in *No Sad Songs* is anything but that. She's a woman who learns that she is fatally ill, and has less than a year of life ahead. Instead of being sorry for herself, she gallantly refuses to let her husband and young daughter know of her illness, goes ahead living the short time left her as fully as possible.[3]

Sullavan flew to Hollywood to meet with the head of Columbia, Harry Cohn. An amusing account of an earlier meeting ten years prior has been recounted so often it has become something of a Hollywood legend. There are many variations to the original incident; my favorite comes from Jerry Asher and Billy Grady:

Prior to making *The Shop Around the Corner*, Sullavan was considered for Columbia's *His Girl Friday*. A meeting was set up with Cohn, who had a reputation for bedding many of his female contract players. The meeting quickly degenerated into crude verbal passes, which Sullavan shot down. Cohn tried to reason with Sullavan, stating that he had heard from several men that she was good in bed. Fed up, Sullavan, heading for the door, assured him that she was, but he was not going to find out. Still, Cohn persisted. Stopping at the door, Sullavan asked if he wanted his answer straight or diluted. Startled, Cohn replied he'd have the answer straight. With brutal honesty, Sullavan responded, "You're not young, handsome or slim enough to get me excited."[4] According to Quirk, Cohn, despite the affront, enjoyed retelling that story over the years.

This time, Sullavan came to terms with Cohn and, by mid–April, Parsons announced, "Margaret Sullavan ... has signed a two-picture contract with Columbia, and her first one will be *No Sad Songs*, which deals with cancer.... It would take a great actress like Margaret to bring such a subject out in the open."[5] It was reported by others that Sullavan signed a $350,000 contract for five pictures. According to Hedda Hopper, "Margaret Sullavan follows *No Sad Songs for Me* at Columbia with one picture a year for that studio. She'll do the films in summer while her three children are at camp."[6]

In June, the *Hollywood Citizen News* reported that veteran director Sam Wood, who helmed such classics as *Kings Row* (1942) and *The Pride of the Yankees* (1942), was to direct upon the completion of *Ambush* for MGM.

Back in 1947, the House of Un-American Activities Committee (HUAC) in Washington investigated subversive Communist activities in Hollywood. During this time, several well-known producers, directors, writers and actors were under heavy scrutiny for Communist ties. HUAC later identified ten people whom they believed engaged in unpatriotic activities. The now famous "Hollywood Ten" included screenwriters Lester Cole and Ring Lardner Jr. and director Edward Dmytryk. In response, many in Hollywood's film community formed the First Amendment committee to support the Hollywood Ten during the hearings. It was founded by screenwriter Philip Dunne, actress Myrna Loy and directors John Huston and William Wyler. The committee included some of Hollywood's biggest names: Humphrey Bogart, Bette Davis, Henry Fonda, John Garfield, Judy Garland, Katharine Hepburn, Groucho Marx, Vincente Minnelli, Edward G. Robinson and Margaret Sullavan.

During most of her life, Sullavan usually remained neutral on political issues. What made this different was the gross injustice inflicted based on paranoia and suspicion. One thing that Sullavan detested was prejudice of any kind. "I find the only prejudice worth having is against people who are prejudiced," Brooke recalled her saying.[7] Sullavan became an outspoken critic of HUAC.

Many in Hollywood believed the HUAC's actions were justified. Among its most fervent supporters were Robert Taylor, James Stewart (whose involvement nearly ended his friendship with Fonda) and Sam Wood. Since the mid–1940s, Wood served as the president of the Motion Picture Alliance for the Preservation of American Ideals, a right-wing organization whose aim was to expose Communist activities in Hollywood. In 1947, Wood was one of the many "patriots" who provided crucial testimony before HUAC.

As Wood and Sullavan worked through early production issues, the differences in their political views made for a contentious relationship. On September 22, they engaged in a heated argument after Sullavan refused to fire a writer who had left-wing views. Later that day, Wood became ill after a meeting at the Alliance. A doctor was summoned and Wood was taken to Cedars of Lebanon Hospital, where he later died from a heart attack. Out of his death came rumors that Sullavan was responsible for his death. As Donald Dewey recounted, Wood "dropped dead from a heart attack shortly after a raging argument with Margaret Sullavan."[8] Offering her perspective, Wood's daughter K.T. Stevens told Tony Thomas, "I think two things contributed to my father's death.... One was the energy he burned up while making *Ambush* on location.... The second thing was politics. His anger was so deep he seethed with it and I believe it affected his health."[9]

Cinematographer Rudolph Maté assumed the directorial chores in his third outing as a director. Wendell Corey was borrowed from the Hal B. Wallis unit at Paramount to play opposite Sullavan. Other important cast members included Swedish-born Viveca Lindfors (on loan from Warner Brothers) and child actress Natalie Wood. Shooting began on October 13, 1949. Early in the production, Sullavan proved highly cooperative with the press. Talking to Sullavan on the set, Bob Thomas remarked, "Hope your return will become a habit." Sullavan replied,

"That's very nice, but we'll wait and see."

"Haven't you signed for one picture a year with Columbia?"

"Yes, but that continues only if they like the first one. I might turn out to be terrible."

"I'm not worried. Maybe you'll become a California resident again."

"I don't know about that. California is the easiest place in the world to live. But I want my children to know what it's like to have seasons. They're in Connecticut."[10]

This interesting tidbit came from columnist Erskine Johnson: "Margaret Sullavan, who was worried about her hearing, is okay following medical treatment."[11] While fellow actors did not notice Sullavan experiencing any trouble, Maté noted definite signs during filming. "Her eyes would scrunch up," he remembered, "and she would tighten up; her shoulders would hunch, and she would look very intently at the other player." During the times she was not on camera, "I would catch her mouthing the other player's lines, very quietly and silently. I don't think the others noticed, but I did. And she seemed to tire very easily, too. But when she was on camera, she was all vitality."[12]

There were times when other players lowered their voices during intimate scenes. Frustrated, Sullavan would erupt and accuse the actor of not "giving" enough in their performance to conceal that she couldn't hear them. Despite this, Maté recalled that it was a privilege to work with her. Likewise, Sullavan had good things to say about her director: "Rudy Maté is a highly intelligent and sensitive person. All of us, all the way through, kept saying, 'Now, let's not be sorry for ourselves.' And we weren't."[13]

Lindfors told Quirk, "She was a really wonderful actress to play off and against, and she carried you along with her in a mutual desire to give the best portrayal possible."[14] Eleven-year-old Wood had fond memories of her interactions with Sullavan, who played her mother. For the youngster, portraying a loved child in a normal family offered her a respite from her dysfunctional and violent family. According to Wood's biographer Suzanne Finstad, the child found Sullavan "was so into her character that it was a little hard to think of her as Margaret Sullavan."[15]

The film had a short production schedule and wrapped on November 19. In late January 1950, Parsons, who saw a rough cut of the film, reported, "Margaret Sullavan is slightly sensational in *No Sad Songs* and you can bet that after the picture conies out every company in the business will be after her. I can't think of anything more gratifying than for Maggie, whom I love and admire, to come back in such a wonderful way."[16]

On April 11, within days of the film's release, Cornelius Sullavan died at the age of 73; Garland later died on April 23, 1952, at 76. Sadly, Frances Fonda committed suicide on April 14. Henry Fonda had been married to her since 1936. Early in their marriage, it became clear that Frances suffered from severe mental illness, and the birth of their two children aggravated the condition. By 1948, Henry moved the family to a house close to Sullavan's in Connecticut while he was appearing on Broadway in *Mr. Roberts*. Sullavan became a sort of surrogate mother to the Fonda children and both have fond memories of her. By then, due to Frances' manic mood swings, Henry wanted a divorce. In January 1950, Frances went into the Austen Riggs Psychiatric Hospital for treatment. It was there she slashed her throat. Both Jane and Peter were told she died of a heart attack. To spare them, Fonda arranged a private funeral with only him and his mother-in-law present. Peter recalled, "No one talked about her. It was as if she hadn't lived." Sullavan was concerned and encouraged Henry to talk honestly to his kids about their mother's death. She reasoned the children would be unable to cope with their mother's death if he remained quiet. Henry never took her advice: "I thought it was better not to tell them. They were too young."[17]

Before *No Sad Songs'* engagement in New York City, Adler talked to *The New York*

Times. Adler believed the film "isn't even a picture about cancer. It's a picture about bravery, about how to live, about defying fears that can destroy lives quicker and even more thoroughly than a dread disease."[18]

Heavily promoted as "The Brave Picture of the Year!," *No Sad Songs for Me* was anticipated to be a box office winner due to Sullavan's return to the big screen.

Mary Scott (Sullavan) is preparing breakfast for her husband Brad (Corey) and their daughter Polly (Wood). There's considerable excitement because Mary has an appointment with the doctor to confirm a long-hoped-for pregnancy. There are a few references to Mary's physical fatigue and the viewer senses something is wrong. Mary is told by Dr. Ralph (John McIntire) that it is impossible for her to have a baby. Ralph is curiously preoccupied and does not maintain eye contact with Mary. Ralph advises her to take it easy the next few months and would like to see her in two weeks.

Ralph's last comment bothers Mary, so she returns to his office and confronts him. This entire scene is handled in a restrained manner that is enormously effective. Ralph is evasive, which makes Mary all the more convinced he's withholding something. She persists in her questioning. Ralph finally reminds her of her symptoms. In an extremely tight close-up, Mary whispers in a barely audible voice, "Ralph, is it … it couldn't be … *cancer?*" One can feel the life drain from Mary's face as the horrible reality sinks in. In a moment that could have degenerated into overwrought theatrics, Sullavan plays with simplicity and restraint, thereby making the moment more powerful.

But the scene's not over yet. Disbelieving, she pleads, "You could have made a mistake, you could be wrong … couldn't you?" Ralph assures her that all of the tests confirm the diagnosis. She asks about treatment options, but he tells her it's too late. She only has ten months. This entire sequence is magnificently played by Sullavan in a *tour de force* performance as she navigates emotions from concern to shock to desperation to resignation in a sequence highly worthy of an Academy Award nomination that never came her way. There's a similar scene in Metro's *The Miniver Story* (released later in 1950), in which Greer Garson's character is diagnosed with cancer. Framed mostly in medium shots, the scene comes across with too much "stiff-upper-lip" sentiment and is dull and uninvolving.

Mary, keeping her illness a secret, decides to live her life to the fullest in the remaining time. She makes it her mission to ensure that Brad and Polly will be prepared for a life without her.

Brad, a civil engineer, hires a new draftsman for an urgent project. Chris (Lindfors) proves to be extremely capable and wins the admiration of Brad and other co-workers. During the Christmas season, Mary runs into Ralph, whom she has been avoiding. Mary, letting down her guard, says, "Once in a while, when I stop fighting it, I get a flash of … I guess you call it … philosophy. Suddenly I realize that what really matters is not how long you live, but *how*." In a tight close-up, Mary continues, "I don't know if I can explain … the feeling that you have nothing more to lose, so you're completely *alive*, every last minute of it." With her subtle, quiet playing, Sullavan beautifully conveys Mary's new perspective on life, a sublime example of the "clarity of vision" in which Sullavan was such an expert— it also reinforces the notion that no one other than Sullavan could have wrought such emotional power with a minimum of gestures.

Brad and Mary include Chris in their social circles and it's not long before gossip about Brad and Chris circulates. Mary is initially reluctant to believe the rumors, despite the change in Brad's work hours and behavior. Eventually suspecting the worst, she visits her father in San Francisco for a few weeks. While there, Mary meets an old friend, a recent widower. He, struggling to readjust to life after his wife's sudden death, is dating a woman, to whom Mary takes an instant dislike. This chance encounter spurs her to contemplate what will happen to her family, so she decides to return home earlier than planned.

Mary's nerves fray when Brad does not come home for dinner that night. Brad calls from a diner to tell Mary he needs to talk to her later. He then rejoins Chris at a table. Convinced that Brad no longer loves her, Mary drives off intending to kill herself. The car runs out of gas and Mary breaks down in tears. It's a startling moment as Sullavan goes full throttle with the emotions, but it is still an affecting moment.

When Mary returns home, she finds Brad frantically worried. Brad admits his affair with Chris, but has decided he loves his family too much to continue. The job is finished and Chris will be leaving town. Brad and Mary make plans to go to Mexico for a vacation.

Mary visits Chris at her boarding house. Despite being contrite, Chris is defensive. Still in love with Brad, she does not believe Mary's request for her to stay is sincere. Mary leaves, feeling that she has made a mess of things. This scene borders on soap opera dramatics, but the absolute sincerity of the actresses keep the suds from forming.

Chris arrives at the Scott home to apologize. Chris reveals she was once married, but lost her newlywed husband during the war. Burying her grief in work, she believed she would never love anyone else again until she met Brad. Mary asks Chris to consider staying. Mary's plan of Brad marrying Chris is set in motion. Mary encourages Chris to become an active part of the community as well as her daughter's life.

One day, Brad finds Mary's painkillers and calls Ralph. In Ralph's office, Brad learns

Sullavan with Wendell Corey in *No Sad Songs for Me* (1950). Her performance in her final motion picture was highly praised, but audiences were put off by the serious subject matter of cancer.

of Mary's illness. He becomes distraught and feels helpless—as well as a little guilt-ridden over his affair. Ralph assures Brad that there is nothing that can be done and Mary only has a few weeks. Ralph reminds him that Mary has made peace with her death and he and Polly must find a way to live on afterwards. "You've had five months without this hanging over your heads," Ralph tells him. "Mary made that possible. Now, you make the next few weeks possible for her."

Brad takes Mary to Mexico and they enjoy their remaining days in bliss. One day, Chris receives a call from Brad at the house that Mary has died. Sitting at the piano with Polly, Chris asks if she remembered what her mother said when she left. "No," Polly answers, "I only remember that she smiled." With that, Chris beams at the knowledge that Polly will never forget her mother—a tear-provoking moment which is handled with intelligence and restraint.

Both the film and its star received glowing reviews. The *Washington Post* was one of the few that disliked it: "Although acted by a splendid cast, headed by the too-long absent Margaret Sullavan, [it] stacks up as dreary soup.... [While] it is good to have the sincere quality of Miss Sullavan back on the screen, and the playing of Viveca Lindfors and Wendell Corey is notably restrained, *No Sad Songs for Me* makes only a soap opera out of what might have been a warm and intelligent film." The *Winnipeg Free Press* disagreed: "Around a theme which could easily have become a dreary soap opera has been built a movie which explores tragedy with the hands of a sensitive, conscientious artist. When it has been acted with such poignant skill by Margaret Sullavan and other members of the cast, it assumes the proportions of a rare emotional experience.... [Sullavan] will certainly be nominated for an Academy Award." The *Detroit Free Press* declared, "Here and now, early in the year as it is, I'll nominate Margaret Sullavan for next year's Oscar as best actress.... She makes this a great picture of love and triumph." The *Motion Picture Herald* magazine was profuse in its commendations: "Columbia has cast this great star in a poignant, heartbreaking story of infinite box office appeal. It is a film of which the industry can be proud." In regards to Sullavan, "Hollywood has produced many stars, but few can match the charm and personality of Miss Sullavan. It is on her performance that the picture takes its dramatic foundation and she does this confidence justice."

Variety predicted that the combination of Sullavan's return and the film's high quality would generate hefty business. But this was not the case. Although Sullavan's name on the marquee drew nostalgic moviegoers, many were turned off by the subject matter. At that time, little was known about cancer and effective treatment options. The fact that Sullavan portrayed an ordinary housewife and mother reinforced the notion that cancer could strike its next victim with no regard to social status or wealth. It was easier to let glamorous stars like Kay Francis (*One Way Passage*, 1932), Bette Davis (*Dark Victory*, 1939) and Maureen O'Hara (*Sentimental Journey*, 1946) languish under their exotic, rare, and unidentified diseases. Cancer, on the other hand, was too close for comfort for the average moviegoer and they stayed away in droves. The film earned a modest return due to initial interest, but nowhere near the anticipated results.

While the film was playing in New York City, Sullavan's children begged her to take them to see it. As she recalled a few years later, "My two daughters and my son saw me for the first time in a picture when they saw *No Sad Songs for Me*":

> The day I took them to the picture, I walked out after a few minutes and went across the street to a restaurant where I drank six cups of black coffee while I waited for the children to come out. After they came out they were so upset that I had to take them with me to our family doctor to assure them that I didn't have cancer.[19]

Despite the numerous predictions of an Oscar nod, Sullavan was left out of the final voting in a year that saw many notable comebacks, particularly Bette Davis in *All About Eve* and Gloria Swanson in *Sunset Blvd*. The only nomination the film received was for George Duning's musical score. In 1955, *No Sad Songs for Me* was presented as a *Lux Video Theatre* television episode with Claire Trevor.

In subsequent years, *No Sad Songs for Me* has been unfairly relegated to low status. In this age where "Dreaded Disease" movies have become a staple of the Lifetime's Movie of the Week, parts of the film are familiar. However, the movie tackles a mawkish situation with intelligence that steers away from obvious soap opera tactics. To fully appreciate this film's achievement, one only needs to compare it to *Sentimental Journey* or the unmoving *The Miniver Story*. Koch's script deals with the subject matter in an insightful, subtle manner. Likewise, Maté's skillful direction keeps the plot from wallowing in melodramatic suds. His handling of the scene in which Mary receives the news is pure genius. As a result, the film becomes real with honest, human emotions. One is frequently moved by Mary's story, but rarely do the emotions feel manipulated or forced. A large measure of the film's effectiveness comes from the sincere, understated performances of the entire cast, from Corey and Lindfors to the bit players.

As Mary, Sullavan shines in a dazzling manner. Her performance gives the movie its heart and deep emotional connection. The beauty of Sullavan's heartbreaking portrayal is that one is rarely aware that she is giving a performance. Rather, one feels like a privileged observer into a woman's innermost thoughts and emotions. Her performance as Mary endures as one of Sullavan's masterpieces alongside Patricia Hollman and Klara Nowak. It is a fitting ending to a short but brilliant film career.

31

Renewed Interest

For the first time since Voice of the Turtle, *I really want to work.*[1]

After *No Sad Songs for Me*, Sullavan was again a hot commodity. Movie and stage offers poured in with a return to Broadway in Samson Raphaelson's *Hilda Crane* the most persistent offer. However, the star proved elusive. "It will take wild horses to drag Margaret Sullavan away from Connecticut while her children are in school," Parsons cautioned.[2]

Columbia tried to entice Sullavan with *Homeward Borne*, based on a bestseller by actress-turned-author Ruth Chatterton. Sullavan's interest was piqued and she agreed to star in it. But the screenplay did not satisfy her and the project was abandoned by mid–1951. *Homeward Borne* was produced as a *Playhouse 90* TV episode starring Linda Darnell in 1957.

As she fended Columbia off, Sullavan and Kenneth Wagg were married on August 30, 1950, with little media attention. According to an article, "A maid in the home of former actress Margaret Sullavan said her employer and Kenneth Arthur Wagg, a London businessman, were married yesterday somewhere on Long Island. Miss Sullavan telephoned the news to her, the maid said, but she insisted 'I didn't get any information whatever' when pressed for more details."[3]

Kenneth Arthur Wagg, the son of Henry John Wagg and Georgie Eleanor Lister, was born in England on March 6, 1909. While attending Eton College, a private boarding school for teenage boys, he discovered a talent for rackets. Considered one of the fastest game in the world, rackets (sometimes spelled racquets) is an indoor sport played on an enclosed granite court with a hard ball which travels at speeds exceeding 100 miles an hour. Wagg proved an outstanding player and part of a winning pair of both British and American doubles championships over a 20-year period. He was once described by the *London Times* as "a brilliant player with one of the best backhand strokes seen since the [first world] war."[4]

Wagg went into his family's banking business after graduating from Magdalen College. In 1933, he married Rachel Katherine Horlick and became a director of her family's food-making firm, Horlick's Malted Milk. They had four sons: Jeremy (born 1933), Timothy (1934), Anthony (1941) and Michael (1942). During World War II, Wagg served with the Rifle Brigade in North Africa and achieved the ranks of lieutenant-colonel. After the war, he became chairman of Horlick's subsidiary located in Racine, Wisconsin, despite his divorce in 1946. After his marriage to Sullavan, Wagg split his time between his English estate, where the boys resided, and Greenwich.

The Hayward children viewed Wagg as a gentle man with a quiet sense of humor and a tremendous amount of patience. More importantly, Brooke reflected, "He gave to our lives a structure and continuity if not the excitement we longed for."[5] Despite their fondness for Wagg, however, the children felt he was no match for their mother's temperament. While perceived as a fawning lapdog by others, Wagg was exactly what Sullavan needed in her life. The marriage lacked the passion and excitement of her other marriages, but Sullavan found a man who was devoted and provided a secure, stable relationship.

The newlyweds honeymooned at Wagg's English estate. Parsons reported in early November that "she's not giving up the screen as has been printed, even though her bridegroom ... spends a great deal of time in the United States, so she'll make a picture now and then."[6] However, the unpredictable star had other ideas. According to another report, "Miss Sullavan said she had no immediate plans for returning to the stage or screen."[7]

On April 20, 1951, Sullavan appeared in a TV production of "Touchstone," based on Edith Wharton's novel. *Variety* wrote, "[Sullavam] turned in a fine portrayal, with that throaty voice and starry-eyed gaze being particularly suited to the role."

In late August, it was reported that Sullavan signed to appear on *Schlitz Playhouse of the Stars* at a salary up to $5000 per show. The first program was an adaptation of Noël Coward's "Still Life" with Wendell Corey. The program was aired on October 26, 1951, despite a near postponement due to the death of Corey's father. *Variety* had special praise for the leading lady: "Miss Sullavan turned in a top-drawer performance." The program was a rating success, and there was a repeat telecast on November 6. On December 7, Sullavan appeared in a second *Schlitz* presentation, "The Nymph and the Lamp" with Robert Preston. Despite the high-powered marquee names, there were no *Variety* or *Billboard* reviews of this program.

Hollywood was again interested in securing Sullavan's services. Under consideration were such projects as *The Girl with the Golden Mandolin*, *The Gardenia* and *Miss Brown, My Mother*. As Parsons ruminated, "When Margaret finished *No Sad Songs for Me* her friends thought it might be her Hollywood swan song. Not that she didn't like it—but she's just so much happier in the East with her husband and children and Broadway close by."[8]

In February 1952, Sullavan was nominated for an Emmy Award along with Helen Hayes, Maria Riva, Mary Sinclair and Imogene Coca. Although no specific performance was given for any of the nominees, it is assumed that Sullavan received the nomination for "Still Life." There was considerable controversy when the winners were announced. "Much professional criticism followed the Academy of Television Arts and Sciences recent selection of Sid Caesar and Imogene Coca as the best TV actor and actress of the year," sniped one columnist. "Caesar and Miss Coca, both comics, won gold-tinted 'Emmys' away from such stellar competition as Robert Montgomery, Thomas Mitchell, Walter Hampden, Helen Hayes and Margaret Sullavan."[9] Television critic Mark Barron likewise deplored the "mixed-up TV Academy-Emmy classifications…. There's only one answer: Separate awards for dramatic and comedy."[10] The following year, the two categories were implemented.

By this time, Sullavan was restless and bored. Her children were getting older and were away at various private schools. Wagg was traveling to Racine and England for business. She needed something artistically creative, but none of the movie, television or stage scripts interested her. One day she received an unmarked transcript of a new play called *The Deep Blue Sea*. When she read it, she knew that it was time to return to Broadway.

The play was written by English playwright Terence Rattigan, who had tremendous success in London with plays like *The Winslow Boy* and *The Browning Version*. However, with the exceptions of *The Winslow Boy* and *O Mistress Mine*, Rattigan did not fare as well in New York. He desperately wanted to establish his reputation in New York and he was hoping his latest play would help him achieve that elusive dream.

A closeted homosexual, Rattigan originally conceived the play about a doomed relationship between two men. This scenario mirrored his real-life relationship with Kenneth Morgan, who left Rattigan for a younger man. Morgan eventually committed suicide by gas when the affair abruptly ended. Rattigan was hesitant to proceed with this idea as he was fearful of revealing his true sexual orientation when homosexuality was viewed as a psychologically deviant disease. Secondly, he knew the Lord Chamberlain would never approve the play for public performance. Instead, Rattigan centered the play around a married woman and her much younger lover. Over the years, rumors suggested Rattigan had written a play about a homosexual couple and then rewrote it. In his extensive research, Geoffrey Wansell found no evidence to support that claim. Nonetheless, those closest to Rattigan noted obvious parallels to the playwright's private life. An intensely personal piece of work, *The Deep Blue Sea* represented, as Rattigan confided to friend Laurence Olivier, "the phenomenon of love is inexplicable in terms of logic."[11] Rattigan completed his play in August 1951, with Broadway as its destination. However, he was unwilling to risk another New York snub, so he made plans for its London debut.

While the London production was in rehearsals, Rattigan decided Sullavan would be the actress who could ensure its critical and financial success in New York. After she expressed interest, Rattigan made a trip to New York to discuss the play in further detail with her and producers Alfred de Liagre and John C. Wilson. It was arranged for Sullavan to attend a performance in London.

The Deep Blue Sea begins with Hester Collyer's neighbors discovering that she has made a failed suicide attempt. A doctor who lives upstairs, Mr. Miller, is summoned. Hester reveals she had recently left her husband, a respectable High Court Judge, for an irresponsible, hard-drinking former RAF pilot, Freddy Page. Their relationship began as a physical and passionate one, but his feelings for her cooled over time. Hester desperately tried to hold on to him. The painful aftershocks of her suicide attempt cause Freddy to withdraw even further, thus jeopardizing any hopes of reconciliation. Through Miller's intervention, Hester realizes that Miller, too, has been hurt by unequal love (although, in his case, it was a homosexual relationship). These social outcasts, with their emotions raw with pain, form a common bond with each other. Rattigan originally intended for Hester to kill herself at the end. However, when he finished the script, he came to the conclusion that it would be better for her to live.

The Deep Blue Sea opened in London on March 6, 1952, and was a tremendous critical and box office success as it struck a deep chord with audiences. The cast, particularly Peggy Ashcroft as Hester, was lauded for their heartbreaking performances. The critics hailed it as one of Rattigan's more introspective and mature works as it perfectly conveyed the overall mood of post–World War II life in England.

News of Rattigan's triumph reached New York and Sullavan found the justification to leave her family behind. In April, Sullavan and Mrs. de Liagre made the voyage to England. Upon seeing Ashcroft's performance, Rattigan observed that Sullavan was "very frightened of the part."[12] In an interview with Quirk in 1952, Sullavan said that she fell in love with the play. Within weeks, it was reported that Sullavan had agreed to star in the production.

What really excited Sullavan was that her character was close to her age. As she later remarked, "I have nearly always had the problem of playing roles that were younger than I really was. In *The Deep Blue Sea* I am a mature woman, something more in the nature of my true age and I feel more comfortable and genuine doing it." More importantly, she admired the play because "it is a play about serious, intelligent people, about life simply within our own families and the lives of our friends and neighbors." With her usual dedication to her craft, Sullavan began learning her lines long before rehearsals commenced.

"I learned the lines for *The Deep Blue Sea* in my own home between sessions of mowing the grass, making plans with the children and doing my housework. It was difficult, because I learn so much faster when I am rehearsing with other players and we can exchange cues."[13]

The original director, Frith Banbury, was brought over from England. Rattigan and Banbury hoped that Kenneth More would recreate his role as Freddie, but a film commitment prevented this. In his place, Banbury convinced his original choice for the London production, Jimmy Hanley, to leave his acting gig in Australia.

Banbury recalled that Sullavan "was this enchanting, tiny little thing." However, as rehearsals progressed, he felt she was unable to play the part as envisioned. Banbury found that Sullavan "could not capture the tragedy at the heart of Hester" as Ashcroft had so beautifully done. Banbury tried to persuade Sullavan to stop acting like a little girl, which was her conception of the part. Sullavan did not deal well with Banbury's direction and "there were screams and shouts all the time" during rehearsals, recalled Banbury.[14]

VOLUME 52   APRIL 13, 1953   NUMBER 24

The PLAYGOER
TRADE MARK

A Magazine for the Cass Theatre

Despite the playwright's misgivings about her performance, Sullavan received excellent notices while *The Deep Blue Sea* (1952) was widely panned.

Sullavan demanded a different director, preferably Joshua Logan, but Rattigan kept Banbury.

Prior to the try-out tour, Sullavan became more agitated and uncomfortable with the role. She did not trust Banbury and was fearful of being unfavorably compared to Ashcroft. To complicate matters, she hated the actor who played her lover. Since the time Banbury had seen Hanley last, he had let his appearance and weight go. Sullavan was horrified to act opposite an actor who did not fit her conception of Freddie.

The play opened in New Haven on October 8, 1952. *Variety* opined that Sullavan fans "will be treated to a good performance, but unless the scripting end develops into sturdier fare, the verdict will probably be regret over not selecting a worthier vehicle.… It is simply a case of not containing enough meat, fire or sustained power to lift an audience to dramatic heights—a requirement that seems to be synonymous with Broadway success these days." Despite fine notices for Sullavan, Rattigan and Banbury believed she was not playing the part correctly. After two weeks in Boston, the play traveled to Washington, D.C., with little change in her performance. While there, Rattigan wrote his mother:

> She's not a good enough actress to play it. She has only two approaches to the part and both are inadequate. Either she plays it all out for "pathos," using her famous tearful voice (put on), in which case she is dull and self-pitying, and the play goes down the drain, or she plays it with her own voice

and personality, in which case the play equally goes down the drain because the part becomes hard and matter of fact, and you lose patience with Hester, and can't see what all the fuss is about.

Distressed, Rattigan considered cancelling the Broadway opening. The producers persuaded him otherwise. Due to Sullavan's reputation, there was a substantial advance in ticket sales, therefore assuring a profitable opening. Rattigan reluctantly agreed. "Our single hope of success is to get good notices for her—which she'll get at the expense of the play—and let people think she's being wonderful in a banal little vehicle."[15]

The play opened at the Morosco on November 5 and the reviews confirmed Rattigan's worst fears. While Sullavan scored a personal success, the play was deemed unworthy of her talents. The *New York Journal-American* effusively wrote that Sullavan had "scored a tumultuous triumph" as the part "offers a more challenging and profound role than those usually associated with her, and in her mastery of the central character one has the conviction that she indeed reached the full maturity as an actress of depth and stature." The critic believed that *Deep Blue Sea* "may not be Mr. Rattigan's best play, but it is certainly Miss Sullavan's." Columnist Inez Robb likened Sullavan's appearance to a "theatrical landslide" and said that the play "seems destined to repeat its [London] triumphs here with the aid of an incandescent and moving performance by Miss Sullavan." Robb concluded her critique by asserting, "Miss Sullavan's Hester is triumphant acting from beginning to end." Her comment "the husky voice, with the familiar catch in the throat, is still Miss Sullavan's particular trademark" must have caused Rattigan and Banbury to throw their hands up in defeat.[16]

There were those who felt Sullavan was miscast. Dorothy Kilgallen sniped, "*The Deep Blue Sea* is a major disappointment. [Sullavan] struggles valiantly with the dullest and most dilatory dialogue of the season, but all her sobbing, screaming, choking and emotional gymnastics fail to lift a single scene above the level of simple boredom."[17]

Despite his misgivings about Sullavan's performance, Rattigan wrote, "In spite of all this, I find I like her very much. She genuinely loves the play, and wants to play it honestly." However, Rattigan sensed she was incapable of playing the role honestly. As a result, she became "hysterical because she knows she can't."[18]

Sullavan brought in the "Standing Room Only" crowds. As for Rattigan, this run was a failure. As columnist Jack Gaver noted, "Rattigan has been one of the brighter successes in the British theater and most of his works have been done here, but so far as this reviewer is concerned he has yet to come up with a really first-rate job."[19] In the mid–1950s, Rattigan finally hit pay dirt when *Separate Tables* ran for almost a year on Broadway.

During *Deep Blue Sea*'s run, Sullavan revealed to one reporter, "Every night when the curtain goes down, I think 'I can't do this again.' But the next day, after a good night's sleep, I have changed my mind and I'm Hester again."[20] Other interviews reflected Sullavan's conflicting feelings about being away from her family:

> I think women—especially women in the theater—are particularly admirable who can manage career, a home and children simultaneously. I can't…. The children mind me not being home…. The other night, Bridget went to her first dance in her first real party dress, and she had to get all dressed up at five in the afternoon so I could see her before I ran for the theater.[21]

By mid–January, ticket sales began to drop off. To re-stimulate interest, Sullavan and some cast members appeared on Ed Sullivan's television show *The Toast of the Town*, and enacted a brief scene on January 11, 1953. *Variety* observed that Sullavan "scored solidly in one of the play's most dramatic moments. Star demonstrated her fine thesping abilities by building to a peak pitch in the scene, *sans* the lead-in she would have in the show itself."

The play closed on February 28, 1953, after 132 performances. Believing Sullavan's name would be a potent draw on the road, the producers sent the play on a tour. Opening on March 9 in Baltimore, *The Deep Blue Sea* also played in Philadelphia, Cincinnati, etc. Reviews were mixed and box office receipts were spotty. According to the *Pittsburgh Post-Gazette*: "The Nixon [Theater] is too big and the play there is too little for Miss Margaret Sullavan. Her smoldering emotional style of acting needs a more intimate sounding board than the theater, and something with more substance than *The Deep Blue Sea*. It is a plainly workaday drama and terribly hackneyed." There was some reserved praise for Sullavan, but the critic felt "she has been saddled to an insincere role and the strain of trying to pull together a scrubby part shows…. She is an actress of strength and overpowering conviction all right, with the most hypnotic voice in the theater today, but in *The Deep Blue Sea*, Miss Sullavan has settled for work beneath her station." The *Detroit News* found much to admire:

> Miss Sullavan, being favored with the indefinable show of authority which none but our first actresses possess, plus charm and patrician ways and obvious intelligence, is admirably suited to the part of Hester; making even its extravagances credible; running a noteworthy emotional and voice range.

When Sullavan's contract was up, she left the play after its Milwaukee engagement on May 3. Uta Hagan substituted for Sullavan in Chicago, but she lacked name recognition and failed to draw theatergoers. The producers shut the play down shortly after.

In addition to numerous theatrical revivals, including two major British productions in 2011, Rattigan's play has been seen several times on the small screen. The first television film was broadcast in 1954 for BBC Television with Kenneth More. More BBC versions aired in 1974 and 1994. There were also two film versions. The first, released in 1955, was directed by Anatole Litvak and starred Vivien Leigh as Hester and More as Freddie. Rattigan felt that Litvak was the wrong director for the project and disliked his association with the film. Leigh, too, was miscast as the tormented woman. It's distressing watching her switch from high-gear dramatic angst to calm, cool authority in seconds. Leigh's interpretation suggests that Hester must have been mentally unhinged long before her affair.

A second British film version was released in 2011 with Rachel Weisz and Tom Hiddleston. Lush production values and exquisite photography cannot disguise the fact that Rattigan's dissertation on the iniquity of love is still a tiresome bore.

During the Broadway run, Sullavan told a reporter, "Under the circumstances, I find it impossible to do a play more often than once every eight or ten years."[22] But after leaving Rattigan's play, Sullavan received the unlikely offer to star in Samuel A. Taylor's *Sabrina Fair*. This association proved to be one of the happiest in her career and personal life.

32

The Happiest Time

In spite of the anguish with which she regarded her profession, Mother, when actually working, was fiercely dedicated to it.[1]—*Brooke Hayward*

Samuel A. Taylor worked many years as a play doctor and re-writer in New York. He worked on the Clifford Goldsmith play *What a Life* (1938), which was later adapted into the radio series *The Aldrich Family* which ran for 14 years. During his time as a radio writer, Taylor spent several years working on a play, *The Happy Time*. That play made its Broadway debut in 1950 and proved to be a smash that ran for nearly two years. His second play, *Nina*, which opened in 1951 with a disgruntled Gloria Swanson, was poorly received and lasted 45 performances. His third play, *Sabrina Fair*, solidified his reputation as a playwright.

Sabrina Fair's premise is deceptively simple: Sabrina Fairchild, the daughter of a chauffeur to the wealthy Larrabee family of Long Island, returns from a long stay in Paris. Her experience has transformed the once-awkward teenager into a young woman of beauty, and sophistication, with an infectious zest for living. Having long ago ignored Sabrina, the Larabee family cannot help but pay attention to her now. Sabrina once had a crush on David, the young, irresponsible playboy of the family. This time, however, she finds herself attracted to the elder son, Linus, because of his intelligence, practical nature and knowledge of the world. Linus, on the other hand, encourages Sabrina to pursue David out of a perverse sense of amusement. David confides to his mother, Maude, that he wants to marry Sabrina. Maude discusses it with Sabrina's father, who disapproves of David. When Sabrina learns what's been happening without her knowledge, she comes to the conclusion that she does not love David after all. After it is disclosed that Sabrina's father has amassed a fortune on the stock market over the past decades (keeping the Larrabee family financially solvent), she decides to return to Paris. Linus finally admits his love and the couple seems destined for a fairy tale ending.

Barbara Bel Geddes, who had just completed a two-year Broadway run in *The Moon Is Blue*, was originally cast as Sabrina. But prior to rehearsals, she bowed out. Taylor thought of Sullavan, but director H.C. Potter (who directed *The Shopworn Angel*) did not believe she could convincingly play a 24-year-old woman. Neither did the 44-year-old Sullavan.

Taylor would not be dissuaded. According to a *Saturday Review of Literature* article, which sounds suspiciously like fabricated publicity, Taylor and Potter went to Sullavan's home on a hot summer day. They found her at the pool with Brooke and Bridget. Supposedly, Potter was unable to distinguish the middle-aged mother from her teenage daughters. Sullavan signed for the play that day.

Hayward recalled, "Mother claimed that *Sabrina* was one of the happiest theatrical experiences of her life."[2] One of the reasons was that, according to Sullavan, the producers assembled the "best cast I've ever worked with": Joseph Cotten as Linus, Scott McKay as David, Russell Collins as Fairchild, John Cromwell as Oliver, the Larrabee patriarch, and Cathleen Nesbitt as Maude, the Larrabee matriarch.[3] Sullavan formed many lasting relationships, including Joseph and Lenore Cotten, Samuel and Suzanne Taylor, and Nesbitt. Cotten felt that playing with Sullavan was one of the most delightful experiences he ever had as an actor.

English actress Nesbit reflected on her association with the play in her autobiography: "What a happy year that was."[4] This was in spite of the fact that she "found the play delightful but my part dull. I nearly turned it down till I heard that two of my favorite film stars, Margaret Sullavan and Joseph Cotten, were going to be in it." On her relationship with Sullavan:

> People told me that Maggie was "difficult" in the theater. I discovered it was for the same reason that Marie Tempest was said to be difficult; she was an absolute perfectionist. At rehearsals she would almost drive everyone mad, most of all herself, in her quest for truth. She had mannerisms of speech that made people say that she was affected. But she was the most honest actress I have ever played with.

What was most remarkable about Sullavan, according to Nesbitt, was that while "immensely disciplined on the stage, she was not so in life. I have always been fascinated by people who vent their emotions unrestrainedly."[5] She elaborated:

> Maggie could flare up suddenly like a thunderstorm; if the lightning blasted you, you suffered for a moment, but forgave her long before she came begging forgiveness like a child.... Sometimes when she said something to her director or fellow actor that I thought unforgivable, I would find myself within a few hours trying to make her forgive herself![6]

Reflecting on Sullavan's untimely death, Nesbitt reminisced, "Maggie died so tragically young and so suddenly that I felt I had lost a beloved sister.... There was so little I could give to her, I like to think that loving someone is itself a gift, that loved ones do take beauty from those who loved them."[7]

Also in the cast was an old friend of Sullavan's, blacklisted Hollywood director John Cromwell who directed *So Ends Our Night*. After being ostracized by the Hollywood colony, Cromwell returned to Broadway in 1952 and appeared in *Point of No Return*, which starred Henry Fonda. Cromwell won a Tony for best supporting actor.

When *Sabrina Fair* opened in New Haven on October 8, it was obvious it was lacking something crucial in its performance. According to *Variety*, "Commenting in terms of initials, before *Sabrina Fair* can hope to approximate SRO, it's going to require an MD.... This one can become either a moderately amusing play or a distinct theatrical disappointment. It doesn't seem to have the makings of a solid click.... It is a matter of two sterling players [Sullavan and Cotten] wasting their histrionic fragrance on the air of a literary desert." By the time the play moved to Boston for two weeks, things were not any better according to this report: "The Margaret Sullavan-Joseph Cotten marquee power overcame the ho-hum reports for *Sabrina Fair* in Boston."[8] The New York critics could be notoriously harsh on a weak vehicle, despite the star power of its performers, and tensions ran high.

During the last days of the Philadelphia engagement, the situation was getting worse as the play began to fall apart. Potter was working so closely with Taylor that he neglected his role as director. The producers decided Potter should leave. Two years earlier, Potter was fired from *Point of No Return* during its try-out tour. Robert Sherwood was brought in from New York to salvage the play, but things continued to worsen. The producers looked

Sabrina Fair (1953) with (*left to right*) Scott McKay, Michael Steele and Sullavan. Sullavan regarded her association with this play as one of the happiest times of her life.

for another director with little success. Finally, Sullavan had enough. She knew that, if Potter was fired from this play, his career would be ruined. She didn't think he deserved to be fired and wanted no part of the decision. She threatened that she would walk out on the play if they carried through with the dismissal. The producers threatened legal action with Actors' Equity. "Do whatever you want," she countered, "kick me out, but I'll be damned if I'll be responsible for Hank Potter's being buried as a director."[9] Potter was brought back and everyone held their breath.

Sabrina Fair opened at the National Theatre on November 11, 1953, and received mixed reviews. The *Daily Mirror* raved, "Miss Sullavan, one of our brightest stars, has one of her best roles in years, and is dazzling in it…. *Sabrina Fair*, in our book, is a delightful, sparkling hit." The *Post* opined, "Once more a lot of fine actors, a handsome production and a general expertness of staging are lavished on an undistinguished play…. I have a suspicion that Margaret Sullavan has grown a trifle mannered as an actress and she may be slightly mature for her role, but she is a highly accomplished and effective performer, and she portrays the chauffeur's daughter with all of her celebrated guile and charm." *Variety* weighed in: "Miss

Sullavan is unquestionably miscast as the girl of about 26 or 27.... But Miss Sullavan is thoroughly convincing as the romantic, but level-headed Sabrina, and of course her magnetic stage personality and potent box office draw will help the show enormously."

Despite the odds, *Sabrina Fair* emerged as the smash hit of the season and drew SRO crowds for many months, much to the bewilderment of the critics. According to columnist John Crosby, the answer was obvious. Calling the play a "plush, sparkling" updated version of the Cinderella fable, he reasoned that "it's just possible we are the mood for fairy stories again."[10]

More remarkable than the play's success was that Sullavan was able to completely inhabit a role that she was too old to play. This is by no means an easy feat to pull off, as any actor will testify. In the early 1990s, my wife and I were fortunate enough to see Debbie Reynolds' performance in a touring production of *The Unsinkable Molly Brown* in Rochester, New York. Although Reynolds was close to 60 at the time, the audience was so mesmerized by her star power that they were willing to wholeheartedly accept her in the role of a woman in her twenties. Likewise, since the part of Sabrina was so close to the audience's perception of the "Margaret Sullavan Persona," many were willing to disregard the obvious and revel in the presence of a magnetic stage performer. Brooke came from Madeira to see for herself if her mother could pull off this seemingly impossible feat. "She was flawless in the play," Hayward recalled, "and not a day over 20.... It was the most extraordinary illusion I have ever seen."[11]

In an interview, Sullavan called *Sabrina Fair* a "dull, gay play."[12] She was conflicted between acting and motherhood and resented that her acting career kept her away from her children. As a perfectionist with nagging self-doubts, she continually struggled with her desire to perform while being the "perfect" mother.

On May 29, 1954, she and Cotten left the play and Leora Dana and Tod Andrews assumed their roles. Without the star power of the Sullavan-Cotten teaming, the play closed on August 31 after 318 performances. Taylor's play has not been revived much over the years and has languished in relative obscurity.

The play's rights were bought by Paramount in March 1953. It was stipulated that the film would not be released until the play ran on Broadway for a year. The film, titled *Sabrina*, began production in late September 1953. The role of Sabrina was envisioned for screen newcomer Audrey Hepburn, who made a sensation in her Hollywood film debut, *Roman Holiday*, a few months earlier. Billy Wilder, director of such hard-hitting classics as *Double Indemnity* (1944) and *Sunset Blvd.* (1950), wrote the screenplay, produced and directed. Taylor was hired to help adapt the play for the screen. However, Taylor was so dismayed by Wilder's tendency to rewrite his original work that he eventually quit. The considerably reworked film emerged as a scintillating romantic comedy that has stood the test of time most remarkably. A radiantly luminous Hepburn is perfectly cast as Sabrina, while Humphrey Bogart (a last-minute replacement for Cary Grant) and William Holden offer splendid support in the roles of Linus and David Larrabee. The extraordinary star presence and Wilder's subtle but insightful direction enable the film to transcend its ordinary tale into a magical experience. *Sabrina* was one of Paramount's biggest hits in 1954 and garnered several Academy Award nominations.

Sabrina inspired three foreign-language films: the Tahitian-produced *Manappandal* (1961); the Telugian-produced *Intiki Deepam Illaley* (1961); and the Hindu-produced *Yeh Dillagi* (1994).

A second English-language version (bearing the same name as the 1954 film) was released in 1995 with Harrison Ford, Julia Ormond and Greg Kinnear. It suffered in comparison to its famed predecessor as evidenced by its critical reviews and box office receipts. While an enjoyable. lushly produced romcom film and competently played by a good-looking cast, this *Sabrina* is often earthbound due to its lack of sheer star power. The fairy tale theme seems lost amidst the gritty reality of the '90s.

Once Sullavan was back in Connecticut, film offers came her way. Wilder hoped she would appear opposite Fredric March and Humphrey Bogart in *The Desperate Hours*, but Martha Scott eventually played the role. Other movie offers were turned down because Sullavan wanted to devote herself to her children.

In mid–September 1954, it was announced that Sullavan would headline the cast of the *Producers' Showcase* presentation of the 1945 stage hit *State of the Union*, for television. There was considerable surprise as columnist Jack O'Brian caustically commented, "Ralph Bellamy seemed a cinch to play his B'dw'y lead in NBC TV's upcoming 'State of the Union,' but Margaret Sullavan refused to star in same unless Joseph Cotten played opposite. Joe gets the job."[13] In an interview, Sullavan claimed that she did not think Bellamy looked "presidential" enough to be convincing. Perhaps the real reason behind Sullavan's insistence on Cotten had to do with her hearing issues: Cotten had a richer, deeper voice than Bellamy did. She was thrilled to be working with Cotten (in his television debut) and John Cromwell again.

"That should make it easier," she joked to an interviewer. "If we blow a line, we can

Left to right: Nina Foch, Joseph Cotten and Sullavan in TV's *State of the Union* (1954). Sullavan's insistence on Cotten over Ralph Bellamy (who originated the role on Broadway) raised some eyebrows in the industry.

always go right into *Sabrina*."[14] To another interviewer, she enthused, "This is the first time in 17 or 18 years that I don't have any acting commitments or children at home. And I'm enjoying every minute of it."[15] Otherwise, she still hated performing on live television. "It's hellish," she said in a *New York Times* interview:

> You rehearse for three weeks and then you get no chance for a real try-out. It's awful. We're like stock company actors who don't know their lines. A television program is badly paced as a rule, just like a Broadway play when it opens in New Haven. With a play, it often takes a week or ten days to get it right. When a television performance is over, it is most dissatisfying.

When asked why she performed on television if she despised it so, Sullavan replied matter-of-factly, "I don't want to work. By doing [television], I can afford not to." As for her current assignment, she conceded, "My part in 'State of the Union' is a perfectly nice part."[16]

On November 15, NBC aired the 90-minute color production. Supporting Sullavan, Cotten and Cromwell were veteran screen and television performers Nina Foch, Ray Walston, Muriel Kirkland and Royal Beal. The television adaptation was hailed a success. The *San Mateo* (CA) *Times* raved that it "proved to be 90 minutes of top television drama…. Margaret Sullavan proved again that she is one of America's greatest actresses. The support she received from Joseph Cotten did much to make last Monday's event top television fare." Also enthusiastic was the *New York Times* television critic: "The magic of theater touched television on Monday evening. Miss Sullavan was a joy, bringing charm, excitement and tenderness to the role of the candidate's lady."

Completing her latest commitment, Sullavan resumed her role as a mother of three teenagers.

33

Deeper Into Despair

We all felt very badly that her life seemed to be coming apart.[1]*—Jerry Asher*

Sullavan had begun to experience issues with her children in the early 1950s. As it is usually experienced in divorces, the children suffer greatly from the fall-out from a bitter split. Sullavan attempted to compensate for this with stricter discipline. Brooke recalled in an interview, "Mother didn't influence me nearly as much as Father did because I was ten years old when they divorced and my sister and brother were like eight and six, so I suspect Mother's tyrannical nature probably affected them more than it did me.... It did crush my sister but I don't know why. And it certainly crushed my brother."[2]

Leland's wife "Slim" found the children "bright, eccentric and bordering on the neurotic—a combination that provides a lot of irresistible surface charm." The children were internally tormented; in particular, "Slim" believed that Bridget and Billy were "deeply disturbed."[3] The adolescents were in constant conflict between asserting their burgeoning independence and questioning the parents' authority. What compounded the situation was that Leland was not any better emotionally equipped to deal with the two younger children. That was a recipe for disaster.

By 1955, the children spent most of the time away: Brooke (now 18) was attending Madeira College; Bridget (16) was abroad in Switzerland; and Bill (14) was at Lawrenceville, New Jersey. As "Slim" recalled, Brooke was the "most like her father—very sure of herself and capable of charming anything and anyone" (an apt description of Sullavan in her youth). As the peacekeeper, it was Brooke who was most sensitive to her mother's needs.

The other children had troubles of their own. Bill was struggling academically in school. It was believed that he was capable of doing better, but lacked the motivation or drive. In his early teenage years, the effects of the rancorous divorce wreaked havoc on his emotional state. As "Slim" recalled, Bridget was "quiet, shy and ethereal. It was if she'd drawn a circle around herself which you felt you wouldn't dare intrude."[4] She became more combative with her mother and challenged what she perceived as hypocritical behavior. In this case, Bridget embodied Sullavan's life at its unhealthiest and most emotionally fragile. It's no wonder Sullavan had difficulty dealing with Bridget.

By the summer of 1955, the deteriorating situation finally imploded. Sullavan came across a letter that Bridget had written; Brooke believed Bridget had intentionally left it out in the open. In the letter, Bridget described her hatred for her mother in no uncertain terms. The shock of reading her daughter's viperous words sent Sullavan reeling. "If you feel that way about me," she told Bridget, "then perhaps you should live with your father."[5] Sullavan was stunned when Bridget and Billy decided to leave. This impulsive decision sent Sullavan into severe depression. Close friends believed this was the beginning of the declining physical and mental health that led to her nervous breakdown. Her guilt over being an unfit mother was finally validated and she was devastated.

Almost undetected among this chaos was the fact that Sullavan was experiencing deafness in the right ear as she had in the left; it was later revealed that this condition manifested itself around 1952.

Back in December 1954, an newspaper item stated that Sullavan "would like to appear in *Janus*.... At present, José Ferrer is considering directing the play for a spring tour to be followed by a Broadway opening next season."[6] However, given the turmoil at the time, it was not a surprise when Sullavan put the play off. She later wrote friends, "This time I mean I've got enough money to retire. No more acting on stage or [in movies]."[7] Her family and close friends were caught off-guard, however, when Sullavan unex-

While Sullavan's marriage to Kenneth Wagg lacked the passion of the other three marriages, he provided stability and unwavering devotion as her personal life unraveled during the 1950s (Brooke Hayward Papers, 1911–1977, Billy Rose Theatre Division, The New York Public Library for the Performing Arts).

pectedly committed to star in *Janus* and serve as one of the financial backers. She had not recovered from Bridget and Bill's departure and it was feared she was neither physically nor mentally ready to tackle the grueling schedule of a new play.

Written by a housewife, Carolyn Green, *Janus* explores the idea of the *wife* who enjoys the benefits of marriage and a secret affair. Jessica (Sullavan) is the respectable wife of a midwestern tycoon, Gil (Robert Preston). She spends every summer alone in New York so she can focus on her "studies." What her husband does not realize is that she is involved with a quiet teacher, Denny (Claude Dauphin). Under the pen name of Janus, the two write best-selling "lusty, busty" historical fiction novels. Gil, who is supposed to be on an ocean voyage, decides to drop in unannounced and is astonished to find another man in the apartment. Not only does Jessica come clean, but she also takes the opportunity to convince her bewildered husband there is nothing wrong with her double life. Taken at face value, *Janus* doesn't seem to warrant much attention beyond a pleasant evening at the theater.

During its try-out tour from mid–October to mid–November, the play was judged a pleasant but unremarkable time-filler. In reviewing its Wilmington performance, *Variety* opined, "It's not yet ready for Broadway, but has possibilities as a laugh show." Sullavan was judged "charming" as "she handles her comedy moments with her familiar ease." What pushed the production into high gear, however, was the glittering performances by the players. The tour's box office business exceeded everyone's expectations.

When *Janus* opened at the Plymouth Theatre on November 24, 1955, there was no doubt it would enjoy a profitable run. Most of the critics were enthusiastic about Sullavan's performance. The *Commonweal* opined, "Miss Sullavan has, by now, transmuted all the mundane stuff of her daylight personality into the glowing dramatic image by which we know her; in this, she is at one with Hepburn, with Dietrich, with Bette Davis, with any performer who seeks to project his imaginative vision of reality." The *New Yorker* observed, "Sullavan obviously has one of the most gratifying parts in her distinguished career, and she does full justice to it.... [T]he voice that can switch so fetchingly from a growl to the tinkle of bells has never been employed to better effect; the manner, at once coltish and worldly, has never been more charming; the acute theatrical intelligence that can make the flattest lines sound sharp almost literate has never been more convincingly displayed." According to *Variety*,

> Not at all bad with Miss Sullavan looking as incredibly, impossibly young and trim and fervent as ever.... The star remains fetching, with a sort of level look and the familiar throaty intensity, individual voice modulations and knack with a laugh line. The combination is as captivating as ever.

On December 18, 1955, early in the play's run, Sullavan made her final television appearance as the Mystery Challenger on *What's My Line?*. Sullavan, while radiant and in good spirits, looks tired. Most interesting is her difficulty in understanding panelist Dorothy Kilgallen's questions, which were repeated by the host. (As a hearing-impaired person, I too find Kilgallen's diction periodically hard to decipher.)

Despite the play's success, Sullavan was miserable. What was lacking was the sense of camaraderie she enjoyed during *Sabrina Fair*. She and Preston did not get along. As Harold J. Kennedy recalled, "Maggie was the undisputed box office draw and I don't think Bob cared for that and Bob had the unquestionable show-stealing part and I know Maggie didn't care for that. At the end of one of their little 'discussions,' Bob said, 'Let's leave it this way, Maggie. You keep on bringing them in and I'll keep on entertaining them.'"[8]

Despite her assured, merry performance, production crew and cast members were shocked to witness lightning-quick changes in her demeanor once she stepped off the stage. Many were amazed that she held up during the performance as, off-stage, she looked as if she was suffering greatly from mental anguish. Years later, Preston recalled, "I know a lot of people in this business who go crazy.... I was in a play once with Margaret Sullavan and she hated performing so much I often wondered why she did it."[9]

By Christmas, Sullavan decided to leave the play when her contract ran out in April. She let the producers know of her decision, so they could find a replacement who would be a worthy box-office draw. Her last performance was on April 1, 1956. Claudette Colbert, the producers' original choice, was hired. Colbert, who had not performed on Broadway since 1929, disclosed, "When you replace another actress, you have to follow all her stage business so as not to throw the cast off. And my personality is very different from Maggie's. She has a fey quality in her comedy."[10] In reviewing Colbert's performance, *Variety* decided, "If she's not quite the practiced player of stage farce that Miss Sullavan is, she's obviously an excellent choice to hold the hit show together ... particularly since she's undoubtedly a substantial box office draw." Colbert left the show on June 9. She was replaced by Imogene

Coca, who apparently did not have that kind of draw as *Janus* closed on June 30, after 251 performances.

Back in Greenwich, Sullavan rested as she indulged in activities such as reading, long walks and meditation. She arranged a short vacation in Virginia with her old school friend Martha Justice Pender. While there, she caught up with old childhood friends. Sullavan told her friends, "There is no place in the world like Virginia. Some day I must have a bit of land here to retire to in my old age." Ironically, Louisa Venable Kyle mused, "Can the blithe spirit that is Margaret Sullavan ever grow old?"[11]

The other excitement that intruded into Sullavan's self-imposed exile occurred when Brooke, 19 years old, eloped with a Yale sophomore, Michael Thomas, in June. Thomas later cynically reflected, "This family was characterized by a total lack of love. Gestures were made, but I think it was impossible for Maggie or Leland to focus on any of their children for more than ten seconds without thoughts of themselves breaking in."[12]

For the moment, Sullavan was content to retire from acting. "After *Janus*, I said, 'No more.' I said that I was never going to work in the theater again."[13] By fall, however, she was restless and bored. She needed something to spark her creative energy. Old friend Felix Jackson approached her about a *Studio One* television program. Entitled "The Pilot," it told the story of Sister Mary Acquinas, a Roman Catholic nun who learned to fly. During World War II, she was contracted by the government to instruct novice pilots on various aerial maneuvers. Intrigued by the offer, Sullavan agreed to star, despite quiet objections from family and friends.

With obsessive dedication, Sullavan delved into the role with a fervor that surprised those close to her. Also surprising was her cooperation with the press. One interviewer noted, "She is unchanged, as lovely as ever.... Miss Sullavan is a delightful conversationalist." Asked why she was doing the episode, she replied, "Because the character of Sister Acquinas interests me."[14]

Unfortunately, she soon became dissatisfied. She requested the services of a Roman Catholic priest to help her with the details inherent in being a nun. Instead, much to her irritation, the producers consented to the services of a Methodist parson. Other issues arose and Sullavan was disheartened. After ten days of rehearsals, Sullavan was agitated after rehearsal on October 7. After a blow-up on the set, she stormed off to her dressing room. Sullavan later claimed to reporters she did not feel she could adequately play the part, but there may have been an incident which sparked her outburst. According to Kennedy, "What I was told, and what I believe, is that the talk-back mike in the control room was inadvertently left open and that as Miss Sullavan was leaving the sound stage she heard a voice saying: 'We'll never make that old hag look 40.'"[15] Jackson recalled, "I didn't take her seriously, because other actresses have said [they would walk out] under strain and calmed down later. In her dressing room and in the presence of her husband, I concluded that she would calm down by Monday morning and everything would be all right."[16]

On Monday, Sullavan failed to report for the final dress rehearsal at 2:30 p.m. Frantic, the producers phoned Sullavan's agent, who tried contacting the actress at her Greenwich home. Finally, Wagg was reached but there are conflicting accounts of his explanations for his wife's disappearance. According to one report, Wagg stated, "My wife was taken ill this morning. She hasn't been well for some time. I think it's probably the strain again."[17] However, other reports indicated Wagg denied having seen his wife that day. With hours to spare, it was decided to rerun an old *Studio One* production, "The Remarkable Incident at Carson Corners." On October 10, the *New York Times* reported, "The failure of Miss Sullavan to show up for her scheduled television performance continued to baffle the entertainment world." It also reported that Sullavan was not in a hospital as reported earlier, but "was safe and well and staying with friends."[18] In one report, two cab drivers accounted for Sullavan's whereabouts that Monday afternoon. One disclosed he picked her up in front of her River-side Drive home and drove her to the 125TH Street New York Central Railroad station. The other driver said he picked her at the Greenwich station, stopped at a bank, then drove her home. "She seemed in good spirits," he remarked.[19] Many who worked with her were shocked by these reports as they have always known her to be a consummate professional. "Margaret's too much of a trouper for that," said Claude Dauphin's wife, actress Norma Eberhardt. "After all, she was ill when she did [*Janus*] with my husband, she was exhausted and run down."[20] The negative publicity mounted.

After three days, Sullavan finally spoke to reporters. Her main line of defense was she did not feel that she could give the role "the kind of performance it deserved" and had told Jackson on Sunday night that she would not perform. Sullavan elaborated:

> I regret the inconvenience it has caused anyone, including my non-availability to the press. Last Sun-day … I concluded that I was unable to give it the kind of performance it deserved and informed the producer of my dissatisfaction in general and with myself in particular and advised him that I did not feel up to the role and could not appear the next day for further rehearsals or the performance. The producer, a veteran and excellent producer, as well as a friend of mine, assured me that, the next day, the causes of my dissatisfaction would disappear. However, I insisted that I be replaced.… The next day, in order to avoid pressure from the studio and my associates to appear, I decided to leave town and, in order to spare my husband, told him that I would not disclose where I was going for a few days.

Sullavan claimed, "While driving to the home of mutual friends … I overheard a radio report that I was missing, and immediately telephoned my agent, Miriam Howell, to tell her that I was well, safe, and on the way to friends. My lawyer, H. William Fitelson, advised CBS of this. I regret the incident and I am glad it is closed."[21]

Not everybody believed her story. Jackson asserted, "At no time did she ask me to replace her.… She couldn't possibly have thought there was someone ready to step into her role." Hubbell Robinson, vice-president of CBS programming, reasoned, "When you have $40,000 invested in a production, the star just doesn't whimsically walk out.… [W]e can't understand why an actress, Miss Sullavan included, can be condoned in signing and con-tracting to star in a show costing $40,000 in production expenses and another $100,000 in network charges and then leave everything hanging on a whim."[22] The executives were ready to engage in legal action unless Sullavan could prove she was ill and under medical attention as previously reported. Sullavan remained at the Osborns' Connecticut home until Wagg arrived. The gravity of the situation hit and she suffered from serious bouts of depression. Wagg consulted her doctor, who recommended she be taken to the Austin Riggs Foundation, a private sanitarium in Stockbridge, Massachusetts. "The Pilot" was broadcast on November 12 with Nancy Kelly and Barbara O'Neil.

In mid–November, the *New York Times* revealed that Sullavan had been "resting" in a sanitarium dedicated to the study and treatment of psychoneurosis. According to her agent, "Miss Sullavan went to the center about two or three weeks ago to get a rest. She will be there at least two more weeks."[23] Those who knew the actress were shocked. "Breakdown? With a strong personality like hers! It's hard to believe." one unidentified actor was quoted as saying.[24] Sullavan remained at Austin Riggs for two and a half months. When she returned home after Christmas, she impulsively sold the house and all of her household possessions to make a fresh start elsewhere.

In January, 1957, it was reported the Waggs flew to California to set up a film deal, but nothing came of it. In early February, Sullavan became a grandmother to Brooke's son, Jeffrey. Later that month, things appeared better as it was reported that Sullavan "is now fully recovered. She played her favorite card game. Hearts, with David Selznick and Ben Hecht this past week."[25] This recovery was short-lived as indicated by this news item: "The Margaret Sullavan saga, which was dramatized in headlines when she walked out on a television show because of 'nerves,' has taken another, even sadder turn."[26] Various reports chronicling the ups and downs of her health continued sporadically until early summer of 1958.

In July, Parsons reported the surprising news of Sullavan's return to the stage via summer stock in *Sabrina Fair* with Joseph Cotten, Cathleen Nesbitt and Luella Gear from the Broadway production. After an absence of two years, she was eager to act again despite her fragile mental health. Her agent arranged for three one-week engagements beginning in mid–July. It was Cotten who recommended starting the tour at Kennedy's Grist Mill Playhouse in Andover, New Jersey. Cotten previously worked with Harold J. Kennedy in Orson Welles' Mercury Theater troupe in the late 1930s and knew he possessed the directorial technique and patience to handle Sullavan. Kennedy was contacted by Sullavan's agent, who explained, "Miss Sullavan, as you know, has been ill and now she wants to find out whether she still has what it takes to work on the stage. She thinks summer stock would be the place to find out." Kennedy needed little time to mull over the offer: He said, "Margaret Sullavan had always been my favorite actress."[27] Kennedy accepted the offer and plans were made for a meeting between Sullavan, Cotten and her director.

When Kennedy met Sullavan, he found that "she seemed in very high spirits, looked 18, ate ravenously, and seemed to enjoy my stories about the rigors of summer stock." However, when Sullavan showed up at a pre-rehearsal gathering, "she seemed very nervous but quietly so and was apparently in control. She ate very little and after a while she came over to me in the corner and said, 'I know I don't have to explain to you but I have to be by myself for a while.'"

As opening night approached, Kennedy worried about Sullavan despite Cotten's reassurances. "A genuine superstar in every medium and then a year in a sanitarium," Kennedy pondered. "And now, would [her acting talent] come back or wouldn't it? I think she knew less than any of us."[28] After the dress rehearsal,

> I didn't see her again until she walked on the stage that night. 'Hello, hello,' called Sabrina off-stage in that unmistakable voice and the applause started. When she hit the stage there was an ovation. When it quieted down, she said her first lines and I knew it was there. But the revelation came after she said a few more lines. And then she knew it. I could see her knowing it, disbelieving it for a minute, then tasting it and savoring it.... Everything she had ever had that had gone away had come back and come back in full flower.[29]

Kennedy characterized his association with *Sabrina Fair* as "one of the most rewarding experiences I have ever had in the theater."[30]

The advance ticket sales made the play one of the most highly anticipated events of a summer season that touted big draws like Don Ameche, Dorothy Lamour, Jeanette MacDonald, Groucho Marx and Mae West. According to the *Falmouth Enterprise*, the play

> is a surefire hit. Last night's opening was a sell-out. The glamor of Margaret Sullavan and Joseph Cotten, who came to the Playhouse complete with an aura of Hollywood and Broadway about them, a rollicking Cinderella comedy embellished with sophisticated and funny lines, add up to surefire summer fare.... Perhaps it was 29 years ago that Margaret Sullavan made her debut on Cape Cod. After last night's performance no one really believes it. She was far too starry eyed and pretty.

After three weeks of glowing reviews and SRO crowds, it was undeniable that Sullavan had made a triumphant return.

34

The Final Bow

I loathe acting. I loathe what it does to my life.[1]

Throughout the rest of 1958 and most of 1959, little was heard of Margaret Sullavan. As her hearing continued to worsen, she retreated from life. Sullavan found it difficult to cope with the prospect of losing her hearing completely and this took its toll on her mental and physical health. She reached out to Dr. Lempert, who confirmed she only had 50 percent hearing in her right ear. He suggested that she'd undergo the same procedure done in 1948 to correct the problem.

To preserve whatever fragment of self-esteem she had left, Sullavan confined herself to a diminishing circle of friends and family. Wagg felt particularly helpless in this situation. "Poor Kenneth, poor gentle, sweet man," Kent Smith remarked to Quirk. "He was the soul of patience with her" as Sullavan sank into deeper bouts of depression.[2]

That fall, without warning, Sullavan made the surprise announcement that she was returning to acting. She received a script by Ruth Goetz, *Sweet Love Remember'd*, that appealed to her. It was the first solo effort by Goetz after the 1957 death of her husband Augustus. They were a prolific playwriting team most noted for *Washington Square* (1947) and its screen incarnation, *The Heiress* (1949). This film was directed by William Wyler and starred Olivia de Havilland (an Oscar winning performance).

Sweet Love Remember'd was an semi-autobiographical account of the couple's last days before the husband's untimely death. Julia and Jamie Garland are successful husband-and-wife playwrights. After the opening of their new play, they decide to vacation in Havana. Their idyllic time is cut short when Jamie learns he has an advanced case of hypertension. With his imminent death, Jamie uses his remaining time to prepare his wife for his death. He hopes to instill in her the courage and confidence to go on as a solo writer. The play's title comes from Shakespeare's twenty-ninth sonnet: "For thy sweet love remember'd such wealth brings; That then I scorn to change my state with kings."[3]

Sullavan knew she had to do the play: "I haven't been as anxious to go to work in a play since I was young and just beginning." Wagg tried to talk her out of it, citing that she was healthy and happy for the first time in a long time. Sullavan was adamant. "I'll be miserable if I don't do this script," she reasoned. Then she prophetically added, "And it will probably kill me if I do."[4]

Sullavan agreed to star in the play and preparations were made. Longtime friend Kent Smith was assigned as her co-star and Harold Clurman was selected to direct. The play would tour in New Haven, Philadelphia and Boston for four to five weeks with the Broadway opening scheduled for the Billy Rose Theater on February 4, 1960. Prior to rehearsals, Sullavan underwent a physical examination and was deemed healthy enough to handle the rigors of the play. She took a two-week vacation in Jamaica to mentally prepare herself.

Rehearsals began on December 1, 1959. On that day, Sullavan conducted her final magazine interview with John Keating of *Theatre Arts* magazine, in which she was her usual brutally honest self. She admitted, "I have something of a reputation of not wanting to go to work." In regards to the play, however, she shared, "This is a play about good people— I mean people you can have respect for."[5]

As rehearsals progressed, Sullavan found herself anxious and stressed due to the difficulty of trying to give a performance with her progressive hearing loss. The simple task of listening for her cues became a daunting challenge and this resulted in more frequent bouts of prolonged depression. James Stewart, who was also suffering from mild hearing loss, was sympathetic and provided some suggestions. As his wife recalled, "Jim gave her as much support and encouragement and advice as he could. He had learned to make sure he had learned everybody else's lines and he had reached a point where in rehearsals he would watch rather than listen for his cues so he could go straight into his lines. But Margaret just found that too difficult, and she grew depressed."[6] Stewart reached out to Fonda to help Sullavan. Fonda, who was still scarred by Frances' suicide in 1950, felt he was incapable of doing so.

Sullavan's worsening condition did not go unnoticed by co-workers. The debilitating pressure of trying to act without making a mistake caused her such anxiety that she became moodier and more depressed. Prior to rehearsals, she threw tantrums.

Millicent Osborn shared with Brooke that her mother often came to dinner during rehearsals. Osborn recalled that Sullavan "was gay and charming; we were having a perfectly lovely time talking about all kinds of things." Osborn continued,

> Suddenly she took me into my bedroom and she said, "Millicent, I can't go on and I can't get out." And I had such a sense of horror—there was something in the way she said it that implied more than the play. Because then I took her by the shoulders, and I held her, and I said, "You must go on." And I didn't mean the play. But there was that crazy confusion, that ambiguity....[7]

As the cast and crew prepared for New Haven, Sullavan consented to her last newspaper interview with Wayne Robinson of the *Philadelphia Sunday Bulletin*. During the interview, Robinson noticed that Sullavan appeared depressed. The difference between the Keating article and this interview is startling. "The theater is a cruel place, a horrible place. Oh, you don't know how difficult it is for me to make myself come back to it. It is hell." Conceding that she wanted to do the play, she admitted, "I have to force myself to come to these rehearsals."[8]

Sweet Love Remember'd premiered at the Shubert Theatre on Monday, December 28, 1959. The critics found it lacking in content, but praised the performers. "In this new play, Ruth Goetz has combined a tender love story with a sometimes absorbing clinical study of a heart condition," The *New Haven Evening Register* noted. "She has been given eloquent support in her endeavor by Margaret Sullavan, Kent Smith and Joseph Wiseman. But the passion and the pathology in her text are, in this tryout stage, never quite fully merged into a satisfying and understandable whole." Among the play's merits were the performances of the leading actors as they "develop every nuance of tenderness that Miss Goetz has put into the play." The *Variety* critique echoed a similar sentiment: "There is the foundation for an interesting story in *Sweet Love Remember'd* but at present, the playwright takes too long to tell it.... The drama seems a good vehicle for Margaret Sullavan, who lends warmth to the sentimental scenes, defiance and determination to the stronger passages, and the right quality for the role of the wife who hopes against hope."

Despite her positive personal notices, Sullavan's anxiety was not assuaged. An alarmed cast member was shocked at her irrational behavior off-stage. "I couldn't believe it was Maggie when she began to tell me that the audience didn't like her."[9] By Wednesday, Sullavan called Wagg and asked him to join her in New Haven as she needed his support. When he arrived at her room at the Taft Hotel, he found her "tired and exhausted, and she said she was fed up with show business."[10] She was having trouble sleeping and this undoubtedly fueled her acute anxiety. By Thursday, Wagg was concerned enough to call a local physician, Rafi Tofig. Based on Tofig's evaluation of her condition (which he described as "nervous and upset"), he prescribed barbiturates to help her sleep. He also gave her an injection to calm her nerves.[11]

By this time, Sullavan had secluded herself in her room when she wasn't performing on stage. A cast member tried to coax her into coming to the cast's New Year's Eve party. She turned down the invitation, stating, "I just can't do it. I just can't face them. I'll try to sleep."[12] At two o'clock in the morning, she called the party and asked if someone could bring her a sandwich.

On Friday, New Year's Day, Dr. Tofig paid two more visits, once at two in the morning and the other in the early afternoon. At his last visit, he still found her "highly nervous." Meanwhile, Wagg was determined to get his wife out of the play. After leaving her room around two p.m. after she had finally fallen asleep, he met with the producers to arrange for her release. When he arrived back at her room around 5:30, he found her door locked. When she failed to respond to his knocking, Wagg sought the help of hotel employees and the producers. After they had unlocked the door, they found that the chain latch prevented them from entering. When they were able to get into her room, she was unconscious in bed. The open script of the play and a copy of *The Adventures of Mark Twain* were found by her side along with several half-full bottles of medication. Sullavan was rushed to Grace New Haven Community Hospital. Shortly after six p.m. on January 1, 1960, Margaret Sullavan, luminous screen and stage star, was pronounced dead at the age of 50.

Later that evening, Sullavan's body was released to the Beecher and Bennett Funeral Home in New Haven. It was Wagg's duty to notify family members and close friends. Brooke, who had recently made her acting debut in the Off-Broadway play *Marching Song*, learned of her mother's death when she called her stepfather to wish him Happy New Year. The stunned 22-year-old then visited her father and his current girlfriend, Pamela. During this time with Leland, it was suggested that Sullavan may have committed suicide. At the time, Brooke refused to consider such a notion.

The following day, the headlines of the nation's newspapers told of the sad passing. The front page of the *New York Times* read "Margaret Sullavan Dead; Overdose of Pills Is Hinted." New Haven County Coroner James J. Corrigan was quoted as saying that he believed that the actress' death was caused by an accidental overdose. "I do not believe it was a suicide," he stated. Corrigan noted that an official cause of death would not be determined until laboratory results were completed. "No one at this time can call this death by barbiturates," he cautioned.[13]

Several of her friends were shocked and saddened by her passing. When James Stewart learned of her death, he was devastated. "He did become something of a recluse for a while," reported Gloria. For several months afterwards, Stewart considered retiring from acting. "He had lost the spark that had always been there. I think that spark went out, not with the failure of his [recent] films, but with the death of Margaret Sullavan," said Gloria.[14]

Equally hard-hit was Fonda, who learned about Sullavan's death while listening to the radio. "I switched off the radio," Fonda recalled. "I couldn't listen any more. That lovely woman, gone. The room wasn't as bright as before."[15] His daughter Jane was in Boston rehearsing a play, *There Was a Little Girl*, with Joshua Logan directing. She recalled that her father came to the theater and the two men hugged. Logan then called for a break in rehearsals. Jane went with her father to a nearby bar, where they sat in silence for over an hour.

The New Year's performance of *Sweet Love Remember'd* play was cancelled. Producer Martin Gabel announced to the press that the play would resume on Saturday, January 2, with Sullavan's understudy, Priscilla Gillette, assuming the role. The cast and crew struggled through the matinee performance. Afterwards, the atmosphere backstage was hushed and somber. "We were all pretty tense," Gillette recalled. "It has been pretty hectic."[16]

The tour was then put on hold as the producers figured out how to proceed. Several actresses, including Julie Harris, Diana Wynyard, and Constance Cummings, were considered, before Gabel's wife Arlene Francis signed a contract as Sullavan's replacement. "We decided to go on because we believe in the play and believe that Miss Francis will be marvelous in in it," reported Gabel.[17] The producers appealed to Actors' Equity to allow them to cancel the Philadelphia and Boston engagements in order to begin rehearsals with Francis on January 25. Nothing ever came of it.

On January 4, coroner Corrigan reported that the toxicology report indicated that Sullavan had died from an overdose of barbiturates. However, he noted that there was not "such a massive overdose as one would expect in a suicide attempt." Furthermore, the absence of a suicide note supported his theory that her death was accidental. Corrigan made the assumption that, due to her extreme emotional state, Sullavan most likely "took an overdose to speed relief" when the initial dosage had proven ineffective in calming her nerves.[18] Based on this, Corrigan officially ruled Sullavan's death an accidental overdose.

That same day, a private memorial service was held in Greenwich at the Christ Protestant Episcopal Church, conducted by the Rev. John W. Price and the Rev. Donald Crawford. In attendance were friends and former co-workers, among them Joan Crawford, David O. Selznick and his wife Jennifer Jones, Worthington Miner and his wife Frances Fuller, Kent Smith, Norris Houghton, Joseph L. Mankiewicz and producers Henry Margolis and Gabel, among others. The Reverend Prince began the service by saying a few words about her illustrious career as a leading stage and film actress. She was buried at Saint Mary's Whitechapel Episcopal churchyard in Lancaster, Virginia, the following week.

In the days and weeks after Sullavan's death, many of her close friends wondered if there was anything they could have done to help her. Audrey Christie reflected to Burrows, "Many times I wish I had been with her in New Haven, a new play, its problems, overtired, possibly depression, forgetting one had taken a sedative earlier. Who knows?" Then, referring to both Sullavan and Patricia Neal (who were the subjects of Burrows' book), Christie mused, "Two tragic stories … two such enchanting gals. Both of their life stories are heartbreakers, aren't they?"[19] About a week after Sullavan's death, a callous reporter asked Henry Fonda what it was like to have been married so many times and to have had two ex-wives commit suicide. Fonda calmly replied, "Well, I loved them all, in a way I still do. I could've not saved any one of them. And they could not have been saved. Everyone has to save themselves."[20]

The most touching and fitting tribute came from Charlton Harrell in his article "Impish Peggy Hated Fuss," published in a local Virginia newspaper. "She'll be missed by her friends here," he wrote. "She'll be a hard person to forget, perhaps because she was a sprite, someone a little different from everyone else. Not because she was a famous actress, but because she was herself an unusual and rare individual."[21]

35

Preserving the Legacy

Mother was very conflicted. She wanted to be a mother but she was also an actress.[1]*—Brooke Hayward*

On January 8, 1960, *The New York Post* revealed that Sullavan was nearly totally deaf at the time of her death. "The tumultuous applause of a delighted audience—was it only a dim murmur over the years to Margaret Sullavan?" the article conjectured. "Did the poised and confident mien of the beautiful actress mask a sick fear … that she'd missed an important cue?"[2] Only those who knew Sullavan intimately knew that this was the case as she fiercely guarded this secret. For the majority of acquaintances and colleagues, the news came as a complete surprise. Even Brooke never suspected how serious this problem was. As she related to a *New York Times* reporter the following day, "It is possible that mother's ear trouble affected her more deeply than she cared to show."[3]

Sullavan bequeathed her temporal bones to Dr. Lempert for further study. Lempert was surprised as "she had never said anything to me about it. I was deeply shocked by her death and I am deeply appreciative of what she has done." Lempert revealed that, while the 1948 operation was successful, she had developed the same problem in the other ear during the early 1950s. He had promised her that he would keep her condition a secret during her lifetime. This was painful for him since there was "so much misunderstanding of some of the things she did, the nervousness, the worry—which were simply a result of her deafness…. She suffered as do most who are hard of hearing who try to keep it a secret and make themselves nervous wrecks. Particularly in her profession, the dread of missing a cue, or not hearing."[4] As a result, Lempert noted, she was "moody, nervous, and tended to shun society. She was apt to throw tantrums before going on the stage."[5] Her gift was a tremendous asset to his studies, since a temporal bone on which a fenestration operation was performed, and the other bone in the beginning stages of deafness, became available for study for the first time in history.

Sullavan's will was filed in Greenwich on January 12, 1960. Wagg was the principal beneficiary of her estate. She bequeathed $5000 to each of his sons. Her brother Sonny received $25,000. Her children received the remainder of the estate, which was put in a trust until they turned 35.

Of her husbands, Leland Hayward died first in 1971 at the age of 68 after a series of debilitating strokes. After his 1960 divorce from "Slim," he married his fourth wife, Pamela Harriman, later that same year. They remained married until his death. Up until a few years prior to his death, he continued his career as a theatrical, TV and motion picture producer. Notable credits include his stage production of *The Sound of Music* (1959) and the 1957 film *The Spirit of St. Louis*, which starred James Stewart.

William Wyler died in 1981 at 79. He achieved prominence as a motion picture director during a 45-year period. He amassed 12 Academy Award nominations for Best Director (making him the record holder), in addition to three wins (*Mrs. Miniver, The Best Years of Our Lives* and *Ben-Hur*). He married actress Margaret Tallichet in 1938. Their marriage, which lasted until his death, produced five children.

Henry Fonda died a year later at 77. After Frances Seymour's death in 1950, Fonda married Susan Blanchard. After their 1956 divorce, he married Afdera Franchetti in 1957. That marriage lasted only four years. He married his fifth wife, Shirlee Adams, in 1965. Their marriage lasted until his death. Both of his children from his union with Seymour, Jane and Peter, are prominent in the acting profession. With Blanchard, the couple adopted a daughter, Amy. Fonda continued his prolific career as a motion picture, TV and stage actor, amassing over 125 credits. While receiving many awards and nominations for film and stage work, he received his only Academy Award for his final motion picture, *On Golden Pond* (1981); he was previously nominated for *The Grapes of Wrath* in 1940. He was also honored with the American Film Institute Lifetime Achievement Award in 1978. Fonda is today recognized as one of the top ten actors in the history of film.

Kenneth Wagg died in 2000 at 91. Although Sullavan's death was a devastating blow, he learned to treasure "the memories of an all too brief life with the most upright, unique and attractive character I had ever met."[6] He became involved in producing and backing plays in London's West End. These included *South* (1961) and *Belle, or The Ballad of Doctor Crippen* (1961). After his marriage to Clare Lady McEwen in 1973, he converted to Roman Catholicism and became a highly effective fundraiser for Roman Catholic causes.

Sullavan's brother Sonny died on November 12, 1991, at age 77 in Norfolk. According to his obituary in the *Virginia Pilot*, Sonny, a graduate of the University of Virginia Law School, lived in San Francisco after World War II and worked for Southwest Airways as a general counsel until he moved back to Norfolk in the late 1940s. He was employed by the Goodman, Segar and Hogan Insurance Company first as an insurance man and later as president before the company merged with Ezra Summers and Co. Sonny never married.

Little is known of Lewise, Sullavan's half-sister, except that she was married to William H. Davies and lived in Cambridge, Massachusetts, until she died on December 12, 1985. The couple apparently had no children as no immediate survivors were noted in the *Cambridge Chronicle*.

Two of Sullavan's children died as tragically as their mother. For years, Bridget had stints in mental institutions, battled depression, and suffered from epileptic seizures. On October 17, 1960, less than a year after Sullavan's death, Bridget was found dead in her midtown New York apartment at the age of 21. Brooke recalled that she spoke with Bridget the previous night. Bridget was in a romantic relationship with Bill Francisco and was excited about the possibility of being pregnant. Brooke became concerned when Bridget failed to come home at an appointed time the following day. It has been reported that either Leland or Francsico or both discovered Bridget's body in her apartment around 4:30 p.m. Her death made national news. According to one account, it was determined that Bridget had apparently committed suicide. The report noted that "an incoherent note was found in the room, but its contents were not disclosed."[7] Francisco later stated, "I am convinced Maggie's suicide set the idea in Bridget's head. It was Maggie's death plus her own illness that drove her to suicide."[8] Peter Fonda recalled learning of Bridget's death from his father. "My very special Bridget, my very secret love was dead," he recalled.[9] Peter was devastated by the loss and mourned her passing for a long time. He later named his daughter (born in 1964) Bridget.

After spending time in mental institutions as a teenager, Bill Hayward also struggled to find his bearings in life. In 1969, Bill, along with Peter Fonda and Bert Schneider, produced the cult classic *Easy Rider*. He also produced *The Hired Hand* (1971), *High-Ballin* (1978) and *Wanda Nevada* (1979), all starring Peter Fonda. He earned a law degree from the University of West Los Angeles in 1989 and became an entertainment lawyer. He was married and divorced three times: first to Fiona Lewis; then Rita Marie Rosate; and finally Marilla Nelson. He had two children, Leland and Bridget. After he dropped out of the limelight, little was heard of him until March 9, 2008, when his body was found in his trailer home outside of Los Angeles. According to police reports, he fired a handgun into his heart. He was 66 years old.

Brooke has been dubbed the "legendary survivor," but her life has not been easy. Her marriage to Michael Thomas ended in mid–1960, leaving her to raise two young sons, Jeffrey and William. Brooke believed that she and Michael succeeded where her parents failed. "We put up a united front. Our sons knew that they had been the product of a relationship between two people who cared for each other."[10] She continued her acting career and made her television debut on *The United States Steel Hour* in "The Devil Makes Sunday" in 1961. She later made her Broadway debut in the short-lived *Mandingo*. In this play, she was cast opposite Dennis Hopper, who became her second husband in August 1961. Later that year, she made her motion picture debut in Burt Balaban's *Mad Dog Coll*. She made a few more appearances in feature films and on television until 1964 when she decided to devote herself to raising her three children (daughter Marin Brooke Hopper was born in 1962). Her most memorable appearance was in a 1962 *Bonanza* episode entitled "The Storm," in which she played the doomed love interest of "Little Joe" Cartwright (Michael Landon), therefore becoming an elite member of the "Cartwright Curse" club. This is the notorious designation for any unlucky female love interest of the Cartwright men as these female characters rarely survived longer than two episodes during its 14-year run. Her last screen appearance was in a small role in the 1993 feature film *Six Degrees of Separation* with Stockard Channing, Donald Sutherland and Will Smith.

Hayward and Hopper were divorced in 1968. Brooke recalled, "Dennis is an extremely interesting character, for whom I have some regard—although he terrified me."[11] In 1977, Hayward remarked that she was "getting older and more eccentric by the minute, and used to stumbling around by myself. I have a series of splintered relationships. Why should I get married again? It's a miserable compromise at best. But I believe in marriage and still have fantasies about it."[12] Soon she became seriously involved with bandleader Peter Duchin, son of bandleader Eddy Duchin. In 1985, they married. During their 26 years of marriage, the couple was referred to as the "perfect blend of Hollywood, Broadway and New York poetry ... possessing those three glorious worlds."[13] By Hayward's admission, she was not an easy person to live with. "Peter is incredibly long-suffering with me. I'm thorny, moody and very difficult," she told *People* magazine.[14] They divorced in 2011 after separating in 2008. Today, Hayward divides her time between Manhattan and Connecticut.

Hayward's most memorable accomplishment came in 1977 when her memoirs, *Haywire*, was published. A personal account of growing up in a dysfunctional family with two famous parents, *Haywire* came about after a conversation with a *New York Times* reporter more than a decade earlier. She revealed to the journalist, "I'm the daughter of a father who's been married five times. Mother killed herself. My sister killed herself. My brother has been in a mental institution. I'm 23 and divorced with two kids." The journalist's response provided the impetus for the novel: "Brooke, either you've got to open the window right now and jump out, or say 'I'm going to live,' because you're right, it's the worst family history that anybody ever had, and either you jump out the window or you live."[15] Writing the book proved a difficult task. "Everybody said, 'This is just going to make you feel wonderful at the end of it.' But it didn't," reflected Hayward. "I don't know how I managed to finish it. It was not a pleasant experience."[16]

Equally unsettling was the notion that she was writing publicly about two people who had a strong aversion to having their private lives "out there" for public consumption. Sullavan in particular detested anything printed about her relationship with her children. As Brooke explained to *People*, "I would weep. I had never confronted my parents with the true feelings I had for them, and I had certainly never expressed the depth of my feeling for my mother, being too selfish to try when I should have."[17] Balancing out the theme of painful childhood memories were the series of interviews Hayward conducted with many of her parents' friends and colleagues. As Hayward explained later, "How could I have possibly written a book about my mother and father without talking to William Wyler, who had been married to my mother and my father's client? Or how could I not talk to Henry Fonda, who had been married to my mother and was father's client?"[18]

Still, Hayward had a cautionary tale to tell. "The moral of my book is that you pay for everything," she remarked at the time the book was published. "They were rich, accomplished, famous and beautiful. We were drowned in privilege, yet it ended in all this hideous tragedy."[19]

Brooke believed one of the reasons she was never in a mental institution was "because I was the oldest, and had a full decade of mother and father when they were happy and before they were divorced. [Those years] gave me a kind of strength. The divorce was a tragedy, and my brother and sister had less of a cushion than I did."[20]

Haywire, published in February 1977, quickly proved a success. It was a #1 *New York Times* bestseller for 17 weeks. According to the *Times*' book review, it was "a glowing tapestry spun with equal parts of gold and pain. As a book it is an absolute beauty—a Hollywood beauty, to be precise—with all the charm that term implies, the deceptive simplicity, the complex hidden machinery and, above all, the terrible cost."[21]

Some took offense to the book. In her autobiography, Myrna Loy made it a point to denounce Hayward's book along with Christina Crawford's *Mommie Dearest*. "It makes me wild when I think about the rubbish that's printed!" Loy wrote. "Most of it's trash, believe me."[22] In regard to *Haywire*: "The book Margaret Sullavan's daughter wrote is just as bad. Maggie gave up the best years of her career to raise those children, and that's what she gets."[23] While Loy was entitled to her opinion, she is mistaken in comparing *Mommie Dearest* to *Haywire*. Crawford's book, published in 1978, focused heavily on the emotional and physical abuse she allegedly suffered at the hands of her mother Joan Crawford. While highly defamatory and malicious in tone, her account has been substantiated by some who knew Joan well. On the other hand, *Haywire* is a unflinchingly honest, but sympathetic, look at family dynamics, warts and all. Hayward manages to create a complex and multifaceted depiction of both parents and her memoir does not read like a one-sided diatribe.

Within months of *Haywire*'s successful release, plans were made to adapt the book into a television movie. *Haywire* was presented as a two-part miniseries on CBS in May 1980. Produced by Bill Hayward and Anna Cottle and directed by Michael Tuchner, *Haywire* stars Lee Remick (as Margaret Sullavan), Jason Robards (Leland), Deborah Raffin (Brooke), Dianne Hull (Bridget) and Hart Bochner (Bill). The miniseries was an ambitious undertaking as it told a story using snippets of incidents from the book in a non-chronological fashion. Adding to the overall impact were frequent, awkward flashbacks and interminable talk. The end result was a well-produced bore that made for an uninvolving viewing experience. Fortunately, most members of the cast are above reproach, particularly Raffin and

Remick, who enacted her role with enough sensitivity and restraint to create a convincing portrait. On playing Sullavan, Remick remarked, "I loved playing her. She was so crazy—with the assurance of her own sanity running through everything she did. She was an irrepressible flirt—and had an affair with any man she felt like."[24] In preparation, Remick watched many of Sullavan's films. For her performance, she was nominated for a Primetime Emmy Award for Outstanding Lead Actress in a Miniseries. Bill Hayward also watched many of his mother's movies for the first time. "She was a good actress," he recalled. "She was a phenomenally *interesting* actress."[25]

In the years following her death, Sullavan remains a largely underappreciated and forgotten figure from Hollywood's Golden Age despite some posthumous honors: a star on the Hollywood Walk of Fame (located at 1751 Vine Street) and an induction into the American Theater Hall of Fame in 1981. Many of the personal materials Sullavan meticulously maintained of her film and stage career are a part of the Brooke Hayward papers collection in the Billy Rose Theatrical Division at the New York Public Library.

Despite being fondly remembered by noted film critics and historians like Andrew Sarris, David Shipman and David Thomson, Sullavan continues to be ignored by mainstream moviegoers. Over the past decades, many articles and chapter selections written about her carried the same message: Margaret Sullavan, one of the most luminous and accomplished actresses of her time, has been unfairly relegated to undeserved "forgotten" status. Even *Child of Fate*, a well-written biography by Lawrence J. Quirk, failed to make much of an impact. For years, her films received very little play, even on late night television. There were a few occasions, San Francisco in 1991 and New York in 1997, when Sullavan and Frank Borzage were honored with a film retrospective entitled "American Romantics."

Fortunately, with cable channels like American Movie Classics and Turner Classic Movies, many of Sullavan's films receive air time. Thirteen of Sullavan's films are available on commercially made DVDs; of the three films currently unavailable (*Only Yesterday*, *So Red the Rose* and *Appointment for Love*), they can be found on YouTube. For those who are interested in starting a collection of her films, I have compiled my own ranking from most to least important with a one- to four-star ratings. I have also included the three unavailable films in the event they become available.

4 stars: *The Shop Around the Corner*
3.8 stars: *The Mortal Storm*
3.75 stars: *Three Comrades*
3.5 stars: *The Good Fairy*
3.5 stars: *So Ends Our Night*
3.25 stars: *The Moon's Our Home*
3.0 stars: *The Shopworn Angel*
3.0 stars: *No Sad Songs for Me*
3.0 stars: *Cry "Havoc"*
3.0 stars: *Back Street*
3.0 stars: *Little Man, What Now?*
2.75 stars: *Only Yesterday*
2.5 stars: *So Red the Rose*
2.25 stars: *Next Time We Love*
2.25 stars: *Appointment for Love*
2 stars: *The Shining Hour*

∽∽∽

Who exactly was Margaret Sullavan? On the shimmery surface, she was a devoted mother and a highly regarded actress in all media. Below the surface, she was a complex woman, alternately loved or hated by those who knew her. At the core, however, she was a woman plagued by nagging doubts and conflicting emotional needs. She never found that elusive inner peace, that "clarity of vision," that she craved all her life. Her death, with its pervasive whispers of "suicide" (although never officially ruled as such), left a profoundly painful and troubling legacy to those she left behind.

To paraphrase Ben Cartwright (Lorne Greene) in the *Bonanza* episode in which Brooke Hayward's character dies so valiantly: "Don't carry her on your shoulders for the rest of your life, but keep a warm spot in your heart for her."[26] Margaret Sullavan's impressive body of film work allows us to do just that.

Appendix A
Film Appearances

Only Yesterday
Universal
Released November 7, 1933
Director: John M. Stahl
105 minutes
Cast: Margaret Sullavan (Mary Lane), John Boles, Edna May Oliver, Billie Burke, Reginald Denny, Jimmie Butler, Benita Hume, George Meeker, June Clyde, Jane Darwell

Little Man, What Now?
Universal
Released May 31, 1934
Director: Frank Borzage
95 minutes
Cast: Margaret Sullavan (Lammchen), Douglass Montgomery, Alan Hale, Catherine Doucet, Fred Kohler, Mae Marsh, DeWitt Jennings, Alan Mowbray

The Good Fairy
Universal
Released February 18, 1935
Director: William Wyler
81 minutes
Cast: Margaret Sullavan (Luisa Ginglebusher), Herbert Marshall, Frank Morgan, Reginald Owen, Alan Hale, Beulah Bondi, Cesar Romero, Eric Blore

So Red the Rose
Paramount
Released November 22, 1935
Director: King Vidor
91 minutes
Cast: Margaret Sullavan (Valette Bedford), Walter Connolly, Randolph Scott, Janet Beecher, Elizabeth Patterson, Robert Cummings, Harry Ellerbe, Dickie Moore, Daniel Haynes, Clarence Muse

Next Time We Love
Universal
Released January 27, 1936
Director: Edward H. Griffith
87 minutes
Cast: Margaret Sullavan (Cicely), James Stewart, Ray Milland, Anna Demetrio, Grant Mitchell, Robert McWade, Hattie McDaniel

The Moon's Our Home
Paramount
Released May 20, 1936
Director: William A. Seiter
80 minutes
Cast: Margaret Sullavan (Cherry Chester), Henry Fonda, Beulah Bondi, Henrietta Crossman, Charles Butterworth, Walter Brennan, Margaret Hamilton, Spencer Charters

Three Comrades
MGM
Released May 25, 1938
Director: Frank Borzage
100 minutes
Cast: Margaret Sullavan (Patricia Hollman), Robert Taylor, Franchot Tone, Robert Young, Guy Kibbee, Lionel Atwill, Henry Hull, George Zucco, Monty Woolley

The Shopworn Angel
MGM
Released July 13, 1938
Director: H.C. Potter
85 minutes
Cast: Margaret Sullavan (Daisy Heath), James Stewart, Walter Pidgeon, Nat Pendleton,

Alan Curtis, Sam Levene, Hattie McDaniel, Charley Grapewin, Jimmie Butler

The Shining Hour
MGM
Released November 16, 1938
Director: Frank Borzage
76 minutes
Cast: Margaret Sullavan (Judy Linden), Joan Crawford, Melvyn Douglas, Robert Young, Fay Bainter, Allyn Joslyn, Hattie McDaniel, Frank Albertson

Land of Liberty
Opened April 30, 1939, at the New York World's Fair and the San Francisco Exposition and shown daily from April to October of 1939 and from April to October of 1940. *Land of Liberty* was later re-edited and put into general distribution in January, 1941.
Sponsored by the Motion Picture Producers and Distributors of America
Supervised by Cecil B. DeMille
98 minutes
Margaret Sullavan was seen in a clip from *So Red the Rose*

The Shop Around the Corner
MGM
Released January 10, 1940
Director: Ernst Lubitsch
97 minutes
Cast: Margaret Sullavan (Klara Nowak), James Stewart, Frank Morgan, Joseph Schildkraut, Sara Haden, Felix Bressart, William Tracy, Inez Courtney, Charles Smith

The Mortal Storm
MGM
Released June 12, 1940
Director: Frank Borzage
100 minutes
Cast: Margaret Sullavan (Freya Roth), James Stewart, Robert Young, Frank Morgan, Irene Rich, Maria Ouspenskaya, Robert Stack, Bonita Granville, Ward Bond, Dan Dailey

So Ends Our Night
United Artists
Released January 29, 1941

Director: John Cromwell
120 minutes
Cast: Margaret Sullavan (Ruth Holland), Fredric March, Frances Dee, Glenn Ford, Anna Sten, Erich von Stroheim, Allan Brett, Joseph Cawthorn, Leonid Kinskey, Roman Bohnen

Back Street
Universal
Released February 12, 1941
Director: Robert Stevenson
89 minutes
Cast: Margaret Sullavan (Ray Smith), Charles Boyer, Richard Carlson, Frank McHugh, Tim Holt, Esther Dale, Samuel S. Hinds, Cecil Cunningham

Appointment with Love
Universal
Released October 29, 1941
Director: William A. Seiter
89 minutes
Cast: Margaret Sullavan (Dr. Jane Alexander), Charles Boyer, Rita Johnson, Eugene Pallette, Ruth Terry, Reginald Denny, Cecil Kellaway

Cry "Havoc"
MGM
Released November 9, 1943
Director: Richard Thorpe
97 minutes
Cast: Margaret Sullavan (Lieutenant "Smitty" Smith), Ann Sothern, Joan Blondell, Fay Bainter, Ella Raines, Frances Gifford, Diana Lewis, Heather Angel, Dorothy Norris, Connie Gilchrist, Gloria Grafton, Fely Franquelli

No Sad Songs for Me
Columbia
Released April 12, 1950
Director: Rudolph Maté
88 minutes
Cast: Margaret Sullavan (Mary Scott), Wendell Corey, Viveca Lindfors, Natalie Wood, John McIntire, Ann Doran, Richard Quine, Jeanette Nolan, Dorothy Tree

Appendix B
Radio Appearances

*A comprehensive, yet by no means complete, listing
of Margaret Sullavan's radio appearances.*

Roses and Drums
This series premiered on May 1, 1932. The actual
date of Sullavan's performance is not known,
but it is believed to have occurred later in the
spring of 1932.

Fleischman Yeast Hour
November 16, 1933
"Strictly Dishonorable" with Tonio Stewart

The Royal Gelatin Hour
January 6, 1934
Host: Rudy Vallee; guests included Margaret
Sullavan, Leslie Howard and Carmel Myers

Hollywood Hotel
June 14, 1935
Host: Louella Parsons; Scenes from *So Red the
Rose* with Margaret Sullavan, Randolph Scott;
other guests included Dick Powell, Frances
Langford, Igor Gorin, Anne Jamison and
Raymond Paige's Orchestra

Hollywood Hotel
January 17, 1936
Host: Louella Parsons; scenes from *Next Time
We Love* with Margaret Sullavan and James
Stewart

Hollywood Hotel
April 11, 1936
Host: Louella Parsons; scenes from *The Moon's
Our Home* with Margaret Sullavan and Henry
Fonda

The Shell Chateau Hour
August 8, 1936
Host: Wallace Beery; scenes from *The Constant
Nymph* with Margaret Sullavan; other guests
included Joe Cook, Judy Garland and Larry
"Buster" Crabbe

Magazine of the Air
October 30, 1936
Host: Brock Pemberton

Columbia Workshop
March 2, 1937
Sullavan appeared in a broadcast of *Macbeth*

Kate Smith Radio Program
March 12, 1937
Host: Kate Smith; Sullavan performed with cast
members in a broadcast of *Stage Door*

Hit Parade Radio Program
March 27, 1937
Sullavan made a guest appearance

Jergens Hollywood Playhouse
October 3, 1937
Host: Tyrone Power, who also played with Margaret Sullavan in an adaptation of *Her Cardboard Lover*

Lux Radio Theatre
November 22, 1937
"The Petrified Forest"
Hosted by Cecil B. DeMille; starred Herbert
Marshall (Alan Squire), Margaret Sullavan
(Gaby), Eduardo Ciannelli (Duke Mantee),
Donald Meek (Gramps), Wallace Clark
(Mr. Chisholm), Frank Milland (Boze), Wally
Mayer (Jackie), George Trevell (Hank),
Martha Wentworth (Mrs. Chisholm), Mar-
garet Breacham (Doris), Frank Melton (Line-

man), Lew Merrill (Doctor), Frank Nelson (Radio Announcer)
Available on YouTube

Chase and Sanborn Program
January 9, 1938
Directed and Hosted by Don Ameche; guest stars: Edgar Bergen, Nelson Eddy, Margaret Sullavan, Loretta Lee, Strout Turns, Ned Sparks

Good News of 1938
June 2, 1938
Scenes from *Three Comrades* with Margaret Sullavan, Robert Taylor, Franchot Tone, Robert Young; other guests included Fanny Brice, Frank Morgan, Una Merkel and Meredith Willson's Orchestra

Good News of 1938
June 30, 1938
Scenes from *The Shopworn Angel* with Margaret Sullavan, James Stewart and Walter Pidgeon

Silver Theater
October 8, 1938
"The Moon's Our Home"
Host: Conrad Nagel, with Margaret Sullavan (Cherry Chester), Bill Goodwin (Anthony Amerton)
Available on YouTube

Hollywood Hotel
October 21, 1938
"Of Human Bondage"
Host: William Powell, who also played with Margaret Sullavan

Magazine of the Air
October 30, 1938

Lux Radio Theater
November 7, 1938
"Next Time We Love"
Hosted by Cecil B. DeMille; starred Margaret Sullavan, Joel McCrea

Good News of 1939
November 17, 1938
Scenes from *The Shining Hour*, with Margaret Sullavan, Joan Crawford, Melvyn Douglas, Robert Young; hosted by Young; other guests included Frank Morgan and Meredith Willson
Available on YouTube

Campbell Playhouse
December 9, 1938
"Rebecca"
Margaret Sullavan (Mrs. de Winter), Orson Welles (Max de Winter), Agnes Moorehead (Mrs. Van Hopper), Mildred Natwick (Mrs. Danvers), Alfred Shirley (Frith), Ray Collins (Frank Crawley), Frank Readick (The Idiot), George Coulouris; with a guest appearance by Daphne Du Maurier
Available on YouTube

Campbell Playhouse
March 31, 1939
"Show Boat"
Margaret Sullavan (Magnolia "Maggie" Hawks/ Ravenal), Orson Welles (Capt. Andy Hawks), Helen Morgan (Julie), Ray Collins (Windy), Everett Sloane (Schultzy), William Johnston (Gaylord Ravenal), Grace Cotton (Kim), with a guest appearance by Edna Ferber (Parthy Ann Hawks)
Available on www.oldradioworld.com

Forecast
August 26, 1940
"Bethal Merriday"
Margaret Sullavan, Howard Da Silva, Bob Burleson, Norman Corwin, Norman Field, Byron Kane, Lurene Tuttle, Paula Winslowe

Screen Guild Theater
September 29, 1940
"The Shop Around the Corner"
Starred Margaret Sullavan (Klara Nowak), James Stewart (Mr. Martin), Frank Morgan (Mr. Matushek/Narrator)
Available on YouTube

Family Theater
March 8, 1947
"I Give You Maggie"
Host: Donald Crisp; starred Margaret SullaVan (Maggie), Van Heflin (Tom)
Available on YouTube

Guild's Radio Theater on the Air
January 11, 1948
"Holiday"
Margaret Sullavan and Kent Smith

Screen Guild
May 3, 1948
"Next Time We Love"
Margaret Sullavan, Joseph Cotten

The Electric Theater
October 17, 1948
"Rebound"

Theatre USA
April 29, 1949

The MGM Theatre of the Air
October 14, 1949
"The Shopworn Angel"

Today's a Great Day
December 13, 1950
Featured: Margaret Sullavan, John Garfield, Burgess Meredith, Melvyn Douglas, Anita Louise, Mildred Natwick

Playhouse on Broadway
April 26, 1951
Featured Margaret Sullavan in scenes from No Sad Songs for Me

Calvacade of America
May 15, 1951
"Militant Angel"

Appendix C
Stage Appearances

The Queen of Youth
Presented at Chatham Episcopal Institute, May 1, 1927
Cast: Margaret Sullavan (Puck), Anne Ramsey, Margaret Huffard, Ruth Carwile

The Girl with the Green Eyes
Presented at Sullins College, Spring 1928 (exact date unknown)

Close Up
Presented by the Harvard Dramatic Society at Brattle Hall, Boston on May 8–10 and at the Repertory Theatre in Boston on May 11, 1929
Cast: Margaret Sullavan (chorus), Henry Fonda

UNIVERSITY PLAYERS GUILD
Falmouth, MA
Summer Stock, 1929

Summer stock troupe also included Henry Fonda, Kent Smith, Joshua Logan, Charles Leatherbee, Bretaigne Windust, Bartlett Quigley, Elizabeth Fenner, Lillie Brayton, Charles Arnt Jr., Julia Dorr and Elizabeth Johnson

The Devil and the Cheese
Presented from July 1–6, 1929
Margaret Sullavan (Goldina Quigley)

The Last Warning
Sullavan's appearance is unconfirmed.
Presented from July 29–August 3, 1929

Crime
Presented from August 5–10, 1929
Margaret Sullavan (Annabelle Porter)

The Constant Nymph
Presented from September 2–7, 1929
Cast: Margaret Sullavan (Teresa Sanger)

LITTLE THEATER
Norfolk, VA
Winter Stock 1930

Dear Brutus
Directed by Rose Johnson Willis
Presented February 4–6, 1930
Cast: Margaret Sullavan (Lady Caroline), Mrs. Aurenger, Finlay Ferguson, Read Wilkins, M. Dally Walsh, William Lachin Beaton

Lady Windermere's Fan
Directed by Rose Johnson Willis
Presented May 13–15, 1930
Cast: Margaret Sullavan (Lady Plymdale), Florian Pelote, Finlay Ferguson, Read Wilkins, William Lachlan Beaton, Helen D. Whitehead

UNIVERSITY PLAYERS GUILD
Falmouth, MA
Summer Stock 1930

The summer stock troupe included Henry Fonda, Bretaigne Windust, Kent Smith, Myron McCormick, Charles Leatherbee, Elizabeth Johnson, Christine Ramsey and Elizabeth Fenner

The Makropoulos Secret
Directed by Bretaigne Windust
Presented from July 28–August 2, 1930

The Firebrand
Presented from August 11–16, 1930
Margaret Sullavan (Emilia)

The Marquise
Presented from August 25–30, 1930
Margaret Sullavan (Adrienne)

A Kiss for Cinderella
Directed by Henry Fonda
Presented from September 2–7, 1930
Margaret Sullavan (Miss Thing)

Strictly Dishonorable
National Tour
Tour included: October 6–9, 1930: Norfolk, VA; November 27–29, 1930: Memphis, TN; December 8–13, 1930: Atlanta, GA; December 29, 1930–January 3, 1931: Indianapolis, IN; *January 12–March 21, 1931: Philadelphia, PA
Sullavan left the tour early in February.
Cast: Margaret Sullavan (Isabelle Parry), Cesar Romero, Willard Dashell, Rudolph Radaloni, Edward Hartford, Leo Leone and Joseph McCallion

Three Artists and a Lady
Directed by Myron McCormick for the Princeton Theatre INTIME
Presented on February 23, 1931

A Modern Virgin
Broadway performance
Pre-Broadway tour began on April 27, 1931: Atlantic City, NJ; ended May 16, 1931: Brooklyn, New York
Presented at the Booth Theatre on May 20, 1931; closed after 53 performances
Directed by Stanley Logan
Cast: Margaret Sullavan (Teddy Simpson), Roger Pryor, Boris Nicholai, Nicholas Joy, Herbert Rawlinson and Cynthia Rogers

UNIVERSITY PLAYERS REPERTORY
Falmouth, MA
Summer Stock 1931

Coquette
Directed by Joshua Logan
Presented from July 20–25, 1931
Cast: Margaret Sullavan (Norma Besant), Henry Fonda, Kent Smith, Mary Lee Logan

A Modern Virgin
The national tour began on August 3, 1931, in Brighton Beach, NY; then August 17 in Chicago; closed on October 11 in Detroit
Cast: Margaret Sullavan (Teddy Simpson), Roger Pryor, Boris Nicholai, Nicholas Joy, Herbert Rawlinson, Cynthia Rogers

If Love Were All
Broadway
Presented at the Booth Theatre, November 13, 1931; closed after 11 performances

Directed by Agnes Morgan
Cast: Margaret Sullavan (Janet Bryce), Walter Kingsford, Aline MacMahon, Hugh Buckler, Mabel Moore, Donald Blackwell

UNIVERSITY PLAYERS REPERTORY
Baltimore, MD
Winter stock 1931–1932

Winter stock troupe included Henry Fonda, Kent Smith, Joshua Logan, Myron McCormick, Barbara O'Neil, Johnny Swope, Merna Pace, Charles Leatherbee, Peter Wayne, Alfred Dalrymple and Katherine Hastings

The Constant Nymph
Presented November 30–December 5, 1931
Margaret Sullavan (Teresa Sanger)

Death Takes a Holiday
Presented December 7–12, 1931
Margaret Sullavan (Grazia)

It's a Wise Child
Presented December 14–19, 1931
Margaret Sullavan (Joyce Stanton)

The Royal Family
Presented December 28, 1931–January 2, 1932
Margaret Sullavan (Gwen)

Holiday
Presented January 4–9, 1932
Margaret Sullavan (Linda Seton)

Coquette
Presented January 11–16, 1932
Margaret Sullavan (Norma Bresant)

Mary Rose
Presented February 1–6, 1932
Margaret Sullavan (Mary Rose)

The Second Man
Presented February 8–13, 1932
Margaret Sullavan (Monica Grey)

Let Us Be Gay
Presented February 22–27, 1932
Margaret Sullavan (Kitty Brown)

Paris Bound
Presented February 29–March 5, 1932
Margaret Sullavan (Mary Hutton)

The Trial of Mary Dugan
Presented March 7–12, 1932

Happy Landing
Broadway Performance
Presented at the Chanin's Forty-Sixth Street

Theatre, March 26, 1932; closed after 25 performances

Directed by Lawrence Marston

Cast: Margaret Sullavan (Phyllis Blair), Russell Hardie, Harry Davenport, Catherine Dale Owen, Edwin Redding, Marjorie Wood

SUMMER STOCK
1932

There's Always Juliet

Presented at the Nyack Broadway Theater, Nyack, NY, from July 4–9, 1932

Cast: Margaret Sullavban (Leonora Perrycoste); Geoffrey Kerr, Phillip Tonge, Elmonia Nollay

Strictly Dishonorable

Presented at the Croton River Playhouse, Harmon-on-Hudson, NY, from July 18–23, 1932

Cast: Margaret Sullavan (Isabelle Perry), Tullio Carminati, Edward Potter, Roy Gordon

Paris Bound

Presented at the Millbrook Playhouse, Poughkeepsie, NY, from July 25–30, 1932, and the Westchester Playhouse, Mt. Kisco, NY, from August 2–7, 1932

Cast: Margaret Sullavan (Mary Hutton), Roland Drew, Martha Mayo, Day Tuttle, John Eldredge, George Lessey, Edith Van Cleve

Men Must Fight

Presented at the Millbrook Playhouse, Poughkeepsie, NY, from August 8–13, 1932, and the Westchester Playhouse, Mt. Kisco from August 15–20, 1932

Cast: Margaret Sullavan (Peggy Chase), Lily Cahill, Alma Kruger, John Eldredge, Martha Mayo, Day Tuttle, Kent Smith

There's Always Juliet

Presented at the Millbrook Playhouse, Poughkeepsie, NY, from August 22–27, 1932, and the Westchester Playhouse, Mt. Kisco, NY, from August 29-September 3, 1932

Cast: Margaret Sullavan (Leonora Perrycoste), Geoffrey Kerr, John Eldredge, Elmonia Nollay

Chrysalis

Broadway performance

Pre-Broadway tour: November 7–12, 1932: Newark, NJ; presented at the Martin Beck Theatre, November 15, 1932; closed after 23 performances

Directed by Theresa Helburn

Cast: Margaret Sullavan (Lyda Cose), Humphrey Bogart, Osgood Perkins, June Walker, Elisha Cook Jr., Elia Kazan

Bad Manners

Broadway performance

Premiered on Broadway at the Playhouse Theatre, January 30, 1933; closed after eight performances

Directed by William A. Brady Jr.

Cast: Margaret Sullavan (Lois Aiken), Bert Lytell, Leona Maricle, William David, Harold Vermilyea, Franklin West

Dinner at Eight

Broadway replacement

Presented at the Music Box Theatre, October 22, 1932; closed after 232 performances. Sullavan replaced Marguerite Churchill on March 24, 1933.

Directed by George S. Kaufman

Cast: Margaret Sullavan (Paula Jordan), Conway Tearle, Ann Andrews, Constance Collier, Gregory Gaye, Malcolm Duncan, Cesar Romero, Judith Wood, Sam Levene

Coquette

Summer stock performance

Directed by Day Tuttle

Presented at Mt. Kisco, NY, July 2–7, 1934

Cast: Margaret Sullavan (Norma Bresant), Henry Fonda, Montague Love, Myron McCormick, Joshua Logan, Mildred Natwick

Stage Door

Broadway performance

Pre-Broadway tour began on September 28, 1936: Philadelphia, PA; ended October 17, 1936: Baltimore, MD; presented at the Music Box Theater, October 22, 1936; closed after 169 performances

Directed by George Kaufman

Cast: Margaret Sullavan (Terry Randall), Lee Patrick, Frances Fuller, Onslow Stevens, Phyllis Brooks, Mary Wickes

Voice of the Turtle

Broadway performance

Pre-Broadway tour began November 4, 1943: New Haven, CT; ended December 4: Philadelphia, PA; presented at the Morosco Theatre, December 6, 1943; closed after 1558 performances. Sullavan left the play on December 16, 1944.

Directed by John van Druten

Cast: Margaret Sullavan (Sally Middleton), Elliott Nugent, Audrey Christie

Voice of the Turtle
Broadway engagement
Performed at the Morosco Theatre, May 26–29, 1947, prior to London engagement

Voice of the Turtle
London performance
Pre-London tour began June 16, 1947: Manchester; ended July 5, 1947: Glasgow; presented at the Picadilly Theatre, July 9, 1947; closed after 69 performances
Directed by John van Druten
Cast: Margaret Sullavan (Sally Middleton), Wendell Corey, Audrey Christie

The Deep Blue Sea
Broadway performance
Pre-Broadway tour began October 8, 1952: New Haven, CT; ended November 2, 1952: Washington, D.C.; presented at the Morosco Theatre, November 5, 1952; closed after 132 performances
Directed by Frith Banbury
Cast: Margaret Sullavan (Hester Collyer), Alan Webb, James Hanley, Herbert Berghoff, Betty Sinclair, John Merivale, Stella Andrew

The Deep Blue Sea
National tour
Tour began March 9, 1953: Baltimore, MD; ended May 3, 1953: Milwaukee, WI
Directed by Frith Banbury
Cast: Margaret Sullavan (Hester Collyer), Alan Webb, Kevin McCarthy, James Hanley, Herbert Berghoff, Betty Sinclair, John Merivale

Sabrina Fair
Broadway performance
Pre-Broadway tour began October 8, 1953: New Haven, CT; ended November 7, 1953: Philadelphia, PA; presented at the National Theatre, November 11, 1953; closed after 318 performances. Sullavan left the play on May 29, 1954.
Directed by H.C. Potter
Cast: Margaret Sullavan (Sabrina Fairchild), Joseph Cotten, John Cromwell, Scott McKay, Cathleen Nesbitt, Russell Collins, Luella Gear

Janus
Broadway performance
Pre-Broadway tour began October 19, 1955: Wilmington, DE; ended November 17, 1955: Washington, D.C., presented at the Plymouth Theatre, November 24, 1955; closed after 251 performances. Sullavan left the play on April 1, 1956.
Directed by Reginald Denham
Cast: Margaret Sullavan (Jessica), Robert Preston, Claude Dauphin, Mary Finney, Robert Emhardt

Sabrina Fair
Summer stock
Tour began July 14, 1958: Andover, NJ; ended August 3, 1958: Nyack, NY
Cast: Margaret Sullavan (Sabrina Fairchild), Joseph Cotten, John Cromwell, Scott McKay, Cathleen Nesbitt, Donald McKea, Luella Gear

Sweet Love Remember'd
Pre-Broadway performance
Presented at the Shubert Theatre in New Haven, CT, December 28, 1959; closed on December 31, 1959
Directed by Harold Clurman
Cast: Margaret Sullavan (Julie Garland), Kent Smith, Joseph Wiseman, Sylvia Gassell, Daniel Ades, Norma Crane, Rae Allen, Steve Pluta

Appendix D
Television Appearances

Studio One
"The Storm"
CBS, November 7, 1948
Director: Worthington Miner
60 minutes
Cast: Margaret Sullavan (Janet Wilson), Dean Jagger, Harry Bellaver, Alan MacAteer, Maurice Manson, Mary Wickes, John Forsythe

Chevrolet on Broadway
"The Twelve Pound Look"
NBC, April 11, 1949
30 minutes
Cast: Margaret Sullavan (Kate), Ralph Forbes, Valerie Cossart

The Ford Theatre Hour
"Touchstone"
CBS, April 20, 1951
Director: Franklin Schaffner
60 minutes
Cast: Margaret Sullavan (Alexa Trent), Paul McGrath, Jerome Cowan, Nydia Westman, Jacqueline DeWit, Francis Compton

Schlitz Playhouse of Stars
"Still Life"
CBS, October 26, 1951
Director: Frank Telford
60 minutes
Cast: Margaret Sullavan, Wendell Corey, Bibi Osterwald, Ruth Gilbert, Henry Jones, Fredd Wayne

Schlitz Playhouse of Stars
"The Nymph and the Lamp"
CBS, December 7, 1951
60 minutes
Cast: Margaret Sullavan, Robert Preston

The Toast of the Town
CBS, January 11, 1952
Host: Ed Sullivan, with guest appearances by Sullavan, Alan Webb, James Hanley, Robert Taylor, Guy Mitchell and Ogden Nash

Producers' Showcase
"State of the Union"
NBC, November 15, 1954
Director: Arthur Penn
90 minutes
Cast: Margaret Sullavan (Mary Matthews), Joseph Cotten, Nina Foch, John Cromwell, Ray Walston, Muriel Kirkland, Royal Beal

What's My Line?
CBS, December 18, 1955
Host: John Daly, with panelists Arlene Francis, Dorothy Kilgallen, Bennett Cerf and Fred Allen. Sullavan was the Mystery Challenger.

Chapter Notes

Introduction

1. John Keating, "Margaret Sullavan's Last Interview," *Theatre Arts*, April 1960.
2. Gladys Hall, "Not a Problem Child," *Motion Picture*, May 1938, 73.
3. Joanna Ney, "American Romantics: Frank Borzage and Margaret Sullavan" program notes from film retrospective series, 1997.

Chapter 1

1. Lawrence J. Quirk, *Child of Fate: Margaret Sullavan* (St. Martin's Press, 1986), 10.
2. Howard Sharpe, "Beautiful Brat-Part One," *Photoplay*, October 1938, 19.
3. Brooke Hayward, *Haywire* (Alfred A. Knopf, 1977), 203.
4. Virginia Lane, "'I Can't Pretend!' Says Margaret Sullavan," *Movie Classic*, October, 1935, 27.
5. Hayward, *Haywire*, 205.
6. Ruth Biery, "You'd Like to Shake Her—But You Can't Help Loving Peg Sullavan," *Hollywood*, May 1934, 62.
7. Hall, "Not a Problem Child," 71.
8. Lane, "I Can't Pretend!," 27.
9. "What Lies Ahead for Miss Sullavan?," *Albany Times-Union*, May 31, 1957.
10. Lane, "I Can't Pretend," 27.
11. "Margaret Sullavan Still Can't See How She Scored Hit in Her First Picture," *Los Angeles Times*, December 31, 1933. See also Hamann, G.D., *Margaret Sullavan in the 30s* (Filming Today Press, 2014) 29.
12. Lane, "I Can't Pretend," 27.
13. Louisa Venable Kyle, "Childhood Friendship with Margaret Sullavan Revived at Edgewood After a Quarter Century," *Virginian Pilot and Chronicle*, June 3, 1956.
14. Quirk, *Child of Fate*, 7–8.
15. Connie Hindmarsh, "We Remember Margaret Sullavan," *Tidewater Virginian* 1, no. 2 (July 1977): 25.
16. Quirk, *Child of Fate*, 11.
17. Michael Munn, *Jimmy Stewart: The Truth Behind the Legend* (Barricade Books, 2006), 53.
18. Hayward, *Haywire*, 188.

19. Hindmarsh, "We Remember Margaret Sullavan," 24.
20. Lane, "I Can't Pretend," 27, 68.
21. Hindmarsh, "We Remember Margaret Sullavan," 25.
22. Sharpe, "Beautiful Brat-Part One," 80.

Chapter 2

1. Keating, "Margaret Sullavan's Last Interview."
2. Marcella Burke, "She Lives Life HER Way," *Universal Weekly*, February 10, 1934, 9.
3. Quirk, *Child of Fate*, 14.
4. Keating, "Margaret Sullavan's Last Interview."
5. Burke, "She Lives Life HER Way," 9.
6. Quirk, *Child of Fate*, 12.
7. Wilbor Morse, "The Lady Who Laughed at Hollywood," *Photoplay*, February 1934, 77.
8. Henry Fonda and Howard Teichman, *Fonda: My Life* (Orion Publications, Inc., 1981), 34.
9. Hayward, *Haywire*, 208.
10. Fonda and Teichman, *Fonda*, 54.
11. *Harvard Crimson*, May 8, 1929, www.thecrimson.com.
12. Norris Houghton, *But Not Forgotten: The Adventure of the University Players* (William Sloan Associates, 1951), 84.
13. John Springer, *The Fondas: The Films and Careers of Henry, Jane and Peter Fonda* (Citadel Press, 1970), 17.
14. Houghton, *But Not Forgotten*, 315.
15. "Norris Houghton," Wikipedia, https://en.wikipedia.org/wiki/Norris_Houghton.
16. "The University Players of Cape Cod," Tragedy and Comedy in New England, http://tragedyandcomedyinnewengland.blogspot.com/2009/04/university-players-of-cape-cod.html.
17. Houghton, *But Not Forgotten*, 83.
18. Fonda and Teichman, *Fonda*, 55.
19. Houghton, *But Not Forgotten*, 95–96.
20. Ibid., 106.
21. Joshua Logan, *Josh: My Up and Down, In and Out Life* (Delacourt Press, 1976), 33.
22. Howard Sharpe, "Beautiful Brat-Part Two," *Photoplay*, November 1938, 64.
23. Munn, *Jimmy Stewart*, 39.
24. Hayward, *Haywire*, 212.

233

25. Quirk, *Child of Fate*, 16.
26. Logan, *Josh*, 32–33.
27. Hayward, *Haywire*, 212.
28. Devin McKinney, *The Man Who Saw a Ghost: The Life and Work of Henry Fonda* (St. Martin's Press, 2012), 45.
29. Hayward, *Haywire*, 212.
30. Houghton, *But Not Forgotten*, 116.
31. Logan, *Josh*, 32.
32. Morse, "The Lady Who Laughed at Hollywood," 77.
33. Logan, *Josh*, 32.
34. Ibid., 35.
35. Houghton, *But Not Forgotten*, 125.
36. Ibid., 126.
37. Burke, "She Lives Life," 9.
38. Helen Klump, "Little Girl, What Now?," *Picture Play*, February 1934, 58.

CHAPTER 3

1. Munn, *Jimmy Stewart*, 27.
2. Sharpe, "Beautiful Brat-Part Two," 65.
3. Ibid.
4. Burke, "She Lives Life," 9.
5. "Margaret Sullavan: The Quality She Had," *The Virginian-Pilot*, January 4, 1960.
6. Houghton, *But Not Forgotten*, 159.
7. Ibid., 162.
8. Fonda and Teichmann, *Fonda*, 62.
9. Hayward, *Haywire*, 212.
10. Radie Harris, "Original!," *Screenland*, February 1934, 94.
11. Kyle Crichton, "She Says It's Spinach," *Collier's*, March 17, 1934, 54.
12. Munn, *Jimmy Stewart*, 27.
13. Donald Dewey, *James Stewart* (Turner Publishing Inc., 1996), 295.
14. Unidentified newspaper clipping, Brooke Hayward Papers, 1911–1977, Billy Rose Theatre Division, The New York Public Library for the Performing Arts.
15. Burke, "She Lives Life," 9.
16. Telegram, Brooke Hayward Papers, NYPL.
17. "Margaret Sullavan Tells Highlights of Her Career," *Brownville* (TX) *Herald*, July 1, 1938.
18. *Smithfield* (VA) *Times*, April 12, 1934.
19. McKinney, *The Man Who Saw a Ghost*, 49.
20. Biery, "You'd Like to Shake Her," 62.
21. Burke, "She Lives Life," 9.
22. "And That's How It's Spelled," *Brooklyn Daily Eagle*, August 2, 1931.
23. *Brooklyn Daily Eagle*, May 12, 1931.
24. Newspaper clipping, Brooke Hayward papers, NYPL.
25. *San Antonio* (TX) *Light*, June 7, 1931.

CHAPTER 4

1. Faith Service, "Margaret Sullavan Isn't Afraid to Have Babies," *Motion Picture*, April 1941, 72.
2. Gilbert Swain, "Volstead Ingénue is Standard Role," *Charleston* (WV) *Daily Mail*, June 9, 1931.

3. "Margaret Sullavan Star in Spite of Family's 'No!,'" *Vidette* (IN) *Messenger*, July 3, 1931.
4. Houghton, *But Not Forgotten*, 190.
5. Ibid.
6. Logan, *Josh*, 48.

CHAPTER 5

1. Houghton, *But Not Forgotten*, 260.
2. Fonda and Teichmann, *Fonda*, 65–66.
3. Donald Kirkley, "University Group's Plane Remains High," *Baltimore Sun*, December 13, 1931.
4. Houghton, *But Not Forgotten*, 261.
5. Logan, *Josh*, 50.
6. McKinney, *The Man Who Saw a Ghost*, 45.
7. Scott Eyman, *Hank and Jim: The Fifty-Year Friendship of Henry Fonda and James Stewart* (Simon & Schuster, 2017), 30.
8. Houghton, *But Not Forgotten*, 255.
9. Ibid., 257.
10. Logan, *Josh*, 51.
11. Fonda and Teichmann, *Fonda*, 67.
12. Water Winchell, "On Broadway," *Port Arthur* (TX) *News*, January 22, 1932.
13. Logan, *Josh*, 52–53.
14. Houghton, *But Not Forgotten*, 318.
15. Logan, *Josh*, 53.
16. "Norris Houghton," Wikipedia, https://en.wikipedia.org/wiki/Norris_Houghton.
17. Morse, "The Lady Who Laughed at Hollywood," 104.
18. Fonda and Teichmann, *Fonda*, 68.
19. Quirk, *Child of Fate*, 20.
20. Fonda and Teichmann, *Fonda*, 58.

CHAPTER 6

1. Gilbert Swain, "In New York," *Indiana* (PA) *Evening Gazette*, April 26, 1932.
2. "At the Movies" by Lawrence Van Gelder, December 18, 1987, www.nytimes.com/1987/12/18/movies/at-the-movies.html.
3. "Three Actresses Pine for Authors," *San Antonio Express*, May 22, 1932.
4. Fonda and Teichmann, *Fonda*, 68–69.
5. McKinney, *The Man Who Saw a Ghost*, 52.
6. Service, "Margaret Sullavan Isn't Afraid," 73.
7. Munn, *Jimmy Stewart*, 38.
8. Hindmarsh, "We Remember Margaret Sullavan," 25.
9. *Long Beach* (CA) *Independent*, November 21, 1951.
10. Munn, *Jimmy Stewart*, 42.
11. Ibid., 53.
12. Newspaper clipping, Brooke Hayward Papers, NYPL.
13. Ibid.

CHAPTER 7

1. Robin Coons, *Kalispell* (MT) *Daily Inter-Lake*, February 1, 1933.

2. Old Movie Section, http://gdhamann.blogspot.com.

3. Gregory Mank, "The Tragedy of Sidney Fox," http://www.classicimages.com/people/article_a8aaed75–4fc2–5c36–9c10–c4552ed70494.html.

4. George Morris, "John M. Stahl: The Man Who Understood Women," *Film Comment*, May/June 1977, 50.

5. Coons, *Kalispell Daily Inter-Lake*.

6. Wood Soanes, *Oakland Tribune*, February 2, 1933.

7. Elizabeth Yeamann, *Hollywood Citizen News*, November 18, 1933. See also Hamann, *Margaret Sullavan in the 30s*, 20.

8. Margaret Sullavan, "The Making of a Movie Star," *American Magazine*, July, 1934, 51.

9. Jerry Lane, "Peg Runs Away!," *Hollywood*, April 1934, 54.

10. Chalres Beahan, "How a Star Was Created," *Modern Screen*, January 1934, 50.

11. Reginald Tanner,, "She Abhors Being Beautified," *Photoplay*, October 1933, 69.

12. Beahan, "How a Star Was Created," 50.

13. Sullavan, "The Making of a Movie Star," 51.

14. Beahan, "How a Star Was Created," 103.

15. Michel Mok, "Extra! Movie Star Knocks Movies," *New York Post*, November 10, 1936.

16. Hayward, *Haywire*, 212.

17. Peter Collier, *The Fondas: A Hollywood Dynasty* (G. P. Putnam's Sons, 1991), 36

Chapter 8

1. Walter Winchell, *Corpus Christi* (TX) *Times*, May 19, 1942.

2. Sullavan, "The Making of a Movie Star," 51.

3. Tanner, "She Abhors Being Beautified," 91.

4. James Robert Parish and Ronald L. Bowers, *The MGM Stock Company* (Arlington House, 1975), 690.

5. Sullavan, "The Making of a Movie Star," 51.

6. Ibid., 112.

7. John Boles, "John Boles Introduces Margaret Sullavan," *Picturegoer Weekly,* April 16, 1934, 10.

8. Klump, "Little Girl, What Now?," 32.

9. Quirk, *Child of Fate*, 30.

10. "Margaret Sullavan Tells Highlights," *Brownville* (TX) *Herald*, July 1, 1938.

11. Jerry Lane, "Peg Runs Away!," 54.

12. "Margaret Sullavan Still Can't See How She Score Hit in Her First Film," *Los Angeles Times*, December 31, 1933. See also Hamann, *Margaret Sullavan in the 30s*, 25.

13. Tanner, "She Abhors," 98.

14. Jerry Lane, "Peg Runs Away!," 54.

15. Klump, "Little Girl, What Now?," 32.

16. "Reform on the Way in Hollywood's Job Racket," *Ogden* (UT) *Standard Examiner*, October 10, 1933.

17. "Notes," *Only Yesterday*, http://www.tcm.com/tcmdb/title/85799/Only-Yesterday/notes.html.

Chapter 9

1. Jerry Lane, "Peg Runs Away!," 54.

2. Elizabeth Yeaman, *Hollywood Citizen News*, 9/15/33 See also Hamann, *Margaret Sullavan in the 30s*, 15.

3. Ida Zeitlin, "That Girl's Here Again," *Modern Screen,* July 1938, 85.

4. *Syracuse Herald*, September 29, 1933

5. Hamann, *Margaret Sullavan in the 30s*, 109.

6. Elizabeth Yeaman, *Hollywood Citizen News*, November 11, 1933. See also Hamann, *Margaret Sullavan in the 30s*, 19.

7. Harris, "Original!," 33.

8. Andrew Sarris, *You Ain't Heard Nothin' Yet: The American Talking Film History and Memory, 1927–1949.* (Oxford University Press, 1998), 414.

9. David Thomson, *A Biographical Dictionary of Film* (William Morrow and Company, Inc., 1981), 589.

10. David Shipman, *The Story of Cinema* (St. Martin's Press, 1980), 425.

11. Review of *Little Man, What Now?* http://www.time.com/time/magazine/article/0,9171,762198–2,00.html.

12. Burke, "She Lives Life," 9.

13. Sonia Lee, "Margaret Sullavan Explains Herself," *Screen Play,* April 1934, 64.

14. "Margaret Sullavan, Film Find, Back on the Job." *Xenia* (OH) *Evening Gazette*, January 5, 1934.

15. Elza Schallert, "Hollywood Will Tame Margaret Sullavan," *Motion Picture*, July 1934, 78.

16. Jerry Lane, "Peg Runs Away!," 20.

17. Martin Gottfried, *Jed Harris: The Curse of the Genius* (Little, Brown, and Company, 1984), 147.

18. Lee, "Margaret Sullavan Explains Herself," 65.

19. *Oakland Tribune*, January 5, 1934.

20. *Burlington* (N.C) *Daily Times News*, January 19, 1934.

21. Harrison Carroll, "Behind the Scenes in Hollywood," *Tyrone* (PA) *Daily Herald*, January 25, 1934.

22. *Hammond* (IN) *Times*, January 25, 1934.

23. Elizabeth Yeaman, *Hollywood Citizen News*, February 9, 1934. See also http://gdhamann.blogspot.com. Old Movie Section.

Chapter 10

1. William F. French, "Margaret Sullavan, Hollywood's Pet Peeve," *Movie Classic*, July 1934, 64.

2. Sarris, *You Ain't Heard Nothin' Yet*, 365.

3. Klump, "Little Girl, What Now?," 32.

4. Schallert, "Hollywood Will Tame Margaret Sullavan," 44.

5. Jack Smalley, "Sullavan, the Untamed!," *Hollywood*, July 1934, 54.

6. Patricia Keats, "Can She Repeat?" *Silver Screen*, June 1934, 63.

7. Smalley, "Sullavan, the Untamed!," 54.

8. Ginger Rogers, *Ginger Rogers: My Story* (Harper Collins, Publishers, 1991), 266.

9. Klump, "Little Girl, What Now?," 58.

10. Jenny Williams, *More Lives Than One: A Biography of Hans Fallada* (Libris, 1998), 114.

11. Williams, *More Lives Than One*, XVII.
12. Eileen Creelman, *New York Sun*, February 22, 1934.
13. Herve Dumont, *Frank Borzage: The Life and Films of a Hollywood Romantic* (McFarland and Company, Inc. Publishers, 2006), 28–29.
14. Dumont, *Frank Borzage*, 217.
15. Keats, "Can She Repeat?," 22.
16. Sarris, *You Ain't Heard Nothin' Yet*, 365.
17. Keats, "Can She Repeat?," 22.
18. Schallert, "Hollywood Will Tame Margaret Sullavan," 78.
19. Quirk, *Child of Fate*, 33.
20. *Universal Weekly*, April 14, 1934.
21. Williams, *More Lives Than One*, 278.
22. Steven Scheuer, *Movies on TV* (Bantam Books, 1980), 384.

CHAPTER 11

1. French, "Margaret Sullavan, Hollywood's Pet Peeve," 64.
2. Ibid., 65.
3. Elizabeth Yeaman, *Hollywood Citizen News*, February 20, 1934. See also Hamann, *Margaret Sullavan in the 30s*, 29.
4. French, "Margaret Sullavan, Hollywood's Pet Peeve," 64.
5. Michael Burrows, *Patricia Neal and Margaret Sullavan* (Formative Film Series Publications, 1971), 25.
6. Fonda and Teichmann, *Fonda*, 79.
7. Fonda and Teichmann, *Fonda*, 81.
8. Joan Davidson, "Hank's Dark Years," *Picture Play*, September 1936, 93.
9. Fonda and Teichmann, *Fonda*, 89.
10. Quirk, *Child of Fate*, 43.

CHAPTER 12

1. Jan Herman, *A Talent for Trouble: The Life of Hollywood's Most Acclaimed Director* (G.P. Putnam's Sons, 1995), 126.
2. French, "Margaret Sullavan, Hollywood's Pet Peeve," 65.
3. Hayward, *Haywire*, 202.
4. "William Wyler," Wikipedia, https://en.wikipedia.org/wiki/William_Wyler.
5. Axel Madsen, *William Wyler: The Authorized Biography* (Thomas Y. Cromwell Company, 1973), 109.
6. Ibid.
7. Herman, *A Talent for Trouble*, 127.
8. Quirk, *Child of Fate*, 47.
9. Herman, *A Talent for Trouble*, 127.
10. Howard Sharpe, "Beautiful Brat-Part Three." *Photoplay*, December 1938, 72.
11. Madsen, *William Wyler*, 109.
12. Herman, *A Talent for Trouble*, 128.
13. Ibid., 128–129.
14. Ibid., 129.
15. Madsen, *William Wyler*, 110.

16. Quirk, *Child of Fate*, 49.
17. *Logansport* (IN) *Press*, December 4, 1934.
18. Robbin Coons, "Hollywood Notes," *Lowell* (MA) *Sun*, December 20, 1934.
19. Michael A. Anderegg, *William Wyler* (Twayne Publishers, 1979), 40, 42.
20. *Reno* (NV) *Gazette*, January 12, 1935.
21. Shipman, *The Story of Cinema*, 425.
22. John DiLeo, *100 Great Film Performances You Should Remember—But Probably Don't* (Limelight Editions, 2002) 53.
23. Herman, *A Talent for Trouble*, 130.
24. Ibid., 131.
25. Ibid., 132.

CHAPTER 13

1. Frank Miller, "The Big Idea Behind *Gone with the Wind*," http://www.tcm.com/this-month/article/136725%7C0/The-Big-Idea.html.
2. Louella O. Parsons, *Kingston* (Jamaica) *Gleaner*, April 27, 1935.
3. Sarah E. Gardner, "The Monstrous Wilderness of Mr. Faulkner's Imagination: Stark Young and the Popular Struggle for Southern Identity," Mercer University, https://www.bu.edu/historic/conf2012/Gardner.doc.
4. Nancy Dowd and David Shepard, *King Vidor* (The Scarecrow Press, Inc., 1998), 157.
5. Harrison Carroll, *Tyrone* (PA) *Daily Herald*, May 16, 1935.
6. *San Mateo* (CA) *Times*, June 10, 1935.
7. James B. Fisher, "Hollywood's Aloof Lady," *Screenland*, November 1935, 78.
8. Hayward, *Haywire*, 217.
9. Jeanne DeKoty, "Who Says High Hat?," *Picture Play*, September, 1935, 53.
10. Leon Baron, "Gossips About Hollywood's Film Folks," *Vidette* (IN) *Messenger*, May 23, 1935.
11. Dowd and Shepard, *King Vidor*, 57.
12. Quirk, *Child of* Fate, 55.
13. Herman, *A Talent for Trouble*, 133.
14. *Madison* (WI) *State Journal*, May 23, 1935.
15. Herman, *A Talent for Trouble*, 133–134.
16. *Sandusky* (OH) *Register*, July 16, 1935.
17. Quirk, *Child of Fate*, 51.
18. "William Wyler Deny Rift," *Los Angeles Examiner*, June 7, 1935. See also Hamann, *Margaret Sullavan in the 30s*, 45.
19. "Margaret Sullavan Admits Separation," *Los Angeles Evening Herald Express*, June 25, 1935. See also Hamann, *Margaret Sullavan in the 30s*, 45.
20. Eileen Creelman, "Stark Young Delighted That He Likes Film," *New York Sun*, November 26, 1935.
21. John Douglas Eames, *The Paramount Story* (Crown Publishers, Ltd., 1985), 109.
22. Walter Winchell, *San Antonio Light*, December 20, 1937.
23. Jimmy Starr, *Los Angeles Evening Herald Express*, July 11, 1938. See also Hamann, *Margaret Sullavan in the 30s*, 99.

CHAPTER 14

1. Robbin Coons, "Margaret Sullavan Shuns Glamor But Won't Bite Hollywood," *Moberly* (MO) *Monitor Index and Democrat,* August 2, 1935.
2. DeKolty, "Who Says High Hat?," 52.
3. Margaret J. Bailey, *Those Glorious Glamour Years* (Citadel Press, Inc., 1982), 13.
4. Gladys Hall, "He Gets Away With Murder!," *Modern Screen,* November 1936, 82.
5. Jerry Hoffman, *San Antonio Light,* October 18, 1935.
6. Munn, *Jimmy Stewart,* 63.
7. Ibid., 64.
8. Quirk, *Child of Fate,* 63.
9. Jerry Lane, "Peg Runs Away!," 68.
10. Sara Hamilton, "The Stormy Heart of Margaret Sullavan," *Photoplay,* June 1936, 68.
11. Herman, *A Talent for Trouble,* 136.
12. Donna Risner, "Margaret Sullavan Still a Problem; Won't Conform to Hollywood Ideas!," *Centralia* (WA) *Daily Chronicle,* February 29, 1936.
13. Arthur Blythe, "'My Life is My Own!' Says Margaret Sullavan," *Motion Picture,* April 1936, 88.
14. Hamilton, "The Stormy Heart," 99.
15. Hayward, *Haywire,* 218.
16. Hall, "He Gets Away with Murder!," 80.
17. Parish, *Hollywood's Great Love Teams,* 377.
18. Pauline Kael, *5001 Nights at the Movies* (Henry Holt and Company, 1991), 522.

CHAPTER 15

1. Fonda and Teichmann, *Fonda,* 113.
2. James Robert Parish, *The R.K.O. Gals* (Rainbow Books, 1974), 283.
3. Quirk, *Child of Fate,* 66.
4. Ibid., 67.
5. George Stevens, "Why I Will Not Re-Marry Margaret Sullavan," *Photoplay,* May 1936, 36.
6. Hamilton, "The Stormy Heart," 30.
7. Risner, "Margaret Sullavan Still a Problem."
8. Jimmy Starr, *Los Angeles Evening Herald Express,* February 27, 1936. See also Hamann, *Margaret Sullavan in the 30s,* 56.
9. "Margaret Sullavan and Wyler Divorced," *Los Angeles Examiner,* March 13, 1936. See also Hamann, *Margaret Sullavan in the 30s,* 57.
10. Quirk, *Child of Fate,* 52.
11. Charles Higham, *Marlene: The Life of Marlene Dietrich* (Pockets Books, Inc., 1977), 119.
12. Louella O. Parson, *San Antonio Light,* May 25, 1936.
13. Fonda and Teichmann, *Fonda,* 112–113.
14. Harrison Carroll, *Los Angeles Evening Herald Express,* April 22, 1936. See also Hamann, *Margaret Sullavan in the 30s,* 62.
15. Fonda and Teichmann, *Fonda,* 113.
16. Springer, *The Fondas,* 61
17. Elvis Mitchell, "Under the Influence," www.tcm.com/.../Elvis-Mitchell-Under-the-Influence-Clip-Bill-Murray-Margaret-Sullavan.html.
18. McKinney, *The Man Who Saw a Ghost,* 52.

19. Ted Sennett, *Lunatics and Lovers* (Arlington House, 1973), 105.
20. Risner, "Margaret Sullavan Still a Problem."
21. *San Antonio Light,* May 21, 1936.

CHAPTER 16

1. George Ross, "In New York," *Lowell* (MA) *Sun,* November 5, 1936.
2. *Centralia* (WA) *Chronicle Advertiser,* July 17, 1936.
3. Quirk, *Child of Fate,* 77.
4. Jimmy Starr, *Los Angeles Evening Herald Express,* July 17, 1936. See also Hamann, *Margaret Sullavan in the 30s,* 65.
5. Rogers, *Ginger Rogers,* 194.
6. Hayward, *Haywire,* 187.
7. Edna Ferber, *A Peculiar Treasure* (Doubleday, Doran and Company, Inc., 1939), 387.
8. Malcolm Goldstein, *George S. Kaufman: His Life, His Theater* (Oxford University Press, 1979), 253.
9. Ferber, 387.
10. Jack Gaver, *Hollywood Citizen News,* November 7, 1936. See also Hamann, *Margaret Sullavan in the 30s,* 69.
11. Franklin J. Schaffner, *A Directors Guild of America Oral History: Worthington Miner* (The Directors Guild of America and the Scarecrow Press, 1985), 198.
12. Ross, "In New York."
13. Quirk, *Child of Fate,* 77.
14. Louella O. Parson, *Los Angeles Examiner,* November 16, 1936. See also Hamann, *Margaret Sullavan in the 30s,* 70.
15. Robbin Coons, "Miss Sullavan is Newest Queen of Unpredictability," *Port Arthur* (TX) *News,* November 29, 1936.
16. Julie Goldsmith Gilbert, *Ferber: A Biography of Edna Ferber and Her Circle* (Doubleday and Company, 1978), 323.
17. Quirk, *Child of Fate,* 76.
18. Gilbert, *Ferber,* 323.
19. Ferber, *A Peculiar Treasure,* 387.
20. Louella Parsons, *Los Angeles Examiner,* January 28, 1937. See also Hamann, *Margaret Sullavan in the 30s,* 73.
21. Louella O. Parsons, *Tell It to Louella* (G. P. Putnam's Sons, 1961), 19.
22. *The Vidette Messenger,* February 12, 1937.
23. Harrison Carroll, *Los Angeles Evening Herald Express,* March 8, 1937. See also Hamann, *Margaret Sullavan in the 30s,* 73.

CHAPTER 17

1. Quirk, *Child of Fate,* 71–72.
2. George Lewis, *Los Angeles Post-Record,* January 1, 1934. See also Hamann, *Margaret Sullavan in the 30s,* 25.
3. Louella Parsons, *Los Angeles Examiner,* January 4, 1934 See also Hamann, *Margaret Sullavan in the 30s,* 26.

4. William J. Mann, *Kate: The Woman Who Was Hepburn* (Holt and Company, 2006), 208.

5. Ronald Berghan, *Katharine Hepburn: An Independent Woman* (Arcade Publishing, 2013), 43.

6. Berghan, *Katharine Hepburn*, 42.

7. Mann, *Kate*, 304.

8. Eyman, *Hank and Jim*, 74.

9. *Portsmouth* (OH) *Times*, June 10, 1934.

10. Parish, *The RKO Gals*, 284.

11. Katharine Hepburn, *Me: The Stories of My Life* (Alfred A. Knopf, 1991), 183.

12. Hepburn, *Me*, 184.

13. Mann, *Kate*, 210.

14. Harrison Carroll, *Los Angeles Evening Herald Express*, November 18, 1936. See also Hamann, *Margaret Sullavan in the 30s*, 71.

15. Mann, *Kate*, 260.

16. Barbara Leaming, *Katharine Hepburn* (Crowns Publishers, Inc, 1995), 335.

17. Mann, *Kate*, 260.

18. Ibid., 259.

19. Ibid., *Kate*, 379.

20. Hepburn, *Me*, 190.

21. Mann, *Kate*, 220.

Chapter 18

1. Zeitlin, "That Girl's Here Again," 86.

2. Hall "Not a Problem Child," 73.

3. *San Mateo* (CA) *Times and Daily News Leader*, August 10, 1937.

4. Harriet Parsons, *San Antonio Light*, August 11, 1937.

5. "Miss Sullavan's Next Picture Picked," *San Antonio Light*, November 15, 1937.

6. Louella O. Parsons, *Rochester* (NY) *Democrat and Chronicle*, October 2, 1937.

7. Paul Danai, "Radio Short Circuits," *Hammond* (LA) *Times*, October 6, 1937.

8. *Oakland Tribune*, November 7, 1937.

9. Sheila Graham, *Syracuse Herald-Journal*, October 24, 1937.

10. *New York Times*, January 16, 1938.

Chapter 19

1. Hall, "Not a Problem Child," 73.

2. James Robert Parish and Gregory Mank, *The Best of MGM: The Golden Years* (*1928–59*) (Arlington House Publishers, 1981), X.

3. Jimmie Fidler, *Joplin* (MO) *Globe*, June 26, 1938.

4. Dumont, *Frank Borzage*, 267.

5. Dumont, *Frank Borzage*, 259.

6. Aaron Latham, *Crazy Sundays: F. Scott Fitzgerald in Hollywood* (The Viking Press, 1971), 123.

7. David Denby, "Hitler in Hollywood," *New Yorker*, September 16, 2013, 7, https://www.newyorker.com/magazine/2013/09/16/hitler-in-hollywood.

8. Andrew Turnbull, ed., *The Letters of F. Scott Fitzgerald* (Charles Scribner's Sons, 1963), 560.

9. Dumont, *Frank Borzage*, 259.

10. Latham, *Crazy Sundays*, 23.

11. Turnbull, *The Letters*, 563.

12. Ibid., 564.

13. Kenneth L. Geist, *Pictures Will Talk: The Life and Films of Joseph L. Mankiewicz* (Scribners, 1978), 89–90.

14. Cheryl Bray Lower and R. Barton Palmer, *Joseph L. Mankiewicz: Critical Essays with an Annotated Bibliography and a Filmography* (McFarland & Company, Inc., Publishers, 2001), 218.

15. "Notes," *Three Comrades*, http://www.tcm.com/tcmdb/title/453/Three-Comrades/notes.html.

16. Hall, "Not a Problem Child," 31.

17. Ibid., 73.

18. Charles Tranberg, *Robert Taylor: a Biography* (Bear Manor Media, 2011), 103.

19. Zeitlin, "That Girl's Here Again," 86.

20. Tranberg, *Robert Taylor*, 112.

21. Dumont, *Frank Borzage*, 269.

22. Wood Soanes, *Oakland Tribune*, February 8, 1939.

23. Danny Peary, *Alternate Oscars* (Delta Books, 1993).

24. "Fritz and the Oscars, Best Actress 1938: Margaret Sullavan," http://fritzlovesoscars.blogspot.com/2011/10/best-actress-1938.html.

25. http://www.tcm.com/tcmdb/title/453/Three-Comrades/notes.html; Dan Callahan, "Review of Three Comrades," *Slant Magazine*, July 26, 2006, https://www.slantmagazine.com/film/three-comrades/.

Chapter 20

1. Quirk, *Child of Fate*, 93–94.

2. Eliot Marc, *Jimmy Stewart: A Biography* (Rebel Road, Inc., 2006), 143.

3. Munn, *Jimmy Stewart*, 88.

4. Jimmie Fidler, "In Hollywood," *North Adams* (MA) *Transcript*, April 27, 1938.

5. *Marshan* (MI) *Evening Chronicle*, December 21, 1938.

6. Service, "Margaret Sullavan Isn't Afraid," 73.

7. Geist, *Pictures Will Talk*, 94.

8. Ibid., 95.

9. Frank Miller, *Leading Couples: The Most Unforgettable Screen Romances of the Studio Era* (Chronicle Books, 2004), 169.

10. Dewey, *James Stewart*, 295.

11. Frank Neal, "In Hollywood," *Long Beach* (CA) *Independent*, February 14, 1949.

12. Munn, *Jimmy Stewart*, 195.

13. James Robert Parish and Don E. Stanke, *The All-Americans* (Arlington House Publishers, 1977), 386.

14. Dewey, *James Stewart*, 314

Chapter 21

1. Radie Harris, "Why Margaret Sullavan Will Forsake the Screen for Motherhood," *Screenland*, December 1938, 22.

2. Louella O. Parsons, *Charleston* (WV) *Gazette*, July 6, 1938.

3. Harris "Why Margaret Sullavan Will Forsake," 22.

4. Alexander Kahn, "Hollywood Film Shop," *Dunkirk* (NY) *Evening Observer*, October 1, 1938.

5. Lawrence J. Quirk and William Schoell, *Joan Crawford: The Essential Biography* (The University Press of Kentucky, 2002), 84.

6. Joan Crawford and Jane Kesner Ardmore, *A Portrait of Joan* (Paperback Library, Inc., 1962), 87.

7. Latham, *Crazy Sundays*, 121.

8. Quirk and Schoell, *Joan Crawford*, 91.

9. Robbin Coons, "Hollywood Speaks," *Mansfield* (OH) *News Journal*, December 2, 1938.

10. Crawford and Ardmore, *A Portrait of Joan*, 88.

11. Coons, "Hollywood Speaks."

12. Crawford and Adrmore, *A Portrait of Joan*, 88.

13. Quirk and Schoell, *Joan Crawford*, 92–93.

14. Ronald Haver, *David O. Selznick's Hollywood* (Alfred A. Knopf, 1980), 325.

15. Sarris, *You Ain't Heard Nothin' Yet*, 246.

CHAPTER 22

1. Service, "Margaret Sullavan Isn't Afraid," 72.

2. Louella Parsons, *San Antonio Light*, August 17, 1939.

3. Herman G. Weinberg, *The Lubitsch Touch: A Critical Study* (Dutton, 1968), 151.

4. Weinberg, *The Lubitsch*, 211.

5. William Paul, *Ernst Lubitsch's American Comedy* (Columbia University Press, 1987), 163.

6. Scott Eyman, *Ernst Lubitsch: Laughter in Paradise* (Simon & Schuster, 1993), 200.

7. Munn, *Jimmy Stewart*, 102

8. Ibid., 103.

9. Paul, *Ernst Lubitsch*, 169.

10. "Ernst Lubitsch," Wikipedia, https://en.wikipedia.org/wiki/Ernst_Lubitsch.

11. Ibid.

12. Dewey, *James Stewart*, 210.

13. Tony Thomas, *A Wonderful Life: The Films and Career of James Stewart* (Citadel Press, 1988), 83.

14. Weinberg, *The Lubitsch*, 266–267.

15. Eyman, *Ernst Lubitsch*, 356.

16. Lawrence Van Gelder, "Chronicles,"(www.nytimes.com).

17. Kael, *5001 Nights*, 677.

18. Eyman, *Ernst Lubitsch*, 279.

19. Dewey, *James Stewart*, 208.

20. Eyman, *Ernst Lubitsch*, 281.

CHAPTER 23

1. Phyllis Bottome Quotes, https://www.goodreads.com/author/quotes/124760.Phyllis_Bottome.

2. *Biloxi* (MS) *Daily Herald*, May 26, 1938.

3. Quirk, *Child of Fate*, 107.

4. Scott Eyman, *Lion of Hollywood: The Life and Legend of Louis B. Mayer* (Simon & Schuster, 2005), 277.

5. Alexis Pogorelskin, "Phyllis Bottome's The Mortal Storm: Film and Controversy," in *The Space Between*, 39, https://www.monmouth.edu/department-of-english/documents/phyllis-bottomes-the-mortal-storm-film-and-controversy.pdf/.

6. Pam Hirsch, *The Constant Liberal: The Life and Work of Phyllis Bottome* (Quartet Books Limited, 2010), 245.

7. Roy Mosely, *Evergreen: Victor Saville in His Own Words* (South Illinois University Press, 2000), 140–141.

8. Dumont, *Frank Borzage*, 288.

9. Robert Stack and Mark Evans, *Straight Shooting* (Macmillan Publishing Co., Inc., 1980), 77.

10. Dewey, *James Stewart*, 219.

11. Dumont, *Frank Borzage*, 288.

12. Service, "Margaret Sullavan Isn't Afraid," 72.

13. Quirk, *Child of Fate*, 107.

14. Ibid., 108.

15. Mosely, *Evergreen*, 141.

16. Hirsch, *The Constant Liberal*, 251.

17. Parish and Mank, *The Best of MGM*, 145.

18. Hirsch, *The Constant Liberal*, 152.

19. Phyllis Bottome, "Speaking as One Who Should Know," *New York Times*, June 16, 1940.

20. Frederick Othman, *Middleboro* (KY) *Daily News*, June 26, 1940.

21. David Thomson, *Have You Seen? A Personal Introduction to 1,000 Films* (Alfred A. Knopf, 2008), 571.

22. Steven Schneider, ed., *1001 Movies You Must See Before You Die: The Mortal Storm*. See also https://1001moviesblog.blogspot.com/2014/04/the-mortal-storm-1940.html.

CHAPTER 24

1. Burrows, *Patricia Neal and Margaret Sullavan*, 35.

2. Kingsley Canham, "John Cromwell: Memories of Love, Elegance and Style," in *The Hollywood Professionals, Volume Five: King Vidor, John Cromwell, Mervyn LeRoy* (A.S. Barnes & Co, 1976), 95.

3. Stanley Kramer, *A Mad, Mad, Mad, Mad World: a Life in Hollywood* (Harcourt Brace, 1997), 6.

4. Peter Ford, *Glenn Ford: A Life* (University of Wisconsin Press, 2011), 33–34.

5. "Film Actress Under Restraining Order," *Cumberland* (MD) *Sunday Times*, August 25, 1940.

6. Quirk, *Child of Fate*, 110.

7. Ford, *Glenn Ford*, 34.

8. Kramer, *A Mad, Mad*, 6–7.

9. Harrison Carroll, *San Mateo* (CA) *Times*, September 27, 1940.

10. George Howard, "Mischievous Mother," *Hollywood*, May 1941, 37.

11. Dan Callahan, "Margaret Sullavan: The Art of Dying," *Bright Lights Film Journal*, August 2005, https://brightlightsfilm.com/margaret-sullavan-art-dying/#.XOg6RRS7DHg.

12. *Port Arthur* (TX) *News*, January 17, 1941.

13. "Overview for Films in World War II," Digital History, http://www.digitalhistory.uh.edu/disp_film.cfm?mediatypeid=1&eraid=15&psid=2962.

14. Joe Morella, Edward Z. Epstein and John Griggs, *The Films of World War II* (The Citadel Press, 1973), 15.

CHAPTER 25

1. Jimmie Fidler, "In Hollywood," *Charleston* (WV) *Gazette*, February 5, 1941.
2. "Notes," *Back Street* (1932), http://www.tcm.com/tcmdb/title/67910/Back-Street/notes.html.
3. Andrea Passafiume, "Notes," *Back Street* (1941), http://www.tcm.com/tcmdb/title/67911/Back-Street/notes.html.
4. Louella O. Parsons, *Charleston* (WV) *Gazette*, October 4, 1940.
5. Margaret Sullavan, "Star Contends Good Direction Key to Successful Film," *Lowell* (MA) *Sun*, January 17, 1941.
6. Louella O. Parson, *Charleston* (WV) *Gazette*, October 10, 1940.
7. Sullavan, "Star Contends."
8. Eileen Creeland, "Stevenson on His Film Work," *New York Sun* (unidentified date).
9. Fidler, "In Hollywood," February 5, 1941.
10. Creeland, "Stevenson on His Film Work."
11. Joe Fisher, "Review of Reviews," *Edwardsville* (IL) *Intelligencer*, February 14, 1941.
12. Quirk, *Child of Fate*, 13–14.
13. Fidler, "In Hollywood," February 5, 1941.
14. Eve Golden, *Vamp: The Rise and Fall of Theda Bara* (Enterprise Publishing, Inc., 1995).

CHAPTER 26

1. Howard, "Mischievous Mother," 27.
2. Louella Parsons, *Charleston* (WV) *Gazette*, March 29, 1941.
3. Louella Parsons, *Charleston* (WV) *Gazette*, March 19, 1941.
4. Ibid.
5. Louella Parsons, *Waterloo* (IA) *Daily Courier*, May 9, 1941.
6. Larry Swindell, *The Reluctant Lover: Charles Boyer* (Doubleday and Company, Inc., 1983), 171.
7. Swindell, *The Reluctant Lover*, 175.
8. Quirk, *Child of Fate*, 123.
9. Charles R. Moore, "Hollywood Film Shop," (Butte) *Montana Standard*, September 17, 1941.

CHAPTER 27

1. "Margaret Sullavan Likes Role of Mother," *San Antonio Light*, September 1, 1941.
2. "Margaret Sullavan, Already Mother of 3, Wants More," *Helena* (MT) *Independent*, August 31, 1941.
3. Hindmarsh, "We Remember Margaret Sullavan," 27.
4. Jimmie Fidler, (Reno) *Nevada State Journal*, October 23, 1942.
5. Jimmie Fidler, *Joplin* (MO) *Globe*, October 28, 1942.
6. Jimmie Fidler, *Joplin* (MO) *Globe*, November 24, 1942.

7. Louella Parsons, "Screen Star Plans End to Film Career," *San Antonio Light*, January 10, 1943.
8. "Trivia," *Cry "Havoc,"* https://www.imdb.com/title/tt0035770/trivia.
9. Frederick C. Othman, *Hollywood Citizen News*, May 22, 1943. See also Hamann, *Margaret Sullavan in the 30s*, 124.
10. Louella Parsons, *Waterloo Daily Courier*, May 6, 1943.
11. Othman, *Hollywood Citizen News*.
12. Quirk, *Child of Fate*, 126.
13. *Traverse City* (MI) *Record Eagle*, September 22, 1946.
14. Quirk, *Child of Fate*, 125.
15. Hayward, *Haywire*, 96.
16. Marsha Hunt, *The Way We Wore: Styles of the 1930s and '40s and Our World Since Then* (Fallbrook Pub Ltd., 1993), 151.
17. Eric Marchese, "*Cry Havoc* in Anaheim Hills Needs More Grit," www.ocregister.com.
18. *Waterloo Daily Courier*, July 27, 1943.

CHAPTER 28

1. Collier, *The Fondas*, 31.
2. Ward Morehouse, *Matinee Tomorrow: Fifty Years of Our Theater* (McGraw-Hill Book Company, Inc., 1949), 278.
3. Elliott Nugent, *Events Leading Up to the Comedy* (Trident Press, 1965), 170.
4. Nugent, *Events*, 171.
5. Clayton Irwin, *Charleston* (WV) *Gazette*, March 10, 1944.
6. Nugent, *Events*, 174–175.
7. Ibid., 175.
8. Ibid., 176.
9. John Van Druten, "The Voice of the Turtle—Margaret Sullavan," *Theatre Arts*, May 1944, 278.
10. Morehouse, *Matinee Tomorrow*, 278.
11. Nugent, *Events*, 176.
12. Harold J. Kennedy, *No Pickle, No Performance* (Doubleday & Company, Inc., 1978), 230.
13. Nugent, *Events*, 176.
14. Quirk, *Child of Fate*, 130.
15. Burrows, *Patricia Neal and Margaret Sullavan*, 35.
16. Van Druten, "The Voice of the Turtle," 273.
17. Ibid., 279.
18. Clayton Irwin, *Charleston* (WV) *Gazette*, March 10, 1944.
19. Hayward, *Haywire*, 88.
20. Jimmie Fidler, *Joplin* (MO) *Globe*, February 9, 1944.
21. Nugent, *Events*, 176.
22. Hedda Hopper, *Salt Lake Tribune*, May 10, 1944.
23. Sarris, *You Ain't Heard Nothin' Yet*, 412.
24. *New York Times*, November 14, 1954.

CHAPTER 29

1. Erich Brandels, *Lebanon* (PA) *Daily News*, July 27, 1945.

2. Hedda Hopper, "Free as a Breeze," *Salt Lake Tribune*, May 28, 1945.

3. Bedell S. Smith, *Reflected Glory: The Life of Pamela Churchill Harriman* (Simon and Schuster, 1996), 201.

4. Hayward, *Haywire*, 68.

5. Fonda and Teichmann, *Fonda*, 139–140.

6. Hayward, *Haywire*, 159.

7. Fonda and Teichmann, *Fonda*, 140.

8. Jane Fonda, *My Life So Far* (Random House, Inc., 2006), 36.

9. Ibid., 48.

10. Colliers, *The Fondas*, 65.

11. Louella Parsons, *Lowell* (MA) *Sun*, August 28, 1946.

12. *Ibid.*

13. Jack Gaven, *Dunkirk* (NY) *Evening Observer*, August 9, 1945.

14. Hayward, *Haywire*, 187.

15. Ibid., 185.

16. Dorothy Kilgallen, *Lowell Sun*, July 21, 1947.

17. Hayward, *Haywire*, 161.

18. "London Gets Lift," *Big Spring* (TX) *Weekly Herald*, January 2, 1948.

19. Burrows, *Patricia Neal and Margaret Sullavan*, 34.

20. Hayward, *Haywire*, 187.

21. Ibid., 186–187.

22. Ibid., 187.

23. "Margaret Sullavan Granted Divorce," *Oakland Tribune*, April 29, 1948.

24. Hayward, *Haywire*, 188–189.

25. Tennessee Williams, *Memoirs* (Doubleday and Company, Inc., 1975), 132.

26. Louella Parsons, *Lowell Sun*, December 1, 1947.

27. Erskine Johnson, *Mattoon* (IL) *Daily Journal-Gazette*, January 9, 1948.

28. Louella Parsons, *Lowell Sun*, May 29, 1948.

29. Dick Kleiner, *Pampa* (TX) *Daily News*, November 29, 1954.

30. Schaffner, *A Directors Guild*, 198.

31. Ibid., 198–199.

32. Ibid., 199.

33. Louella Parsons, *Lowell Sun*, December 1, 1948.

34. "Miss Sullavan Seeks Release," *New York Times*, December 22, 1948.

Chapter 30

1. "What Lies Ahead for Miss Sullavan?," *Albany Times-Union*, May 31, 1957.

2. Frank Daugherty, "Buddy Adler, Exhibitor-Producer," *New York Times*, April 16, 1950.

3. *Brooklyn Daily Eagle*, May 28, 1950.

4. Quirk, *Child of Fate*, 138.

5. Louella Parsons, "Miss Sullavan in Movies Again," *Galveston* (TX) *Daily News*, April 15, 1949.

6. Hedda Hopper, *Newark* (NJ) *Advocate*, September 29, 1949.

7. Hayward, *Haywire*, 227.

8. Dewey, *James Stewart*, 285.

9. Clive Denton, Kingsley Canham and Tony Thomas, *The Hollywood Professionals: Henry King, Lewis Milestone, Sam Wood* (A. S. Barnes and Company, 1974), 172–173.

10. Bob Thomas, *Bakersfield* (CA) *Californian*, October 22, 1949.

11. Erskine Johnson, "Margaret Sullavan No Longer Worried About Her Hearing," *Miami* (OK) *Daily News Record*, November 7, 1949.

12. Quirk, *Child of Fate*, 140.

13. *Brooklyn Daily Eagle*, May 28, 1950.

14. Quirk, 137.

15. Suzanne Finstad, *Natasha: The Biography of Natalie Wood* (Harmony Books, 2001), 72.

16. Louella O. Parsons, *Bakersfield Californian*, January 28, 1950.

17. Patricia Bosworth, *Jane Fonda: The Private Life of a Public Woman* (Houghton Mifflin Harcourt, 2011), 73.

18. Daugherty, "Buddy Adler."

19. Marl Barron, "Star Of *Deep Blue Sea* Off Stage 8 Years," *Cumberland* (MD) *Times*, November 16, 1952.

Chapter 31

1. Inez Robb, "Christmas Eve Gift to Close Hit Show," *Binghamton* (NY) *Press*, December 22, 1952.

2. Louella O. Parsons, *San Antonio Light*, February 15, 1950.

3. "Margaret Sullavan Reported Married," *Syracuse Post-Standard*, 8/31/50.

4. "Kenneth Wagg Obituary," The Telegraph, last modified June 24, 2000, https://www.telegraph.co.uk/news/1344643/Kenneth-Wagg.html

5. Hayward, *Haywire*, 240.

6. Louella O. Parsons, *Cedar Rapids* (IA) *Gazette*, September 14, 1950.

7. *Racine* (WS) *Journal Times*, October 25, 1950.

8. Louella O. Parsons, (Phoenix) *Arizona Republic*, February 13, 1952.

9. "Critics Unhappy Over TV Awards," *Abilene* (TX) *Reporter News*, March 9, 1952.

10. Mark Barron, *Fitchburg* (MA) *Sentinel*, March 21, 1952.

11. Geoffrey Wansell, *Terence Rattigan* (Fourth Estate Limited, 1995), 216.

12. Ibid., 229.

13. Barron, "Star of *Deep Blue Sea*," November 16, 1952.

14. Wansell, *Terence Rattigan*, 229.

15. Ibid., 230.

16. Inez Robb, *Cedar Rapids Gazette*, November 9, 1952.

17. Dorothy Kilgallen, *Charleston Gazette*, November 9, 1952.

18. Wansell, *Terence Rattigan*, 230.

19. Jack Gaver, "Sullavan Stars In *Deep Blue Sea* By Terry Rattigan," *Kingsport* (TN) *Times-News*, November 30, 1952.

20. Henry Ward, "Margaret Sullavan Plans for a Future—at Home," *Pittsburgh Press*, April 8, 1953.

21. Inez Robb, "Margaret Sullavan Given Christ-

mas Eve," *Syracuse Herald-Journal*, December 22, 1952.

22. Ibid.

Chapter 32

1. Hayward, *Haywire*, 261.
2. Ibid., 263.
3. *New York Times*, November 14, 1954.
4. Cathleen Nesbit, *A Little Love and Good Company* (September House Publishers, Inc., 1977), 206.
5. Ibid., 204.
6. Ibid., 204–205.
7. Ibid., 206.
8. *Zanesville* (OH) *Signal*, October 27, 1953.
9. Hayward, *Haywire*, 262.
10. John Crosby, "TV Fairy Tales Romances Now in Vogue," *Oakland Tribune*, November 30, 1953.
11. Hayward, *Haywire*, 260.
12. *New York Times*, November 14, 1954.
13. Jack O'Brian, "Radio TV Chatter," *Tipton* (IN) *Tribune*, September 24, 1954.
14. Dick Kleiner, "The Marquee," *Pampa* (TX) *Daily News*, November 29, 1954.
15. Steven H. Scheuer, "Margaret Sullavan Just a Book Seller at Heart," *Brooklyn Daily Eagle*, October 28, 1954.
16. *New York Times*, November 14, 1954.

Chapter 33

1. Quirk, *Child of Fate*, 161.
2. Sian Ballen and Lesley Hague, "Brooke Duchin," New York Social Diary, www.newyorksocialdiary.com/social-diary/2011/haywire-and-humble.
3. Slim Keith and Annette Tappert, *Slim: Memories of a Rich and Imperfect Life* (Simon and Shuster, 1990), 186.
4. Ibid., 180.
5. Ibid., 191.
6. Fred H. Russell, "Gossip of the Rialto," *Bridgeport* (CT) *Post*, December 19, 1954.
7. *Rocky Mount* (NC) *Evening Telegram*, February 24, 1955.
8. Kennedy, *No Pickle*, 230.
9. David Richards, "At Age 66, an Actor Looks Back at His Career," *The Journal-News*, September 9, 1984.
10. James Robert Parish, *The Paramount Pretties*, 116.
11. *Virginian Pilot and Chronicle*, June 3, 1956.
12. Smith, *Reflected Glory*, 197.
13. *Virginia-Post and Portsmouth Star*, January 3, 1960.
14. Charles Mercer, "Margaret Sullavan Meets Her 'Beau,'" *The Albany Knickerbocker News*, October 9, 1956
15. Kennedy, *No Pickle*, 61–62.
16. *New York Times*, October 11, 1956.
17. "Miss Sullavan Misses T.V. Show," *New York Times*, October 9, 1956.
18. *New York Times*, October 10, 1956.
19. Earl Wilson, "The Margaret Sullavan Mys-

tery—A Tantrum or Is She Really Sick?," *New York Post*, October 10, 1956.
20. Ibid.
21. *New York Times*, October 11, 1956.
22. "Miss Sullavan Didn't Ask for Replacement, CBS Replies," *Buffalo Evening News*, October 11, 1956.
23. *New York Times*, November 29, 1956.
24. "What Lies Ahead ... Sullavan?" *Albany Times-Union*, May 31, 1957.
25. Leonard Lyons, *Long Beach* (CA) *Independent*, February 13, 1957.
26. Dorothy Kilgallen, *Anderson* (IN) *Daily Bulletin*, May 2, 1957.
27. Kennedy, *No Pickle*, 62.
28. Ibid., 63.
29. Ibid., 64.
30. Ibid., 61.

Chapter 34

1. Keating, "Margaret Sullavan's Last Interview."
2. Quirk, *Child of Fate*, 163.
3. "Sonnet 29," www.shakespeare-online.com/sonnets/29.html.
4. Deborah Marshall, "Peace Comes at Last to a Tortured Soul," *Modern Screen*, April 1960, 73.
5. Keating, "Margaret Sullavan's Last Interview."
6. Mann, *Kate*, 243.
7. Hayward, *Haywire*, 221.
8. *Virginia Post and Portsmouth Star*, January 3, 1960.
9. Marshall, "Peace Comes at Last," 73.
10. *New York Times*, January 2, 1960.
11. *Reading* (PA) *Eagle*, January 5, 1960.
12. Marshall, "Peace Comes at Last," 73.
13. *New York Times*, January 2, 1960.
14. Mann, *Kate*, 248.
15. Marshall, "Peace Comes at Last," 74.
16. Fonda and Teichmann, *Fonda*, 290.
17. *Virginia Post and Portsmouth Star*, January 3, 1960.
18. *New York Times*, January 4, 1960.
19. Burrows, *Patricia Neal and Margaret Sullavan*, 36.
20. Bosworth, *Jane Fonda*, 161.
21. "Impish Peggy Hated Fuss," (Unidentified newspaper), Norfolk Public Library.

Chapter 35

1. Christine Spines, "Legendary Survivor: Brooke Hayward Was Born to Hollywood Royalty, Married and Divorced Dennis Hopper and Lived to Tell the Tale," March 8, 2011, www.hemi-syncproductsandprograms.com/haywire/haywire.html.
2. Quirk, *Child of Fate*, 168–169.
3. Paul Hoffmann, "Death Discloses Actress' Secret," *New York Times*, January 9, 1960.
4. Judith Cirst, "Star Was Deaf; Leaves Ears to Science," *Winnipeg Free Press*, January 9, 1960.
5. Hoffmann, "Death Discloses."
6. "Kenneth Wagg" (obituary) 24 Jun 2000; www.

telegraph.co.uk/news/obituaries/1344643/Kenneth-Wagg.html.

7. "Bridget Hayward Is Found Dead," *Owosso* (MI) *Argus-Press*, October 18, 1960.

8. Smith, *Reflected Glory*, 224.

9. Peter Fonda, *Don't Tell Dad: A Memoir* (Hyperion, 1998), 142.

10. Robert Windeler, "The Eldest Daughter Remembers When Filmland's Golden Family, the Haywards, Went Haywire," *People*, May 23, 1974, https://people.com/archive/the-eldest-daughter-remembers-when-filmlands-golden-family-the-haywards-went-haywire-vol-7-no-20/.

11. Andrea Chambers, "The Combo's a Little Haywire, but Brooke Hayward and Bandleader Peter Duchin Play a Good Duet," April 14, 1986, https://people.com/archive/the-combos-a-little-haywire-but-brooke-hayward-and-bandleader-peter-duchin-play-a-good-duet-vol-25-no-15/.

12. Windeler, "The Eldest Daughter."

13. "Sad Marital Split," Page Six, https://pagesix.com/2008/09/07/sad-marital-split/.

14. Chambers, "The Combo's a Little Haywire."

15. Brooke Hayward quotes, https://www.goodreads.com/author/quotes/803964.Brooke_Hayward.

16. Spines, "Legendary Survivor."

17. Windeler, "The Eldest Daughter."

18. Spines, "Legendary Survivor."

19. Windeler, "The Eldest Daughter."

20. Judy Klemesrud, "*Haywire-* Or What It's Like With Everything and Nothing," *Ocala* (FL) *Star-Banner*, April 6, 1977.

21. "*Haywire* (book)," Wikipedia, https://en.wikipedia.org/wiki/Haywire_(book).

22. James Kotsilibas-Davis and Myrna Loy, *Myrna Loy: Being and Becoming* (Alfred A. Knopf, 1987), 143.

23. Kotsilibas-Davis and Loy, *Myrna Loy*, 144.

24. "Trivia," *Haywire* (1980 TV Movie), https://www.imdb.com/title/tt0080849/trivia?ref_=tt_ql_trv_1.

25. Eyman, *Hank and Jim*, 314.

26. "The Storm," *Bonanza,* video, 00:44:50–00:44:57, www.youtube.com/watch?v=o7Wn5P1uxH8.

Bibliography

BOOKS

Anderegg, Michael A. *William Wyler*. Twayne Publishers, 1979.

Bailey, Margaret J. *Those Glorious Glamour Years*. Citadel Press, 1982.

Belton, John. *The Hollywood Professionals: Howard Hawks, Frank Borzage, Edgar G. Ulmer*. A. S. Barnes and Co., 1974.

Berghan, Ronald. *Katharine Hepburn: An Independent Woman*. Arcade Publishing, 2013.

Bosworth, Patricia. *Jane Fonda: The Private Life of a Public Woman*. Houghton Mifflin Harcourt, 2011.

Burrows, Michael. *Patricia Neal and Margaret Sullavan*. Formative Film Series Publications, 1971.

Canham, Kingsley. *The Hollywood Professionals, Volume Five: King Vidor, John Cromwell, Mervyn LeRoy*. A.S. Barnes & Co, 1976.

Chandler, Charlotte. *I Know Where I'm Going: Katharine Hepburn, a Personal Biography*. Simon & Schuster, 2010.

Collier, Peter. *The Fondas: A Hollywood Dynasty*. G. P. Putnam's Sons, 1991.

Crawford, Joan, and Jane Kesner Ardmore. *A Portrait of Joan*. Paperback Library, Inc., 1962.

Darlow, Michael, and Gillian Hobson. *Terence Rattigan—The Man and His Work*. Quartet Books, 1979.

Denton, Clive, Kingsley Canham, and Tony Thomas. *The Hollywood Professionals: Henry King, Lewis Milestone, Sam Wood*. A. S. Barnes and Co., 1974.

Dewey, Donald. *James Stewart*. Turner Publishing, Inc., 1996.

Dick, Bernard F. *Joseph L. Mankiewicz*. Twayne Publishers, 1983.

Dowd, Nancy, and David Shepard. *King Vidor*. The Scarecrow Press, Inc., 1988.

Dumont, Herve. *Frank Borzage: The Life and Films of a Hollywood Romantic*. McFarland & Company, Inc., Publishers, 2006.

Durham, Weldon B., ed. *American Theatre Companies, 1888–1930*. Greenwood Press, 1987.

Eames, John Douglas. *The Paramount Story*. Octopus Books, Ltd., 1985.

Eliot, Marc. *Jimmy Stewart: A Biography*. Rebel Road, Inc., 2006.

Eyman, Scott. *Ernst Lubitsch: Laughter in Paradise*. Simon & Schuster, 1993.

Eyman, Scott. *Hank and Jim: The Fifty-Year Friendship of Henry Fonda and James Stewart*. Simon & Schuster, 2017.

Eyman, Scott. *Lion of Hollywood: The Life and Legend of Louis B. Mayer*. Simon & Schuster, 2005.

Felleman, Susan. *Botticelli in Hollywood: The Films of Albert Lewin*. Twayne Publishers, 1997.

Ferber, Edna. *A Peculiar Treasure*. Doubleday, Doran and Company, 1939.

Finstad, Suzanne. *Natasha: The Biography of Natalie Wood*. Harmony Books, 2001.

Fonda, Henry, and Howard Teichman. *Fonda: My Life*. Orion Productions, Inc., 1981.

Fonda, Jane. *My Life So Far*. Random House, Inc., 2005.

Fonda, Peter. *Don't Tell Dad: A Memoir*. Hyperion, 1998.

Ford, Peter. *Glenn Ford: A Life*. University of Wisconsin Press, 2011.

Geist, Kenneth L. *Pictures Will Talk: The Life and Films of Joseph L. Mankiewicz*. Scribners, 1978.

Gilbert, Julie Goldsmith. *Ferber: A Biography of Edna Ferber and Her Circle*. Doubleday & Company, Inc., 1978.

Golden, Eve. *Vamp: The Rise and Fall of Theda Bara*. Enterprise Publishing, Inc., 1995.

Goldstein, Malcolm. *George S. Kaufman: His Life, His Theater*. Oxford University Press, 1979.

Gottfried, Martin. *Jed Harris: The Curse of the Genius*. Little, Brown, and Company, 1984.

Hamann, G. D. *Margaret Sullavan in the 30s*. Filming Today Press, 2014.

Haver, Ronald. *David O. Selznick's Hollywood*. Bonanza Books, 1987.

Hayward, Brooke. *Haywire*. Alfred A. Knopf, 1977.

Hepburn, Katharine. *Me: The Stories of My Life*. Alfred A. Knopf, 1991.

Herman, Jan. *A Talent for Trouble: The Life of Hollywood's Most Acclaimed Director*. G.P. Putnam's Sons, 1995.

Higham, Charles. *Bette: The Life of Bette Davis*. Macmillan Publishing Co., 1981.

Higham, Charles. *Marlene: The Life of Marlene Dietrich*. Pockets Books, Inc., 1977.

Hirsch, Pam. *The Constant Liberal—The Life and Work of Phyllis Bottome,* Quartet Books, 2010.

Hirschhorn, Clive. *The Universal Story*. Crown Publishers, Inc., 1983.

Houghton, Norris. *But Not Forgotten: The Adventure of the University Players*. William Sloan Associates, 1951.

Hunt, Marsha. *The Way We Wore: Styles of the 1930s and 1940s and Our World Since Then*. Fallbrook Publishing, Ltd., 1993.

Kael, Pauline. *5001 Nights at the Movies*. Henry Holt and Company, 1991.

Keith, Slim, and Annette Tappert. *Slim: Memories of a Rich and Imperfect Life*. Simon & Schuster, 1990.

Kennedy, Harold J. *No Pickle, No Performance*. Doubleday & Company, Inc., 1978.

Kerbel, Michael. *Henry Fonda*. Pyramid Communications, Inc., 1975.

Kotsilibas-Davis, James, and Myrna Loy. *Myrna Loy: Being and Becoming*. Alfred A. Knopf, 1987.

Kramer, Stanley. *A Mad, Mad, Mad, Mad World: A Life in Hollywood*. Harcourt Brace, 1997.

Lamster, Frederick. *Souls Made Great Through Love and Adversity: The Film Work of Frank Borzage*. The Scarecrow Press, Inc., 1981.

Latham, Aaron. *Crazy Sundays: F. Scott Fitzgerald in Hollywood*. Vikings Press, 1971.

Leaming, Barbara. *Katharine Hepburn*. Crowns Publishers, Inc., 1995.

Logan, Joshua. *Josh: My Up and Down, In and Out Life*. Delacorte Press, 1976.

Madsen, Axel. *William Wyler: The Authorized Biography*. Thomas Y. Cromwell Company, 1973.

Mann, William J. *Kate: The Woman Who Was Hepburn*. Henry Holt and Company, 2006.

Mcgilligan, Patrick. *Alfred Hitchcock: A Life in Darkness and Light*. It Books, 2004.

McKinney, Devin. *The Man Who Saw a Ghost: The Life and Work of Henry Fonda*. St. Marti's Press, 2012.

Miller, Frank. *Leading Couples: The Most Unforgettable Screen Romances of the Studio Era*. Chronicle Books, 2008.

Molyneaux, Gerard. *James Stewart: A Bio-Bibliography*. Greenwood Press, 1992.

Morehouse, Ward. *Matinee Tomorrow: Fifty Years of Our Theater*. McGraw-Hill Book Company, Inc., 1949.

Morella, Joe, Edward Z. Epstein, and John Griggs. *The Films of World War II*. The Citadel Press, 1973.

Mosely, Roy. *Evergreen: Victor Saville in His Own Words*. South Illinois University Press, 2000.

Munn, Michael. *Jimmy Stewart: The Truth Behind the Legend*. Barricade Books, 2006.

Nesbit, Cathleen. *A Little Love and Good Company*. Stemmer House Publishers, Inc., 1977.

Nott, Robert. *The Films of Randolph Scott*. McFarland & Company, Inc., Publishers, 2004.

Nugent, Elliott. *Events Leading Up to the Comedy*. Trident Press, 1965.

Parish, James Robert. *Hollywood Great Love Teams*. Arlington House, 1974.

Parish, James Robert. *The Paramount Pretties*. Arlington House, 1972.

Parish, James Robert. *The R.K.O. Gals*. Rainbow Books, 1974.

Parish, James Robert, and Don E. Stanke. *The All-Americans*. Arlington House Publishers, 1977.

Parish, James Robert, and Gregory Mank. *The Best of MGM: The Golden Years (1928–59)*. Arlington House Publishers, 1981.

Parish, James Robert, and Ronald L. Bowers. *The MGM Stock Company*. Arlington House, 1975.

Paul, William. *Ernst Lubitsch's American Comedy*. Columbia University Press, 1987.

Peary, Danny. *Alternate Oscars*. Delta Publishers, 1993.

Quirk, Lawrence J. *Child of Fate: Margaret Sullavan*. St. Martin's Press, 1986.

Quirk, Lawrence J., and William Schoell. *Joan Crawford: The Essential Biography*. University Press of Kentucky, 2002.

Robinson, Alice M., Vera Mowry Roberts, and Milly S. Barranger, PhD., eds. *Notable Women in the American Theatre: A Biographical Dictionary*. Greenwood Press, 1989.

Rogers, Ginger. *Ginger Rogers: My Story*. Harper-Collins, Publishers, 1991.

Sarris, Andrew. *You Ain't Heard Nothin' Yet: The American Talking Film History and Memory, 1927–1949*. Oxford University Press, 1998.

Schaffner, Franklin J. *A Directors Guild of America Oral History: Worthington Miner*. The Directors Guild of America and the Scarecrow Press, 1985.

Scheuer, Steven, ed. *Movies on TV*. Bantam Books, 1981.

Sennett, Ted. *Lunatics and Lovers*. Arlington House, 1973.

Shipman, David. *The Great Movie Stars: The Golden Years*. Bonanza Books, 1970.

Shipman, David. *The Story of Cinema: A Complete Narrative History from the Beginnings to the Present*. St. Martin's Press, 1980.

Smith, Sally Bedell. *Reflected Glory: The Life of Pamela Churchill Harriman*. Simon & Schuster, 1996.

Springer, John. *The Fondas: The Films and Careers of Henry, Jane and Peter Fonda*. Citadel Press, 1970.

Stack, Robert, and Mark Evans. *Straight Shooting*. Macmillan Publishing Co., Inc., 1980.

Sturges, Preston. *Preston Sturges on Preston Sturges*. Simon & Schuster, 1980.

Sweeney, Kevin. *Henry Fonda: A Bio-Bibliography*. Greenwood Press, 1992.

Swindell, Larry. *The Reluctant Lover: Charles Boyer*. Doubleday and Company, Inc., 1983.

Taylor, Harley U., Jr. *Erich Maria Remarque: A Literary and Film Biography*. Peter Lang Publishing, Inc., 1977.

Thompson, Howard. *James Stewart*. Pyramid Communications, Inc., 1974.

Thomson, David. *A Biographical Dictionary of Film*. William Morrow and Company, 1981.

Thomson, David. *Have You Seen? A Personal Introduction to 1,000 Films*. Alfred A. Knopf, 2008.

Tranberg, Charles. *Robert Taylor: A Biography*. Bear Manor Media, 2011.

Turnbull, Andrew, ed. *The Letters of F. Scott Fitzgerald*. Charles Scribner's Sons, 1963.

Vermilye, Jerry. *Bette Davis*. Galahad Books, 1973.

Wansell, Geoffrey. *Terence Rattigan*. Dourth Estate Limited, 1995.

Weinberg, Herman G. *The Lubitsch Touch: A Critical Study*. Dutton, 1968.

Williams, Jenny. *More Lives Than One: A Biography of Hans Fallada*. Libris, 1998.

Williams, Tennessee. *Memoirs*. Doubleday & Company, Inc., 1975.

PERIODICALS

American Magazine
Sullavan, Margaret. "The Making of a Movie Star." July 1934.

Collier's
Crichton, Kyle. "She Says It's Spinach." March 17, 1934.

Films in Review
Jacobs, J. "Margaret Sullavan." April 1960.

Hollywood
Biery, Ruth. "You'd Like to Shake Her—But You Can't Help Loving Peg Sullavan." May 1934.

Howard, George. "Mischievous Mother." May 1941.

Lane, Jerry. "Peg Runs Away!" April 1934.

"Margaret Sullavan: An Armbreaking Interview." July 1936.

Smalley, Jack. "Sullavan, the Untamed!." July 1934.

Warwick, Lee. "You Can't Beat a Girl Like That!." February 1934.

Modern Screen
Beahan, Charles. "How a Star Was Created." January 1934.

Hall, Gladys. "He Gets Away with Murder!" September 1936.

Harris, Radie. "Never a Dull Moment." September 1936.

Marshall, Deborah. "Peace Comes at Last to a Tortured Soul." April 1960.

Zeitlin, Ida. "That Girl's Here Again." July 1938.

Motion Picture
Blythe, Arthur. "'My Life is My Own!' Says Margaret Sullavan." April 1936.

Hall, Gladys. "Not a Problem Child." May 1938.

Schallert, Elza. "Hollywood Will Tame Margaret Sullavan." July 1934.

Service, Faith. "Margaret Sullavan Isn't Afraid to Have Babies." April 1941.

Movie Classic
French, William F., "Margaret Sullavan, Hollywood's Pet Peeve." July 1934.

Lane, Virginia. "'I Can't Pretend!' Says Margaret Sullavan." October 1935.

Photoplay
Baskette, Kirlley. "Margaret Sullavan Wants None of It!." January 1935.

Hamilton, Sara. "The Stormy Heart of Margaret Sullavan." June 1936.

Morse, Wilbor. "The Lady Who Laughed at Hollywood." February 1934.

Sharpe, Howard. "Beautiful Brat-Part One." October 1938.

Sharpe, Howard. "Beautiful Brat-Part Three." December 1938.

Sharpe, Howard. "Beautiful Brat-Part Two." November 1938

Stevens, George. "Why I Will Not Re-Marry Margaret Sullavan." May 1936.

Tanner, Reginald. "She Abhors Being Beautified." October 1933.

Picture Play
DeKoty, Jeanne. "Who Says High Hat?." September 1935.

Klump, Helen. "Little Girl, What Now?." February 1934.

Picturegoer Weekly
Boles, John. "John Boles Introduces Margaret Sullavan." April 16, 1934.

Screenland
Fisher, James B. "Hollywood's Aloof Lady." November 1935.

Harris, Radie. "Margaret Sullavan Forsakes the Screen for Motherhood." December 1938.

Harris, Radie. "Original!." February 1934.

Screen Play
Lee, Sonia. "Margaret Sullavan Explains Herself." April 1934.

Silver Screen
DeKolty, Jeanne. "On Location With a Best Seller." November 1935.

Karel, Paul. "Three Chances for Happiness." July 1938.

Keats, Patricia. "Can She Repeat?." June 1934.

Theatre Arts Monthly
Keating, John. "Margaret Sullavan's Last Interview." February 1960.

Van Durten, John. "The Voice of the Turtle–Margaret Sullavan." May 1944.

Tidewater Virginian
Hindmarsh, Connie. "We Remember Margaret Sullavan." Volume 1, Issue 2, July 1977.

Universal Weekly
Burke, Marcella. "She Lives Life HER Way." February 10, 1934.

ON-LINE RESOURCES

Callahan, Dan. "Margaret Sullavan and the Art of Dying." *Bright Lights Film Journal*. https://brightlightsfilm.com/margaret-sullavan-art-dying/#.XO7rgBS7DHg.

Gardner, Sarah E. "'The Monstrous Wilderness of Mr. Faulkner's Imagination:' Stark Young and the Popular Struggle for Southern Identity." Mercer University. https://www.bu.edu/historic/conf2012/Gardner.doc.

Phyllis Bottome Quotes. https://www.goodreads.com/author/quotes/124760.Phyllis_Bottome.

Pogorelskin, Alexis, "Phyllis Bottome's The Mortal Storm: Film and Controversy," *The Space Be-*

tween. https://www.monmouth.edu/department-of-english/documents/phyllis-bottomes-the-mortal-storm-film-and-controversy.pdf/.

Schneider, Steven, ed. *1001 Movies You Must See Before You Die: The Mortal Storm*. https://1001moviesblog.blogspot.com/2014/04/the-mortal-storm-1940.html.

Stokes, Melvyn. "Slavery in Hollywood Film: an exclusive extract from 'American History through Hollywood Film'." https://bloomsburyhistory.typepad.com/bloomsbury-history/2014/02/american-history-through-hollywood-film.html.

Thomson, David. "Remembering Margaret Sullavan, Who would Have Been 100 (or 102) This Year." https://newrepublic.com/article/95359/sullivan-sterwart-shop-around-the-corner-hollywood.

Urwand, Ben, "The Chilling History of How Hollywood Helped Hitler (Exclusive)." From *The Collaboration: Hollywood's Pact with Hitler*. https://www.hollywoodreporter.com/news/how-hollywood-helped-hitler-595684.

Wikipedia. "Margaret Sullavan." https://en.wikipedia.org/wiki/Margaret_Sullavan.

Index